SEAMANSHIP SECRETS

JOHN JAMIESON

185 TIPS & TECHNIQUES

for Better Navigation,
Cruise Planning,
and Boat Handling
Under Power
and Sail

INTERNATIONAL MARINE | McGRAW-HILL

CAMDEN, MAINE   NEW YORK   CHICAGO   SAN FRANCISCO   LISBON
LONDON   MADRID   MEXICO CITY   MILAN   NEW DELHI
SAN JUAN   SEOUL   SINGAPORE   SYDNEY   TORONTO

The McGraw·Hill Companies

1 2 3 4 5 6 7 8 9 FGR FGR 3 2 1 0 9

Library of Congress Cataloging-in-Publication Data may be obtained from the Library of Congress
ISBN 978-0-07-160578-6
MHID 0-07-160578-9

Questions regarding the content of this book should be addressed to
www.internationalmarine.com

Questions regarding the ordering of this book should be addressed to
The McGraw-Hill Companies
Customer Service Department
P.O. Box 547
Blacklick, OH 43004
Retail customers: 1-800-262-4729
Bookstores: 1-800-722-4726

Illustrations by the author unless noted otherwise.
Please visit the author's website at www.skippertips.com.

CONTENTS

8 DIESEL ENGINE MAINTENANCE AND POWERBOAT SEAMANSHIP

9 SAILBOAT SEAMANSHIP

10 DOCKING SEAMANSHIP

11 ANCHORING AND MARLINSPIKE SEAMANSHIP

# ACKNOWLEDGMENTS

Thanks to Jennifer Castle Field, President of Chapman School of Seamanship—for providing the opportunity to reach for the stars and beyond . . .

Thanks to the top-notch staff of instructors, mechanics, maintenance, and administrative personnel at Chapman School of Seamanship—for their knowledge, dedication, and professionalism . . .

Thanks to John Vigor, Dan Spurr, and Karen Larson for your kindness, encouragement, and shared wisdom . . .

Thanks to Jon Eaton and Molly Mulhern, editorial directors at International Marine, for guiding an apprentice wordsmith to landfall . . .

 INTRODUCTION

A Note to My Fellow Skippers

How many times have you wished for a system of easy-to-learn, easy-to-remember techniques that work the first time, the second time, and every other time you try them? This book was written for skippers by a skipper who has been frustrated by the crushing amount of information that—for the most part—doesn't seem to quite measure up to what I call the *repeatability factor*.

Several years ago, commercial fishermen petitioned the Coast Guard to keep its Loran-C navigation system active because of its superior repeatability. Once they'd found a lucrative fishing ground, these hardy seamen wanted to return to it again and again. Loran-C earned their highest respect for its ability to take them back to those exact coordinates time after time after time.

Repeatability is the essence of seamanship under power or sail. What works today should work tomorrow on my boat, your boat, or any other boat out there—without a whole lot of fuss. In fair weather or storm, in pea soup fog or a sparkling night under a canopy of stars, simple is good and simpler is better.

So it is with navigation skills. You need a system that works in a comfy cabin or—because small crews rarely have the luxury of navigating from the cabin—in the cockpit or flying bridge, exposed to wind, rain, and spray. I once captained a Bertram 47 that took spray all the way back to the flying bridge, even in moderate weather, yet I still had to navigate with traditional chart and compass. This book will show you how to set up the series of charts for an entire trip and fit them onto a portable, one-handed clipboard. We'll explore the quickest, most accurate ways to navigate to the next marina, across the Gulf Stream, or to islands beyond the horizon. If your electronics go on the blink, this book will show you the easiest, fastest methods to find your way from Point A to B.

We'll look at the vital skill of short tacking up a narrow channel with shoals or boats on both sides. I've often observed apprehension in even the most experienced sailors when they're forced to practice this important skill. And yet, time and again, I've welcomed guys and gals from the desert who have never set foot on a boat, taken them aboard a sailboat of nearly 30 feet, and had them short tacking like a racing crew in less than 20 minutes. The secret to success lies in preparation, coordination, and crystal-clear communication.

In this book I'll show you the secrets to mastering this skill along with entering a slip under sail.

On the powerboat side, we'll solve problems like how to ease a twin-engine powerboat alongside a pier or into a slip after losing one engine. Though the thought of a one-engine landing might curl your toes a bit, there are ways to do this successfully using the secrets of preparation, coordination, and communication.

Then we'll look at emergency skills such as getting things under control after a collision or a fire and how to respond to flooding or a crewmember overboard. Throughout the book you'll find proven methods to step through any emergency quickly and logically. Much has been written about various ways to return to a person who has fallen overboard, but the best approach of all is to keep your crew on the boat, safe and sound. Thus, we look at recovery methods, but we also discuss prevention.

Each chapter ends with a short list of questions designed to test your ability to make decisions on your feet. There are no absolute right or wrong answers to most questions, but I give you feedback on how I might handle each situation.

This book doesn't attempt to be everything to everyone. More knowledgeable mariners than I have written voluminous books covering every aspect of navigation and seamanship. Nevertheless, this carefully selected collection of tips and techniques will boost you to the next level of nautical knowledge and confidence, making you a better skipper in all respects.

So here's wishing only the best of nautical experiences to you. Have a great read, enjoy your boating, and stay safe and sound out there.

The primary and essential ingredient of sea sense is a thorough awareness of safety afloat. Every skipper has the responsibility of seamanlike management of his vessel under adverse as well as favorable conditions.
—RICHARD HENDERSON, *Sea Sense*

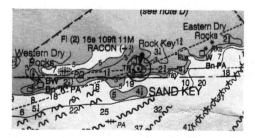

CHART AND PUBLICATION SECRETS

What mystery lies behind chart colors, water and seabed notations, or those dangerous-looking wreck and reef symbols sprinkled in our path? When searching for a buoy or marker at night or in the fog, what five things do you want to know before steering the direction your calculations point to? How do you gather all the latest information you need before leaving on that long-awaited cruise?

In This Chapter, You'll Learn How To:
- Solve the mystery behind chart colors, shapes, and symbols
- Instantly identify any buoy, beacon, or lighthouse
- Avoid dangerous shoals, reefs, and wrecks
- Make certain you are purchasing the newest editions of the charts you need
- Obtain the best cruising guides published in the United States for free!

A Navigator's Most Trusted Companion

Navigation begins with the ability to look at a two-dimensional nautical chart and imagine how the seascape would look in three dimensions. This skill gives you the confidence to plot a safe course, plan an enjoyable cruise, find a safe anchorage, take shelter in a storm or an emergency, and avoid dangers.

You'll find symbols and abbreviations for any chart in the world in a little booklet called Chart No. 1. It's a bit smaller than a medium-sized magazine, so adding it to your list of most valuable books aboard should be a cinch. Chart No. 1 is available by electronic download from the National Ocean Service at **http://www.nauticalcharts.noaa.gov/**. Follow these three easy steps:

1. Click on "View NOAA Charts" on the right side.
2. Find the "Nautical Charting Publications" section on the left side blue column.
3. Click on "U.S. Chart No. 1."

The U.S. government no longer provides printed versions, but these are available commercially through marinas or nautical bookstores. (Note from the publisher: Nigel Calder's *How to Read a Nautical Chart* contains the full contents of Chart No. 1.)

If you're using British Admiralty Charts, order Chart 5011, "Symbols and Abbreviations Used on Admiralty Charts," from the United Kingdom Hydrographic Office (Tel: +44 (0)1823 723366, e-mail: helpdesk@ukho.gov.uk, website: http://www.ukho.gov.uk/amd/standardNavigationalCharts.asp).

Chart No. 1 and Chart 5011 are not nautical charts, but they provide the keys to interpreting virtually every printed or electronic nautical chart you are likely to use. Let's check out the must-knows from these amazing dictionaries of nautical symbology. (Note: unless otherwise indicated, all symbols discussed apply to charts throughout the world.)

Chart Tints and Coloring

A darker shade of blue could mean danger for you.
—ANONYMOUS MARINER

Cartographers use five color backgrounds on most nautical charts. Three of these represent above-tide and intertidal land masses and two represent water areas. (Some other colors are used on foreign charts, but for now, we will concentrate on U.S charts.)

Buff. Most land areas show a dull yellowish color. This buff-colored topography remains visible at all stages of the tide. Elevated regions, such as cliffs and mountains, offer excellent visual and radar targets for landfall and positioning.

Gold. This distinctive tint, which shows up as a darker hue of buff, indicates highly developed areas. If you need repairs, reprovisioning, or just a night on the town, lay your course for these areas.

Green. Look just inside, along, or just off any coastline. Green tinting indicates areas that cover or uncover with the tide, such as marshland, mudflats, sandbars, and oyster beds. At low tide such areas may or may not be visible; they may remain covered on a higher-than-normal neap low tide (the low tide at the time of the quarter moon, when low-water heights average higher than normal). At high tide, however, they're completely underwater. Give green-tinted areas a wide berth.

White. White is the primary background color for deeper water. The white areas on a chart indicate water deep enough for most small craft. Never assume, however. Always check out any area you plan to travel to and make sure it's safe.

Blue. Blue denotes shoal water. Depths decrease as the shade of blue darkens. Study the depth marked on the chart inside any blue-tinted area before deciding to pass that way. Also examine the curve that often encloses an area of blue water. Trace this solid curved line, called a *contour line*, and you'll find a depth, or *sounding*, printed in bold type in a break along the curve. The waters outside the curve will have low-water depths greater than that sounding. Dashed or dotted curves bounding blue water are less trustworthy and should be given a wide berth. Some charts show different tints of blue.

Flat Beach, High Cliffs, or Soaring Peaks?

In a blow, would you want to anchor off a flat beach or in the shelter of a hill or cliff? On the one hand, a steep cliff sometimes blocks an onshore breeze so effectively that you'll find no wind at all for some distance seaward of it. On the other hand, when you're sailing you should be aware that winds sometimes tumble down steep cliffs like snowballs down a mountain, creating gusty katabatic winds called *williwaws* near their bases. The wind velocity could double when funneled between two steep-sided islands or headlands. (In Chapter 11 you will learn which land features offer the best protection for anchoring.)

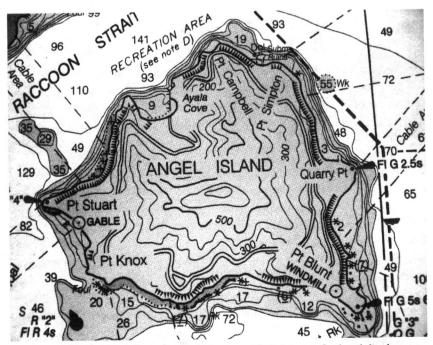

This chart of Angel Island illustrates several geographic features. A flat beach lies between Pt. Stuart and Pt. Knox. Hachures show the location of cliffs. The highest mountains peak at 500 feet above sea level, providing good visual and radar targets from well out at sea.

You will want to take advantage of or avoid such effects once you recognize their potential by examining your charts when planning a passage. These are the three most common land profile symbols.

Flat beach. Black, smooth lines wrapped around a land mass indicate flat beach areas. These lines represent the average high-tide mark. When the tide goes out, this line expands out toward the water. Study the chart and give beaches a wide berth to avoid rip currents and dangerous surf.

High cliffs. Teeth set just inside the land's edge—tiny black triangles that look like the serrations on a saw blade—indicate high cliffs. Cartographers refer to these symbols as *hachures*. High cliffs might provide shelter for anchoring, but vessels under sail should stay well clear; high winds or wind eddies may exist near their bases.

Mountain elevations and peaks. Many charts show mountains with elevations along their contours. In some atmospheric conditions, tall mountain peaks can be seen from far at sea. Note the 300- and 500-foot elevations on Angel Island in the illustration on page 3.

How to Interpret Water Depths and Seabed Characteristics

Nearing Nantucket, fog blanketed the square-rigger. The captain ordered the boatswain forward to begin casting the lead. Each cast solved three mysteries—water depth, nature of the sea bottom, and the distance off the ship-killing reefs ahead.

DEPTHS

Every tiny number located against a background of white or blue shows the water depth, or sounding, at an average low tide. On U.S. charts the usual low-water *datum*, or reference level, is *mean lower low water*, or *MLLW*, which is the long-term average of the lower of the two low tides that occur in each 24-hour period. (In some regions, such as the U.S. Pacific Coast, one low tide is significantly lower than the other; this is called a *mixed tide*.) British Admiralty charts and many other charts around the world use *lowest astronomical tide*, or *LAT*, as the datum for soundings. LAT is a slightly more conservative datum measurement than MLLW. Both measures, however, are more than ample for safe navigation.

MLLW and LAT serve as baselines, or starting points, for determining how much water you'll have available in any given place, at any given time. The actual depth will be greater at mid-tide or high tide. At an extremely low tide, the depth might be less that what is indicated on the chart (see Chapter 5 for more on tides).

U.S. charts show soundings in feet, fathoms, or meters, with the latter becoming more prevalent as charts are revised. Some charts in other countries combine two or more of these units. Look in the chart's title block or along one of the white borders to find which units apply.

Charts that combine soundings, such as fathoms and feet, show a normal-sized base number followed by a subscripted number, such as 2_4. The base number indicates the major depth and the subscripted number the minor depth. For example, in this case we have 2 fathoms and 4 feet, or 16 feet, of water over this particular spot. A sounding of 1_5 on the same chart would indicate 1 fathom and 5 feet, or 11 feet, over that spot. For more examples, see below.

- **SOUNDINGS IN FATHOMS**

  How many feet of water do these soundings represent?

  (*One fathom equals 6 feet.*)

  2   Answer: $2 \times 6 = 12$ feet

  8   Answer: $8 \times 6 = 48$ feet

- **SOUNDINGS IN METERS AND FEET**

  How many feet of water do these soundings represent?

  (*One meter is about 3.3 feet.*) Round the final answer *down* to the closest lower whole number; this gives you a margin of safety.

  3_4 Answer: $3 \times 3.3 = 9.9 + 4 = 13.9$, or about 13 feet

  1_1 Answer: $1 \times 3.3 = 3.3 + 1 = 4.3$, or about 4 feet

- **SOUNDINGS IN FATHOMS AND FEET**

  How many feet of water do these soundings represent?

  1_4 Answer: $1 \times 6 = 6 + 4 = 10$ feet

  3_5 Answer: $3 \times 6 = 18 + 5 = 23$ feet

THE IMPORTANCE OF BECOMING SEA BOTTOM SAVVY

Seabed characteristics continue to play a vital role for the modern-day navigator. With this information you'll know exactly which anchor you need to put down to hold your boat overnight or in a blow. If you run aground, knowing whether the bottom consists of mud, sand, rocks, or coral helps you choose the best way to free your boat without damage.

Three descriptions paint a picture of the sea bottom: *type, texture,* and *color* or *contrast.* Sometimes your chart will show only the basic bottom material or type, but in other areas it might further describe the material color and textures. The most common abbreviations used for sea bottoms are found in the accompanying table.

CHART SEABED ABBREVIATIONS

Bottom Type	Bottom Texture	Color/Contrast
S—Sand	f or fne—fine	wh—white
M—Mud	bk or brk—broken	bl or bk—black
Cl or Cy—Clay	sy or stk—sticky	bu—blue
Sh—Shells	so or sft—soft	gn—green
Grs—Grass	h or hrd—hard	yl—yellow
K—Kelp		gy—gray
Rk or Rky—Rocky		br—brown
Co—Coral		lt—light
Co Hd—Coral Head		dk—dark
Blds—Boulders		
Oys—Oysters		
Ms—Mussels		

SEA-CRET TIP

▶ You'll sometimes find a bottom texture—such as so, sft, h, or hrd—alone on the chart, with no bottom type indicated. Look around the symbol out to about a half mile for an S, M, or Cl.

▶ As an alternative, discover the nature of the seabed yourself with a lead line—a traditional but handy tool that should be carried aboard. This instrument consists of a cylindrically shaped piece of lead with a hollow bottom. A long length of light line is attached to the top. Mark the line every fathom or every two meters. Smear a bit of grease or peanut butter inside the hollowed bottom. Cast the lead out ahead of the boat. When the line goes slack, read the marks for water depth. Pull the lead back up and turn it over. You should find a sample of the sea bottom embedded in the grease or peanut butter. Now you know for sure what kind of sediment is down there.

Height Measurements for Safe Passage

Nautical charts show heights of bridges, powerlines, and overhead cables at *mean high water* or *MHW*. This datum is the average of all high waters over a nineteen-year period. British Admiralty and many other international charts show heights at *mean high water springs*, abbreviated *MHWS*, which is the long-term average of the local spring high tides. Both measures are conservative for safe navigation provided that you use caution before attempting to pass beneath a structure. For example, if you are counting on a 6-foot tide range to squeeze your 60-foot mast under a bridge with a charted vertical clearance of 55 feet, you are not exercising prudent, conservative navigation.

This leads us to ask, how do you know how much clearance you must have to keep from accidentally and permanently shortening your mast, antenna, or flying bridge?

Look on the chart next to bridge and power cable symbols for both vertical and horizontal clearances. Determine the state of the tide (see more on tides in Chapter 5). U.S. federal law requires bridges to show tide gauges on each entrance side, telling mariners the vertical clearance at any moment. You must know the height of the highest projection of your mast, antennas, cabintop, flying bridge, or tuna tower. Use all of these factors to decide whether or not it is safe to pass beneath.

Sailing Vessels

Use your sailplan to determine mast height. This often shows the height from the waterline to the top of the mast. If in doubt, contact the manufacturer or class association for the exact specifications. If you carry instrumentation atop your mast such as an apparent wind indicator or VHF whip antenna, add a generous margin for safety.

SEA-CRET TIP

▶ If you are sailing a boat under 30 feet long and are unsure of its mast height, use a rough estimate by multiplying the boat's length × 1.5. If the mast is extremely tall, add several feet for safety.

Power Vessels

You'll need two measurements for powerboats: one with all antennas and instruments up, and one excluding any equipment that is easily lowered for safe passage beneath bridges (such as many VHF whips). If you are unsure, try these easy steps for accurate measurement:

1. Attach a small block to the end of a boathook.
2. Pass a line through the block. Attach a weight to the end of the line.
3. Get up as high as possible and extend the device over the water.
4. Feed the line out until the weight touches the water. Tie off the line.
5. Pull the line aboard and measure from the end of the boathook to the weight. Add any gear extensions to the measurement.

SEA-CRET TIP

▶ U.S. federal law requires vessels with easily lowered antennas to lower them before requesting a bridge opening. That's another reason to always know the "antenna-up" and "antenna-down" height of your vessel.

Symbols That Shout "Danger!" and "Beware!"

Learn to recognize rocks, coral, wrecks, and obstructions at a glance on your chart. Some rock symbols are accompanied by the abbreviation *Rk* or *Rky*—but not always. Here's a quick summary of the four primary danger categories you'll want to become familiar with:

ROCKY ROADS

Plus sign. Dangerous rocks that lie underwater at all stages of the tide. Avoid these hazards like the plague.

Plus sign with dots. Dots in all four corners of the plus-sign symbol indicate rocks that are barely visible, or just awash, at MLLW or LAT.

Asterisk or squiggly-edged, rounded shape, accompanied by underlined number. These rocks cover and uncover with the tide. The symbol is usually accompanied by an underlined number to indicate height above the low-water datum.

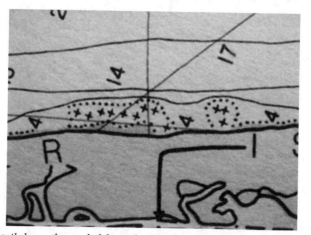

This chart detail shows the symbol for rocks that lie underwater at all stages of the tide.

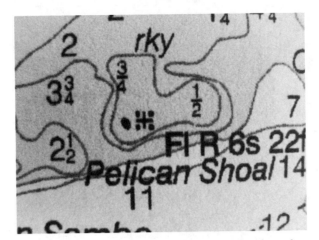

This symbol indicates rocks that are barely visible or just awash at low tide.

If the number doesn't fit inside the symbol, parentheses enclose the number next to the symbol.

Rocks that cover and uncover. The underlined number gives the height above low-water datum. If no number accompanies the symbol, uncovering information is unknown.

Smooth-edged, rounded shape with number enclosed in shape (or appearing next to it in parentheses). These rocks or islets are always visible. Even at high-tide they stick out of the water, and the numbers indicate their height above the high-water datum.

Rocks shown this way on a chart are always visible. The number is the height of the rock above high-water datum.

Stand-alone Rk abbreviations. Depths accompanied by the abbreviation *Rk*—with or without a bracket beneath—show rocks covered by that depth at low-water datum. Use caution when navigating close to these areas.

WRECKS

Undersea currents and surface waves and swells constantly shift many wreck positions. Cartographers can only plot the original reported position of a wreck. Some wreck symbols indicate danger to mariners, while others are safe to pass over.

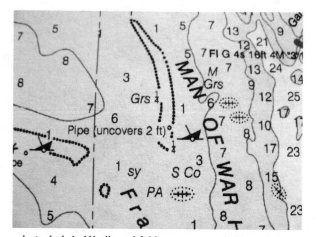

Dangerous wrecks include half hulls and fishbones surrounded by a dotted circle.

Stand-alone Wk abbreviations, circled or bracketed. The abbreviation *Wk* is shown along with the known or least-known depth. It's best to avoid this obstruction altogether if it's enclosed by any type of circle.

Half-hull symbols. Avoid these dangerous wrecks at all costs. Part of the hull is always visible. At high tide, however, only the top of the mast, cabin, or gunwale might show above the water.

"Fishbone" symbols enclosed by dotted circles. Stay away from these wrecks. Uncertain depths cover the hulk during all tidal stages. When accompanied by the word *Masts*, some portion of a mast or masts—but not the hull or superstructure—is visible above chart datum.

"Fishbone" symbols without dotted circles. This is the one and only wreck symbol safe to lay your course across and is usually found in deep water. Chartmakers plot these for the benefit of commercial fishermen (whose nets might snag) or to warn larger ships not to anchor near such foul ground.

OBSTRUCTIONS
Stakes, spoils, beds, traps, nets, stumps, posts, and piles provide the sailor with the same challenges as a slalom racecourse. Hazards such as underwater pilings, deadheads (floating logs or trees), and submerged stumps plot as small enclosed circles. Circles with dotted boundaries and numbers inside show the least depth over the obstruction at all tidal stages. The abbreviation *Obstn* complements many smaller obstructions.

Fish stakes, traps, or nets. Dashed magenta (light purple) lines mark the boundaries of fish-stake or fish-trap areas. These wooden stakes with underwater nets strung between them proliferate in areas such as the Chesapeake Bay, where fishermen use them for catching baitfish. Sometimes you'll find the words *Fish Traps* within the boundary lines. More often, however, you'll see the warning *See Note*, which is an indication to look at one of the descriptive blocks of text on your chart. Be extra cautious when sailing at night near fish-trap areas; they're unlighted!

Spoils, dumping grounds, and fish havens. Inland and coastal charts often show circular or square areas of blue water with no soundings. Ever wonder where old cars, boats, ships, dredge material, and excess garbage end up? These spoil areas or dumping grounds are subject to changing depths, so surveyors rarely bother trying to keep them updated with soundings. Sometimes you'll find the words *Least depth__ft* printed over the middle of such an area, but don't trust it. Stay clear and go around—not aground.

Sparse Soundings

It's always a good idea to avoid any charted area showing sparse, widely spaced, or missing soundings. You never know what underwater monsters lurk there, just waiting to ruin your perfect underway day.

Solve the Mystery of Aid-to-Navigation Symbols

Charted aids to navigation (ATONs) give the mariner a clear picture of their basic characteristics. All buoys are anchored to the bottom and swing in a small radius.

BUOYS

Two shapes represent a buoy body on U.S. charts: the first is a diamond; the second, much-less-common shape is a pie-pan viewed in cross section. Diamonds make up the majority of floating-aid chart symbols, while pie-pan shapes represent mooring buoys. On one end of the buoy symbol is a small open circle known as the *swing circle*. The buoy's actual position at any time lies within this swing circle.

Diamond-shaped buoy bodies may be white, green, red, yellow, red and white, red and green, or red and black. The diamond may be segmented horizontally or vertically with a line or color change. Some diamond symbols show one or more tiny circles on the end opposite the swing circle. These represent a

Chart symbols for buoys, from left to right: unlighted buoy, unlighted mooring buoy, buoy with vertical stripes, buoy with horizontal stripes, and two buoys with topmarks.

topmark—a lollipop shape on a pole sticking out of the top of the buoy. Pie-pan shaped mooring buoy symbols are always black.

LIGHTED BUOYS
The symbology for lighted buoys is the same as that for unlighted buoys except that a large magenta (light purple) disk covers the swing circle. Only lighted diamond-shaped buoys show a purple disk.

DAYBEACONS
Small triangles or squares represent unlighted dayboards atop pilings called daybeacons. These symbols may be white, green, or red. The shape and color of a dayboard is the same as its charted symbol.

LIGHT STRUCTURES
Fixed lighted structures—structures that don't move, such as lights or lighthouses overlooking the sea—show a magenta teardrop shape with a black dot on the tapered end. The dot represents the aid's exact position. Cartographers sometimes enclose light symbols with a squiggly, irregular circle to indicate that riprap (broken rock, shale, or concrete slabs) surrounds the light. This material helps cut down on erosion from waves pounding onto the lighthouse's foundation. Give such lights a wide berth.

ELECTRONIC AIDS
Larger floating or fixed aids sometimes carry a radar beacon, called a RACON. Pulses transmitted from your radar trigger the RACON, and an image of a Morse code letter appears on your radar receiver. For instance, the Dry Tortugas Lighthouse carries a RACON with the Morse code symbol for K (—.—). When activated, a long dash, dot, and long dash appear on your radar display, identifying the exact position of the light. It's possible to pick up RACON signals up to 17 miles away.

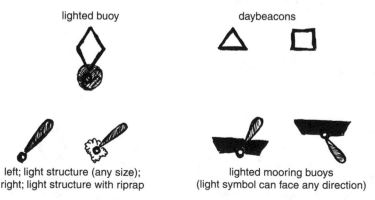

lighted buoy   daybeacons

left; light structure (any size);   lighted mooring buoys
right; light structure with riprap   (light symbol can face any direction)

Chart symbols for various lighted and unlighted buoys.

Ranges Lead You to Safety

Among the mariner's best friends are *ranges,* either those that are man-made or those that form by the natural coincidence of charted objects. Use ranges whenever possible to increase the safety of navigation, to position your vessel, or to check your compass.

Natural ranges are everywhere—a charted church spire over a point of land; a bold rock in front of the highest elevation of a more distant island; a bell buoy directly in front of a lighthouse; and so forth. Once you start looking for them, you'll spot natural ranges all around your boat. Any range like this can give you the most accurate line of position on earth, as we'll see in Chapter 4. For now, though, let's talk about man-made ranges.

A Coast Guard–established range usually comprises two fixed, lighted structures placed at the far end of a channel. The front light (i.e., the light nearer the channel) is shorter than the rear (more distant) light. When you align the lights so that the nearer one is directly beneath the farther one, you are *on range*—i.e., you are in the center of the channel.

When the lights don't line up, you are said to be *off range.* If you want to return to the center-of-channel, you must know which way to turn. Follow these simple rules to find out where you are and how to stay on range:

If the range lights are over your bow, follow the nearer, shorter object or light to get back on range.

If the front object is to the left of the back object, turn left to get back on range.

If the front object is to the right of the back object, turn right to get back on range.

If the range lights are over your stern, follow the more distant, taller object or light to get back on range.

If the back object is to the left of the front object, turn left to get back on range.

If the back object is to the right of the front object, turn right to get back on range.

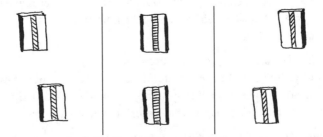

When you are steering toward a range, the two structures will line up (center). When you are off range to the left (left on illustration), turn right to get back on range, when you are off range to the right (right portion of illustration), turn left to get back on range.

The Five Secrets for Visualizing Any Aid to Navigation

Aids to navigation follow a specific sequence of abbreviations and text, giving you a clear visual picture of any buoy, beacon, or light. A buoy or beacon may be referred to as a *navigational aid*, *navaid*, or *aid to navigation* (abbreviated ATON). Look at this typical buoy description as it appears on a chart:

G "7" Fl. G 4s BELL

This is a green bell buoy with the number 7 painted on it, and it has a green light that flashes once every 4 seconds. In general, these are the questions to answer when you look at an ATON description on a chart.

1. **What is the painted color?** Notice the description starts with a G. Buoys and smaller lights always list the painted color of the buoy body *first*. This buoy is painted a solid green color. These colors provide important navigational information, as detailed below.

   Red or Green Denotes Safe Side to Pass On
   Lateral navaids   Solid red or green aids—called *lateral buoys, beacons,* or *lights*—designate the safe side of passage. Throughout the Western Hemisphere and in Japan, Korea, and the Philippines (collectively, Region B of the International Association of Lighthouse Authorities, or IALA-B), when returning from seaward, keep solid red aids on your right side and solid green aids on your left side. "Red, right, returning" is the handy mnemonic for remembering this. In IALA Region A (i.e., the rest of the world), these directions are reversed, and you keep red navigational aids on your left when returning from sea.
   When it isn't clear which direction is seaward and which is landward, it pays to remember that the clockwise direction around North America is considered "landward"—thus, when traveling south along the Canadian and U.S east coasts, west along the Gulf Coast, and north along the Pacific Coast of North America, keep red aids on your right. But in all cases where you harbor any doubt at all, let your chart be the final arbiter as to which side to pass an aid to navigation.

   Yellow Denotes a Special-Purpose Area
   Solid yellow buoys have no lateral significance. Rather, they designate areas such as anchorages and seaplane landing strips. You'll often find a chart note nearby that describes the area in question.

   Multiple Colors Denote Special-Purpose Navaids
   Special-purpose aids carry more than one color. Depending on the color combination, they may indicate safe water, a split channel, or extreme danger.

Safe water all around

RW = red and white vertical stripes. Such a navaid is often called a
midchannel buoy, or beacon.

Channel splits into two (one with deeper water)

RG = red and green horizontal bands (the top band being red). In
North America, keep the buoy to your right when returning from
seaward to stay in the preferred (deeper-water) channel.

GR = green-and-red horizontal bands (the top band being green). In
North America, keep the buoy to your left when returning from
seaward to stay in the preferred channel.

Extreme danger nearby

BR = black and red horizontal bands.

2. **What is the name?** Smaller lights and all buoys are identified with numbers,
letters (single or dual), or number-letter combinations bracketed in quotation
marks. Common examples might be the number "7," letter "F" or "CB," or a
combination such as "16E."

   Lateral aids are numbered from seaward (or in a clockwise direction
around North America), with the sequence beginning anew each time you
leave one cove, harbor, or channel and enter another. Green aids carry
odd numbers and red aids carry even numbers. Thus, the first aid you
encounter when entering a channel, river mouth, or harbor entrance from
seaward will usually be numbered "1" if it's green or "2" if it's red. You
should closely track your position to prevent confusion.

3. **What is the light pattern?** A light pattern helps an aid stand out from
nearby lighted aids. Aids marking channels use one of four flashing
patterns. Each light pattern includes specified intervals of light and
darkness, called a *light period*. Here are the abbreviations used to indicate
the light pattern. Look back at our sample light characteristic. Which one
of these standard characteristics describes it?

   Fl = flashing (flashes at a set interval)

   Q = quick flashing (flashes once per second)

   Oc = occulting (light stays on longer than it stays off)

   Iso = isophase (exhibits equal periods of light and darkness)

   Our example buoy has a flashing 4-second light period. This means
its total period of light and darkness equals four seconds. You would
time the buoy from the first flash of the pattern, to the first flash of the
pattern's next repetition. Check the timed period against that shown on
the chart.

A light that flashes every 4 seconds has a period of 4 seconds. A quick-flashing light has a period of 1 second. Other aids use special patterns. A midchannel lighted buoy shows a distinctive Morse code letter A (a dot and a dash—i.e., a brief flash followed by a longer one). You would not need to time such an aid because its character reveals how it is used. That is why you never see a midchannel buoy with a period noted next to its light characteristic.

4. **What is the light color, if any?** Look at the sample buoy description above. The color that immediately follows the characteristic is the light color. For instance, Fl. G. 4s shows a green light. If you have a light characteristic without a color indicated, it shows a white light. For example, Fl 4s indicates a white light. Red or green lights are used only on aids that tell you the safe side of passage (though not all lateral navaids are lighted). These lights, when present, will be the same color as the navaid itself. On red-and-green or green-and-red preferred-channel aids, the light, when present, always matches the color of the top band. Yellow aids carry only yellow lights. Lighted special-purpose aids—such as red-and-white midchannel buoys—carry white lights with unique flashing patterns (see number 3 above).

These abbreviations are used to indicate light color:

R = red
G = green
Y = yellow
W (or no color indicated) = white

5. **What is the sound, if any?** Aids marking dangerous shoals and those located in geographic areas where fog prevails often carry a bell, gong, whistle, or horn signal. Note in the example that sound, if indeed the ATON has it, comes last in the description. There's a lot of comfort in hearing the clang of a bell buoy or the raspy sound of a gong buoy in a pea soup fog. And there's a lot to be said for laying a course to a buoy that you don't have to pinpoint in order to locate—especially a midchannel buoy surrounded by deep water. If you don't find the buoy where and when you expected to, shut down the engine or engines and listen. Ah, there it is, about a hundred yards to starboard. Bells, gongs, and whistles operate by wave or swell action. Clappers strike bell domes or gong disks to activate the sound. The up-and-down action of swells causes whistles to produce their unique "sighing" tone by compressing air through a diaphragm. The horn stands alone as the only electronic signal. It's usually reserved for large lighthouses located along fog-shrouded coasts.

SEA-CRET TIP

▶ If searching for a wave-actuated buoy in low visibility, send a crewmember up to the bow, away from engine noise.

▶ You can also turn your boat in a tight circle to create a wake. Stop and listen. Your wake may help actuate the buoy's clappers or diaphragm.

LIGHTS ALWAYS CARRY TWO EXTRA DESCRIPTIONS

Both small and large fixed-light structures give height and range information after the basic aid information. Take a look, for example, at the charted description for Dry Tortugas Light:

DRY TORTUGAS LIGHT
Fl W 20s 151ft 20M

Height. The vertical distance of the *eye* of the light above datum high water is 151 feet.

Range. The charted visibility of this light, called its *nominal range*, is 20 nautical miles. Nominal range depends only on candlepower of the light, however, and doesn't take into account the height of the light or the observer's eye. The earth's curvature will often prevent you from seeing a light at its full nominal range. For example, the distance of the horizon from the 151-foot-high Dry Tortugas Light is 14.3 nautical miles. If your height of eye as you attempt to view the light is 9 feet above the water, your horizon distance is 3.5 nautical miles. Since 14.3 + 3.5 = 17.8, the *geographic range* of the Dry Tortugas Light for you is 17.8 miles—more than 2 miles short of its nominal range. Even in clear weather, you will not see the light from 20 miles away. (Learn more about using height to find range to any object in Chapter 4, How to Determine When You Will Make Landfall.)

Chart Notes: Nuggets of Hidden Gold

Look all around the land mass and margin section on your chart and you'll notice navigational notes. Take time to scan the notes when you first purchase a chart. They're specific to the geographical area displayed, and you'll want to use your highlighter for the most critical data. Here are examples of common notations and their meanings.

"LOCAL MAGNETIC DISTURBANCE—Differences of as much as 3 degrees from the normal variation have been observed on Cuttyhunk Island between Buzzards Bay and Vineyard Sound."

What it means: Near this island, the normal compass variation indicated in the chart's compass rose may be off by as much as 3 degrees. Check your position frequently and adjust your course as necessary. (See Chapter 2 for more on magnetic variation and how to account for it when steering compass courses.)

"CAUTION RIPRAP—Mariners are warned to stay clear of the protective riprap surrounding navigational light structures."

What it means: Riprap is erosion-reducing material such as shale, brick, concrete pieces, or rock built up around the base of a light structure. Without this protection, the base would quickly crumble from the pounding of waves and swell. It's best to stay well clear of the squiggly circle surrounding the light's position circle.

"FOR OFFSHORE NAVIGATION ONLY—Detail within the 10-fathom curve is not shown on this chart except on the off-lying shoal and the Bahama Islands."

What it means: This one tells us not to rely on any depth equal to or less than 10 fathoms or 60 feet. Shoal banks surround the Bahama Islands, extending many miles to sea, showing soundings. The cautious navigator should pull out a larger-scale chart before attempting a passage over these areas. (A large-scale chart covers a small area in great detail; for more on chart scales, see Chapter 2.)

"TRAFFIC SEPARATION ZONE—Mariners are requested to stay outside the circular separation zone centered on the San Francisco Sea Buoy."

What it means: You'll find traffic separation zones in the approaches to most major ports that accept deep-draft ships. A zone is charted with inbound and outbound lanes separated by a centerline. Both inbound and outbound ships stay to the right, just as on U.S. highways. Small vessels not using the traffic lanes should stay clear of the zone and maintain a careful lookout.

Are Your Charts Up-to-Date?

When is the last time you checked your chart edition dates? Before using any chart, glance at the lower left-hand corner. This lists the edition number, month, and year of issue. You probably won't see the current year. This doesn't mean the chart is outdated; governments find it too expensive to resurvey and reissue charts annually unless major topographical changes have occurred. But you'll need to check for the most current edition.

For example, in August 2005 Hurricane Katrina shifted shoals and channels, destroyed aids to navigation, and permanently altered land profiles along the Louisiana and Mississippi coasts and rivers. After the disaster, cartographers and surveyors worked for months to put together new editions for the region.

One of the best-kept secrets on the web is the DOLE listing, or Dates of Latest Editions. The National Oceanic and Atmospheric Administration (NOAA) maintains this valuable free tool at **http://www.nauticalcharts.noaa.gov/**. Follow these steps:

1. Click on "View NOAA Charts" on the right side.
2. Find the "Nautical Charting Publications" section on the left side blue column.
3. Click on "Dates of Latest Editions (DOLE)."
4. Click on "Dates of Latest Editions (Current Listing)."

Make this site your first stop before purchasing paper or electronic charts. If you are purchasing in person, carry a copy of the DOLE printout with you. Ask the vendor to pull the chart, then check your DOLE list against the chart's lower-left corner edition information. If you are buying over the phone or online, compare edition numbers and dates with the DOLE.

Note the two links directly above the DOLE box referring to "recent" editions. These are the newest editions available from NOAA. Make sure to check these and see if your area of interest has a brand-new edition. If so, make sure the vendor has that edition on hand.

NOAA Chart Dates of Latest Editions

This List Updated 10/15/2008

Click Here for the NOAA Chart Dates of Recent Traditional Paper Chart Editions.
Click Here for the NOAA Chart Dates of Recent Print on Demand Editions.

NUMBER	TITLE	SCALE	EDITION	PAPER DATE	POD DATE
11434	Florida Keys Sombrero Key to Dry Tortugas	180,000	28	Jun /08 (NM:6/14/2008) (LNM:6/17/2008)	Jun /08 (NM:6/14/2008) (LNM:6/17/2008)
11438	Dry Tortugas;Tortugas Harbor	30,000	13	Jan /08 (NM:1/26/2008) (LNM:1/22/2008)	Jan /08 (NM:1/26/2008) (LNM:1/22/2008)
11439	Sand Key to Rebecca Shoal	80,000	26	Jul /04 (NM:7/31/2004) (LNM:7/13/2004)	Jul /04 (NM:7/31/2004) (LNM:7/13/2004)
11441	Key West Harbor and Approaches	30,000	41	Sep /06 (NM:9/30/2006) (LNM:9/26/2006)	Sep /06 (NM:9/30/2006) (LNM:9/26/2006)

Sample entries from NOAA Chart Dates of Latest Editions (DOLE) page. Note the different columns for paper charts versus POD (print-on-demand) charts.

THREE CHART FORMATS

After finding your chart or charts, go to the columns headed Paper Date or POD Date.

Paper Date. These are the common paper nautical charts issued by the National Ocean Service (a department of NOAA) in the United States and by corresponding agencies in other countries. Paper charts provide exceptional accuracy and reliability.

POD (Print-on-Demand) Date. Print-on-demand charts are updated versions of paper charts. When you place an order for a print-on-demand chart, the vendor prints your chart on a machine linked to a chart correction database. Your chart contains all updates to changes in aids to navigation, shoals, and wrecks through the date of order. The cost is about 10% to 15% more than a standard paper chart.

Raster Nautical Charts. A raster nautical chart, or RNC, is a scanned electronic version of a traditional chart. Because raster charts are scanned from a traditional chart, their edition dates are the same as that shown in the DOLE listing under the heading "PAPER DATE". Dozens of RNCs can be scanned onto a CD or DVD for use in a laptop or onboard computer, which displays the chart and drives the associated navigation software. Raster charts are too memory-hungry to be compatible with most electronic chart plotters. RNCs have the same level of precision as traditional charts—no less and no more. The electronic alternative to RNCs is vector charts, which we'll discuss in Chapter 2.

NOTICES TO MARINERS: VITAL DATA FOR KEEPING CHARTS UPDATED

In the DOLE listing, in each column under the edition date you'll find dates preceded by the designations *NM* or *LNM*. NM stands for Notices to Mariners and LNM for Local Notices to Mariners. Both contain vital information on new, revised, relocated, and removed aids to navigation, reports of wrecks, dangerous shoaling, or bridge operation status.

Notices to Mariners cover waters worldwide. Local Notices to Mariners cover only those waters within a U.S. Coast Guard District Boundary. The Coast Guard issues both versions of notice to mariners once a week. As long as you're sailing in U.S. waters, you'll only need the Local Notices to Mariners to keep your charts up-to-date.

How to Download Free Weekly LNMs

1. Type in the Coast Guard Navigation Center's site address (**http://www.navcen.uscg.gov/lnm/default.htm**).
2. Click on your area on the Coast Guard Districts map.

3. Scroll down to the latest LNM (sorted by month).
4. Click on the latest notice. The first two numbers indicate the week of the year; the last two indicate the year.
5. Save or print the pdf file.

Free Code-Breaker for 36,000 Mariners' Friends

The U.S. Coast Guard maintains about 36,000 light and unlighted aids to navigation in the United States and its possessions. Your chart describes the major characteristics of each buoy, beacon, and light.

When making landfall or sailing in unfamiliar waters, you'll need more detailed information. The Coast Guard publishes six volumes of Light Lists, available online and updated frequently. Download any volume free of charge from the Coast Guard Navigation Center site (see steps below). To understand what information the Light Lists include, let's look at an example.

We're planning a coastal cruise from Miami to the Chesapeake Bay. Chesapeake Light, a prominent offshore light structure, marks the entrance to the bay. On our chart, the description next to the symbol reads:

> **CHESAPEAKE LIGHT**
> **117' Fl (2) W 15s 19M HORN**
> **RACON: N (-.)**

What We Know from This Description
- The light is 117 feet above mean high water (MHW).
- The light flashes in groups of 2, with a total period of light and dark of 15 seconds.
- The nominal range of the light is 19 nautical miles. (To see it at that range on a clear evening, however, we would have to be watching from 31 feet above the water. We can learn this by consulting a distance to horizon table, found in Appendix I. We will discuss these methods in Chapter 4).
- The light carries a horn signal.
- If we have radar, we could receive a signal from the RACON. This will paint an image on our radar display shaped like the Morse code symbol for N (long flash–short flash).

What We Still Need to Find Out
- What is the color and shape of the physical structure?
- What is the interval of darkness between flashes?
- How often does the horn sound, and for how long?

DOWNLOADING LIGHT LISTS: DIGGING UP A FREE TREASURE CHEST OF INFORMATION

1. Type the Coast Guard Navigation Center website address (http://www.navcen.uscg.gov/pubs/LightLists/LightLists.htm).
2. Find your location on the geographic locator map. For our example, click on District 5, which covers the Midatlantic Region, including the Chesapeake Bay. The pdf file will download.
3. Click the Save icon (floppy disk symbol on the toolbar). This takes you to My Documents (or elsewhere, depending on your computer system's default) and assigns a file name, such as V2Complete.pdf. Keep or change the name as desired. Then click on save; close the website pdf file.
4. Open My Documents (or whatever folder your system saves to) and retrieve the pdf file.
5. Click the search field and type in the words *Chesapeake Light*. Press the enter key on your keyboard.

Physical appearance during daylight. In the Light List, under column 7, which is labeled *Structure*, the physical appearance of this offshore beacon is described. Four giant legs rise from the seabed to support a flat, square platform. A blue tower protrudes skyward from the platform. In giant capital letters, the word *CHESAPEAKE* adorns the sides of the structure, welcoming mariners to the entrance of the largest estuary in the United States.

Periods of light and darkness. In the Light List, look under column 4, which is labeled *Characteristic*. This breaks each group into intervals of light and darkness (eclipse). In this case, each flash lasts 0.1 second, and 2.9 seconds of darkness separate the first and second flash of the group. Then 11.9 seconds of darkness intervenes until the pattern starts again. The period of the light (sum of light and darkness) is 15 seconds.

Horn blast and interval. The last column, labeled Remarks, provides information on any extra equipment or restrictions. The horn gives one 3-second blast every 30 seconds. I believe the importance of knowing this cannot be overstated. Container, cargo, and military ships frequent this area, and low visibility dominates during certain times of the year. All of these vessels will sound fog signals in accordance with the prescribed International Rules for the Prevention of Collisions at Sea (COLREGS). Knowing our light's horn characteristic, we should easily be able to pinpoint its location among a cacophony of other foghorns.

Free Cruising Guides to Take You Anywhere

Every year new cruising guides fill the bookstores, covering the more popular coastal and inland waterways. Many of these offer excellent advice that is tailored for the small-boat sailor. But it's best to use caution when using a recreational guide unless you're confident in the reliability of the information.

(1) No.	(2) Name and Location	(3) Position	(4) Characteristic	(5) Height	(6) Range	(7) Structure	(8) Remarks
			SEACOAST (Virginia) - Fifth District				
325 6730	QUINBY INLET ENTRANCE LIGHT	37 27 50 N 75 40 12 W	Fl W 4s	28	8	NB on skeleton tower on structure.	
330 6800	*Great Machipongo Inlet Lighted Whistle Buoy GM*	37 23 36 N 75 39 06 W	Mo (A) W		5	Red and white stripes with red spherical topmark.	
335	*Hog Island Lighted Buoy 12*	37 17 40 N 75 34 39 W	Fl R 2.5s		5	Red.	
340 6965	*Sand Shoal Inlet Lighted Whistle Buoy A*	37 17 49 N 75 41 09 W	Mo (A) W		5	Red and white stripes with red spherical topmark.	
345	*Cape Charles Lighted Bell Buoy 14*	37 07 24 N 75 40 59 W	Fl R 2.5s		4	Red.	
347	*Navy Surface Gunnery Area 8 Lighted Buoy GA*	37 12 00 N 74 52 00 W	Fl Y 4s		5	Yellow	
348	*Surface Gunnery Area 8 Lighted Buoy GB*	37 12 00 N 74 51 40 W	Fl Y 6s		4	Yellow.	
349	*Surface Gunnery Area 8 Lighted Buoy GC*	37 12 15 N 74 51 49 W	Fl Y 2.5s		4	Yellow.	
350	**Cape Charles Light**	37 07 23 N 75 54 23 W	Fl W 5s	180	24	Octagonal, pyramidal skeleton tower, upper part black, lower part white. 191	Operates 24 hours.
360	**Chesapeake Light**	36 54 17 N 75 42 46 W	Fl (2) W 15s 0.1s fl 2.9s ec. 0.1s fl 11.9s ec.	117	19	Blue tower on white square superstructure on four black piles, CHESAPEAKE on sides.	Emergency light of lower intensity will be displayed when main light is inoperative. RACON: N (– •). HORN: 1 blast ev 30s (3s bl). Operates continuously.
365	*Navy SESEF Lighted Buoy A*	36 55 02 N 75 38 14 W	Fl Y 2.5s		5	Yellow.	
370	**Cape Henry Light**	36 55 35 N 76 00 26 W	Mo (U) W 20s (R sector) 1s fl 2s ec. 1s fl 2s ec. 7s fl 7s ec.	164	W 17 R 15	Octagonal pyramidal tower, upper and lower half of each face alternately black and white. 163	Red from 154° to 233°, covers shoals outside Cape Charles and Middle Ground inside bay. Emergency light of lower intensity will be displayed when main light is extinguished.

This is some of the information for the Chesapeake Light—use the first column to find its light number (360)–as it appears in the Light List.

The Office of Coast Survey, a division of NOAA, offers sailors a free cruising guide that's hard to beat for accuracy and detail. Issued annually, the nine volumes (listed below) of the *U.S. Coast Pilot* cover all navigable waters within the United States and its possessions, including Hawaii, the U.S. Virgin Islands, Puerto Rico, and the Pacific Islands.

CP1 Eastport, Maine, to Cape Cod, Massachusetts
CP2 Cape Cod, Massachusetts, to Sandy Hook, New Jersey
CP3 Sandy Hook, New Jersey, to Cape Henry, Virginia
CP4 Cape Henry, Virgnia, to Key West, Florida
CP5 Gulf of Mexico, Puerto Rico, and Virgin Islands
CP6 Great Lakes and Connecting Waterways
CP7 California, Oregon, Washington, Hawaii, and Pacific Isles

CP8 Alaska: Dixon Entrance to Cape Spencer
CP9 Alaska: Cape Spencer to Beaufort Sea

HOW TO DOWNLOAD YOUR FREE CRUISING GUIDE

You can download an entire volume or just the chapter that applies to your cruising area. Below is one example for a New England cruise.

We're planning a cruise from Provincetown, Massachusetts, on the tip of Cape Cod, to Martha's Vineyard, an island to the south of Cape Cod. Select the charts and chapters needed to safely plan your cruise.

Access the NOAA website at **http://www.nauticalcharts.noaa.gov/**.

1. Click on "View NOAA Charts" on the right side
2. Find the "Nautical Charting Publications" section on the left side blue column
3. Click on "United States Coast Pilot"
4. Click on "Download United States Coast Pilot and Updates"
5. Scroll down and read the brief descriptions of each Coast Pilot. Look at the list above. We'll find what we're looking for in Coast Pilot 1 or 2. Take a look at Coast Pilot 2 first, since our cruise runs south from Cape Cod.
6. Click the link labeled Coast Pilot 2 Download Page
7. Scroll down the chapter list and find the one covering your route. Chapters 4 and 5 should cover the entire trip from beginning to end. The first page of each chapter shows an illustration of the area covered by the chapter. Charts are superimposed over the illustration to show every chart you need for safe cruising.

"Your Call, Skipper"

You're the skipper or most knowledgeable crewmember in each of the following situations. What actions would you take?

1. Checking your paper chart or chart plotter, you see several wrecks directly in the way of your destination. It's getting late and you need to find the safest, shortest route through the wrecks to get to the marina. Which wreck symbols could you safely cross over without fear of damaging your boat?

2. The forecast calls for the weather to pick up this evening, with wind, waves, and driving rain from the northeast. Studying your chart, what land profile symbols might offer the best protection for anchoring?

3. On the chart or chart plotter, you see the symbol *so*. No bottom type is shown. You need to know what's down there to choose the right anchor for peace of mind. What two methods could you use to determine if the bottom type is sand, mud, or clay?

4. You're planning a weekend trip to your favorite local cruising ground. What publication would you check to see if any buoys or beacons along the way are missing, changed, damaged, or removed?

5. After a cold winter, you are looking forward to spending a week cruising in the Virgin Islands. You are anxious to read up on the islands, learn what facilities each has to offer, and look at charts of the area. What's the fastest way to find just the information you need?

Answers

1. A fishbone symbol *not* enclosed by a dotted circle.

2. Hachures (teethlike symbols) on the lee side of the island. These indicate high cliffs or a steep hillside.

3. Look on the chart from the symbol out to a radius of about one-half mile; look for the symbol *S* (sand), *M* (mud), or *Cl* (clay). You might also cast an armed lead line (i.e., coated with grease or peanut butter) to take a sample of the seabed.

4. Check the Local Notices to Mariners for the past thirty days.

5. Access the NOAA website. Scroll down to CP 5. Click on the link labeled *Coast Pilot 5 Download Page*. Then, scroll down the link to find the chapters covering the Virgin Islands.

CHART PLOTTING AND PREPARATION

Paper nautical charts are among the most valuable and essential tools we have aboard our vessels.

—SID STAPLETON, *STAPLETON'S POWERBOAT BIBLE*

As fantastic as electronic charts are, how do we best prepare for the unexpected, such as the loss of power? How do we make our paper charts ready to use in an instant, with most of the navigation work completed before casting off? How accurate is your compass? Is there a fast, reliable method of checking this vital instrument, giving us peace of mind in all types of weather—day or night?

In This Chapter, You'll Learn How To:
- Plot latitude, longitude, and distances faster than ever before
- Fit paper charts to a portable clipboard
- Complete 90% of all navigation on your charts before casting off
- Check the accuracy of your compass in three easy steps
- Protect your paper charts and extend their life by a year or more

Skipper's Navigation Tools

Steering Compass. Used for steering the boat. The person at the wheel or tiller uses the steering compass to move the boat along a line (called a *trackline*) from point A to point B.

Handbearing Compass. A portable compass, used for finding the boat's position or checking the steering compass for errors. Some handbearing compasses come with a miniature compass mounted atop a pistol grip. Others look like a rubber-coated hockey puck with a neck lanyard.

Follow these steps to accurately use a handbearing compass:

1. Raise the compass to the eye.
2. Sight an object through the *vanes* or slot that runs across the compass.
3. Read the magnified compass bearing.

Parallel Rulers. Used for measuring direction. This instrument has two thin, flat sections of wood or plastic attached by hinges. You "walk" them across a chart. Place pressure on one leg and hold it steady. Move the other leg. Then, place pressure on the leg you just moved, and move the trailing leg up. Continue the process of alternating pressure from one leg to the other to move from one place to another.

Protractor. Used for measuring direction. This instrument has one flat section, scribed with a half circle that shows increments of degrees. To use the protractor, place it along any vertical line, read the angle, and slide it to the place needed. Some protractors, like the "Weems Plotter," have wheels on one long edge to assist in moving the instrument long distances.

Dividers. Used for plotting positions and measuring distance. This hand-held instrument has two legs attached to a hinge. Sharp metal needles are inserted into the ends of the legs opposite the hinge.

Plotting Compass. Used for plotting positions, measuring distance, and marking the chart. Similar to dividers, but only one leg has a metal needle point. The other leg contains a thin sliver of pencil lead with a pointed end.

Quick-and-Easy Review of Latitude and Longitude

Chartmakers created a system of vertical and horizontal intersecting lines to enable navigators to quickly and accurately plot a vessel's position. They named the horizontal (i.e., east-west) lines *latitude* and the vertical (i.e., north-south) lines *longitude*.

LATITUDE

Picture the earth as a perfect sphere balanced on a vertical axis. The North Pole lies where the axis penetrates the top of the sphere, and the South Pole is located where it penetrates the bottom. Now divide the sphere horizontally into two equal halves. The resultant dividing line—a belt around the waist of the world—is the *equator*.

The equator is the starting point for latitude measurements, which is to say that the latitude of the equator is 0 degrees. If we move north of the equator, the first degree of latitude is named *1 degree north*, the second degree is *2 degrees north*, and so on. Latitude reaches a maximum of 90 degrees north at the North Pole. If we start from the equator and move south, we'll pass 1 degree south, then 2 degrees south, and so forth to a maximum of 90 degrees south at the South Pole. All lines of latitude are parallel with one another, which is why a line of latitude is also called a *parallel*.

Measure Latitude on the Chart's Right or Left Margin Scale

On a nautical chart we measure latitude using the scales on the right- or left-side margins of the chart. These scales show latitude in degrees, minutes, and tenths of a minute or in degrees, minutes, and seconds. One degree of latitude equals 60 minutes; one minute of latitude equals 60 seconds.

$$1 \text{ degree } (°) \text{ of latitude} = 60 \text{ minutes}$$

$$1 \text{ minute } (') \text{ of latitude} = 60 \text{ seconds } (")$$

On charts showing degrees, minutes, and seconds, it's often convenient to change the seconds into tenths of a minute. Simply divide the number of seconds by six. Round oddball seconds to the closest number divisible by six.

Convert 42°25'18"N into degrees, minutes, and tenths.

- Since 18 seconds is exactly divisible by six, we simply divide it by six to convert it to tenths of a minute: 18"/6 = 0.3'
- Our converted latitude is 42°25.3'N

Convert 13°49'26"N into degrees, minutes, and tenths.

- Since 26 seconds is not exactly divisible by six, round it to the closest number divisible by six, which is 24, and then divide by six: 24/6 = 0.4'
- Our converted latitude is 13°49.4'N

LONGITUDE

Now let's go back to our globe, this time dividing it vertically into two equal halves. Imagine that we do this by lowering a giant guillotine, but let's be careful: the blade must pass through both the North and the South poles. The resulting cut will also pass through the earth's center and—because this system was invented in England—we must orient the blade so that it also passes through the city of Greenwich, England, on the earth's surface. That half of the circle that passes through Greenwich is called the *Greenwich meridian* (or *prime meridian*) and labeled 0 degrees. The remaining half of the circle on the opposite side of the globe from Greenwich is labeled 180 degrees. Measurement of longitude begins at the Greenwich meridian.

Now let's use our blade again and make additional slices on each side of the Greenwich meridian. Each of these circles—called meridians—represents one degree of longitude. Traveling west from the Greenwich meridian, we will pass 1 degree west, then 2 degrees west, and so on to 180 degrees. If we travel east from the Greenwich meridian, we will pass 1 degree east, then 2 degrees east, and continue all the way around the globe to 180 degrees.

The 180th meridian coincides more or less with the *international date line* (though the latter is distorted by bumps and jogs so as not to divide certain Pacific island nations into multiple time zones).

Measure Longitude on the Chart's Top or Bottom Margin Scale

Use either the top or bottom scale of the chart to measure longitude. Like latitude, longitude is broken down into degrees, minutes, and tenths of minutes or into degrees, minutes, and seconds. Use the same methods shown above to convert seconds to tenths of a minute of longitude.

How to Choose the Chart Scale You Need

A chart's scale indicates the amount of detail it provides for safe navigation. Think of chart scales like the scale of a model ship. Let's say you go to a craft store looking for a model of the tall ship HMS *Bounty*. The store offers two different models of the same ship. One box states that the model is on a scale of 1:48, and the other is 1:96.

If we open the first box, we'll find rather large pieces of the model. For instance, the ship's wheel will be prominent with good detail, and we won't lose our eyesight straining to see the intricate details of its spokes. Popping open the second box, we'll find much smaller pieces. The ship's wheel on this model has shrunk to half the size of the other wheel. What happened?

If we look at the second number of each ratio, the mystery resolves itself. A larger second number means a smaller representation, or scale, than a smaller second number. This is true regardless of the units of measure.

In a 1:48 scale ship model, each 1/4 inch represents 1 foot of the full-size ship (12" ÷ 48 = 0.25"). HMS *Bounty* was 91 feet long on deck (small for her day and her mission), so a 1:48 scale model would be 1.9 feet or 23 inches long. If her ship's wheel was 5 feet in diameter, it would be 11/4 inches in diameter on the model, and so on. A 1:96 scale model of the *Bounty,* however, would be just 111/2 inches long with a wheel of 5/8-inch diameter.

It is the same with charts. On a 1:80,000 scale chart, 1 inch represents 80,000 inches of actual nautical real estate. On a 1:10,000 scale chart, 1 inch represents 10,000 inches on the earth's surface. The 1:10,000 chart gives you more detail for a tricky harbor entrance, while the 1:80,000 chart gives you a bigger picture for coastal piloting.

When choosing charts, always select the largest scale available. Larger scale charts enable you to enter harbors and anchorages, pass close to or even over shoals (if your draft allows), and give the best detail in restricted waters. Large scale equals larger detail and a smaller area; small scale equals smaller detail and a larger area.

SCALE SELECTION SIMPLIFIED

Use a baseline of 1:80,000 to select the appropriate scale for navigation. This is the most common chart scale used in U.S. coastal waters. If using British Admiralty charts, use the largest scale available for safe navigation. A 1:80,000 scale chart provides excellent detail from about 1 to 10 miles off the coast. Shift to a larger-scale chart—1:60,000; 1:40,000; 1:20,000, or larger—as soon as possible when making landfall. Farther off the coast, you must change to a smaller-scale chart. Ocean-crossing charts often have scales of 1:1,000,000 or smaller.

Skipper Tip—24-Hour Time

Navigators throughout the world use the 24-hour clock to avoid confusion (as do colleges and universities). Remember these two things: 0000 is midnight and 1200 is noon. From midnight until 1200, you add the number of hours past midnight. For instance, 1 hour past midnight is 0100 (1 am), 2 hours past is 0200 (2 am) and so forth until 1200. From 1200 to midnight, add 1 hour to 1200. For instance, 1 hour past 1200 is 1300 (1 pm), 2 hours past 1200 is 1400 (2 pm). Practice until this becomes second nature. Use only 24-hour time for all chartwork, log entries, and talking on the marine radio.

24-HOUR TIME		CLOCK TIME
0000	=	MIDNIGHT
0100	=	1:00 AM
0200	=	2:00 AM
0300	=	3:00 AM
0400	=	4:00 AM
0500	=	5:00 AM
0600	=	6:00 AM
0700	=	7:00 AM
0800	=	8:00 AM
0900	=	9:00 AM
1000	=	10:00 AM
1100	=	11:00 AM
1200	=	12:00 PM
1300	=	1:00 PM
1400	=	2:00 PM
1500	=	3:00 PM
1600	=	4:00 PM
1700	=	5:00 PM
1800	=	6:00 PM
1900	=	7:00 PM
2000	=	8:00 PM
2100	=	9:00 PM
2200	=	10:00 PM
2300	=	11:00 PM

CAUTION AROUND OUTLYING REEFS

Charts produced by foreign agencies often use smaller scales for close coastal navigation. For example, many Bahamas charts lack detail for approaches to islands or off-lying reefs because their scales are much smaller than 1:80,000. Distances between soundings are sometimes hundreds or even thousands of yards. Some areas show no depths at all! When in doubt, use well-traveled routes or seek local knowledge.

Box-Plot Your Position

If you stand back and look at any chart, you'll notice a system of grid lines overlaying the land and water areas. These grid boxes form the basis for navigation. The top and bottom of each box is a line of latitude, or a parallel. The right and left sides of each box are lines of longitude, or meridians. When you box-plot, you use sides of the box to help pinpoint your boat's position inside the box. This makes a fast and accurate way to transfer your position from your GPS to your chart.

Supplies and Tools Needed to Box-Plot Your Position

► pencil
► artist's or draftsman eraser
► straightedge
► plotting compass

1. **Locate the grid box.** Find the pair of latitude lines (parallels) and the pair of meridians (longitude lines) that form a box around your boat and mark the corners for easy reference.

2. **Plot your latitude.** Measure latitude on the right or left chart margin scales. Transfer the measurement to each vertical side of the box by sticking the point of the compass (or dividers) in one corner of the box and sweeping an arc with the compass lead across the corresponding meridian. If using dividers, plant the other divider point on the meridian and mark that spot with a sharp #2 lead pencil. Duplicate this on the other meridian. These are your *latitude marks*. Use any straightedge to draw a line joining the two marks.

3. **Plot your longitude.** Measure longitude on the top or bottom chart margin scales. Follow one of the meridian lines bounding your box until you come to the horizontal latitude line you just drew. Place the compass (or divider) point on that intersection, sweep an arc through the horizontal line (or plant the other divider point there and mark with a pencil), and you're done.

4. **Neaten the plot.** Place a small circle around the intersection of the latitude and longitude. Erase all lines and arcs to neaten up the chart.

How to Convert Minutes, Seconds, or Degrees to Miles

Most nautical charts are based on the projection of a round globe onto a cylinder. This projection, called a *Mercator projection*, thus contains some distortion. For instance, because meridians of longitude appear as straight lines on your nautical chart (on a globe, they converge at the poles), you must take care in measuring distance. Always use the latitude scale (i.e., the right or left chart margin) and get into the habit of taking your distance measurement at a place along the latitude scale, close to your position. For instance, if your position is near the top of the chart, take distance measurements from the top of the chart.

Because each line of latitude parallels all the others, the distance between two such lines is always consistent. Therefore each minute of latitude equals one nautical mile, no matter where on the globe you may be.

$$1' \text{ (minute)} = 1 \text{ nautical mile}$$

$$1° \text{ (degree) (60 minutes)} = 60 \text{ nautical miles}$$

This relationship does not hold true for lines of longitude, since these converge at the north and south poles. They look parallel on a Mercator chart, but only because the chartmakers have distorted things for convenient navigation. A minute of longitude equals one nautical mile only at the equator and diminishes

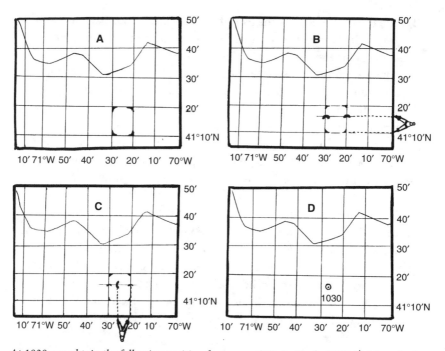

At 1030 you obtain the following position from your GPS: Latitude 41°17.0'N; Longitude 70°26.0'W. Below are the steps to box-plot your 1030 position:

Locate the grid box (A). First eyeball which latitude-longitude box surrounds your vessel. In the accompanying illustration we've marked the four corners of this position box where the 41°10'N and 41°20'N latitude lines intersect the 70°20'W and 70°30'W longitude lines. This way, if you need to put aside the chart temporarily to attend to your boat, a quick glance reorients you when you return.

Plot your latitude (B). Go to the right or left chart margin scale, whichever is closest to your position box. Stick the point of your compass in the latitude mark that forms the bottom of your box, in this case 41°10'N. Now open the other leg of the compass until the pencil point is on your latitude position of 41°17'N. Maintaining that span, slide the compass to your position box. Stick the point into each of the two bottom corners of the box in turn and strike arcs through the corresponding meridians. Grab a straightedge and draw a horizontal line between the two arcs.

Plot your longitude (C). Go to the top or bottom chart margin scale, whichever is closest. Stick the point of your compass in the longitude that forms the right or left side of your position box (it doesn't matter which you choose as long as you're consistent). In our case, we'll stick our needle point in 70°20'W. Then we'll open the other leg until the pencil point falls on our longitude reading of 70°26'W. Slide the compass along the meridian until you reach the line of latitude you drew between the arcs in the position box. Strike an arc over the line to mark your 1030 GPS position.

Neaten the plot (D). Circle your position, label it with the time of the position (1030) and erase all extraneous lines from your chart. Always scrub your chart, which is the nautical term for erasing, to make things as easy to read as possible. Extra lines and marks frequently cause confusion and lead to navigational errors.

to nothing at the poles. Thus, use only the latitude scale (or the chart's distance scale) to measure distances.

Always express distances in nautical miles and tenths of a nautical mile. On charts that show degrees, minutes, and tenths, you can read distances directly from the latitude scale. On charts showing degrees, minutes, and seconds, you'll have to divide the seconds by six to convert them to tenths of minutes.

CHARTS WITH DEGREES, MINUTES, AND TENTHS

1. Open your compass or dividers until the two points fall exactly on the two chart locations whose distance apart you want to measure. Preserving that span, move to the adjoining right or left chart scale.

2. Stick the point of your compass or dividers into an even minute and touch the other leg above. You'll notice each minute is divided into ten small segments, or *tick marks*. Each tick mark represents a tenth of a minute (which is a tenth of a mile).

3. If you measure 4 minutes and 3 additional tick marks, the distance is 4.3 nautical miles. If you measure 12 minutes and 9 additional tick marks, the distance is 12.9 nautical miles.

CHARTS WITH DEGREES, MINUTES, AND SECONDS

1. Open your compass or dividers until the two points fall exactly on the two chart locations whose distance apart you want to measure. Preserving that span, move to the adjoining right or left chart scale.

2. Stick the point of your compass or dividers into an even minute and touch the other leg above.

3. If you measure 4 minutes and 36 seconds, the distance is 4.6 nautical miles (36 divided by 6 equals 0.6 mile). Round off seconds that are not exactly divisible by 6. For example, 27 seconds rounds off to 0.5 mile, and 11 seconds rounds off to 0.2 mile.

True versus Magnetic Directions and Two Ways to Find Variation

True north points to the geographic North Pole. Due to the magnetic field surrounding the earth, the needle on your compass points to the magnetic North Pole, which is some distance from the geographic North Pole (see more, below).

True directions. For example, imagine pointing one arm toward the North Pole and another in the direction you want to go. Measure the angle clockwise from the arm pointing north to the arm pointing toward the direction you want

A Primer on Plotting Terms

When you plot lines on a chart, they might be referred to as *courseline* (course) or *trackline* (track). Many navigators use these interchangeably. In this book, we will use the following terms.

Trackline (or track), abbreviated TR. The plotted direction. You plot the trackline (or track) onto the chart. This is the track you want the boat to follow from point A to B. But sometimes wind or current push the boat to one side or the other. In that case, you have to steer a different course (see next). To label a trackline, precede the direction of the line with "TR"; for example, "TR—233M" means that the trackline direction from A to B is 233 degrees magnetic.

Compass Course (or steering course). The course steered by the person on the wheel or tiller. If it is found that the boat is no longer on the TR, the navigator changes to a new compass course (or steering course), to return the boat to the trackline. If you steer a compass course different from the trackline, plot it onto the chart. Precede the course with a "C"; for example, "C—225M" means that the steering course is 225 degrees magnetic.

Course or Courseline. A general term that covers both steering course and trackline (or track). You plot a course onto the chart. The line itself is the trackline. Or, you could measure the trackline with parallel rules or protractor to find the magnetic course. Then again, someone might ask what course you are steering. You would tell them what compass course you are steering. Many navigators precede all directions with a C on the chart. We will prefix all tracks with "TR" and compass courses with "C" to eliminate confusion.

to go, and you have a true direction. All meridians of longitude on the chart point toward the true, or geographic, North Pole. Thus, to measure true directions, we measure the angle clockwise from a meridian to a course or bearing line drawn on the chart.

Magnetic directions. Most small craft use a magnetic compass. This instrument consists of a compass card with a small magnet attached to its bottom. The card floats in liquid inside an airtight case so that it can turn without friction, and the magnet rotates the card until it lines up with the magnetic North Pole, which is some distance from the true North Pole. Now imagine pointing one arm toward the magnetic North Pole and the other in the direction you want to go. Unless you happen to be standing in a spot from where the magnetic and true north poles line up, you'll find that this magnetic course angle differs from the true angle (i.e., the angle of your course in degrees from the true North Pole). The difference between the two angles can vary from 1 degree to more than 50 degrees, depending on where you are located! This difference, called *variation,* changes when we move from one point to another on the Earth's surface.

LOCATION, LOCATION, LOCATION—VARIATION EXPLAINED

If we sail from Miami to Bermuda, the variation from the beginning to the end of our passage will change by around 12 degrees. If we make a run in a powerboat from Key West across the Gulf of Mexico to Houston, the variation will change around 6 degrees. To account for these changes you must periodically steer a different trackline. Otherwise you'll end up somewhere other than your intended destination.

So how do we find the variation at our location? Fortunately, cartographers have worked this out for us, and all we need to do is know where to look and how to apply it. There are two sources from which you can learn the variation for the waters in which you are boating. *(Note: a GPS receiver can give you bearings and courses in degrees true or degrees magnetic—the choice is yours. And if you choose the latter, the GPS receiver will adjust for local variation automatically. We'll discuss GPS navigation in Chapter 4.)*

Compass rose. Every chart has at least one compass rose overprinted on it, and most have three or four. Printed in magenta, most roses have two concentric rings; the outer one shows true directions and the inner shows magnetic directions. Locate the closest compass rose to your location, and just above its center crosshairs you will find a label noting the local variation (as of the stated year) and its name—east or west. Record this in your log. Just below the crosshairs you will find a note of the annual increase or decrease in variation. Take the difference between the year shown and the current year. Multiply this difference by the minutes of increase or decrease. If increasing, add the difference to variation. If decreasing, subtract the difference. Round your answer to the closest whole degree of variation.

> Variation: 18 degrees east (2002)
> Annual decrease: 5 minutes
> The current year is 2009; what is variation at this location?
> 7 (years) × 5 = 35 minutes
> 18 degrees east – 35 minutes = 17 degrees 25 minutes east
> Round the answer to the closest whole degree. The variation in this instance is therefore 17 degrees east.

Sometimes the annual change in variation is noted as east or west, rather than increasing or decreasing. If the annual change has the same name (east or west) as the variation, variation is increasing. If the names are opposite, variation is decreasing. For example: If your compass rose says 12°14'W (10'E), this indicates a decrease of 10 minutes a year because the names, W and E, are opposite. If it says 12°14'W (10'W), that would indicate an increase by 10 minutes a year because the names are the same.

Isogonic lines. On small-scale charts covering large areas over which variation changes markedly—most notably, on offshore charts—look for curved magenta lines (dashed or solid) running across the chart. Using the curve closest to your position, scan along it to find the noted variation.

APPLYING VARIATION TO FIND YOUR MAGNETIC TRACKLINE

You can read true directions from the outermost ring of the compass rose and then convert these to magnetic directions, or you can use the inner ring to plot magnetic directions directly. Many small-boat navigators prefer the latter, but I find the inner ring difficult to read because the degree hash marks are densely packed and often labeled only at 30-degree intervals (in contrast with 10-degree intervals for the outer ring). It's a simple process to find magnetic directions from true. You begin by plotting the true direction, then add a westerly variation or subtract an easterly one.

The only tricky part is remembering when to add and when to subtract. Some navigators use the mnemonic "East is least (–); west is best (+)." When converting from true (indicated as T) to magnetic (indicated as M), you subtract an easterly variation and add a westerly one.

Inner Ring versus Outer

I rarely use the inner (magnetic variation) ring on charts, and here's why.

First, on many charts, it's on a smaller scale than the outer ring, and shows degrees in two-degree versus one-degree increments. That means more chance for a misread, especially if the rose shows the compass points just inside the magnetic ring. More confusion!

Second, you are dependent on a compass rose that may lie far from your position. Trying to walk parallel rulers or a protractor across a large space leads to errors when they slip.

Third, on offshore charts, cartographers don't include the magnetic ring on roses; only true directions are shown. This is because variation changes so quickly offshore (smaller-scale charts) that your chart would be cluttered with compass roses. That's why magnetic variation on offshore charts is shown with diagonal isogonic lines.

The true course to Shelter Cove is 135 degrees true. If the local variation is 17 degrees east, then your magnetic course would be: 135 degrees true – 17 degrees east = 118 degrees magnetic.

Check Your Steering Compass in Three Easy Steps

It is utterly reckless to rely upon an uncorrected compass.
—MALCOLM PEARSON, *REED'S SKIPPER'S HANDBOOK*

The small magnets on the bottom of a compass card love to interact with metals and electrical currents on your boat. This can pull the compass card away from its proper reading by several degrees. The resultant error is called *deviation*. Unlike variation, deviation is peculiar to each boat and changes with your heading.

I remember being sent out on a Coast Guard rescue case offshore on an open 40-foot patrol boat. Our

SEA-CRET TIP

▶ Many small-craft navigators prefer to plot in degrees magnetic. It's a personal choice, but use care not to mix true and magnetic tracklines or bearing lines. Consistency is the key. Plot all lines using magnetic directions or all lines using true directions.

navigational equipment consisted of a magnetic compass, chart, and radar. As we cleared the jetties, the pre-plotted tracklines and compass weren't jibing at all. As a matter of fact, the compass consistently read 5 or 6 degrees high or low, depending on our heading. Luckily the disabled vessel was only a few miles offshore, and we picked them up on radar, but I was determined to solve the mystery back at the docks. As it turned out, a tiny 2-inch flathead screwdriver had dropped into a slot behind the compass mounting.

Always mount the compass in a location several feet away from electronic instruments, including depth sounders, radar, VHF radio, or GPS receivers. Also, check your jewelry, knife location, cell phones, calculators, cameras, wire-rimmed glasses, earrings, necklaces, stereo speakers, and anything else close to the compass. Keep metals and electronics 36 inches from the compass, if practicable. If that's not possible, minimize electrical interference by twisting electronic instrument wiring beneath the console or binnacle housing. Twisted wire pairs cancel each other's fields and leave your compass free to do its job.

Every boat needs its compass periodically checked for deviation. After making a course change, get into the habit of checking the deviation. Use a handbearing compass for comparison against any steering compass.

HOW TO CONSTRUCT A DEVIATION
TABLE FOR ANY BOAT

1. **Turn on standard equipment.** Energize any electronics that you normally use while underway, such as radios, GPS, chart plotter, or radar.
2. **Find your boat's deviation-free zone.** To find deviation, you must first locate your boat's deviation-free zone, or DFZ, a spot that is completely free of magnetic influences. On power vessels, move aft of the console or into the cockpit. On sailing vessels, move aft toward the backstay. On any boat, stay as close as possible to the boat's centerline. Find a distant object at a range of 1 to 2 miles. It's not necessary that the object be charted, as long as

it is stationary. Sight the object with a handbearing compass and keep the compass up to your eye. Have your mate turn the boat slowly in a circle while you pivot your body to follow the object. If the bearing remains constant, you've found your DFZ. If it changes, move to a different spot and try again. Take your time. You need to find your boat's DFZ before going to the next step.

3. **Make a three-column recording log.** Make three columns on a piece of paper. Label the first column *"Boat Heading (Handbearing Compass),"* the second column *"Deviation,"* and the third column *"Steering Compass (Boat Compass)."* Under the Steering Compass column, enter 000°, then 015°, then 030°, and so forth at 15-degree intervals down the column. When you are done, attach your log to a clipboard.

4. **Steer your "Steering Compass" tracklines.** Sight down the centerline and onto the headstay or bow rail with the handbearing compass. Have the helm

BOAT HEADING (Handbearing Compass)	DEVIATION	STEERING COMPASS (Boat Compass)
001	1E	000
018	3E	015
027	3W	030
043	2W	045
063	3E	060
077	2E	075
088	2W	90
103	2W	105
122	2E	120
136	1E	135
149	1W	150
163	2W	165
182	2E	180

A partial deviation table. Always swing your compass through a complete 360-degree circle. Our table shows intervals of 15 degrees between headings (far right column). Some navigators prefer intervals of 30 degrees or even 45 degrees. Smaller intervals give more accurate results.

steady up on 000° on the steering compass. Have the helm call out "Mark!" the exact moment the steering compass reads 000°, and write down the corresponding handbearing compass reading in the Boat Heading column. Now steer 015°. Repeat the process as before. Continue doing this for each heading. When you are finished, go to the next step.

5. **Find the deviation.** Compare the Boat Heading and Steering Compass columns. Record the difference in the Deviation column. Name each deviation east or west. Use this mnemonic: Compass least, error east; Compass best, error west. This means that if the Steering Compass column is less (least) than the Boat Heading column, you should label deviation east. If it is higher (best), label deviation west.

It's a good idea to have your compass professionally adjusted, especially before going on an extended cruise. Deviations of less than 3 degrees can be ignored. Because of the amount of swing of the compass card, you'll find that even the best helmsmen can only steer a course within 2 degrees. This is just one more reason you should update your position on the chart every so often.

Using Your Deviation Table to Find the Course to Steer

1. Plot the trackline from starting point to destination. Convert the true course to a magnetic course.
2. Enter the table and look under the Boat Heading column. Find the closest boat heading to your magnetic trackline.
3. Read the deviation in the second column. If the deviation is west, add the number to the magnetic trackline. If the deviation is east, subtract the number from the magnetic trackline.

The magnetic trackline from point A to B is 057 degrees magnetic.

Choose the closest number to 057 degrees magnetic in the Boat Heading column (i.e., 063°).

Look across from 063 degrees and read the deviation: 3 degrees east. Apply the deviation to the magnetic trackline to find the course to steer:

057 degrees magnetic − 3 degrees east = 054 degrees.

SEA-CRET TIP

▶ Don't make the mistake of using a number from the Boat Heading column as your course to steer. Use the table only to find the deviation. Then apply the deviation to your magnetic trackline to find the course to steer.

Vector Charts for Precision Electronic Navigation

I mentioned vector charts in Chapter 1. Unlike raster charts, which are simply scanned versions of traditional paper charts, vector charts pull information from a database within their software. Many chart plotters and GPS systems use a *vector display*, but it does take some getting used to. The first thing you will notice is that the display may show much less detail than a nautical chart or raster display of the same area. Here's a summary of the pros and cons of this remarkable technology.

PROS

Razor-sharp adjustable display. The display appears with unmatched clarity but looks a bit "computerized" to some mariners. Land profiles and imagery appear with less detail than a raster scan but retain the same positioning accuracy. GPS plotters normally carry a menu function, allowing users to adjust the screen for viewing in bright sunlight or darkness.

Selective layering. The user retains control over how much data he wants displayed on the screen. Don't want to see depth contours or landmark names cluttering up the display? Simply open up the Chart Display Options menu and deselect that function.

Depth unit selection. Choose from feet, fathoms, or meters, and the display instantly converts every sounding and depth curve to your selection.

Text font consistency. Raster chart text enlarges when you zoom in for detail. This sometimes obliterates important information such as wrecks, navigation aids, or soundings. With vector displays, the text stays the same size when you zoom in or out.

Memory storage. Vector compression technology allows storage of massive amounts of data using a mere fraction of the memory required to store the same amount of data in a raster display. In his book *GPS for Mariners,* author Robert Sweet states that a set of raster charts requiring 200 megabytes of memory only requires 20 megabytes of memory through vector compression. Using this technology, every chart in the world could fit onto one tiny CD-ROM disc!

Info dialog box pop-ups. Do you want to know the hours the fuel pier is open at the marina 5 miles ahead? Or how about the range of visibility on the lighthouse ahead? Simply move the cursor, place it over the object desired, and a pop-up dialog box shows amplifying information, similar to that of a cruising guide, Light List, or coast pilot.

CONS

Display limited by screen size. As with all displays, the monitor-screen size limits the amount of screen real estate available. When zooming in, you'll need to scroll right, left, up, or down to move the display. It's easy to lose your place when zooming in. If this happens, zoom out, find a reference landmark, and then try zooming in again.

Cursor movement. With layering technology, you need to move the cursor over areas of interest for more detailed information. Save time by doing as much of this as possible before casting off. For instance, check marina data along your route and make note of information such as the hours of fuel dock operation and the ship's store, or radio contact information. Enter this into a logbook for instant reference.

Bulletproof Your Charts for Longer Life

Crazy as it sounds, I consider Scotch Magic Tape (or any tape with a dull finish that allows writing and erasing) an important navigational tool. In the Coast Guard, we maintained hundreds of charts. The latitude and longitude scales wore out after time from repeated perforating by divider and compass points. We needed a solution to make our charts last longer.

So we started taping the scales with the Magic Tape and found that it protected them from perforations for several months. When the tape showed signs of wear, we simply laid another strip of tape over the first one. You can write and erase on this tape in both pencil and pen. Try this solution to keep your charts going and going and going.

Paper Chartlets for Cockpit Ease

To imagine that installing a GPS does away with any need for navigational expertise is a grave mistake.
—TOM CUNLIFFE, *THE COMPLETE YACHTMASTER*

You must keep traditional charts on hand in case of electronic chart failure. All electronic instruments require a constant source of power and are vulnerable to vibration or accidental breakage. No instrument is 100% waterproof and salt-air proof—no matter what the manufacturer claims.

Supplies Needed to Make Paper Chartlets

▶ one piece of posterboard
▶ pencil
▶ soft (kneadable) eraser
▶ Exacto knife
▶ artist sketchboard
▶ duplicate charts of your area

But how do you make a bulky, full-size paper chart usable in a small cockpit or flying bridge? Here's a solution that will keep things simple, efficient, and hassle-free in wind and spray.

Sources for chart copies. Purchase the original full-scale color charts you need for your trip. Next, find an engineering or architectural design company that can handle copying full-scale charts. Make two copies of each chart in high resolution, either in black and white or in color (which is more expensive).

Another alternative is to purchase duplicate charts from chart printers like Bellingham Chart Printers of Friday Harbor, Washington (**www.tidesend .com**). They offer high-resolution grayscale charts for anywhere in the world, at two-thirds the size of a full-scale chart. These charts contain different shades of gray to make shoals and landmasses stand out.

Even so, you should carry the original full-color chart onboard for reference. Keep the original below in the cabin, protected from wind and spray. Use your black-and-white copies for navigation on deck. Remember, you will need at least two copies of the original color chart. Follow these steps and the accompanying illustrations to set up your chartlets:

1. **Make a posterboard template.** Artist's clipboards, called *sketchboards*, come in two sizes: 18$\frac{1}{2}$ inches × 19$\frac{1}{2}$ inches or 15$\frac{1}{2}$ inches × 16 inches (for short day trips or weekend cruising, an alternative is to use a legal-size clipboard). If you desire, you can waterproof the board with varnish. Next, use a piece of posterboard to make a rectangular template that is $\frac{1}{2}$ to $\frac{3}{4}$ inch shorter and narrower than your clipboard. This will ensure that the edges of the chartlets will be protected inside the clipboard edges.

2. **Plan your route.** Mark all the tracklines for your journey on your chart copies. Double-check the entire length of each track to make sure no hazards lie along your path.

3. **Trace both cutting lines onto copy #1.** Starting at your departure point, lightly trace a cutting line around all four sides of the template. This denotes your first chart segment, or *chartlet*. Within an inch or two of the chartlet's far side, find a transfer point (TP) to use on the next chartlet. When you shift from one chartlet to the next, you want to have a common reference point. Select a prominent aid to navigation, landmark, sounding, contour curve, or point of land as your TP. Move the template to the opposite side of the charted trackline. Make sure it completely covers your TP on one edge. Trace an outline for your second chartlet.

4. **Transfer the cutting line onto copy #2.** Transfer this outline onto your second chart copy. Line up your posterboard template so that it covers the TP and matches the outline from copy #1. Trace a cutting line for your second chartlet.

5. **Cut out your chartlets.** Double-check your work. Then cut out the chartlets with your Exacto knife. Repeat these steps for the remainder of your journey. When you are finished, darken in your tracklines.

Now, go to the next tip to find secrets that will help you complete 90% of all navigation before you cast off your dock lines.

SEA-CRET TIP

▶ Protect your charts and sketchboard with a large zip-top plastic bag. For example, the Ziploc Big Bag is heavy-duty and comes in two sizes: 2 feet × 1.7 feet (XL) and 2 feet × 2.7 feet (XXL). They're good insurance, and they're cheap.

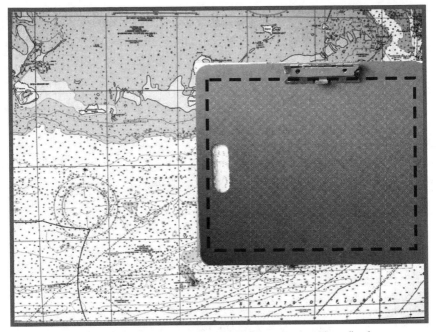

Make the posterboard template ½ to ¾ inch smaller than the sketchboard's edges.

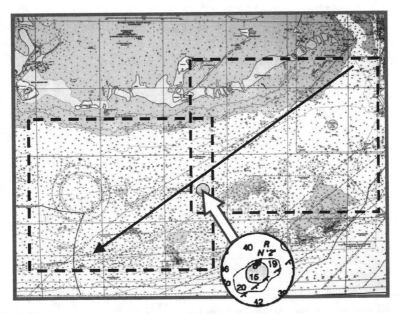

Draw in your trackline or tracklines. Using the posterboard template, outline both chart copies. Choose a prominent object as a transfer point (TP) inside the overlap. Mark the TP on both copies.

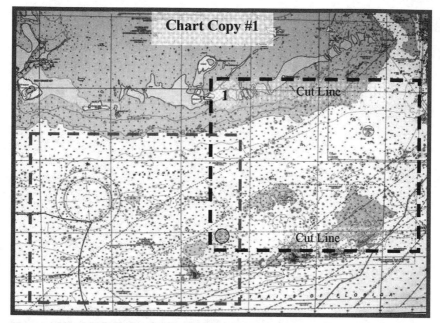

Cut out and number the first chartlet from the first chart copy.

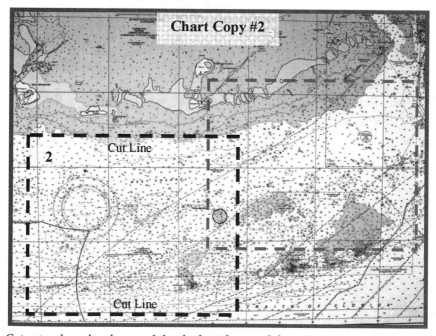

Cut out and number the second chartlet from the second chart copy. Continue this method for any remaining charts.

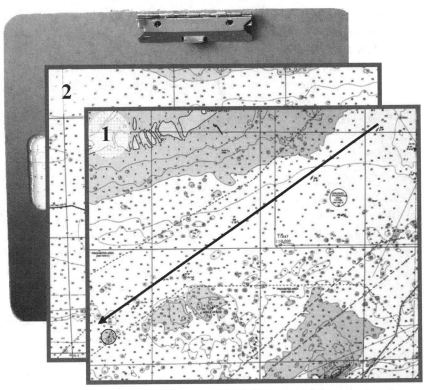

After cutting your chartlets, draw in your tracklines. Use your transfer points for reference. Then, stack the chartlets in order. Finally, lash your chartlets to the sketchboard with rubber bands.

Complete 90% of Your Navigation by Annotation

Many charts contain a confusing web of lines signifying Loran-C time differences, territorial sea boundaries, naval training areas, underwater cables, and so forth.

Supplies Needed for Annotating Charts

▶ colored pencils (except red)
▶ highlighters (except red)
▶ fine or medium felt-tip black marker
▶ removable Scotch Magic Tape (dull-sided clear tape)
▶ duplicate charts as mentioned in previous section

Our tracklines, which we add to our paper charts, make up the foundation of our navigation. What follows is a way to make these stand out boldly from all the other symbols on our charts.

MARKING, LABELING, AND TAPING TRACKLINES

Pencil it. Lightly pencil in your tracklines. Enter these into your logbook, but do not label them on the chart yet (see below).

Tape it. Tape each track with *removable* Scotch Magic Tape (or dull-sided tape). Use continuous strips on short legs and multiple strips on longer legs. Make sure the tape adheres firmly.

Mark and label it. With the fine or medium felt-tip marker, draw over your penciled lines. Add more tape above and below the line where you can write in your trackline information.

How to make changes. If you need to remove the old tape for a course change, simply peel away the old tape, erase the penciled lines beneath, and repeat the steps above.

MARK DANGERS, AIDS, AND ANCHORAGES ALONG THE WAY

You'll need your colored pencils for these next steps, which involve marking, or annotating, the chart to highlight shoals, danger bearings or boundaries, and natural ranges. Try using a dark blue pencil for shoals and magenta or crimson for danger boundaries and bearings. Customize any annotation, but keep it simple so that the crew understands its meaning.

Mark shoal-limit lines. Use a dark blue pencil to highlight shoals or contour curves less than twice your draft. Contour curves show depths in increments of 6 feet. If your draft is 8 feet, you should mark any 18-foot contour curves on the chart ($2 \times 8 = 16'$; for safety, round up to 18'). If you have a depth sounder with an alarm, set it to trigger at your shoal-limit line.

Dashed lines for ranges, bearings, and turns. To highlight a natural range, draw a dashed line from the more distant aligned object through the nearer object and toward your trackline, out to the *stop point*. This is the point where you must stop using the range to avoid standing into danger. Coast Guard–maintained ranges change from a solid to a dashed line at the stop point. Mark each stop point with a distinctive *X* or circle.

Draw danger marks and bearings. Use the magenta-colored pencil to draw in danger bearings (or danger arcs, if you are using radar—see Chapter 4).

Designate emergency anchorages. Study water depths and seabed characteristics on either side of every trackline. Pockets of white indicate deeper water off the main channel. Use a dark-colored pencil to draw an anchor symbol surrounded by a circle for possible emergency anchorages, then highlight the nearest bottom characteristics.

More information to come. After reading Chapters 4 and 5, you'll want to add other valuable annotations to your charts. Try to keep things simple to avoid clutter or confusion. Always remember that everyone aboard should be able to understand your information, in case you are incapacitated.

SEA-CRET TIP

▶ Stay away from using red markers when annotating charts. Flashlights and cabin or bridge lights with red lenses, which are favored because they do not degrade your night vision, make red markings invisible. This is why magenta is used on charts.

Save Time with Custom Distance Scales

Measuring distances on a 1:80,000 scale coastal chart is a snap, because the latitude scale is broken down into degrees, minutes, and tenths of minutes. Larger-scale charts (such as harbor charts) make distance plotting more challenging, however, because their latitude scales are often shown in degrees, minutes, and seconds. I find it convenient to draw my own scale line divided into miles and tenths on such charts, making distance measurements faster and more accurate.

1. **Selecting a spot for the scale.** Locate an area on the chart that is not needed for navigation. This keeps the scale from interfering with tracks and annotations, or covering important navigation information.
2. **Tape the scale.** Pull off a few inches of dull-sided tape and lay it down over the area where your scale will reside. If you use removable tape, you can peel it off later if necessary. (You can remove more permanent tape by rubbing a heated piece of metal over the tape, peeling as you rub.)
3. **Make the distance scale.** Draw a line onto the tape equivalent to about 2 to 3 miles in distance. Mark one end of the line with a small tick mark and label it 0. Next, find that part of the latitude scale on the right or left margin that breaks down a minute into seconds. Using your dividers or compass, pick off 6 seconds of latitude. Starting at the 0 point, strike arcs in 6-second (tenth-of-a-mile) increments to the other end of the line.
4. **Label the distance scale.** Starting at the first mark above the 0 baseline, label each tenth of a mile 0.1, 0.2, and so forth, continuing to the 1-mile mark. Then continue above the 1.0-mile mark with 1.1, 1.2, and so forth, up to the 2-mile mark. Make the whole- and half-mile tick marks longer than those that indicate tenths of a mile. Tape over the scale to protect it from smudging.

Invaluable Copilot: The Navigator's Log

Enter anything into the log that directly or indirectly influences the navigation of the vessel.

Logbooks provide a record of the past for use in the future. In a court of law, they're legal documents, carrying enough weight to prove your case if the need arises. Underway, they give a clear picture of the vessel's travels and serve the navigator as well as any chart or publication. Indeed, for hundreds of years they served as the *only* guide for navigators and ship captains because of the scarcity of usable nautical charts.

Keep entries clear, specific, and easy for every crewmember to understand. Reserve the first column for times (using the 24-hour clock time) and the subsequent columns for true course, variation, and magnetic course. Make columns for your distance log (or speed). Keep an open column for comments.

Sample Sailing Vessel Navigation Log

Time	True	V	Mag.	Log Dist.	Lat.	Long.	Method	Comments
1200	330	6W	336	5.5	36–42.2N	73–16.8W	GPS.	Wind W @ 12; Seas 2-3 Main (full); 135 Lapper 1220 made visual landfall with Pt. Judith Light
1300	330	7W	337	5.5	36–48.0N	73–18.2W	Vis/Rad.	Wind WNW @ 16–18; Seas 3 Main (2 reefs); 135 Lapper.

Sample Power Vessel Navigation Log

Time	True	V	Mag.	Log Dist.	Lat.	Long.	Method	Engine Hours	Comments
1200	330	6W	336	12.5	36–42.2N	73–16.8W	GPS	1,565	Wind W @ 12; Seas 2-3 1400 RPMs both Engines 1220 made visual landfall with Pt. Judith Light
1300	330	7W	337	12.8	36–48.0N	73–18.2W	Vis/Rad.	1,566	Wind WNW @ 16–18; Seas 3 1400 RPMs both engines

Sample logbook entries for a sailboat and a powerboat.

Some ideas for the sailing comments column might be: sails hoisted, sail changes, and reefing.

Power vessels (or sailing vessels under power) have a separate column for engine hours. Show RPM in another column or in the comments field. All power vessels need a separate engineering log for hourly readings of water temperature, oil pressure, and voltage. Log comments on any problems such as vibration, smoke, leaks, engines out of sync, or unusual noises.

All vessels should log times and details of landfall and sightings of important navigational aids. Enter weather observations or make a separate weather log. (For details on recommended weather entries, see Chapter 12.)

"Your Call, Skipper"

You're the skipper or most knowledgeable crewmember in each of the following situations. What actions would you take?

1. You are at the chandlery and need to purchase a chart showing the best detail of San Francisco Bay. The vendor has three charts for that area with scales of 1:125,000, 1:80,000, and 1:40,000. Which do you buy, and why?

2. Before checking your compass for deviation, what two things must you do?

3. You arrive at a sea buoy and want to know the distance to the turn into the main channel. You measure on the latitude scale 3'22". What is the distance to the channel just ahead?

4. While underway in a narrow channel, you lose engine power and must take immediate action to keep from grounding. Where do you look to find an emergency anchoring spot?

5. Which two places would you look to find the variation at your location on any chart used throughout the world?

Answers

1. A scale of 1:40,000. The second number represents the magnification necessary to show the same relative size of landmass on earth. The smaller the number, the greater the detail.

2. Remove magnetic materials that you are wearing. Stand in an area not influenced by metal (for instance, a metal awning). Energize all equipment you routinely use underway to simulate actual conditions.

3. The distance is 3.4 nautical miles. Divide seconds by 6 and round off.

4. Aim for white pockets of deeper water on the channel edges. Better yet, mark these ahead of time when annotating your chart.

5. In coastal or piloting waters, look in the center of the closest compass rose. On coastal or offshore passages, look for the closest dashed or solid magenta isogonic curve. Find the variation written somewhere on top of the line.

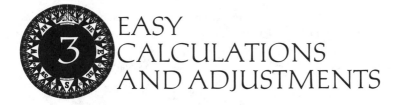

3 EASY CALCULATIONS AND ADJUSTMENTS

I saw this man in his leisure moments, examining and testing
everything that a vessel needs when at sea.
—Xenophon, Greek historian, 427–355 BC

Can you estimate your speed within half a knot at any RPM setting? What three factors must you know when estimating fuel and provisioning for a cruise? How do you adjust vital navigation gear to produce top-notch performance?

In This Chapter, You'll Learn How To:
- ❀ Solve important navigation calculations in seconds
- ❀ Make a super-accurate speed graph for any boat
- ❀ Choose, test, and calibrate three vital navigation tools
- ❀ Adjust your radar like a pro in five easy steps

Lightning Fast Arrival Time Estimates

How long does it take you to travel 1 nautical mile? Know this and you'll be able to quickly estimate your arrival time at waypoints and your favorite anchorages, even without GPS.

To get the answer, just divide your speed into 60. If your speed is 4 knots, you'll travel a mile every 15 minutes. A speed of 5 knots gives a time of 12 minutes per mile. Averaging 6 knots means you'll travel a mile in 10 minutes.

Now try these examples:

You are on a powerboat at a speed of 12 knots. How long will it take you to travel 1 mile?

$$60 \div 12 = 5 \text{ minutes}$$

How long will it take you to travel 2 miles?

$$5 \text{ minutes} \times 2 = 10 \text{ minutes}$$

How long will it take you to travel 30 miles?

$$5 \text{ minutes} \times 30 = 150 \text{ minutes, or 2 hours 30 minutes}$$

Now you can figure the amount of time needed to get to any point. Just multiply the time to travel 1 mile by the number of miles you will travel to reach your waypoint.

Note: these examples give you estimated times in transit based on your speed through the water, and the underlying assumption is that your speed through the water and your speed over ground are the same. This is not true in places with strong current, and you will need to make a few adjustments. Adjustments will also be required on vessels under sail and subject to changing speeds. We will learn how to make these adjustments in Chapter 5.

How to Make a Speed Graph in Three Easy Steps

A customized, ready-to-use speed/RPM table will tell you at a glance what your speed through the water is at any RPM setting. Compare this speed with the speed over ground reading from your GPS receiver to quantify the combined effect of wind and current at any given time. You can also use the table to estimate fuel requirements, time en route to a destination, provisioning needs, and fuel stop-off points.

Supplies Needed to Make a Speed Graph

▶ pencil
▶ graph paper
▶ watch or stopwatch

POINTS TO REMEMBER

- Make your speed runs in little or no wind and current. This keeps the data much more accurate.
- Find two prominent marks about a mile apart with good water all around. You'll need room to make a loop around each mark or near each mark.
- Select an area clear of boat traffic. If you need to slow down, divert your course, or stop for another boat, you'll have to repeat the run at your chosen RPM setting.
- Load the boat for normal cruising. Top off fuel tanks and water tanks; invite some friends.

1. **Make the graph.** List speeds in 2-knot increments up the left side of a piece of graph paper (see art page 54). Label across the bottom with RPMs, beginning at zero and ending at the highest rated RPM for your engine. Displacement power and sailing vessels might want to extend their graphs only as high as the RPM at *hull speed,* since a displacement boat can exceed its theoretical hull speed only by a small margin and only at

the cost of inadvisably high RPMs, fuel consumption, and engine and hull stress. *(Note: to find the theoretical hull speed of a displacement boat, use the formula 1.34 × the square root of the boat's waterline length. A displacement boat with a 36-foot waterline thus has a hull speed of 8.04 knots.)*

2. **Make the speed run.** Time your run from the first mark to the second mark at a steady RPM. Divide the distance by the time (converted to parts of an hour) to find speed. For instance, if you run from A to B in 12 minutes, convert that to hours using the formula 12 ÷ 60 = 0.2 hour. If A and B are 1.2 miles apart, your speed for the run was 1.2 ÷ 0.2 = 6 knots. Now time the run from the second mark back to the first at the same RPM. Calculate the speed for this leg in the same manner.

3. **Plot data onto the graph.** Add the two speeds together and divide by two. This gives you the average speed for that RPM setting. Repeat at 200 to 400 RPM intervals. Remember to calculate the speed for each half of a round trip. Plot your speeds onto the graph and join the dots with a smooth curve. Post your graph at your console, into your logbook, and onto your sketchboard. Try this example.

You will run a 1-mile distance between Marker A and Marker B. Your first run will be at 800 RPM.

1. Bring the boat up to speed at 800 RPM. Make sure the boat is at speed before you start the run.
2. Start the stopwatch the moment you are abeam of Marker A.
3. Read the stopwatch the moment you are abeam of Marker B. Time reads 12 minutes.
4. Make a wide turn and pass close abeam of Marker B. Start the watch when abeam.
5. Read the stopwatch the moment you are abeam of Marker A. Time reads 10 minutes.

Compute the speed on the first leg (A to B): 1 mile ÷ 0.2 hour = 5 knots

Compute the speed on the second leg (B to A): 1 mile ÷ 0.167 hour = 6 knots

Take the average: 5 + 6 = 11 ÷ 2 = 5.5 knots.

Plot 5.5 knots on your graph next to RPM 800.

Repeat this method for any other RPMs desired, all the way to maximum speed. Now you have a gold mine of information for use with navigation, cruise, and voyage planning. (See also Appendix I for Speed over a Measured Mile.)

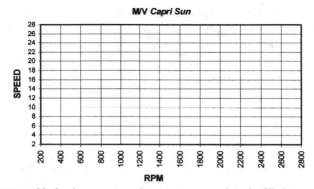

This speed/RPM table for the motor vessel Capri Sun *is ready to be filled out.*

HOW TO USE A GPS RECEIVER FOR YOUR SPEED RUN

If you use the GPS speed function, you won't need fixed landmarks for your run. Run half-mile legs at each chosen RPM setting; this allows the GPS to settle down for more accuracy. Record the GPS speed, make a tight turn, and run a half mile on the reciprocal heading. Add the two speeds, find the average, and plot it onto your graph. Repeat this method for other RPM settings.

Navigation Solutions in Less than 5 Seconds

Smaller than a sheet of paper and almost as thin, completely waterproof and easy to use, the nautical slide rule has but one purpose—to solve time, distance, and speed problems. If you know two of those factors, a nautical slide rule will solve the third for you.

All slide rules come with a base and two wheels. Use the large wheel to find the distance traveled. Use the smaller wheel to find your boatspeed or the time required to travel a given distance. To master the slide rule, remember these three little-known secrets.

1. **Know how each scale breaks down**
   Distance scale (large wheel). Find the printed distance arrow on the base. The distance wheel shows miles on the outside and yards on the inside. For practical navigation, use only the outside miles scale.

   Speed window scale (small wheel). The speed window shows whole knots. Estimate tenths of a knot of speed between the whole mile marks.

   Time window scale (small wheel). The time window has three scales: outside, middle, and inside. The outside shows hours, the middle shows seconds, and the inside shows minutes. For practical navigation, use only hours or minutes.

2. **To find speed or time from distance traveled**
   Set the distance wheel first. Hold it firmly in place with your nondominant thumb.

   Turn the small wheel to the other known factor, either speed or time. Read the window to solve the unknown factor.

   For example: Using the chart, you determine that you must travel 13.5 miles to reach the sea buoy ahead. The GPS shows a speed over ground of 9 knots. If the time now is 1445, what time should you arrive at the sea buoy?

   Because you know the distance, set that first. Set the speed window to 9 knots. Read the time: 1.5 hours. Add 1.5 hours to 1445 to find your ETA of 1615, which should agree with the ETA your GPS receiver is giving you. (I can imagine you thinking, "If my GPS receiver will give

Time, Distance, and Speed—Manual Method

If you don't have a slide rule or calculator, you will still want to work out time, distance, and speed solutions. Follow these steps and work through the examples.

1. Draw a large triangle.
2. Subdivide the triangle with a horizontal line drawn halfway between its base and its apex. Now bisect the lower part of the triangle with a vertical line.
3. Place a D in the upper portion. Place a T in the lower left portion and an S in the lower right portion. These represent the factors of Distance, Time, and Speed.
4. Cover the unknown factor in order to find what to do to solve the problem. For example, if you cover the D, the S and T are side by side. Multiply them together to find D.

If you cover the S, you see that you must divide T into D. If you cover the T, you must divide S into D. If time is a known factor, you must first convert it to hours. For instance,

if the time traveled is 1 hour 36 minutes, convert to hours like this: 36 ÷ 60 = 0.6. Total hours = 1.6.

Example 1
You have 64 miles to go and must arrive in 5 hours 22 minutes. What speed must you make?

Cover up the S (speed unknown); you must divide time into distance.

Convert time to hours first: 22 ÷ 60 = 0.4 (rounded). Total hours = 5.4 hours.

64 nautical miles ÷ 5.4 hours = 11.9 knots (round to 12 knots).

Example 2
You are averaging 5 knots under sail. The next port lies 38 miles downwind. It's 0800 hours. What is your estimated time of arrival?

Cover up the T (time unknown); you must divide speed into distance.

38 nautical miles ÷ 5 knots = 7.6 hours.

Convert tenths of hours to minutes: 0.6 x 60 = 36 minutes; 7 hours 36 minutes.

0800 + 7 h 36 m = 1536, i.e., 3:36 pm.

me an ETA, why go through this calculation?" First, it's always good to check the result of one navigation method against the result of another. And second, a manual speed-time-distance calculation will give you an ETA even when you have no working GPS receiver. All you have to do is estimate your boatspeed some other way—for example, using a speed/RPM table.)

3. **To find the distance traveled from speed and time en route**
   Set the speed factor *first*. Hold it lightly in place with your nondominant thumb to allow the large wheel to turn underneath.

   Turn the large wheel. Watch the time window as you turn it, and stop when you reach your time en route.

   Before reading the distance, check the speed window to make sure it hasn't shifted. Adjust as needed. Then read the distance.

   For example: In this example we do not know our distance traveled. It's 1600 in the afternoon. We've averaged 4.5 knots under sail since 0930 this morning. How far have we traveled?

   Because you do not know distance, set the speed window first. Hold it lightly in place and turn the large wheel until the time window reads 6.5 hours. Check both windows for alignment and then read your distance: 29.25 nautical miles. Round this off to 29.3, since the precision of the method is not high enough to carry to two decimal points.

Harness the Power of the 3-Minute Rule

When you need quick solutions and your nautical slide rule isn't handy, try using the 3-minute rule. Find the distance (in hundreds or thousands of yards) your vessel travels in 3 minutes and move the decimal two places to the left. For instance, if you travel 2,000 yards in 3 minutes, your speed is 20 knots. Travel 620 yards in 3 minutes and your speed is 6.2 knots.

To calculate distance traveled, simply reverse the rule by moving the decimal two places to the right, adding zeroes as necessary. If your speed is 4 knots, you'll travel 400 yards in 3 minutes. If you are traveling at 18.5 knots, you'll travel 1,850 yards in 3 minutes.

Use the same method with one extra step for finding 1-minute increments of travel. For instance, if your speed over ground is 4 knots, in 3 minutes you'll travel 400 yards. Divide 400 by 3 and you'll cover 133 yards every minute. Now try a few examples.

If your speed is 4.6 knots, how far do you travel in 3 minutes? By moving the decimal point two places to the right, we get an answer of 460 yards.

If your speed is 22.7 knots, how far do you travel in 3 minutes? 2,270 yards.

If your speed is 5.8 knots, how far do you travel in 12 minutes? By moving the decimal point two places to the right, we know we travel 580 yards in 3 minutes, and 580 × 4 = 2,320 yards.

If your speed is 7.7 knots, how far do you travel in 5 minutes? We know we travel 770 yards in 3 minutes. Next, figure how far you travel in 1 minute: 770 ÷ 3 = 256 yards in 1 minute. Multiply by 5 to get your answer: 256 yards × 5 = 1,280 yards.

If you travel 300 yards in 1 minute, what is your speed? First factor how far you travel in 3 minutes: 300 yards × 3 = 900 yards. By moving the decimal point two places to the left we get our answer: 9 knots.

If you travel 1,660 yards in 4 minutes, what is your speed? First factor how far you travel in 1 minute: 1,660 ÷ 4 = 415 yards in 1 minute. Next, factor how far you travel in 3 minutes: 415 × 3 = 1,245 yards. By moving the decimal place two places to the left, we know our speed is 12.5 knots (rounded).

This speed is uncorrected for the effects of current or wind. To learn how to do this, see Chapter 5.

SEA-CRET TIP

▶ Apply the 3-minute rule to figure your docking drift rate. At a speed of 1 knot, your drift rate is 33 yards per minute (100 ÷ 3), or about 2 feet per second (100 ÷ 60). Use this to judge when to stop your way and drift to the dock or slip.

How to Select and Calibrate a New Compass

Simplicity and reliability are the hallmarks of any great compass. Carry at least two compasses aboard at all times for safety and peace of mind. If something happens to your steering compass, the handbearing compass can get you home in a pinch. You'll learn more about using this remarkable tool in the next chapter. Test a compass before you buy it to make sure it meets certain standards.

TESTING A COMPASS BEFORE YOU BUY
1. How is the visibility and readability?

Card visibility. Look for a compass with a card diameter of 4 inches or greater. A card of this size has large, easy-to-read degree markings that cut down on fatigue and eyestrain. Numbers spaced at 30-degree intervals are easy to read in a seaway, and you want hash marks at 10- and 5-degree intervals between numbers. The compass dome serves as a magnifier to further enhance the card markings.

Card readability. Stand in front and to the side of the compass. Move the compass to different heights to simulate sitting or standing at the helm. Position the compass to match your likely viewing angle in practice. Step back and look at the display. Is it clear and easy to read without eyestrain? If you like what you see, go to step #2.

Offset lubber lines for sailors. Lubber lines are lines drawn onto or fixed to the compass glass. The person steering the boat lines up the course to the fixed lubber line. For instance, if you wanted to steer 045 degrees magnetic, you would turn the boat until 045 lined up with the lubber line. Some sailors prefer to use two additional lubber lines, offset by 45 degrees to the main lubber line. They use these for tacking and jibing maneuvers.

2. **Test before you purchase**

   Oscillation test. Remove the compass from the box and rotate it in a horizontal plane through 360 degrees. The card should be completely free of friction (sticking) and not bind against any part of the housing. Repeat the test in the opposite direction.

   Recovery test. Place the compass back on the shelf and align the lubber line with one of the numbered 30-degree markings. Hold your magnet to one side of the compass housing. The card will begin to spin toward your magnet. Wait until the card stops all movement, and then quickly remove your magnet to a distance of at least 3 feet.

   Smaller cards should move back to the original mark immediately. Larger cards might make a small swing past the lubber line, but should move back to the original mark without further oscillation. The card should stop within 1 degree of the original reading. If not, the compass pivot, card, or fluid viscosity could be defective.

"ZERO" A STEERING COMPASS BEFORE YOU INSTALL

You'll want to make sure your steering compass is free of internal errors before mounting it on your boat. Most magnetic compasses have internal compensating magnets, which are used for aligning the compass card. These magnets sometimes move during shipping, causing a permanent internal error. Remove all internal error by "zeroing" the compass.

The procedure is fussy but simple. Here it is:

1. **Find a test area.** Find a location without any nearby metals, electrical wiring, or other magnetic influences. The floor or a wooden table might make a good base for zeroing. Sometimes it's easier to locate a good place outdoors.

2. **Find the adjustment screws.** Now locate the compensator-magnet adjustment screws. You'll normally find these beneath small, round caps near the base of the compass. One will be on the side and the other on the front or back of the base. Remove the caps to find the adjustment screws.

> **Tools and Supplies Needed for Zeroing a Steering Compass**
>
> ▸ 1 small nonmagnetic flathead screwdriver
> ▸ 12-inch-square piece of plywood or pressboard
> ▸ duct tape
> ▸ felt-tip pen
> ▸ 1 large hardcover book

3. **Set up board, book, and compass.** Use the felt-tip pen to draw a straight line in the center of the board, parallel to one edge. We'll use this mark to align our compass. Place the compass on the board so that the lubber line aligns with the line you've drawn. Alignment is easier if you look down at the board from above. Screw or tape the compass firmly in place all around its base. Make sure the compass doesn't move even if you move the board from side to side.

4. **Test for north-south error.** The compensator magnets controlled by the side screw are used to remove northerly or southerly compass error. Turn the board until the compass lubber line points to zero degrees. Place the hardcover book along one edge of the board and hold the book firmly in place. Now move the board away from the book, rotate it 180 degrees, and place it firmly against the book's edge again. Does the compass read 180 degrees? If not, *remove exactly one-half of the error*. For example, if the compass reads 176 degrees, turn the compensator screw on the side of the compass until it reads 178 degrees. If it reads 182 degrees, turn the screw until it reads 181 degrees.

   Now we'll start again from a new point. Move your board, aligning the lubber line to 180 degrees. Re-align the book edge along the board. Again turn your board around, placing it firmly against the book's edge. The compass should read zero degrees. If it doesn't, *remove one-half of the error*. Then turn the board to line up the lubber line to zero degrees, reset your book along the edge, and spin the board. Continue in this incremental fashion until you remove all error.

5. **Test for east-west error.** The compensator magnets controlled by the front (forward) or back (aft) screw are used to remove easterly or westerly compass error. Point the lubber line to 90 degrees. Reset your book edge to the board, then rotate the board 180 degrees and place its opposite edge against the book. The new lubber line reading should be 270 degrees. If not, *remove exactly one-half of the error*, this time using the forward or aft compensator screw.

Reset the board to 270 degrees, re-align your book, and spin your board. Repeat the process as before. When you are done, install your error-free compass onboard.

How to Choose and Adjust Marine Binoculars

Select marine binoculars based on quality, comfort, clarity, and ease of adjustment. Good binoculars allow you to see vessels through haze, rain, or low light conditions. From far away, you can identify that buoy you're looking for or the friendly twinkle of a long-awaited landfall.

Field of View (FOV)
When you look through a pair of binoculars, a circle surrounds the object being viewed. The diameter of that circle at a distance of 1,000 yards is called the *field of view*, or FOV. A larger FOV helps keep objects inside the circle when your boat is rolling or pitching. Purchase binoculars with a specified FOV between 350 and 450 feet at 1,000 yards.

Power and Light-Gathering Ability
The most common marine binocular powers are 7 × 50 and 7 × 35. The first number shows the amount of magnification of a viewed object. You'll need magnification of 6 or 7; anything higher causes objects to jump out of the FOV.

The second number is the diameter of the larger lens, or *objective lens*. This indicates the instrument's ability to gather light at twilight or nighttime and in haze or fog. Larger is better. Look for an objective lens diameter of 35 to 50 millimeters.

Is the Rubber Coating Waterproof?
Rubber coating provides the user with a better grip and protects against damage. Waterproof binoculars come charged with nitrogen to prevent intrusion into the prism or lens housing. Read the specifications and avoid binoculars bearing the much less protective "water-resistant" claim. You want waterproof, not just water-resistant, binoculars, and you'll be glad you spent a few dollars more after spray or a squall douses your binocs.

SEA-CRET TIP

▶ Eyeglass wearers should choose rubber-coated binoculars with the fold-down eyecups. These help improve focus and provide comfort when bracing the binoculars against glasses.

FOCUS ADJUSTMENT CHOICES

Binoculars come with *center focus* or *individual focus* eyepieces. Center focus makes adjustment easier and readjusting unnecessary as your viewing range changes. Many fine professional marine binoculars, however, come with individual focus lenses. They just take a bit longer to adjust and need readjustment at different ranges.

Take the time to learn the adjustment process for both types of instruments. Now you can select the perfect pair that will give you satisfaction for years to come.

How to Adjust Individual Focus Eyepiece Binoculars

1. **Focus the left eyepiece.** Close your right eye or cover the right objective lens. Focus the left eyepiece on an object at least 1 mile away. Mark the scale setting between the body and the focus ring.
2. **Focus the right eyepiece.** Close your left eye or cover the left objective lens. Focus the right eyepiece on a distant object at a range of at least 1 mile. Mark the scale setting between the body and focus ring.
3. **Reset the focus when ranges change.** With individual focus settings, you'll need to make incremental adjustments when viewing objects at longer or shorter distances than your original setting. Remember to reset your binoculars back to your personal focus-ring setting.

How to Adjust Center Focus Eyepiece Binoculars

1. **Focus the left eyepiece.** Close your right eye or cover the right objective lens. Use the center focus wheel to focus the left lens while viewing an object at least 1 mile away. Mark the scale setting on the center focus ring.
2. **Focus the right eyepiece.** Close your left eye or cover the left objective lens. Using the right eyepiece focus ring, adjust the focus by viewing the distant object. Mark the scale shown on the body and focus ring.
3. **Fine-tune with the center focus ring.** When you need to make adjustments as viewing ranges change, use only the center focus ring.

How to Adjust a Sextant in Three Steps

Any cautious navigator will see the sense of carrying a sextant and double-checking the GPS ...
—John Vigor, *The Seaworthy Offshore Sailboat*

Long before GPS, the Coast Guard used sextants to position buoys and lights to a tolerance of +/−10 yards. With a bit of practice, it's easy to use a sextant for finding your position or your distance off an object in piloting waters. Out at sea, celestial navigation remains the primary backup to GPS. The sextant requires periodic maintenance, like any fine instrument.

A sextant measures the angle between two objects. For instance, you could measure the vertical angle from the horizon to the sun, and with a few calculations, you could convert this angle to a bearing line (a *line of position* or *LOP*). When you cross that LOP with another obtained by some other means, you'll have fixed your position at the intersection of the two. Or, you could measure the angle from the top of a tall lighthouse down to its base at the water's edge, enter a table with that angle, and (knowing the height of the lighthouse, which will be noted on the chart or in the Light List) find your distance off the lighthouse. You can also measure the horizontal angle between two charted objects, such as a tank and church spire. The angle between them will give you a line of position.

Note: any line of position based on an angular measurement—including the three examples just noted—is in fact a circle of position *or COP. A COP is a specialized instance of an LOP, but the distinction is illusory, as Chapter 4 will make clear.*

Every sextant comes with eight standard parts (see sidebar).

HOW TO READ A SEXTANT

Before beginning adjustments, let's do some practice setting and reading the index arm. Squeeze the levers and slide the arm up and down the arc. Notice an engraved mark on the index arm. Move the index arm until it's close to the 0 on the arc, and release the levers. Just get it close to the zero, not directly on it. Turn the micrometer drum and line up two things: the index arm at zero degrees and the micrometer drum at zero minutes. Next, find out if there is any error in the sextant.

On the arc. Turn the micrometer drum away from you. You'll notice the minutes increase. This is called *on the arc.*

Off the arc. Turn the micrometer drum toward you. You'll notice the minutes decrease. This is called *off the arc.*

Now let's check the sextant to make sure it's properly adjusted and ready to use.

SEA-CRET TIP

▶ Some sextants have a vernier scale next to the micrometer drum. It reads in tenths of a minute or in seconds. Look for an unbroken line formed by the vernier and micrometer scales. Add the vernier scale reading to the micrometer minutes. Many navigators choose to ignore the vernier reading and estimate tenths by eye. This will not affect your accuracy.

The Parts of a Sextant

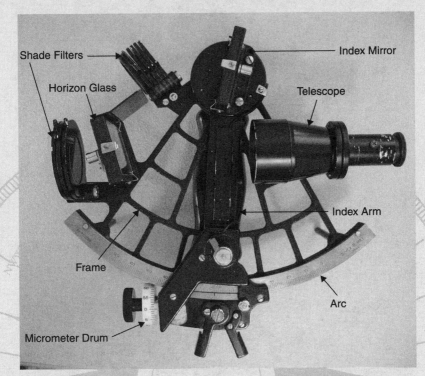

Shade Filters

Horizon Glass

Index Mirror

Telescope

Frame

Index Arm

Micrometer Drum

Arc

A sextant has eight standard parts.

Frame: The weblike structure that holds all other parts. The frame approximates 1/6th of a circle, thus the name *sextant*.

Arc: The curved piece of metal or plastic running along the bottom of the frame. Lines engraved on the arc show whole degrees.

Index Arm: The arm attached to the top of the frame. Squeezing two clamps at the bottom of the arm enables it to move up and down the arc.

Micrometer Drum: The wheel near the index-arm clamps, with marks showing minutes. This is used to fine-tune an observation.

Index Mirror: A small mirror attached to the top of the index arm that captures the reflected image of an observed object.

Horizon Glass: Attached to the front of the frame, one half is clear and one half is a mirror.

Shade Filters: Both the index mirror and horizon glass have shade glasses to protect the eye from water surface glare or direct sunlight.

Telescope: The scope power should not exceed 5X. More powerful scopes have too small a field of view, making the observed image difficult to view.

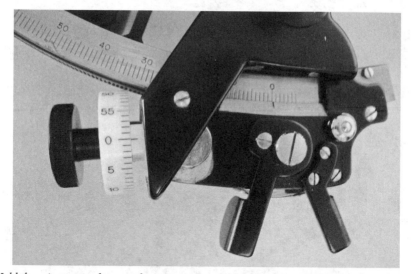

Hold the micrometer drum and spin it one way or the other to perfectly align three things at once: the index-arm mark, the zero-degree mark on the arc, and the zero-minutes mark on the micrometer drum.

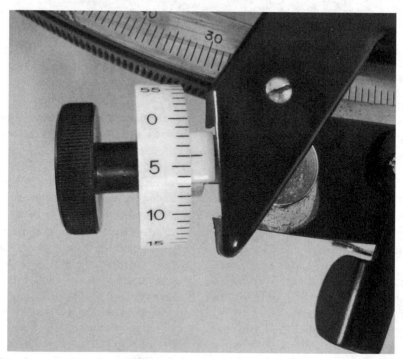

Turn the micrometer drum away from you about a quarter turn. You'll notice the minutes increase. When adjusting or checking for error, this is called on the arc. Subtract the minutes to correct an observation.

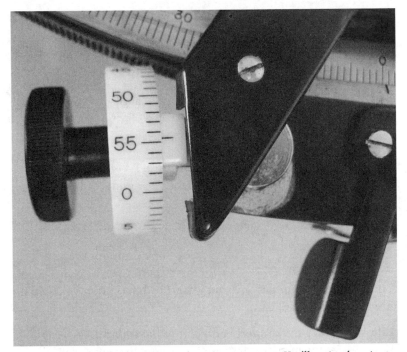

Turn the micrometer drum toward you about a quarter turn. You'll notice the minutes decrease. When adjusting or checking for error, this is called off the arc. *Add the minutes to correct an observation.*

HOW TO CHECK THE INDEX ERROR

Index error is caused by minor alignment errors in the mirror. This causes a sextant to read too high or too low. If you fail to correct the index error, your position could be off by several miles. It's simple to measure and apply index error. Always find index error before using any marine sextant.

- Set the mark on the index arm and micrometer drum to zero (as shown in the first photo).
- Look through the scope and sight the horizon or a distant horizontal surface. Crank the micrometer drum slowly up and down. Watch the image split, then bring it together to form a straight line.
- Now read the micrometer drum as described in the second and third photos. How many minutes is it on or off the arc? Check it once or twice more. You should get similar readings.

To correct a sextant reading with minutes on the arc, you subtract the index error from the observed angle. To correct a sextant reading with minutes off the arc, you add the index error to the observed angle.

Example: You check the index error on your sextant and determine that it has 2 minutes of error **on the arc.** You observe an angle between two objects of 24 degrees 12 minutes. Subtract 2 minutes to correct the reading to 24 degrees 10 minutes.

Example: You check the index error on your sextant and determine that it has 3 minutes of error **off the arc.** You observe an angle between two objects of 98 degrees 54 minutes. Add 3 minutes to correct the reading to 98 degrees 57 minutes.

THREE STEPS TO ADJUST YOUR SEXTANT

Tools Needed to Adjust Your Sextant

▶ jeweler's screwdriver or hex-key wrench set

If the error is more than 2 minutes on or off the arc, you'll need to go through the adjustment process shown below. Follow each step consecutively to reduce or eliminate the index error. First, check the type of screws on the back of the index mirror and horizon glass. Read the sextant manufacturer's recommendation for adjustment tools.

1. **Adjust the index mirror perpendicular to the frame.** Remove the telescope. Set the micrometer drum to zero. Set the index arm to 35 degrees. Turn the sextant around so that you're looking at the index mirror. Hold the sextant up to your eye and look directly into the mirror. Now, rotate the sextant slowly to the left until you see the actual and reflected image of the arc. If you see a broken line, find the screw on the back of the index mirror. You may need a jeweler's screwdriver or Allen wrench. Insert the tool into the screw and hold it. Bring the sextant back up to your eye and once again rotate it to get the actual and reflected image of the arc in the mirror. Turn the screw until you have a straight line. Then go to Step 2.

2. **Remove side error.** Insert the telescope. Set the micrometer drum and index arm to zero. Find a distant vertical object such as a flagpole or water tank. Sight the object through the horizon glass. Now, keeping the sextant vertical, move it slightly to the left and right. You'll see two images, the object itself and its reflected image. As you move the sextant from side to side, they should stay lined up on top of one another. If not, you need to adjust the horizon glass.

   The horizon glass has two screws. Use the horizon glass screw *farthest* from the frame. Insert your tool in the screw and then sight the vertical object again. Adjust the screw incrementally up or down to vertically align the actual and reflected object. Check the adjustment again when you are done. Then go to Step 3.

3. **Remove index error.** Set the micrometer drum and index arm to zero. Look through the scope at the horizon or a distant horizontal surface. If you see a broken line, you must make this adjustment.

   Set your tool into the horizon glass screw *closest* to the sextant frame. Now look at the horizon again and slowly turn the setscrew up or down until you see a straight line.

Always make a final adjustment check. Go back and check all three adjustments again, and if necessary, repeat steps 1 through 3. Remember, you must go through all three adjustment steps in the order shown.

How to Adjust Your Radar for the Best Picture

No other electronic instrument offers the versatility or multitasking of the modern radar. It gives navigational information, tracks targets, allows entry into port during fog, and warns of approaching squalls and storms. (Chapter 7 includes tips on using radar for collision avoidance.) Newer radars even interface with GPS receivers and chart plotters.

Most modern radars have automatic tuning, but knowing how to adjust yours manually puts you in control and often gives a sharper picture.

THE FIVE MAIN CONTROLS TO GET YOU STARTED

Brilliance: Adjust how bright the monitor and text look. Use this control as you would use any computer screen brightness control.

Contrast: As on a computer screen, the contrast control changes the vibrancy of an image or text. Increase contrast to sharpen images and text. Decrease contrast for a softer effect.

Gain: This is the system's main receiver control. Gain measures the ability of the receiver to process the reflected signal properly. Use the gain control to tweak the radar for a good picture.

Sea clutter (STC): Use this control to clear up screen clutter caused by signal reflections from wave or swell faces.

Rain clutter (FTC): Use this control to clear up screen clutter caused by signal reflections from rain, squalls, or storms.

START WITH A WARM-UP

If you'll use the radar with the engine running, start your engine or engines. Turn on all electronic gear. Then turn on the radar receiver. Wait 2 to 3 minutes before beginning adjustments.

ADJUSTING FOR RAIN, SQUALL, WAVES, AND SWELL

Water droplets, when massed together, provide an excellent reflective surface. Rain and squalls appear as clusters of dots anywhere on the scope. Sea waves appear as a mass of clutter at the center of the scope. Make rain clutter (FTC) or sea clutter (STC) adjustments in small increments. The rain clutter control clears interference over the entire scope at once; the sea clutter control clears clutter from the scope center outward.

Use a *turn-stop-watch* method of incremental adjustment with any control. Crank a tad and stop cranking. Watch the scope for several sweeps. Wait for a target to paint more than once in the same spot. If you see nothing, repeat the turn-stop-watch method. Easy does it. You want to adjust for the best picture without washing out small, hidden targets.

PROPER GAIN ADJUSTMENT

Gain determines the ability of your radar receiver to amplify a signal reflected from a vessel, landmass, or buoy. Concentrate on properly adjusting the gain control. Good gain adjustment rewards you with three vital features for safety:

1. Detection of long- and short-range targets.
2. Separation of targets close to one another. For example, two vessels close together appear as individual targets instead of as one large target.
3. Acquisition of weak reflection targets (wooden vessels, targets with round versus flat surfaces).

How to Adjust Your Gain for the Best Picture

Try to adjust gain in relatively calm weather with no rain or wave activity.

1. Turn off the rain and sea clutter controls.
2. Turn the gain control down all the way.
3. Set the range scale to the maximum for your vessel, based on your antenna height (see Appendix I for a table). Find a distant object just inside this range.
4. Turn up the gain very slowly until you just begin acquiring your selected target. You should see a light speckle of dots on the scope.
5. Reset brightness and contrast collectively for the best picture. Take care not to wash out small targets with too much brilliance or lose them with too little brilliance.
6. Mark the gain setting on the radar with tape or a felt-tip pen. That way you can quickly return to the proper setting after changing gain or range scales. Lower the gain a bit when trying to pick up closer targets; raise it for distant targets.

TARGET STRENGTH AND THE ART OF BECOMING "RADAR-VISIBLE"

A radar signal requires a large amount of mass for good reflectivity. It doesn't matter whether the mass consists of wood, paper, plastic, or metal. A large, flat surface that is perpendicular to the radar signal paints a sharp radar image. (Note, however, that sails do not reflect radar signals well.) Smaller, rounded shapes (sailboat hulls and masts) present a poor reflective surface to the signal.

Large ships often miss smaller targets at relatively close range. Their high antennas send out a narrow, cone-shaped signal, skipping over these close targets. In heavy weather, huge seas or swells hide small targets, making detection difficult or impossible.

Hoist one or more radar reflectors to make your boat visible to other radar-equipped vessels. Reflectors come in all sizes and shapes, from simple plates to a vitamin-pill-shaped canister. In recent radar reflector testing, the trihedral-shaped reflector took home the gold. This design consists of three round plates that intersect one another at 90-degree angles. For the strongest signal return, hoist the reflector in a "rain catcher" position. To do this, make sure two of the plates form a "V" shape when pointing skyward.

"Your Call, Skipper"

You're the skipper or most knowledgeable crewmember in each of the following situations. What actions would you take?

1. You are bound from the Miami sea buoy to Charleston, SC. Your GPS indicates the next waypoint to be 3.6 miles ahead. At 12 knots, how long will this take you?

2. Using the 3-minute rule, what is your speed if you cover 1.5 miles in 6 minutes? You have 30 miles to go to the marina ahead. It's now 1545. You need to arrive before the fuel pier closes at 1800. What is your ETA? Do you have enough time?

3. A new crewmember is having a hard time focusing his new, high-quality, center focus binoculars. He can't seem to get the left lens to focus. "The left eyepiece is stuck and won't turn, skipper! Can you help me out?"

4. When looking for a new steering or handbearing compass, what two things do you want to test before buying?

5. What three radar controls are turned all the way *down* before you start to adjust the radar?

ANSWERS

1. The trip will take 18 minutes. There are two ways to arrive at the answer.

To find time needed to cover one mile, divide your speed into 60:

60 minutes ÷ 12 knots = 5 minutes to cover 1 mile; 5 × 3.6 miles = 18 minutes

or

To find time needed to travel known distance at known speed:

3.6 miles ÷ 12 knots = 0.3 hour × 60 minutes/hour = 18 minutes

2. You are traveling 15 knots. With 30 miles to go, this will take 2 hours, so 1545 + 2 = 1745 ETA. You'll need to slow to bare steerage from the marina entrance to the fuel pier. I like to allow at least 20 minutes for this, so I'd increase my speed a bit.

3. The left lens doesn't turn; it's focused with the center focus wheel. Cover the right lens and focus the left lens with the center focus wheel. Cover the left lens and focus the right lens with the right lens eyepiece. That's it!

4. First, roll the compass up and down and from side to side. Watch for friction. Next, use a small magnet to move the card off its heading. Remove the magnet. The card should return to within 1 degree of the original heading without wandering.

5. Gain, rain clutter (FTC), and sea clutter (STC).

PILOTING TIPS AND TECHNIQUES

The navigator's job is a specialized one but not sacred. He or she should never feel above explaining it to shipmates.
—John Rousmaniere, *The Annapolis Book of Seamanship*

What is the fastest way to predict when you will sight the cliff-top lighthouse 17 miles ahead? With our position in doubt, what three things must we know before turning toward land? How can we use GPS to plot our position onto a chart faster than ever before?

In This Chapter, You'll Learn How To:
- Avoid dangers with a single bearing or range
- Pass a treacherous, rock-strewn reef without using a chart
- Turn the sides of your boat into powerful navigation tools
- Plot positions in under 5 seconds—using only a pencil!
- Reach any windward destination quickly and in complete safety

DR Plotting and the Boat-Trackline Connection

Even now, in the age of GPS, you need to back up all other forms of navigation with basic dead reckoning (DR). DR navigation uses the three factors of time, distance, and speed to estimate a boat's movement from one point to another. For instance, if you know your boatspeed and the distance you have to go, you can determine the time of arrival, as we saw in Chapter 3. In Chapter 2 we prepared our charts with tracklines. You can use dead reckoning to plan your trip before casting off. If you measure the trackline distance and predict your speed, you will get a good idea of how much time it should take to reach your destination.

A navigator uses similar techniques in a sailboat tacking upwind, though often for shorter distances. For instance, you can measure the predicted length of each tacking leg (distance), predict your speed on that leg (speed), and then calculate the elapsed time to the next tack. As soon as the next tack is made, the time is started again and the process repeated.

There are five essential ingredients for hassle-free dead reckoning:

1. **Known position.** All navigation begins from a known position, whether a buoy, a jetty, or any other means of positive identification.
2. **Trackline.** A *trackline*, labeled TR, extends from the known position in the desired direction of travel. Plot the TR boldly to make it stand out from other plotted lines. We hope our boat stays on the TR, but forces such as wind and current, or our own steering errors, can move the boat off the TR.

   The connection between your boat and its TR changes all the time. At any given time, your boat is in two of six relationships to its trackline:

   on TR
   to the right of TR
   to the left of TR
   moving at its predicted speed
   moving faster than expected
   moving slower than expected

   Once you have established your boat's relationship to its trackline, you can decide on a course of action. In some cases, being off the TR isn't at all critical, and the boat can continue in safety. At other times, being off the TR by a few yards might place the boat and crew in danger.
3. **Steering course (C).** The *steering course,* or *courseline,* is the course steered by the helmsman. Sometimes wind, current, or steering error can move a boat off its trackline. This means you might very well have to steer a different course to return to the trackline. In Chapter 5 we'll find out how to tell this and how to correct for it. If the TR is 90 degrees but you are steering 85 degrees to compensate for a south-setting current, you plot two lines on the chart. Draw the trackline boldly and label it TR—090°M. Then draw the 85-degree courseline with a lighter solid or dashed line and label it C—085°M.
4. **DR positions require time, speed, and distance.** From the last known position, plot dead reckoning positions along the trackline (or tracklines) being steered. If you are steering the TR, plot DRs along the trackline. Otherwise, plot them along the steering course.

   Time: Pick a time interval based on your proximity to danger or uncertainty of position. Within a mile or two of the coast, use a frequency of every 15 or 30 minutes. Off-soundings (when you are offshore), use an interval of an hour or longer.
   Speed: DR speed is usually taken from speed tables, a knotmeter, or a knot log. Vessels under power can use a speed/RPM table (see Chapter 3). Vessels under sail should use the knotmeter or knot log and take an average of readings. As mentioned in Chapter 3, the speed these methods

give you is speed through the water, which will differ from speed over ground to the extent that your boat's progress is aided or impeded by current. Again, we'll look at these effects in Chapter 5.

Distance: Once you determine an appropriate time interval and your DR speed, calculate the estimated distance traveled (remember the formula, Distance ÷ Speed = Time; see Chapter 3) and plot your DRs ahead of your last known position.

Skipper's Quick Guide to Bearings and Lines of Position (LOP)

If you point your boat at a charted object—a buoy, tank, or lighthouse—and look across your steering compass, you are *sighting a bearing* to the object. For instance, let's say you sight a tank onshore at 350 degrees magnetic. This is the bearing *from* your boat *to* the tank, so draw a line on the chart *from* the water *to* the tank in the direction of 350 degrees magnetic. You have *taken a bearing* on the tank, and you are somewhere along that line.

If you were to wrap that line completely around the earth, it would eventually come back and intersect the tank again. In effect, this proves that bearings are actually circles, but navigators call them *lines of position*, or LOPs, as we saw in Chapter 3. For practical purposes, you only plot a short segment of the circle onto the chart, and that segment looks like a straight line—hence the name line of position.

Getting back to our tank, we need to determine where we are along that bearing line. So we look for a second charted object whose bearing will cross the tank bearing at an angle approaching 90 degrees. Ah—there's a spire over there, and it shows on the chart. We point the boat at the

spire, take a bearing to the spire from the steering compass, plot the bearing on the chart, and note where it intersects our first LOP. This fixes our position (thus the word *fix*). The closer the intersection is to 90 degrees, the stronger the reliability of the fix. Your GPS receiver provides reliable fixes in part because the LOPs—a line of latitude and a line of longitude—intersect at 90 degrees. A fix must be derived from at least two LOPs, and a third LOP provides increased reliability. Seldom will three LOPs intersect at a single spot; more commonly their intersections will form a small triangle that navigators call a *cocked hat*. Your actual position is somewhere in that triangle.

A good handbearing compass makes it easy to sight a bearing. You don't need to point your boat at the sighted object and read the bearing from your steering compass. Instead, just point the handbearing compass at the object and read the bearing through the sighting vane. (Find a spot on deck where the handbearing compass is unaffected by deviation, as discussed in Chapter 3.) When bearings are this easy to get, you'll get more of them, and that will improve your DR navigation.

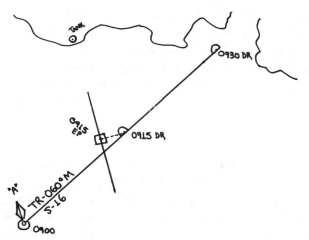

Use the standard international symbols for plotting on your charts. This includes a solid line for your TR (as well as course steered); a dot, half circle, and time (in 24-hour time) for a DR position; a dot, square, and time for an estimated position (EP); and a dot, circle, and time for a fix, or known position.

5. **Use standard international symbols.** Use one of three symbols for any plotted position (see illustration).

   Dead reckoning (DR)—dot, half circle, and time.

   Estimated position (EP)—dot, square, and time. Estimated positions upgrade the reliability of a DR plot. Simply take a bearing and plot a DR position for the same time. The EP lies at the point along the bearing that is closest to the DR position.

   Known/fixed position—dot, circle, and time. Your GPS provides a *fix*, or known position. Alternatively, if you are sitting next to a buoy or light, you know beyond a shadow of a doubt where you are, and that is your fix. More broadly speaking, a fix results from plotting two or more bearing lines (see the sidebar on page 73) and is thus more accurate and reliable than an estimated position. (See "Secrets of the Most Accurate LOP on Earth" later in this chapter to learn why ranges yield the most accurate fixes of all.)

THREE GOLDEN RULES FOR SUCCESSFUL DR PLOTTING

1. Plot a DR at your chosen time interval. If you maintain your DR plot faithfully, you'll have a rough idea of your location in the event your navigation electronics go off-line.

2. Plot a DR *at the same time* you take a bearing or range. If you take a bearing at 0912, plot a DR for 0912. You must do this in order to determine the impact of the current on your boat. In Chapter 5 we'll

discuss how to determine if a current is setting your boat off its trackline, and how to correct for that.

3. Plot new DRs when your speed changes. When this happens, whether by throttle, wind, or current (or any combination of them), erase the old DRs *ahead* of your current position. They no longer apply. Lay down new DRs based on your new speed.

How to Become Piloting Sequence Savvy

At all times, the nautical chart must agree with the visual picture that surrounds you.

Piloting combines three methods of finding one's position: piloting by eye; piloting by visual bearings on charted landforms, landmarks, or navigation aids; and piloting by electronics. The navigator must never rely on only one method—even in the most trying conditions. Checking one method against another keeps your boat and crew safe. The best sequence of these methods depends on whether you are piloting offshore, inshore, or on a coastwise passage.

Piloting by Eye. Use two objects and observe how they appear to move relative to one another. For instance, if steering down a channel, keep the aids to navigation lined up evenly to the right and left. On the other hand, if you were turning into a channel, you might use a line of aids to navigation to turn safely into the channel. In the illustration on page 76, a sharp turn to the left is coming up. Make your turn the moment the left side markers (the 3, 5, and 7 navaids) line up. As you make your turn, concentrate on the navaids to the right, staying inside that line for safety. While navigating, make adjustments for wind and current. Use piloting by eye to prevent a collision with another boat (as discussed in detail in Chapter 7) or with a buoy, beacon, or hazard to navigation. Observe objects ahead as well as those astern. Check abeam to sense speed along your visual TR. Make sure your visual picture agrees with what you see on the chart. If not, slow or stop the boat and work things out.

Piloting by Visual Bearings. Maintain a dead reckoning plot as described above, and update the plot using bearings taken with your steering or hand bearing compass to fixed or floating navaids, charted landmarks, and landform tangents. (Examples of the latter could include the right-hand end of a bold island, the left-hand extremity of a line of cliffs, etc. Any sharp break in topography that you can view in profile and locate unambiguously on a chart makes a good target for a tangent bearing.)

You can also take soundings by electronic transducer or lead line, correct these for the state of tide, and compare them with charted soundings to

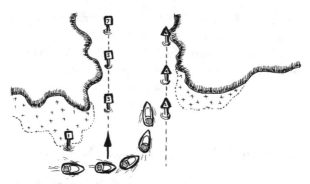

Piloting by eye is one technique for staying on a safe course. When entering a channel, it might mean delaying the turn until the left-hand markers line up, as here.

SEA-CRET TIP

▶ In narrow channels, always glance astern every minute or so. Study the *set* of the boat (how it is moving) relative to aids on the channel edges. This quickly shows if you're in danger of wandering out of the channel.

---

help locate yourself. This method may not be that convenient, but if you find yourself in poor visibility without functioning GPS, it's a good technique to know. You have to correct the sounding from an electronic depth sounder by measuring the distance of the transducer below the vessel's waterline and adding this distance to the instrument sounding (unless the instrument has a programmed offset correction). For instance, if your depth transducer is mounted 4 feet below the waterline and the sounding reads 10 feet, you are in 14 feet of water. You then correct this number by adding or subtracting the present height of tide relative to low-water datum (see Chapter 5). If you measure a 14-foot sounding at low water and the tide tables tell you to expect a low-water height of 1.2 feet (i.e., 1.2 feet above low-water datum), subtract 1.2 from 14 to get 12.8, then round up to 13. Look for a 13-foot sounding on the chart near your DR position—maybe that's where you are. This works best when you're near a rapidly shoaling coast. In such a case, find the 12-foot depth contour, and you can be fairly sure you're just outside it.

Combine soundings with bearings, and take action as needed to keep your vessel in safe water. Use what you have. Advanced techniques include using a sextant.

Piloting by Electronics. Radar is the most versatile electronic navigation instrument in existence. Not only can it provide distance and bearing from a landmass, but it is the primary instrument for collision avoidance, low vis-ibility navigation, and tracking of nearby squalls and storms. GPS units and chart plotters provide an instant and highly accurate assessment of position and speed over ground. Integrated navigation systems include a chart plotter, radar, and depth sounder in one unit.

PRIORITIZING PILOTING INFORMATION BASED ON SCALE

So how does the shorthanded navigator prioritize the relevance of the piloting information gathered by the three means? Make the decision based on the scale of your chart or plotter display. Keep in mind that the 1:80,000 scale serves as the baseline for all coastal piloting. Navigators switch to smaller scales for offshore work and use larger scales for inshore work.

- **OFFSHORE: SCALES SMALLER THAN 1:80,000**
  First priority: electronic (celestial as backup)
  Second priority: visual bearings (as long as practicable)
  Third priority: eye
- **COASTWISE: SCALES CLOSE TO 1:80,000**
  First priority: visual bearings (in good visibility)
  Second priority: eye
  Third priority: electronic (higher priority in poor visibility)
- **INSHORE: SCALES GREATER THAN 1: 80,000**
  First priority: eye
  Second priority: electronic
  Third priority: visual bearings

Some may question the priority of electronic over visual bearings in inshore waters. But in the twenty-first century, the inshore navigator relies heavily on GPS, chart plotter, and radar for navigation in unfamiliar, confined waters. This does not excuse the shorthanded crew from maintaining a dead reckoning plot or taking bearings. The number one form of navigation lies in what you can see.

At all times the navigator should compare the surrounding visual picture with the chart. Even celestial navigation fixes can be confirmed or contradicted by visual means. If for any reason things *look* wrong, stop the boat. If necessary, anchor. Get oriented and comfortable before proceeding.

How to Determine When You Will Make Landfall

There's nothing quite like the crisp, fresh air that accompanies the passage of a cold front on the U.S. east coast. The wind shifts to the northwest, and it looks like you can see for miles and miles. Walk down to the beach and scan that razor-sharp horizon. How far do you think you can see: 20 miles, 15 miles?

If your eyes are 6 feet above sea level, would you believe only 2.9 miles? The distance to the horizon is limited by the earth's curvature, which causes objects beyond the horizon to appear to drop off the earth. In order to see more distant objects, we must raise our *height of eye* (HE) farther above sea level—for example, by climbing to the cabin coachroof or the flying bridge. This of course is why lookouts in the whaling ships and sailing navies were posted in masthead crow's nests. (For more on distance to the horizon, see Chapter 7.)

CHOOSE A PROMINENT LANDFALL OBJECT

Before you make a landfall from offshore, pick a prominent charted object—such as a mountaintop, lighthouse, or offshore light tower—on which to home your approach. If you know the height of the object and your own height of eye, you'll know when to expect it to come into view on your horizon in clear weather. The steps below describe the procedure for making landfall on lighted and unlighted objects.

Making Landfall on a Lighted Object

1. **Find your height of eye and the height of the object.** Estimate your height of eye (HE). Assume, for example, that your HE will be 9 feet when you're standing on your coachroof. That figure includes the height of the coachroof from sea level (3 feet), plus your own height (6 feet). Now read the height of the Dry Tortugas Light from the chart: 151 feet.
2. **Find the geographic range.** Geographic range combines the distance to your horizon and the horizon distance of the other object. The formula is:

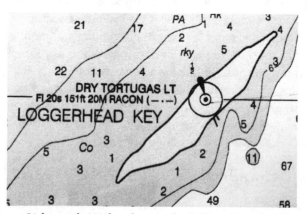

The Dry Tortugas Light stands 151 feet above sea level. The 20M in the abbreviation next to the light indicates the object's nominal range in nautical miles. (This range takes into account the light's candlepower, but not its height; see text.)

[(square root of the height of eye × 1.17) + (square root of the height of the object in feet × 1.17)] = Distance off in nautical miles. In our example:

Observer's horizon distance = square root
of 9 = 3 × 1.17 = 3.5 miles

Dry Tortugas Light's horizon distance = square root
of 151 = 12.288205 × 1.17 = 14.4 miles

Geographic range = 3.5 + 14.4 = 17.9 miles

3. **Draw both range arcs on the chart.** The range at which you actually see an object at sea varies with atmospheric conditions and, in the case of lights, full output of candlepower. You should see a light somewhere between the nominal range (given on the chart) and the geographic range (computed as above). For this reason, it is prudent to plot both of these range arcs on the chart. In this example you would do so by sticking the needle point of your compass into the light's position dot on the chart and swinging a 17.9-mile arc (the geographic range arc) and a 20-mile arc (the nominal range arc) across the TR. The next step is to plot a DR to both of these arcs from your current position. Next set the GPS alarm or a stopwatch to signal when you pass the first arc. Begin scanning the horizon at that time. Set the alarm to sound again when you transit the second arc. If you still don't see the object upon arrival at the second arc, stop the boat, plot a position, and check your math. Raise your height of eye and scan again. Has haze or light fog set in? Try scanning just above or below the horizon.

Making Landfall on an Unlighted Object

You can use points of land, mountains or islands to determine time of landfall, as long as the chart shows the elevation contours. In this example, let's assume you are traveling on a power cruiser toward Angel Island. You want to find out when you can expect to see the highest point on the island.

1. Find your HE and the height of the object. The height of the flying bridge deck on your power cruiser is 20 feet, and your own height is 6 feet. So your HE is 20 + 6 = 26 feet. The height of the highest peak on Angel Island is 500 feet.

2. At what range might you expect to start picking up the highest point on Angel Island? To find the geographic (computed) range:

Your horizon distance = square root of 26 = 5.10 × 1.17 = 6.0 miles

Angel Island's horizon distance = square root
of 500 = 22.36 × 1.17 = 26.2 miles

Geographic range = 6.0 + 26.2 = 32.2 miles

3. Use a straightedge to extend your TR over Angel Island intersecting the 500-foot elevation contour. Mark this point.

The mountains of Angel Island, which the chart shows to be 300 and 500 feet above sea level, could be used as a prominent landfall.

4. Measure 32.2 miles on the chart's right- or left-hand latitude scale with your plotting compass. Stick the compass needle point into the mark at the top of Angel Island and sweep an arc at 32.2 miles across the TR. If the distance is too long for the compass, measure a convenient number of miles and walk the compass back along the TR. For instance, if you measure 5 miles, you would walk the compass back 6 full segments (30 miles), plus an additional 2.2 miles.

5. Estimate your time to that intersection point, label the chart, and set the GPS alarm. When the alarm sounds, scan the horizon with binoculars for Angel Island. In clear weather, Angel Island should appear nearly dead ahead on the horizon.

Secrets of the Most Accurate LOP on Earth

When two charted objects line up as viewed from your boat—say a church spire behind a tank—you have a *range* (also known as a *transit*). A range provides a flawless line of position (LOP). When planning a cruise, look ahead, behind, and to the sides of your track for pairs of charted objects that will line up as you proceed. Natural ranges help you stay on track, show your boat's speed of advance, and strengthen the quality of any position fix. You can use any combination of landform tangents, landmarks, beacons, and buoys as a range. You needn't convert a bearing to true or magnetic or even use a protractor. Just draw a line on the chart through the two objects, extend the line over the water, and you're somewhere on that LOP. No error, no slipped parallel rulers, no fuss, and no doubt about it. Cross that LOP with a bearing to an object off the beam, and you've got a solid fix. Here are some ways to use ranges:

Track drift: Keep in a channel by choosing two objects that are in line and dead ahead of your course. But check dead astern, too. Over-the-shoulder ranges give the quickest warning that your boat is drifting off track. (See below for corrective actions when you drift off-range.)

Track advance: The elapsed time between successive ranges along the side of a trackline will enable you to calculate your boat's speed over ground, or *advance*, along the trackline.

Track turns: Use a natural range to tell you when to turn onto a new trackline. Plot this range onto the trackline ahead of time. Label the line TB for *turn bearing*.

Fast and easy line of position (LOP): When two charted objects line up, write down your time and draw the LOP over your trackline. This gives you an instant *estimated position* (EP). Upgrade it to a fix by taking and plotting a bearing to a charted object 60 to 120 degrees off the range.

HOW TO REGAIN A RANGE AFTER DRIFTING

Range ahead: If you start drifting off a range dead ahead, follow the direction of the *closer* object. If the closer object is to the left of the more distant object, turn left; if it is to the right, turn right.

Range astern (over-the-shoulder): If you start to drift while using an over-the-shoulder range, follow the direction of the *farther* object. If the more distant object is to the left, turn left; if to the right, turn right.

A Simple Solution to Running-Fix Confusion

If you're like me, one of the harder concepts to grasp is the *running fix*. To make a running fix you need three things:

1. A charted object located between your bow and beam
2. A trackline
3. A good estimate of your boatspeed

Let's suppose you have a lighthouse off your bow. You take a bearing to the lighthouse of 350 degrees magnetic. You plot this bearing on your chart and make sure that the bearing line crosses your trackline. Label the time you took the bearing as 1000. Now you steer down your trackline at a speed of 4 knots.

At 1100 you take a second bearing to the lighthouse. This time it bears 300 degrees magnetic. You plot this second line onto the chart and make sure it, too, crosses the trackline. Now you have a trackline crossed by two bearing lines, neither which crosses the other. How do you get a fix from this?

First, figure out how far you traveled from 1000 to 1100 at 4 knots. The answer is 4 miles, of course. Now advance—i.e., "run"—that first bearing line of 350 degrees exactly 4 miles along the trackline. Do this with parallel rulers or a protractor. As in the old Star Trek shows, you want to transport that bearing line from one spot to another without changing anything about it. Once you've done that, extend the bearing line so that it intersects the second bearing line, and the point where they intersect is your running fix. A running fix is more reliable than a DR position but less reliable than a fix based on two or more simultaneous bearings. Still, when faced with a lack of charted objects for bearings, the running fix is a good technique to know.

A running fix can be needlessly confusing when the bearing lines resemble the trackline. In the accompanying illustrations you can see how easy it is to make this mistake, and how simple marking techniques can improve the utility of a running fix. A quick glance at the first illustration might convince you that the boat is in any of four places. In the second illustration, however, the R Fix is more obvious. Here's how to improve your running fix technique:

1. **Make a bold TR.** Start by using a bolder TR. Make the trackline stand out so you won't mistake it for a bearing line. Instead of full-length lines of position (LOP), use short segments that cross the track less than an inch on each side. Label the first bearing line (taken at 1000) as an EP.
2. **Take the second bearing.** At 1100 we take a second bearing. Write the bearing in your log. Before plotting this second bearing, advance the first LOP 4 miles along the TR. This represents the distance traveled from

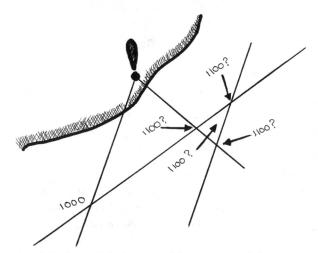

At first glance it is difficult to tell the location of the 1100 running fix.

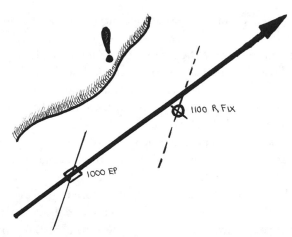

The running fix position lies at the bottom right, where the first and second LOP cross. One way to minimize running fix confusion is by using a bolder TR line. The dashed line represents a mirror image of the first LOP.

1000 to 1100 at a speed of 4 knots. Plot the bearing as a dashed line overlapping the TR by two inches.

3. **Plot and label the running fix.** Plot your second bearing, but instead of drawing a line, place a small tick mark where it crosses the dashed first LOP. Circle the dot and label it with time and position type (e.g., 1100 R Fix).

Longshore Piloting When Landfall Is in Doubt

Approaching landfall after even a short passage is exhilarating, yet it can also be a period of doubt. If visibility is getting worse in squalls, fog, or mist, will you make the sea buoy that marks the entrance between those jetties?

One technique that's been used for decades in such a circumstance is called *longshore piloting*. Simply lay your courseline purposely two or more miles to the right or left of your destination. That way, you'll know—without a doubt—which way to turn to run down your landfall.

One way to ensure further success in longshore piloting is to make your turning point a charted contour line (one of those black continuous lines that indicate constant soundings along the line). Once your fathometer indicates you're on this line, turn toward your destination and sail *down the line*. Follow these easy steps to success in longshore piloting:

1. Lay your trackline two miles upwind or upcurrent of your intended destination.
2. Find a prominent contour curve marked with depth that parallels the shoreline.

3. Measure the distance to the contour curve. Estimate the speed you will use.

4. Determine the time to the contour curve. For example, if the distance is 3 miles and your boatspeed is 5 knots, it should take you 36 minutes. If you make this calculation at 0900, you should arrive at 0936.

5. Mark the contour curve with your estimated time of arrival. In our example, we would label it 0936.

6. Watch your depth sounder during the transit. As soon as your depth sounder (as corrected for transducer depth and height of tide; see earlier in this chapter) reads the sounding of the contour curve (which should be at the approximate time you indicated), turn toward the destination.

7. Measure the distance from this turning point to the destination, estimate your speed, and calculate a new time of arrival at the harbor entrance.

SEA-CRET TIPS FOR LONGSHORE PILOTING LANDFALLS

▶ Correct your fathometer for tide and transducer depth to match the charted datum (MLLW or LAT; see Chapter 1).

▶ Lay your track to the upwind or upcurrent side of the destination. That way, you'll have a fair wind and sea at your back when you make your turn.

How to Avoid Hazards with Danger Bearings

Imagine that a dangerous rock-strewn island lies ahead to starboard. The currents in this area are notorious for sweeping small craft down onto the shoal. We need to make the anchorage on the other side before sunset. How can we do this easily and safely?

When approaching an area with navigational hazards, you can stay safe by plotting bearings to a single object. This *danger bearing* is a reference point to tell us whether we are passing safely by the hazard.

Choose a charted object that lies between you and the danger and on the side of the danger on which you wish to pass. An alternative is to take a tangent bearing to the steep sides of an island or cliffs that lie ahead of the danger. Always check the chart before you make a decision. The accompanying illustration and instructions demonstrate using a danger bearing to pass the hazard safely.

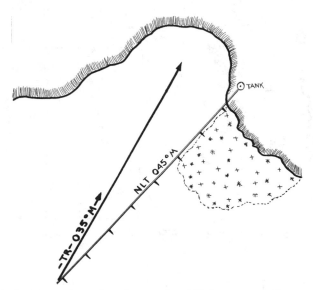

As long as the bearing to the tank reads more than 045 degrees magnetic, you will clear the shoal to starboard. If the bearings start to decrease, turn left to cross the danger bearing line and return to safe water.

1. **Choose a danger bearing.** Pick a charted, visually prominent object such that a line drawn through the object will skirt the shoal's near edge at its far end and pass near your approach point at its near end. This is your danger bearing. Draw short tick marks along the line pointing toward the side of the danger (see illustration). This helps the danger bearing stand out from other lines, such as your trackline.

2. **Determine the direction of the danger bearing.** Measure the direction to the object twice to confirm the bearing. Convert a true bearing to a magnetic bearing by applying variation (add westerly or subtract easterly variation). Label the top of the danger bearing line with the magnetic danger bearing (045°M in the illustration).

3. **Prefix the danger bearing.** If the danger lies to starboard of the bearing, use the prefix *NLT* (not less than) in front of the danger bearing. If the hazard lies to port, use the prefix *NMT* (not more than). In the illustration we write NLT in front of the danger bearing of 045 degrees magnetic. As long as your bearing to the tank reads more than 045 degrees, you'll pass safely. If it reads 045 degrees or less, you need to turn left until you cross the danger bearing.

RADAR DANGER RANGES AND CIRCLES OF POSITION
Radar-equipped vessels often use predetermined range settings to clear shoals. As discussed earlier, lines of position are actually parts of circles. Compare a

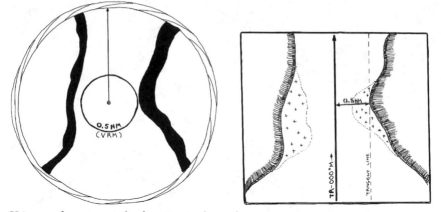

Using a radar-range circle of position to clear a dangerous pass.

radar beam from your antenna to a pebble dropped into a tub of water. Concentric circles emanate from the pebble's splash point (your antenna), bounce off the tub sides, and return to the point of origin. So when we plot a radar range as an arc on the chart, we are actually plotting a segment of a circle of position. The following steps show how to use this secret to plot radar ranges to clear any danger in your path:

1. Determine from the chart a range from a prominent point, cliff, headland, or other feature that will keep you clear of off-lying shoals. If passing between two headlands, pick the one with the more prominent point. This gives a sharper radar picture. In the illustration, we chose the prominent point to starboard.
2. Draw a line parallel to your courseline and tangent to the prominent point. Measure the distance from the tangent line back to your courseline (0.5 NM in the illustration).
3. Adjust the variable-range marker (VRM) on your radar to that distance. The VRM measures distance (range) on a radar. The illustration shows what the radar will look like as you pass between the two shoals. Keep the VRM circle tangent to the prominent point to starboard to clear both shoals.

How to Clear Hazards without Plotting on a Chart

Sometimes we need a quick solution to avoid hazards such as shoals or ships that lie ahead. One blazing-fast solution allows you to do this without plotting on a chart! The *Rule of 60* shows how many degrees to alter course to the right or left to clear a danger. You need to know two terms to use this rule:

Distance off (DO): The distance you need to stay off the shoal to clear it safely.

Distance ahead (DA): How far ahead the shoal lies from your current location.

1. Determine the safe side (left or right) on which to pass the shoal
2. Decide on the required distance off (DO) the shoal to clear it safely
3. Measure how far ahead the shoal lies from your present location (DA)
4. Multiply 60 by the DO
5. Divide by DA.

Apply the result using one of these two rules:

If the safe side is to the left of the shoal, *subtract* the result from the trackline and steer that course.

If the safe side is to the right of the shoal, *add* the result to the trackline and steer that course.

Our course is 045 degrees magnetic. The chart indicates a dangerous shoal off our starboard bow 2 miles ahead (DA). The safe side is to the right of the shoal, and we need to stay 1 mile off (DO) the shoal to clear it safely. How many degrees do we need to turn to starboard to clear the shoal by 1 mile?

Multiply 60 by the DO and divide by the DA. Our calculation would be: $(60 \times 1)/2 = 30$ degrees.

Since the safe side is to the right of the shoal, we add the correction: 045 degrees magnetic + 30 degrees = 075 degrees magnetic.

SEA-CRET TIP

▶ Always use the Rule of 60 with caution. It does not tell you the effect of current or leeway once you change course. Calculate the course alteration and then estimate the effect of current (see Chapter 5). Sailing vessels may also need to estimate leeway if the new course results in heading up.

Depth Contour Secrets

With just a fathometer corrected for tide and transducer location, you can use depth contour curves to estimate your speed and position. Look at any nautical chart and you'll see thin, black lines. Starting along the shore, they closely match the profile of the shoreline. Farther away, these lines take on every shape under the sun—from gentle curves to crazy, out-of-control

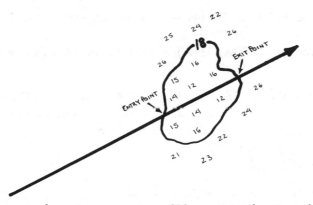

When crossing a circular contour curve, set up a GPS waypoint at the entry and exit points.

squiggles. To find the depth of any curve, look along the line or circle for a bold number. This indicates the depth anywhere along the curve.

Plot your trackline across these contour lines. For circular contours, plot dead reckoning positions at the entry and exit points. Set up waypoints in the GPS or chart plotter at both positions. Correct your fathometer reading to mean lower low water (MLLW) and compare it with the GPS. Do they agree?

Magic Boat Markers for Distance Off

The *bow-beam bearing* gives great position information using just one object. Sight a charted object when it's 45 degrees off your bow to port or starboard. Note the time of the bearing, then hold a steady course and speed until the object draws abeam, or 90 degrees off your bow. Your distance off the object when it's abeam equals the distance run between the two bearings, and that distance run is equal to speed multiplied by elapsed time (see Chapter 3).

Before you leave the dock, set up your boat to do most of the work for you. Follow these two simple steps:

1. Sit or stand at your normal helm position. Using your handbearing compass, sight directly down the centerline of your boat, aiming at the headstay or bow pulpit. Write down that centerline bearing, then calculate the bearings 45 degrees on either side of it. Write down both of these bearings.
2. Now sight over the handbearing compass at the bow once again, making sure it's aligned to the original centerline bearing. Then slowly rotate the compass to each of the bearings 45 degrees from the bow. What part of your boat do you see superimposed in the compass sight at each of these bearings? The upper shroud? A lifeline stanchion? An aft corner of the coachroof? Mark those points port and starboard and you're done!

For example, from your normal helm position, you take a centerline bearing of 125 degrees magnetic. Adding 45 degrees to the centerline bearing gives 170 degrees magnetic. Subtracting 45 gives you 80 degrees magnetic. Sight over the handbearing compass again using these bearings.

You notice that the bearing at 170 degrees magnetic touches one of the lifeline stanchions to starboard, and the bearing at 80 degrees magnetic touches a lifeline stanchion to port. Mark both points, and you have your 45-degree bearing marks.

Now, when you're underway and ready to figure distance off a charted object, sit or stand at this helm position. When the object "touches" one of your preset marks, mark your time, then watch your speed and hold your course. When you can look directly abeam at the object (i.e., when it's off your shoulder if you're facing the bow), mark the time again. Figure the distance sailed from mark to mark. That distance equals your distance off the object when it was abeam. Follow these steps and work through the example:

1. Maintain a steady speed and course (any course will do, as long as you stay steady).
2. Mark the time an object touches your 45-degree boat mark.
3. Mark the time again when you see the same object abeam (off your shoulder).
4. Convert the time (minutes) to fractional or decimal parts of an hour. Multiply by your speed.

You want to find your distance off of an island off your starboard side. The chart shows a prominent church spire on a high hill near the shore.

> You get onto a course of 090 degrees magnetic and a speed of 5 knots.
> At 1035, the church spire touches your 45-degree boat mark.
> At 1123, you can look abeam (off your shoulder) at the church spire.
> How far are you off the island?
> 1123 – 1035 = 48 minutes or 0.8 hour (48 ÷ 60)
> 0.8 hour × 5 knots = 4.0 nautical miles off the island.

Practice this technique using GPS for a precise measurement of the distance run between the bow and beam bearings. Your navigation won't depend on the answer if your GPS receiver is functioning, but the exercise will build your visual memory of how objects appear from various distances off. Practice with islands, rocks, navigation buoys, lighthouses, and so forth. You'll gain a better understanding of how a bell buoy appears from a distance of 1 mile versus 2, or how an island appears from 2 miles versus 3. This knowledge is highly useful when piloting by eye (see earlier in this chapter).

To make the exercise even more useful, estimate your distances run (through the water) between bearings using your knotmeter or an RPM/boatspeed graph, and compare the estimates with the actual distances run (over ground) as reported by your GPS receiver. One day, when GPS isn't working, this practice estimating boatspeed in various conditions of wind, waves, and current will prove valuable.

Make a GPS Grid Highway to Avoid Dangers

Use the latitude and longitude function on any GPS receiver to keep your crew safe and sound. This also works when using an unfamiliar GPS receiver. This method quickly shows your advance along a track and whether you are drifting toward danger.

For example, you need to clear a dangerous ledge off your port bow. Pea soup fog has reduced visibility to a couple of hundred yards. Follow these steps for safety.

1. **Plot your TR on the nautical chart.** Draw the dead reckoning courseline of your approach onto the chart, then plot a turn to due north or due south when you near the ledge but are still safely off it. This north-south trackline marks the center of the grid highway you will use to avoid the danger. Power or sailing vessels should plot the same base courselines. (We'll talk about tacking strategies shortly.)
2. **Make the sides of the highway.** Determine how closely you are willing to approach the ledge. This minimum distance east or west of the ledge establishes one edge of the grid highway you are creating; draw a vertical line (i.e., a meridian) through that point, extending it so as to clear the danger both north and south. Label it with the longitude in degrees and minutes. Draw a second meridian on the opposite side of the north-south trackline you plotted, thus defining the width of the "road" you desire to stay on. Power and sailing vessels simply need to stay between the two meridians in order to pass the hazard safely.
3. **Make the entry and exit gate.** Well north and south of the hazard area, draw in two parallels of latitude. These define the entry point into the hazard area and the exit point when you are clear of the hazard.

TACKING THROUGH THE HIGHWAY

Sailing vessels hard on the wind will need to tack through the grid highway. In the illustration, the vessel enters the gate on starboard tack and sails until the GPS reads 71°54'W. The boat then comes about onto port tack and sails until the GPS reads 71°53'W. Then the boat comes about again, repeating the sequence up the highway until the GPS latitude reads 42°19'N.

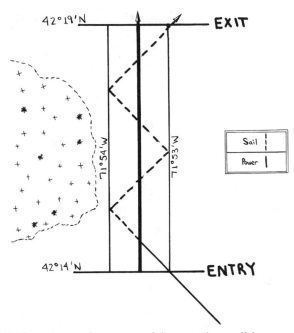

Making a grid highway is a good way to avoid dangers. The parallels serve as the entry and exit gates, and the meridians serve as the east-west boundaries of your highway.

How to Plot a GPS Position in Less than 5 Seconds

Choppy seas make plotting on a high-speed powerboat a challenge. But you can learn to position your boat in 5 seconds using only a pencil and a chart on a clipboard. Called a GPS plotting grid, this backup method is hard to beat for speed, accuracy, and fun.

Supplies and Tools Needed to Plot a GPS Position in Less than 5 Seconds

▶ pencil
▶ plotting compass
▶ parallel rulers, protractor, or plotter
▶ Scotch Magic Tape or any tape with a dull finish that you can write on

1. **Set the primary waypoint, your TR to that waypoint, and radiating lines.** Enter your waypoint into the GPS, then plot it on your chart. Next plot your trackline to the waypoint. Make this line bold so it stands out. Then, as shown in the illustration on page 92, draw lines from the waypoint that radiate at 2-degree intervals either side of the courseline (TR), and label the end of each such line with the magnetic bearing to the waypoint.

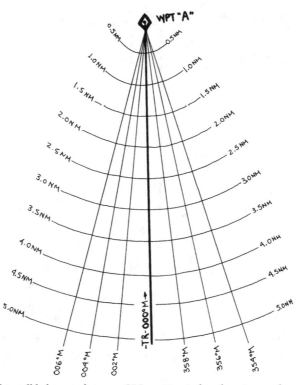

A chart like this will help you plot your GPS position in less than 5 seconds.

2. **Plot range arcs and size the grid based on your speed.** Use your plotting compass to measure 1 nautical mile (or a distance appropriate to your speed, see below) on the latitude scale. Then center the plotting compass needle point on the waypoint and scribe a 1-mile range arc over the bearing lines. Now go back to the scale and pick off 2 nautical miles, then plot a 2-mile arc in the same manner. Draw arcs for each successive mile (or whatever increment of distance you have selected).

Power vessels should extend the grid outward from the waypoint to the distance that will be covered in 30 to 60 minutes at the intended speed of the run. For example, if you plan to make the run at 14 knots, give the grid a radius of 7 to 14 miles. Sailing vessels need a grid size equal to or greater than their average speed. If you anticipate sailing at an average of 4.5 knots, make the grid radius at least 4.5 miles (as in the accompanying illustration). Sailing vessels beating to windward should make the outer boundaries of the grid 10 to 20 degrees on each side of the center trackline. In steady winds, use 10 degrees; in gusty, shifting winds, use 20 degrees. (See "Sail a Tacking Cone to a Windward Destination" below.) If under power or sailing a reach, make the boundaries narrower.

3. **Label the range arcs.** As in the illustration, label the range arcs on both sides of the bold central trackline. To save chart wear, tape over your grid. That's it! Now you're ready to plot any position off your GPS in less than 5 seconds with just a pencil.

4. **Use the waypoint bearing and range function.** Set the GPS menu onto the waypoint bearing and range function. As you steam toward your waypoint, read the bearing and range from the GPS. Place a dot on your grid where bearing and range intersect. If you lose the GPS, you'll instantly know how to get to your destination.

Sail a Tacking Cone to a Windward Destination

You've been reaching on a beauty of a westerly breeze, heading for Cape Landfall dead ahead to the north. But the wind seems determined to continue veering, and you soon find yourself on a close reach. You have 6 miles to go, sunset is in 3 hours, and you are averaging 4 knots. Your 1845 ETA may be hard to make if this wind keeps shifting. If it clocks a few more degrees to the right you'll be hard on the wind, tacking and adding more mileage. Better prepare now for sailing those last few miles close-hauled.

A *tacking cone* helps you zero in on your destination and makes navigation less stressful. Before we delve into the strategy for using a tacking cone, we need to understand the concept of *lifts* and *headers*.

A lift occurs when the wind direction moves *away* from the bow. When lifted, you can point your boat closer to your windward destination. A header occurs when the wind direction moves *toward* the bow. When headed, you can no longer point as close to your windward destination as you could before, and you will need to alter your course or tack. Take advantage of lifts and headers to reach your destination sooner. When going to windward, tack on a header (because a header on one tack is a lift on the other) and point higher on a lift.

Now, review the strategies you'll need to make the best progress toward any windward goal.

- Start on the tack that takes you closest to your destination.
- Sail the longest leg toward the mark first.
- Tack on headers; point higher on lifts. This keeps you near the TR and progressing toward the windward destination.

Find a prominent charted landmark or land feature in line with your destination, and draw a straight line back from the object to represent your TR. Next, draw two bearings from the object to form a narrow cone on each side of the TR. Make your tacking cone between 10 and 20 degrees on each side of the TR, depending on the wind. In steady winds, use 10 degrees; in gusty,

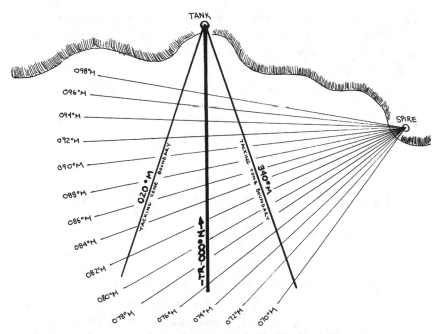

Combining a tacking cone with cross bearings to a landmark outside the cone is a good way to fix your position. As you sail upwind, plot the distance advanced along the trackline.

shifting winds, make the boundaries 20 degrees on either side of the center TR. Measure each cone boundary bearing (in degrees magnetic) and label the boundaries accordingly.

Scan inside and outside for hazards. Before going any farther, check inside and outside the tacking cone's boundaries for shoals, wrecks, or obstructions. The ideal tacking cone will have no hazards within the boundaries. Highlight shoals or obstructions just outside the cone.

Cone boundaries and cross bearings. Find a second prominent charted object to the left or right of the TR. Extend light lines from that object across the cone and label the end of each line with the magnetic bearing. Use these cross bearings to fix your position and show your distance advanced along the TR.

Ask a crewmember to take bearings with a handbearing compass. When you reach one of the tacking boundary bearings, come about and sail to the other boundary-line bearing, and then tack again.

Lift and header tacking strategy. The wind usually blows slightly to one side or the other of the dead-ahead target course. Sail the favored tack first, because this tack takes you closest to the intended destination and keeps you closest to the base trackline. This saves you lots of time and, if you are headed along the way, you will continue to make good forward progress. Draw an arrow onto your tacking cone to indicate the true wind direction. You will see right

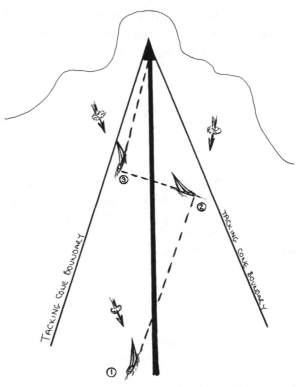

This diagram maps the course of a boat tacking on headers and lifts as it sails upwind to its destination inside a tacking cone. At position 1, the boat sails the longest tack (port here) at an angle that is closest to the target. At position 2, the wind shifts toward the bow, so we tack right away to stay close to the trackline and keep moving toward our destination. At position 3, the wind shifts toward the bow again, so we tack again. Continue this method until you arrive.

away which is the favored tack. The other tack heads off at a 90-degree angle to the mark! Now look at the illustration to see how all this fits together.

ICW Secrets: Channel Jogs and Marker Silhouettes

Supplies Needed for Making Strip Charts

▶ highlighter
▶ black felt-tip pen (fine tip)
▶ dull-sided tape that can be written on

The United States' Intracoastal Waterway (ICW) runs from New Jersey, down the east coast and around the Gulf Coast until it ends in Brownsville, Texas. Charts for the narrow channels with all their accompanying twists and turns are available as foldout government charts or the spiral-bound commercial charts described as chartkits or chartbooks. In Europe, use the techniques described below to track your vessel along that vast inland waterway system of rivers and canals (for an overview, see **http://www.worldcanals .com/english/vne_Europe.html**).

The small print on these charts makes interpreting the aid to navigation (ATON) symbols confusing. Small changes in course between aids become nerve-wracking. But you can simplify things to make your transit of the ICW (or any narrow waterway) an easy and pleasurable experience by making strip charts as outlined below.

1. **Preparing the strip charts.** Lay down three strips of tape along each intended route. Use one for the center and two strips on either side of your route. Next, draw your channel jogs. Using the felt-tip pen, put a dot where one leg begins and another where it ends, and then join your dots.

2. **Custom symbols: squares, triangles, and cones.** Next, draw silhouettes of your ATONs. Draw oversized squares or triangles adjacent to those shown along each leg. Perfection isn't as important as relative position along a leg.

3. **Silhouette labels.** Simplify the descriptions of beacons and lights. For example, if your chart shows a light with the description G "17" Fl G 4 sec, you could shorten it to "17" G4. At a glance, you see the number 17 has a green (G) four-second (4) light. For an unlighted ATON, put the color of the marker before the number like this: R "14" or G "3."

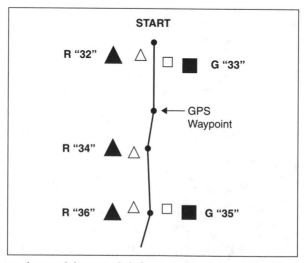

Annotating your chart with large symbols for navaids and enlarged buoyage numbers will help simplify a journey along the ICW or any other turning, twisting passage.

"Your Call, Skipper"

You're the skipper or most knowledgeable crewmember in each of the following situations. What actions would you take?

1. Fog shrouds your boat. The GPS is on the blink, but your fathometer seems to be working. What three steps would you take before turning and heading for land?

2. Your chart shows an 80-foot light on a high cliff dead ahead. The charted nominal range is 12 miles. Your HE is 9 feet. How would you set up the chart to make landfall?

3. A dangerous coral reef lies 2 miles ahead just off your starboard bow. You need to make a quick decision and turn to the left. Swift currents make the reef a lee shore. How many degrees must you alter course to clear the reef by 2.5 miles?

4. You need to beat to windward and pass a mile-long stretch of dangerous shoals to starboard. The skipper has a new GPS unit, no manual, and not a clue as to how to use it. You plot a quick GPS grid highway to clear the shoal. How would you explain to the skipper the method for using this grid highway?

5. On a power vessel traveling at 22 knots, what is the minimum practical size you should make a GPS plotting grid?

Answers

1. First, study the chart and look for a contour curve running along the coast 2 to 3 miles on either side of the destination. Second, correct your depth sounder to the charted depth (using transducer depth and present height of tide information). Third, aim well upwind or upcurrent of the destination.

2. Measure two arcs from the light at 12 miles and 14 miles. Calculate the time to both ranges, and set the GPS alarm.

3. Using the Rule of 60, and knowing that your DO is 2.5 and your DA is 2, you determine that you need to alter course 75 degrees to the left:

$$(60 \times 2.5) \div 2 = 75$$

4. Sail close-hauled until you reach the highway meridian closer to the hazard, then come about and sail until you reach the highway meridian on the opposite side. Continue this procedure until the boat clears the shoal at the GPS latitude exit gate.

5. It should be 11 miles, or half the speed of advance.

TIDES, CURRENTS, AND LEEWAY

The greatest tides occur in the Bay of Fundy, Nova Scotia, where there is an extreme range of 57 feet.
—ROBERT HENDRICKSON, *THE OCEAN ALMANAC*

In unfamiliar waters, how can you accurately determine if you have enough water to enter port, lie alongside a pier, or anchor in a pristine cove? Ahead lies a narrow passage with strong rip currents. When can you safely transit the pass, and how much time will you have to make it through?

In This Chapter You'll Learn How To:
- ❀ Make an easy graph to predict tidal heights and currents worldwide
- ❀ Find the speed of a current without a table or a calculator
- ❀ Determine the window of opportunity to transit an inlet
- ❀ Learn how to steer an accurate course across the Gulf Stream
- ❀ Deal with the mystery of leeway in three simple ways

How to Predict Tides Anywhere in the World

Both the sun and moon exert a gravitational pull on the earth's waters to produce tides. The moon, being the closer of the two heavenly bodies, exerts twice the influence of the sun. The result is a bulge of high water beneath the moon, and this high-water bulge travels around the globe as the earth spins. There is a second high-water bulge on the opposite side of the globe from the first, the result of centrifugal forces in the earth-moon couple. Thus, in the absence of local effects, each spot on the world's oceans would receive two high tides and two low tides each day (a semidiurnal tide). But latitude, shoreline configuration, and seabed topography also affect local tides. While midocean tides are scarcely noticeable, the tides funneled up the Bay of Fundy, through the English Channel, and into other mid- and high-latitude constrictions can achieve truly impressive heights. A big range of tide requires a correspondingly rapid horizontal transport of water, so big tides are associated with strong tidal currents. Along other coastlines, local effects produce only one high and low tide per day (a diurnal tide), or a mixed tide, in which one high water is much higher than the other.

Here are the tide terms you'll want to know:

Tide: The vertical rise and fall of water in coastal regions throughout the world.

Semidiurnal tides: Most of the world, including the U.S. east coast and Europe, experiences two high tides and two low tides each day.

Diurnal tide: Some places, including the U.S. Gulf Coast and Southeast Asia, experience only one high tide and one low tide every day.

Mixed tides: Places along the U.S. and Canadian west coasts receive multiple tides each day—with a high tide followed by a higher high tide, and a similar pattern for low tides.

Stand: The tidal height "pauses" after reaching its highest or lowest point. This high-water or low-water stand may last a few seconds or several minutes, then the tide begins to move down or up.

Spring tides: At or near the time of a full or new moon, the moon is aligned with the sun, and the gravitational pulls of the two bodies are additive. The result is that tidal ranges (the distance a tide rises and falls) increase. High-water heights average higher than normal. Low-water heights average lower than normal.

Neap tides: At or near the times of the moon's first and third quarters, the moon's gravitational pull on the earth is exerted more or less at right angles with the sun's, and the sun's pull partially cancels the moon's. The result is that tidal ranges decrease. High-water heights average lower than normal. Low-water heights average higher than normal.

Charted depth: The charted depth is the "starting depth," or *low-water datum,* for the measurement of tides. (Low-water datum in the U.S. is mean lower low water, or MLLW, the long-term average of the lower of each day's low tides.) Tide tables and publications show how much height (in feet or meters) to add to or subtract from the charted depth to correct for the stage of the tide at a specified time.

Range: The total distance the tide rises or falls from high tide to low tide. If the low-water height is below low-water datum (called a *minus tide),* add low-water height to high-water height to find the range. (For example, if the high-water height as read from a tide table is 10.3 feet and the low-water height is −0.7 feet, the tidal range is 11.0 feet.) If the low-water height is above low-water datum, subtract it from the high-water height to find the range.

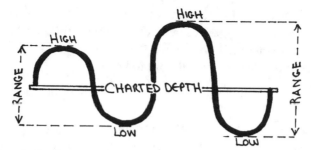

In a semidiurnal tide, there are two high tides and two low tides in each 24-hour period. (Actually, the tidal day is a bit longer than 24 hours—more like 24 hours 50 minutes—because the moon advances about 50 minutes in its orbit with each 24-hour rotation of the earth.) Since the range of the tide often varies from one cycle to the next, you should not assume that the range this evening will be the same as it was this morning.

Slack Tide, Ebb Tide, and Flood Tide Don't Exist

The term *slack* refers to a tidal current, not to the tide itself. A slack current is any current with a velocity less than half a knot. The tide *stands,* but it does not go slack. Similarly, there is no such thing as an "ebb tide" or "flood tide." The *ebb* and the *flood* are tidal currents, but they are not the tide itself. The poets and songwriters have it wrong. Though we all use these terms, they are incorrect. The distinction may seem trivial—after all, tidal currents are the direct result of tides even if they're not the same thing—but maintaining the distinction will better prepare you for those times when, for example, slack current and the nearest low- or high-water stand are hours apart.

HOW TO USE U.S. TIDE TABLE PUBLICATIONS

In the United States, you can order tide tables in book form (they are also available online, see below). These publications show the time and height of the tide at select stations. Surveyors study the tides at large ports, called *reference stations.* They record the time (using Eastern Standard Time) and height of tide for each day of the month. These daily tides are grouped by month and placed into the book in Table 1. Next, surveys are conducted at minor harbors, rivers, and bays called *substations.* Times and heights of tide at substations are compared with those recorded at nearby reference stations, and the differences are placed into the book in Table 2. Follow these three simple Steps to find time and height from the tide tables.

1. **Enter the back index.** Turn to the back of the book and look for the substation of interest. If you don't find the exact location, find one nearby. Write down the substation number you see next to the name.

2. **Enter Table 2 (substations).** Enter Table 2 with your substation number. Look at the middle columns showing time and height differences. Write this information down. Look directly *above* your substation line. You'll see the name of the Table 1 reference station in bold print, along with a page number. Turn to this page.

3. **Enter Table 1 (reference stations).** The page number lands you onto the month of January. Flip through the pages to find the month and date you need. Copy the time and heights. Add or subtract the substation time differences to the reference station high- and low-water times. Add or subtract the substation height differences to the reference station high- and low-water heights. (Occasionally you will see an asterisk in the substation height difference column. This means you must multiply the number shown by the applicable reference station high- or low-water heights. For example, if you find "*0.6" under the substation high-water column, multiply each reference station high-water height by 0.6.)

BRITISH ADMIRALTY AND FOREIGN TIDE TABLES

British Admiralty tide tables are intuitive and easy to follow. Note the few minor differences from the U.S. government tide tables:

Station names. Reference Stations are called *standard ports*. Substations are called *secondary ports*.

Times. British ports use Greenwich Mean Time (GMT). (In the near future, this will be listed as Coordinated Universal Time [UTC]). Foreign ports use the time zone of that country.

Heights. Heights are given in meters. Add or subtract height differences based on their sign (+ or −). Differences are listed under four columns:

MHWS = Mean High Water Springs
MHWN = Mean High Water Neaps
MLWS = Mean Low Water Springs
MLWN = Mean Low Water Neaps

SEA-CRET TIP

▶ U.S. and British Admiralty tide tables list reference station (or standard port) times, respectively, in Eastern Standard Time (EST) or Greenwich Mean Time (GMT). Remember to add 1 hour during periods of Daylight Savings Time (DST).

Another Method to Use Tide Tables

TABLE 2 – TIDAL DIFFERENCES AND OTHER CONSTANTS

No.	PLACE	POSITION		DIFFERENCES				RANGES		Mean Tide Level
		Latitude	Longitude	Time		Height		Mean	Spring	
				High Water	Low Water	High Water	Low Water			
		North	West							
	MASSACHUSETTS, outer coast Time meridian, 75° W	reference station				(on Portland, p.36)				
	Merrimack River									
821	Plum Island, Merrimack River Entrance ..	42° 49.0'	70° 49.2'	+0 06	+0 29	*0.88	*0.88	8.00	9.12	4.30
823	Newburyport	42° 48.7'	70° 51.9'	+0 31	+1 11	*0.86	*0.86	7.8	9.0	4.2
825	Salisbury Point	42° 50.3'	70° 54.5'	+0 55	+1 18	*0.83	*0.56	7.64	8.71	4.01
827	Merrimacport	42° 49.5'	70° 59.3'	+1 26	+2 08	*0.76	*0.50	7.05	8.04	3.70
829	Riverside	42° 45.8'	71° 04.6'	+1 56	+3 30	*0.62	*0.35	5.72	6.52	2.80
831	Plum Island Sound (south end)	42° 42.6'	70° 47.3'	+0 12	+0 37	*0.94	*0.94	8.6	9.9	4.6
833	Essex	42° 37.9'	70° 46.6'	+0 22	+0 31	*1.00	*0.94	9.18	10.47	4.90
835	Annisquam, Lobster Cove	42° 39.3'	70° 40.6'	+0 11	+0 03	*0.97	*0.97	8.81	10.04	4.74
837	Rockport	42° 39.5'	70° 36.9'	+0 06	+0 06	*0.95	*0.97	8.70	9.92	4.71
		reference station				(on Boston, p.40)				
839	Gloucester Harbor	42° 36.6'	70° 39.6'	+0 00	−0 04	*0.93	*0.97	8.80	10.03	4.73
841	Salem, Salem Harbor	42° 31.4'	70° 52.6'	−0 02	−0 05	*0.94	*0.97	8.93	10.18	4.79
843	Lynn, Lynn Harbor	42° 27.5'	70° 56.6'	+0 01	−0 03	*0.97	*1.00	9.16	10.44	4.92
	Boston Harbor									
845	Boston Light	42° 19.7'	70° 53.5'	−0 01	−0 02	*0.95	*0.97	9.05	10.03	4.85
847	Deer Island (south end)	42° 20.7'	70° 57.5'	+0 01	+0 00	*0.97	*0.97	9.3	10.8	4.9
849	BOSTON	42° 21.3'	71° 03.1'	Daily predictions				9.49	11.07	5.09
851	Charlestown, Charles River entrance . . .	42° 22.5'	71° 03.0'	+0 00	+0 01	*1.00	*1.00	9.5	11.0	5.0
853	Amelia Earhart Dam, Mystic River	42° 23.7'	71° 04.6'	+0 01	+0 02	*1.01	*1.01	9.56	10.89	5.11
855	Chelsea St. Bridge, Chelsea River	42° 23.2'	71° 01.4'	+0 01	+0 06	*1.01	*1.01	9.6	11.1	5.1
857	Neponset, Neponset River	42° 17.1'	71° 02.4'	−0 02	+0 03	*1.00	*1.00	9.5	1.0	5.0
859	Moon Head	42° 18.5'	70° 59.3'	+0 01	+0 04	*0.99	*0.99	9.4	10.9	5.0

location — time differences, high and low — height ratios, high and low — ranges

This table of differences from the National Ocean Service's 2008 tide tables for the eastern coasts of North and South America references Neponset, Massachusetts (a subordinate station), to Boston (a reference station). Times of high and low tides at Neponset are 2 minutes earlier and 3 minutes, later, respectively, than at Boston, and their heights are 1.0 times the corresponding heights in Boston—in other words, they're the same.

Boston, Massachusetts, 2008
Times and Heights of High and Low Waters

date   new moon   time of tide   height of tide

	July				August				September			
	Time	Height	Time	Height	Time	Height	Time	Height	Time	Height	Time	Height
	h m	ft cm	h m	ft cm	h m	ft cm	h m	ft cm	h m	ft cm	h m	ft cm
1 Tu	0256	-0.8 -24	16 W 0345	0.9 27	1 F 0432	-1.0 -30	16 Sa 0435	-0.5 -15	1 M 0546	-0.5 -15	16 Tu 0519	-0.3 -9
	0907	9.6 293	0959	8.4 256	1047	10.0 305	1049	9.2 280	1200	10.5 320	1129	10.7 326
	1506	0.3 9	1544	1.8 55	1643	-0.1 -3	1643	0.9 27	1806	-0.3 -9	1742	-0.5 -15
	2120	11.7 357	2201	9.9 302	2300	11.5 351	O 2257	10.3 314			2352	10.6 323
2 W	0353	-1.1 -34	17 Th 0427	0.6 18	2 Sa 0523	-1.1 -34	17 Su 0514	0.1 3	2 Tu 0020	10.6 323	17 W 0601	-0.3 -9
	1006	9.8 299	1042	8.6 262	1139	10.2 311	1127	9.5 290	0628	-0.2 -6	1210	11.0 335
	1602	0.0 0	1627	1.6 49	1736	-0.3 -9	1725	0.5 15	1242	10.5 320	1827	-0.8 -24
	2217	11.9 363	2243	10.1 308	2352	11.4 347	2337	10.5 320	1851	-0.2 -6		
3 Th	0448	-1.3 -40	18 F 0506	0.4 12	3 Su 0611	-1.1 -34	18 M 0552	-0.1 -3	3 W 0105	10.1 308	18 Th 0037	10.5 320
	1102	10.0 305	1122	8.8 268	1227	10.4 317	1204	9.9 302	0710	0.2 6	0644	-0.2 -6
	1658	-0.1 -3	1709	1.3 40	1827	-0.3 -9	1807	0.2 6	1323	10.3 314	1253	11.2 341
	2313	11.9 363	O 2323	10.2 311					1937	0.1 3	1915	-0.8 -24

A portion of a 2008 tide table for Boston. The table provides the time of each high and low tide for each day of the year and also the height of each tide relative to mean lower low water (MLLW), which is the vertical datum used by NOAA's National Ocean Service in its tide tables (and in the soundings printed on nautical charts). The time of low water on the afternoon of August 2 is 1736, which is 1836 Daylight Savings Time. The fact that this is a minus tide (−0.3 feet) suggests that it is a spring tide, and indeed we see that the new moon was on August 1, so a run of spring tides can be expected.

HOW TO USE ONLINE NOAA TIDE TABLES

NOAA offers free online tide and current tables for selected locations through-out the world. Let's look at one example. Let's say you were planning to stay in Charleston, South Carolina, on Saturday, September 20, 2008.

1. Access the NOAA site at **http://tidesandcurrents.noaa.gov/tides08/**.
2. Scroll down the list of states. Click on South Carolina.
3. Click on Charleston Harbor.
4. Click on Predictions, adjacent to CHARLESTON (Customhouse Wharf).
5. Click on the option for a printable version (at the top of the page).
6. Scroll to the September page and highlight the information for September 20. Right click on your mouse, then click to copy.
7. Go to any word processing program, such as MS Word. Open up a new page. Click on File, Page Setup, Landscape, and click OK. Right click your mouse and click on Paste. Print the page.

Note: the NOAA website automatically corrects the times of tides to Daylight Savings Time (DST) when applicable. At the bottom of each month, NOAA refers to this as Local Daylight Time (LDT).

We'll make an easy-to-use graph for our trip and tape it onto a cockpit navigation clipboard to show the expected tides, based on the information below:

SEPTEMBER – CHARLESTON						
Date	**Time**	**Height**	**Time**	**Height**	**Time**	**Height**
09/20/2008	*0600*	*0.1L*	*1220*	*6.3H*	*1853*	*0.9L*
A minus sign before a height would indicate a tide below the charted depth. In our example, all tides for this day are above (added to) the charted depth.						

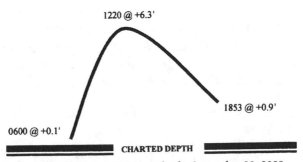

This graph represents the Charleston Harbor tides for September 20, 2008.

The Secret to Understanding Tidal Currents

All the rivers run into the sea . . . yet the sea is not full.
—KING SOLOMON

How will currents influence us as we move from one point to another? Will they push us along or hold us back? Will they set us to the left or to the right of our trackline? We have looked at the vertical rise and fall of water, called tides. Now we'll discover how those tides directly influence the horizontal flow of water, called tidal currents. Other factors, including geography, water depth, and weather, influence tidal current strength and direction. Tidal currents have their own unique prediction tables, called *tidal current tables*. Here's a list of terms you'll want to know.

Flood. The horizontal flow of water from the sea toward inland waters. In most places, but by no means in all, the flood lasts 6 hours.

Ebb. The horizontal flow of water from inland areas back out to the sea. In most places, but by no means in all, the ebb lasts 6 hours.

Maximum current. The highest speed, or velocity, of the flood or ebb during one cycle.

Set. The direction (in degrees true) toward which a current is flowing. For example, if the set is 180 degrees true, the current is flowing toward the south. Note that this convention is the opposite of that applied to winds, which are named for the direction *from which,* not toward which, they blow.

Drift. The speed of a current expressed in knots.

Slack current. When speaking of tidal heights, we talked about a period of rest, called the *stand,* that follows each rise or fall. There is an analogous interval of rest following each flood or ebb, and this is called *slack water.* During this period, currents flow between 0 and ½ knot. It is not unusual for the time of slack water to be offset from the corresponding stand. At river mouths, for example, the ebb—enhanced by river flow—may continue for as much as 2 hours or more after the tide begins to rise.

A DAY IN THE LIFE OF A TIDAL CURRENT CYCLE
Let's look at a typical day of tidal currents on the U.S. East Coast. The dark black horizontal line in the accompanying illustration marks slack water. Flood cycles rise above the slack line; ebb cycles dip below the slack line.

HOW TO USE U.S. TIDAL CURRENT TABLE PUBLICATIONS
Before, we talked about how to find the time and height of the tide from the tide table books. You can use a similar but different book to find the time, direction, and

speed of a tidal current. In the United States, you can order tidal current tables in book form. These show the current at select stations (also available online, see below). Surveyors use the same sequence for mapping tidal currents as they do for tides. They record the times (in Eastern Standard Time) of the maximum ebbs and floods and the slacks at the reference station for each day of the month. Then they determine the maximum speeds of the ebbs and floods. The results are placed into the tidal current book in Table 1. Next they conduct surveys at nearby substations to find time and speed differences for Table 2. Look over the three steps below for finding tidal current information from the Tidal Current Tables. (See page 106 for samples.)

1. **Enter the back index.** Turn to the back of the book and look for the substation of interest. If you don't find the exact location, find one nearby. Write down the substation number next to the geographic name.

2. **Enter Table 2 (substations).** Enter Table 2 with your substation number.

   - Look at the *Time Differences* section. Columns headed *Min. before Flood* and *Min. before Ebb* (Min. means minimum, or slack) show slack-water time differences. Write down each time difference. Now look under the columns headed *Flood* or *Ebb*. These show maximum current time differences. Write down each time difference.
   - Slide over to the column headed *Speed Ratios*. Write down the flood and ebb speed ratios.
   - Move over to the *Average Speeds and Directions* column. Write down the maximum flood and maximum ebb current directions.
   - Look above your substation line to find the Table 1 reference station; turn to this page.

3. **Enter Table 1 (reference stations).** Find the month and date you need. Copy the times of slack water and maximum current. Copy the maximum speed of each flood or ebb. Apply the substation time differences to the appropriate reference station times. Multiply the speed ratios by the appropriate flood or ebb speed. Jot down the flood and ebb direction (set) next to your figures.

SEA-CRET TIP

▶ Wind or sea in opposition to a tidal current creates a steep chop. In an inlet, an ebb current creates rougher conditions than does a flood current. Ocean swells flowing into an inlet collide with an outgoing ebb. Onshore winds add to the danger. In marginal conditions, choose a safer route.

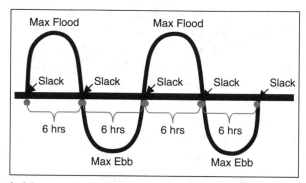

A typical day of tidal currents at a U.S. East Coast location where each flood and ebb lasts 6 hours.

Another Method to Use Tidal Current Tables

SLACK   MAXIMUM FLOOD   SLACK   MAXIMUM EBB

TABLE 2 – CURRENT DIFFERENCES AND OTHER CONSTANTS

No.	PLACE	Meter Depth (ft)	POSITION Latitude	POSITION Longitude	TIME DIFFERENCES Min. before Flood (h m)	TIME DIFFERENCES Flood (h m)	TIME DIFFERENCES Min. before Ebb (h m)	TIME DIFFERENCES Ebb (h m)	SPEED RATIOS Flood	SPEED RATIOS Ebb	AVERAGE SPEEDS AND DIRECTIONS Minimum before Flood (knots)	Dir.	Maximum Flood (knots)	Dir.	Minimum before Ebb (knots)	Dir.	Maximum Ebb (knots)	Dir.
	BOSTON HARBOR–PRESIDENT ROADS–cont. Time meridian, 75° W		North	West	on Boston Harbor, p.16 Current weak and variable													
1321	Charles River	10	42° 22.18′	71° 03.38′														
1326	East Boston, Pier 10, southeast of	10	42° 22.56′	71° 02.80′	+1 35	+0 50	+0 28	+0 16	0.2	0.3	--	--	0.2	017°	--	--	0.4	194°
	do.	25	42° 22.56′	71° 02.80′	+0 01	+1 06	+1 23	+0 51	0.3	0.2	--	--	0.3	030°	--	--	0.2	193°
1331	Chelsea River, west of bascule bridge	10	42° 23.07′	71° 02.53′	+0 02	-0 26	+0 43	-0 46	0.2	0.2	--	--	0.2	048°	--	--	0.2	240°
1336	Chelsea River, below bascule bridge	10	42° 23.03′	71° 01.70′	+0 29	-0 15	+0 37	-0 04	0.2	0.2	--	--	0.2	088°	--	--	0.3	272°
1341	Mystic River Bridge, 0.1 n.mi. west of	10	42° 23.18′	71° 03.02′	+0 31	-0 10	+0 46	-0 16	0.1	0.1	--	--	0.1	267°	--	--	0.1	093°
1346	Mystic River Bridge, northwest of	10	42° 23.15′	71° 02.96′	-0 35	+1 04	+0 22	-0 44	0.1	0.1	--	--	0.1	300°	--	--	0.1	099°
1351	City Point, 0.8 n.mi. SSE of	10	42° 19.22′	71° 03.88′	+0 13	+0 34	+1 19	+1 03	0.5	0.5	--	--	0.6	088°	0.1	170°	0.6	069°
1356	Squantum Point, 0.8 n.mi. northeast of	10	42° 18.63′	71° 01.70′	+0 18	+0 36	+1 16	+0 51	0.4	0.4	--	--	0.4	216°	--	--	0.5	036°
1361	Squantum Point, 0.4 n.mi. NNE of	10	42° 18.38′	71° 02.23′	+0 14	+0 06	+0 56	+0 52	0.4	0.4	--	--	0.4	295°	--	--	0.5	091°
1366	Neponset River	10	42° 18.29′	71° 02.98′	-0 25	-0 32	+0 45	+0 35	0.4	0.4	--	--	0.4	218°	--	--	0.4	029°

Now let's find something about the tidal currents at Neponset on the afternoon of August 2, 2008. In the table of differences in the back pages of the tidal current tables, we find that slack (Minimum before Flood) at Neponset is 25 minutes earlier than in Boston Harbor on August 2, 2008. The following slack (Minimum before Ebb) is 45 minutes later than in Boston Harbor. Maximum flood current is 32 minutes earlier than Boston and maximum ebb current is 35 minutes later than Boston. The speed ratio columns show maximum ebb and flood currents are both 0.4 times as strong as in Boston Harbor.

Boston Harbor (Deer Island Light), Massachusetts, 2008

F–Flood, Dir. 254° True   E–Ebb, Dir. 111° True

July Slack	July Maximum		July Slack	July Maximum		August Slack	August Maximum		August Slack	August Maximum		September Slack	September Maximum		September Slack	September Maximum	
h m	h m	knots	h m	h m	knots	h m	h m	knots	h m	h m	knots	h m	h m	knots	h m	h m	knots
1 Tu 0250 0895 1508 2057	0532 1229 1745	1.3F 1.2E 1.4F	**16** W 0341 0937 1551 2142	0123 0658 1346 1913	1.3E 1.0F 1.1E 1.1F	**1** F 0419 1011 1640 2229	0150 0739 1419 1953	1.5E 1.2F 1.4E 1.3F	**16** Sa ● 0431 1022 1650 2234	0213 0748 1424 2001	1.2E 1.2F 1.1E 1.2F	**1** M 0538 1132 1805 2352	0313 0855 1540 2119	1.5E 1.4F 1.5E 1.3F	**16** Tu 0519 1111 1747 2329	0209 0805 1430 2021	1.3E 1.5F 1.3E 1.4F
2 W ● 0344 0932 1601	0101 0641 1334 1852	1.4E 1.3F 1.3E 1.3F	**17** Th 0423 1015 1636	0206 0741 1429 1955	1.2E 1.1F 1.1E 1.1F	**2** Sa 0510 1104 1734	0242 0827 1501 2047	1.5E 1.3F 1.4E 1.3F	**17** Su 0512 1101 1732	0245 0823 1504 2031	1.2E 1.3F 1.2E 1.2F	**2** Tu 0624 1218 1853	0402 0941 1629 2207	1.4E 1.3F 1.4E 1.2F	**17** W 0601 1152 1831	0238 0835 1502 2057	1.3E 1.5F 1.4E 1.4F

From the National Ocean Service's 2008 tidal current tables for the Atlantic Coast of North America, we learn that the afternoon maximum current in Boston Harbor will be an ebb at 1611 (Daylight Savings Time) on August 2, and that current speed is 1.4 knots. Slack water at Boston occurs at 1204 and 1834.

HOW TO ACCESS YOUR FREE ONLINE TIDAL CURRENT TABLES

1. Access the NOAA site for Tidal Currents at **http://tidesandcurrents .noaa.gov/currents08/**. (Notice the last two numbers for the year 2008; for any other year, change the last two numbers.)
2. Scroll down the page and click on South Carolina.
3. Click on Charleston Harbor.
4. Click on Predictions, adjacent to CHARLESTON HARBOR (off Fort Sumter).
5. Scroll down to the September 2008 listings. Place your cursor over the word *Charleston* in the title at the upper left corner. Double click to mark the word. Scroll down to the bottom right corner of the September page. Hold down the shift key and left click the right corner.
6. Right click and then click on Copy. Go to any word processing program such as MS Word. Click on File, Page Setup, Landscape, then click OK. Then, right click and then click on Paste. Print this page, or go to the next section to print and format your data.

Note: the NOAA website automatically corrects the times of tidal currents to Daylight Savings Time (DST), when applicable.

For cockpit navigation we'll make an easy-to-use graph for Charleston Harbor on September 20, 2008, based on the information obtained from the online tidal current tables.

CHARLESTON HARBOR (off Fort Sumter)																		
Predicted Tidal Current				September, 2008														
Flood Direction, 313 True.				Ebb (-) Direction, 127 True.														
NOAA, National Ocean Service																		

	Slack Water	Maximum Current		Slack Water	Maximum Current		Slack Water	Maximum Current		Slack Water	Maximum Current		Slack Water	Maximum Current		Slack Water	Maximum Current	
Day	Time h.m.	Time h.m.	Veloc knots	Time h.m.	Time h.m.	Veloc knots	Time h.m.	Time h.m.	Veloc knots	Time h.m.	Time h.m.	Veloc knots	Time h.m.	Time h.m.	Veloc knots	Time h.m.	Time h.m.	Veloc knots
20	0013	0335	-2.3	0632	0919	+1.9	1306	1622	-2.5	1933	2148	+1.4						

Tidal current data for Charleston Harbor, South Carolina, on September 20, 2008, as can be found online.

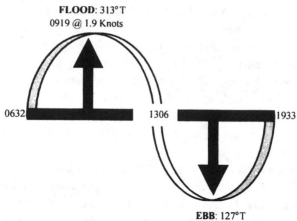

FLOOD: 313°T
0919 @ 1.9 Knots

0632   1306   1933

EBB: 127°T
1622 @ 2.5 Knots

A graph made from the time table and maximum current for the flood and ebb at Charleston Harbor on September 20, 2008.

Make a Tidal Current Graph from Online Data

1. **Slack-water line.** Draw a thick, horizontal slack-water line first. Remember, each current cycle begins and ends at this line.
2. **Max current.** In the column for *Maximum Current* in the online tidal current tables, a plus (+) sign indicates flood current; a negative (–) sign represents ebb current. Use that information to draw each cycle, beginning and ending with a slack-water time marked on the slack-water line. Show flood above and ebb below the slack-water line.
3. **Current direction (set).** Look above the columns on the tidal current table; note the true direction of the flood (313°T) and ebb (127°T). Write these directions onto your graph next to the appropriate flood or ebb. Compare this direction to your tracklines. Current from ahead will slow you down (boatspeed minus current speed = actual speed). Current from behind will add to your boatspeed (boatspeed plus current speed = actual speed). Any current not directly in line with your trackline will set you off course. Check the chart and mark any dangers toward which a tidal current will set you.

BRITISH ADMIRALTY TIDAL CURRENT RESOURCES

Tidal station diamonds. Tidal station diamonds are plotted at various locations on British Admiralty (and some U.S.) charts. Look for a letter enclosed by a diamond border. You will find a tidal stream table printed on the chart nearby. Enter the column to the left with the number of hours before or after high water. For example, for 4 hours after high water, find "4" in the column. Follow this line across to the column that shows the letter diamond of interest. Read the direction and speed of the neap or spring current at that location.

*Tidal stream atlases (also called tidal current atlases).*Tidal stream atlases are published annually from the United Kingdom Hydrographic Office and can be ordered from its website at: **http://www.ukho.gov.uk/amd/paperPublications .asp.** The atlases contain diagrams of current flow at selected areas in northwestern Europe, including Great Britain, Ireland, France, Scotland, and the North Sea. Each area contains a series of diagrams referenced to the time of high water. You enter the diagram based on the number of hours before or after the time of high water. For example, if you were sailing in the English Channel 3 hours after high water, you would turn to the diagram labeled as such. Current arrows show the direction of the current and its speed in knots. Because the current speeds are for spring and neap tides, you would correct the speed using a convenient table. Finally, you could lightly pencil your track onto the page to see how the current would affect you during your transit. Later in this chapter you will learn how to use this information to correct your course.

Tap the Magic of the 50-90-100 Rule

You might expect current to move in a rather lazy motion—taking its time to get from slack water to maximum speed during the first half of the cycle, and then slowly losing strength through the latter half. In fact, however, the current reaches 50% of its maximum velocity by the end of the first hour. The 50-90-100 Rule makes it easy to find current speed during any hour of a cycle.

The numbers 50, 90, and 100 represent percentages of the maximum current during the first half of the cycle. We then reverse the rule—from 90 to 50 to 0—during the last half-cycle. A flood or an ebb might not be exactly 6 hours in duration, so for more accuracy, divide the actual interval between the slack and the maximum current that bracket your time of interest into three equal portions. If the interval between the bracketing slack and maximum current is 2 hours 30 minutes, each portion thereof is 50 minutes. Follow these steps; then go to the example:

1. Find the interval of time between the slack and the maximum current that bracket your time of interest.
2. Divide this time interval by 3. This gives three equal portions of time between slack and maximum current.
3. For the first half of an ebb or a flood, begin with the initial slack and add each interval twice. For instance, if slack is at 0900 and maximum current is at 1212, each interval would be 1 hour 04 minutes. For the first interval, 0900 + 1 h 04 m = 1004. Then once more: 1004 + 1 h 04 m = 1108.
4. For the second half of the ebb or flood, subtract the time of maximum current from the time of the next slack, then proceed as above.

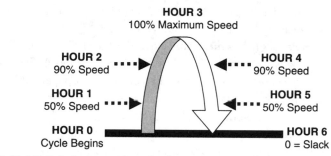

The 50-90-100 Rule during a 6-hour flood.

5. Multiply the 50-90-100 Rule factors by the maximum current and place these next to the appropriate times. For instance, if the maximum current is 2 knots at 1212, the current at 1004 will be 50% × 2 or 1 knot. At 1108, it will be 90% × 2 or 1.8 knots.

Let's apply the 50-90-100 Rule to our graph of Charleston Harbor tidal currents, covering all times and velocities for Charleston Harbor on September 20, 2008. For more accuracy, calculate time intervals for each half-cycle. It looks like this:

Time Intervals

Flood cycle runs from 0632 to 1306

First half of cycle: 0632 (slack) to 0919 (max flood)

2 h 47 m (167 minutes) ÷ 3 = 56 minutes

0632 + 56 m = 0728

0728 + 56 m = 0824

Repeat the process for the last half of cycle: 0919 (max flood) to 1306 (slack)

3 h 47 m (227 minutes) ÷ 3 = 76 minutes

0919 + 1 h 16 m = 1035

1035 + 1 h 16 m = 1151

Repeat this method for the remaining cycles.

Current velocity (round results to closest tenth)

Maximum flood = 1.9 knots

0728 velocity = 50% × 1.9 = 1 knot

0824 velocity = 90% × 1.9 = 1.8 knots

0919 velocity = maximum flood = 1.9 knots

1035 velocity = 90% × 1.9 = 1.8 knots

1151 velocity = 50% × 1.9 = 1 knot

1306 velocity = slack

Repeat this method for the remaining cycles.

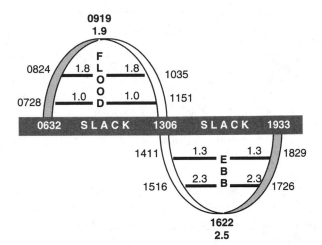

Using the 50-90-100 Rule, we can compute the speed of current flow during flood and ebb cycles.

SEA-CRET TIP

▶ High winds blowing onshore for hours on end increase high- and low-water heights. Flood speeds increase and ebb speeds decrease. The beginning of the ebb may be delayed for hours.

Slack Intervals: Nature's Gift to Mariners

Power and sailing vessels often need to know how much time they have to make it through a narrow passage, bridge, or inlet. Dangerous currents make some transits impossible. In these cases, make your run in slack-water speeds of ½ knot or less. You can plan your passage by calculating slack velocity and duration. Below, we use a midday arrival at Charleston Harbor as an example.

Find the closest slack time to your arrival time. First, look at the tidal current table to find the closest slack water to your planned time of arrival. For example, we plan to arrive at Charleston Harbor around noon on September 20, 2008; the closest slack time to our arrival, based on the table, is 1306.

Estimate the current speed you may encounter at your ETA. On the table, look at the maximum current velocities bracketing the 1306 slack water. The maximum flood velocity is 1.9 knots, and the maximum ebb is 2.5 knots. For safety, use the higher of the two. Remember, this is just an estimate. Let's use 2.5 knots for our calculation.

	Slack Water	Maximum Current		Slack Water	Maximum Current		Slack Water	Maximum Current		Slack Water	Maximum Current		Slack Water	Maximum Current	
Day	Time	Time	Veloc knots	Time	Time	Veloc knots	Time	Time	Veloc knots	Time	Time	Veloc knots	Time	Time	Veloc knots
20	0013	0335	-2.3	0632	0919	+1.9	1306	1622	-2.5	1933	2148	+1.4			

Based on the tidal current table for Charleston Harbor, the closest slack-water time to our arrival is 1306 hours.

We plan to arrive about 1 hour before slack water. Using the 50-90-100 Rule, we estimate that the current will be at 50% velocity about 1 hour before slack and about 1 hour after slack. So our calculation would be:

$$2.5 \text{ knots} \times 50\% = 1.25 \text{ knots}$$

Calculate slack-water duration. From the estimated current speed approximately 1 hour from slack, we can estimate slack-water duration (i.e., the length of time during which the current will run at ½ knot or less). Simply divide 0.5 knot by the estimated current speed 1 hour from slack, convert this result to minutes, and subtract and add the minutes to the slack-water time.

$$0.5 \text{ knot (slack-water velocity)} \div 1.25 \text{ knots (current speed at 1 hour from slack)} = 0.4 \text{ hour} = 24 \text{ minutes.}$$

Now let's apply this to our 1306 slack-water time.

$$1306 \text{ hours} - 24 \text{ minutes} = 1242 \text{ hours}$$

$$1306 \text{ hours} + 24 \text{ minutes} = 1330 \text{ hours}$$

We estimate that our slack-water interval will run from 1242 to 1330 hours. Our total time of slack water will be 48 minutes. (See also the Duration of Slack Water table in Appendix I.)

SEA-CRET TIP

▶ Arrive earlier than your estimated time of slack interval. Use binoculars to study the water inside the transit area. Do you still see current tails streaming from buoys or pilings? If necessary, heave-to or anchor and wait for slack water. Remember, frontal passages, heavy rainfall, or prevailing winds can alter the time, strength, and direction of any current.

How to Measure the Effect of Current in Three Easy Steps

In navigation, the word *current* includes all effects, both mechanical and natural, that combine to push a boat from ahead, astern, or one side. Tidal currents, ocean and wind-generated currents, helm error, engine or engines out of sync, even leeway—all these go into the term "current" as it applies to navigation. Tidal currents are those currents directly affected by the vertical rise and fall of water (tide) in a geographic area. Ocean currents such as the Gulf Stream are not influenced by tide.

Your GPS receiver has a *cross-track error* function—abbreviated XTE or XTK—showing how far right or left you have wandered from your plotted trackline. It also tells you the direction to the next waypoint, but it won't tell you whether steering that course places you in danger. For that reason, it is far preferable to stick to your original trackline (which you presumably have plotted on the chart and know to be hazard-free) than to wander off that trackline and then steer a new course to bring you back to it.

Here too GPS provides a ready answer: You can simply adjust your course until your GPS receiver tells you that your course over ground (COG: see below) and the bearing to the next waypoint (i.e., your trackline) are the same. But how can you stick to your trackline without GPS? Doing so will be easier once you know a quick and easy method that tells you the direction and strength of the current.

FINDING THE DIRECTION AND SPEED OF ANY CURRENT

As mentioned above, the set of a current is noted in degrees true. If the current sets 045 degrees, then it is flowing *toward* 045 degrees true. Also as noted, the velocity of a current is called its drift. Like boatspeed, drift is expressed in knots.

For example, let's say you've used your tidal current tables or atlas to calculate the current. You determine it has a set of 045 degrees true and a drift of 3 knots. If you stopped your boat next to a buoy, what would happen? The current would push (set) the boat in a direction of 045 degrees true, and in 1 hour you would end up 3 miles northeast of the buoy. Once you figure out the set and drift of any current in the world, you can compensate for it. Below is an example.

At 1200 we obtain a fix from crossed bearings and plot a trackline to the next waypoint. The TR is 90 degrees magnetic, and our speed is 4 knots. At 1230 we obtain and plot a second fix. How is the current affecting our boat?

1. **Plot three separate positions.** All set and drift calculations require you to plot three basic positions. Start with a known position. Plot a second position based on information from a reliable navigation source (visual or

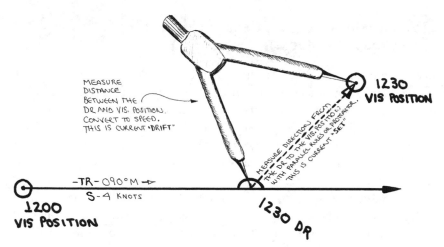

MEASURE
DISTANCE
BETWEEN THE
DR AND VIS. POSITION.
CONVERT TO SPEED.
THIS IS CURRENT "DRIFT"

1230
VIS POSITION

MEASURE DIRECTION FROM
THE DR TO THE VIS POS ITO 6)
WITH PARALLEL RULES OR PROTRACTOR
THIS IS CURRENT "SET"

—TR—090°M—▸
S—4 KNOTS

1200
VIS POSITION

1230 DR

Plot three positions to calculate the set of a current. Because the fix is obtained from visual bearings, it is labeled VIS.

electronic bearings or an electronic or celestial fix). In our example, we are using visual bearings. Plot a DR at the *same time* as the second position.

2. **Always measure current set from the DR.** Use parallel rules or a protractor and measure the direction from the DR to the second position. In our example, we measure the direction from the 1230 DR to the 1230 fix. The current set is 045 degrees true.

3. **Always measure current drift from the DR.** Measure the distance from the DR to the second position. In our example, we measure from the 1230 DR to the 1230 fix. Convert that distance to speed using your nautical slide rule. In the example, the current has set our boat 0.5 nautical mile in 30 minutes, so the drift is 1 knot.

WHAT IS THE CURRENT'S EFFECT ON YOUR COURSE AND SPEED?

Your boat follows a course over the seabed called *course over the ground,* or *COG.* To find COG, measure the direction between two or more consecutive positions. In the example (the dashed line in the accompanying art) this is the actual course of the boat from the 1200 fix to the 1230 fix. Measure this with your parallel rulers or protractor to find course over ground (COG).

Find your *speed over ground,* or *SOG,* the same way. If the distance between the 1200 and 1230 positions measures 2.5 miles, your SOG is 5 knots. Which of the six boat/TR relationships do you see?

boat on TR?
boat to the right of TR?
boat to the left of TR?

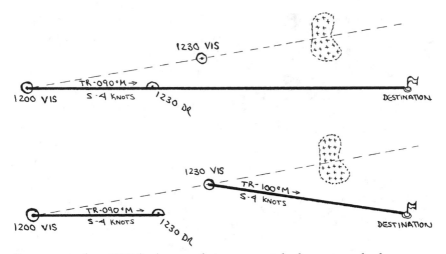

Once we extend our COG (top), we see that our course is leading us toward a dangerous shoal. We must plot a new course (bottom) that will take us safely to our destination.

boat moving at expected speed?
boat moving faster than expected?
boat moving slower than expected?

Current has affected our boat to create two out of the six boat/TR relation-ships: It is to the left of the TR and moving faster than expected.

Extend the TR and check for dangers ahead. Now that you know the effect of the current, predict your track by extending the COG line 1 hour or more ahead of your most recent fix. Check for dangers on all sides of the extended COG line; then plot the safest course to keep you out of danger. Once we know set and drift, we can quickly and accurately calculate the course to steer to keep us in safe water. *Note: this assumes a steady set and drift of current. If you expect the current set or drift to change as the stage of tide changes or as you leave one channel and enter another, you'll want to accommodate the expected change in your calculations. When visibility is poor and the effects of current are significant, run short courses between prominent navaids or landmarks.*

How to Cross the Gulf Stream or Any Other Ocean Current

Solve any current problem by building a *course-to-steer,* or *CTS,* triangle. A CTS triangle has three sides, called *vectors.* All vectors represent a specific direction and speed.

Tools Needed to Build a Course-to-Steer (CTS) Triangle

▶ any convenient compass rose
▶ plotting compass
▶ a consistent scale (see the section on finding a scale, below)
▶ direction measuring tool (Weems plotter, parallel rulers, protractor)

Some electronics allow current data input for crossing areas like the Gulf Stream. For peace of mind, make this simple calculation to ensure the computer doesn't lead you astray.

Find a clear area on the chart. I find it much less confusing to do my calculations well away from the plotted trackline. Many navigators find the center crosshairs of a convenient compass rose ideal.

Find a scale to use for speed. Choose any convenient scale for your calculations. It isn't necessary—and it's often impractical—to use the latitude scale. Use a ruler, graph paper, or the tenths increments on a chart. Just be sure all increments are the same size, and use this scale consistently throughout the calculation. Make sure the plotting compass opens up to your vessel's speed. In a 22-knot power vessel, you'll need a scale with twenty-two increments. In a 6-knot sailing vessel, you'll need a scale with six increments.

THREE EASY STEPS TO SOLVE THE MYSTERY

1. **Draw the set and drift vector.** From any crosshair, draw a vector showing 1 hour of set and drift. In the example above, this vector measures exactly 1 nautical mile long in the direction of 45 degrees true.

2. **Draw the TR vector.** Convert the trackline (TR) from your chart to a true direction (if plotted in degrees magnetic). Next, go to the crosshair and draw a long line that represents the true direction of this TR vector. We'll shorten this line later, but make it long for now.

3. **Draw in the third side and solve the CTS triangle.** Use your plotting compass to measure boatspeed through the water from your scale. Power vessels can calculate speed from engine RPMs; sailing vessels can use speed averaged from a distance or speed log. Place the needle point of the compass in the *end* of your set and drift vector, and sweep an arc across the TR vector. Use a straightedge to join the end of the set and drift vector to the TR vector. In the illustration, the dashed line shows the true course to steer in order to compensate for current and progress along your TR. Apply variation to convert this true course to a magnetic course to steer.

4. **Solve for the boat's speed of advance along the TR.** Will boatspeed remain the same, increase, or decrease in this current? To find out, measure the length of the TR vector. In our illustration you will find that the TR vector is longer than the course-to-steer vector. This means that our speed increases in this case.

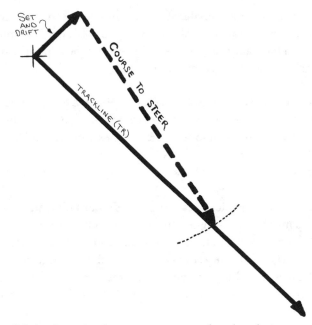

A CTS triangle helps determine the new course to steer based on the impact of the current.

How to Correct for Leeway Wind Drift

All vessels tend to sideslip, or make *leeway*, except with the wind dead ahead or astern. High-freeboard power vessels make leeway at slower speeds when the wind strikes their sides. Sailing vessels make lots of leeway when hard on the wind and less leeway when well off the wind. Light airs and heavy winds have more impact than moderate breezes.

THREE METHODS FOR ESTIMATING LEEWAY

Choose any of these methods to make a rough estimate of your boat's leeway angle.

1. **Take a bearing on your wake trail.** Use your handbearing compass to estimate leeway angle. Sight dead astern with your compass. Wait several minutes, then sight along the wake line to windward. The difference in the two angles gives you your leeway angle.

2. **Take a bearing to an object astern.** Find a landmark, light structure, or buoy dead astern. Take a bearing with the handbearing compass. Hold a steady course for a several minutes, and then take a second bearing. The difference in bearings is your leeway angle.

3. **Leeway by backstay wake angle.** Steady up on a course for a few minutes until you see a wake trail to windward. Swing the boat quickly, lining up the backstay with the wake trail. Glance at the compass heading. The difference between the two headings is your leeway angle.

STEERING UPWIND TO CORRECT FOR LEEWAY ANGLE

To correct for leeway, be sure to apply the correction to your steering course in the proper direction. You want to steer the boat *closer* to the wind to counteract the effect of leeway. If the wind blows from the port side, subtract the angle from your course. If the wind blows from the starboard side, add the leeway angle to the course.

For example, you are close-reaching on starboard tack, steering a course of 350 degrees magnetic. You sight astern with the handbearing compass for a reading of 170 degrees magnetic. Five minutes later, you sight down the wake line, and the bearing is 164 degrees magnetic. The difference gives you a leeway angle of 6 degrees. You'll need to point 6 degrees higher, so add the angle to your 350-degree course and steer a new course of 356 degrees magnetic.

"Your Call, Skipper"

You're the skipper or most knowledgeable crewmember on board. What actions would you take in the following situations?

1.   You are planning to arrive in Marblehead, Massachusetts, late in the afternoon of May 25. Turning to the tide tables, you read the following information: high water will be 9.5 feet at 1335 hours; low water is –0.7 foot at 1940 hours. What final step must you take before making your tidal graph?

2.   Slack water in The Race, at the eastern end of Long Island Sound, is at 1400 hours DST. Three hours later the ebb reaches a maximum of 3 knots. You plan on entering the The Race from the eastward around 1500. You expect the current to be from dead ahead. In a sailing vessel traveling at 5.5 knots, how would this affect your SOG?

3.   You expect a Gulf Stream current of 000 degrees true at 3.5 knots between Miami and Bahama Cay. In a power vessel traveling at 12 knots, you lay a TR of 93 degrees magnetic for Bahama Cay. The variation is 3 degrees west and the distance is 46 nautical miles. You begin the crossing at 0900. What is the initial course to steer and the estimated time of arrival?

4.   Your latest position places you a quarter mile to the right of your TR. You're not too concerned but want to make sure this course will be safe. What is the safest method to use before making a decision?

5.   You are close-reaching on port tack, bound for Martha's Vineyard in a stiff southwesterly. Your estimated leeway is 10 degrees. How do you apply this to your present course?

Answers

1.   Add 1 hour to each tide time for Daylight Savings Time. In the United States, DST lasts from March into November. Then make your tide graph using the listed information. (Note: remember, if using tide data from the NOAA online tide tables, it isn't necessary to add an hour; those times are corrected for Daylight Savings Time when applicable.)

2.   Using the 50-90-100 Rule, you estimate that the current will reach 50% of its maximum during the first hour after slack. At 1500 hours there would be 1.5 knots ebb. This would slow your SOG to 4 knots (5.5 knots of boatspeed – 1.5 knots ebb current).

3.   The true course to steer is 107 degrees. Convert this to a magnetic course to steer: 107 degrees true + 3 degrees west variation = 110 degrees magnetic. Your ETA would be 1300, since the SOG would slow to 11.5 knots (46 miles ÷ 11.5 = 4 hours). (Measure the second side [vector] of the set and drift triangle. This vector shows 11.5 nautical miles, which represents speed over ground.)

4.   Draw a line from your starting point to your latest position. This is your COG. Extend it for one or more hours ahead, and study the resultant track on all sides for danger.

5.   Change course 10 degrees toward the wind, or to port.

BRIDGES, NIGHT PASSAGES, AND OTHER TRICKY NAVIGATION SITUATIONS

Preparedness frees you to enjoy the night passage, guided by wind, sea, stars, and moon.

Up ahead, you see a bridge with three white lights and red and green lights. What does this tell you? How comfortable are you entering an unfamiliar harbor at night with multiple channels and blinking lights? What steps would you take to make this transit safe and easy?

In This Chapter, You'll Learn How To:
- ❀ Instantly identify the four bridge types and what their lights mean
- ❀ Transit any harbor or channel at night in four easy steps
- ❀ Solve the riddle of the invisible lighted range
- ❀ Find a danger bearing to clear a deadly reef—without plotting!

Cracking the Mystery of Bridge Lighting

The U.S. Coast Guard Bridge Administration Division regulates bridge construction and lighting. Nevertheless, most bridges present an array of lights confusing even to the saltiest mariner. You need to find the center span to allow the greatest clearance for your sailboat mast or powerboat antennas. Understanding the various light signals indicating closed or open is essential to avoid catastrophe. The following definitions for bridge terms may help.

Low steel. The lowest part of the bridge superstructure. A chart shows the clearance at mean high water to the bottom of the bridge span, called *low steel.*
Clearance gauges. Vertical white boards, called *clearance* or *tide gauges,* have blue or black numbers showing the height to the low steel. They are installed to the right of the bridge entrance on each side. Newer gauges show an electronic display.
Abutment. The supports on either end of the bridge.

Pier. Support pillars or stanchions between the abutments, which are made of steel, stone, concrete, or wood. Vessels pass between the piers marked for safe passage.

Fenders. Protective walls placed on each side of the piers of passage. These walls consist of wood or composite plastic. They protect the piers if a vessel loses control during its passage.

Dolphins. A cluster of pilings lashed together. Dolphins serve the same purpose as fenders, protecting the piers if a vessel loses control.

BRIDGE SYMBOLS AND DESCRIPTIONS

To quickly learn the four basic bridge shapes—fixed, bascule, swing, and lift—locate the line that crosses open water on your nautical chart.

Bridge Symbols

Bridges that do not move are **fixed bridges**—they show no center span marks over open water. Bridges that move are one of three types: **bascule bridges** (drawbridges) show a gap between center span marks; **swing bridges** show the center span turned 90 degrees; and **lift bridges** show two small arcs to mark the center span. (See illustration.)

Bridge Descriptions

Fixed bridges. The vertical height of the bridge is marked next to the charted symbol. That height doesn't take into account extreme tides at high-water springs. Check the state of the tide and clearance gauge before passing through. Fixed bridges have a central main channel and may have one or more auxiliary channels.

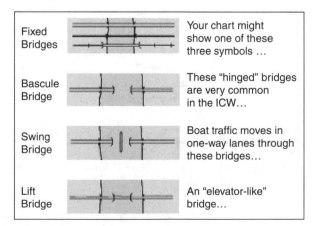

The most common bridge symbols on a nautical chart.

Bascule bridges (drawbridges). These drawbridges have one or two arms—called *leafs*—on hinges. Single-arm bascules have much less horizontal clearance than those with two arms. Check the vertical and horizontal clearances before attempting a passage through this type of bridge. Chart symbols for bascule bridges do not indicate single or double arm (leafs). Look in the Coast Pilot (see Chapter 1) or a local Waterways Cruising guide for more detailed clearance information.

Swing bridges. Swing bridges turn on a vertical axis, allowing one-way traffic on each side. The tall center span acts as a dividing line for the boat traffic that passes on each side.

Lift bridges. These giant elevator bridges have two monster legs on each side. The center span remains horizontal while moving up and down the legs.

BRIDGE LIGHT INTERPRETATION

Bridges display red, green, or white lights to indicate open and closed positions, fender locations, and channel edges. The descriptions below, along with the illustrations of the light patterns on fixed and movable bridges, will provide guidance as you navigate under bridges at nighttime. In general, bridge lighting follows these rules. In any event, always check the Local Notices to Mariners (see Chapter 1) for bridge light outages, construction information, or changes to opening schedules.

Red lights. Red lights mark the edges of the passage beneath a bridge. Installed on fenders or adjacent to the green center span lights, red lights show the width of the channel under the bridge. If the bridge moves, red lights warn the mariner to stop. For example, on a bascule bridge with two arms (or *leafs*), the leaf ends show a red light when closed; when they are opened, the light changes to green. On a lift bridge (the bridge moves up and down), wait until the center span light turns green before passing underneath. (See illustration on page 124.)

Green lights. On fixed bridges: Two rangelike green lights mark the highest vertical clearance of the bridge and show the channel centerline. These lights hang on poles from the top of the highest part of the arc. When in line (range), they help

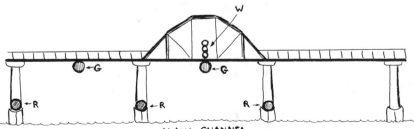

Fixed-bridge lighting. Fixed bridges with multiple channels illuminate each channel separately. The three white lights are always over the center channel.

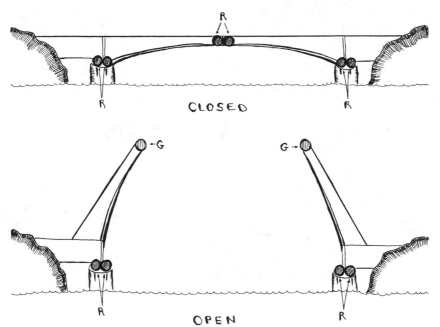

Bascule bridge lighting (closed and open positions).

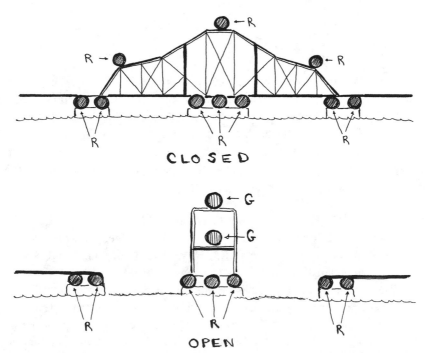

Swing bridge lighting (closed and open positions).

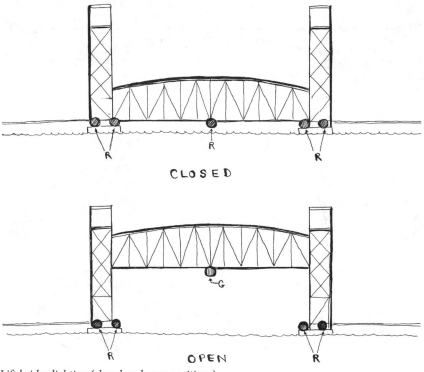

Lift bridge lighting (closed and open positions).

keep you in the center of the channel as you pass beneath the bridge. On moving bridges, green lights indicate that the bridge has opened and it's safe to proceed. On these bridges, always double-check to make sure the structure has opened completely before you attempt to pass through. Call the bridge tender if in doubt.

White lights. On fixed bridges, three vertical white lights over the green center span range lights indicate that another passage exists to the side of the main channel (see illustration on page 122).

MOVABLE BRIDGE OPENING REQUIREMENTS
If you need to pass under a bascule, swing, or lift bridge, you have two options. Call the bridge tender on your VHF-FM radio or sound and receive the appropriate whistle signal.

VHF-FM radio. If your boat has a radio, try this method first. Call the bridge tender to establish communications on Channel 16. Then shift to Channel 13 and request an opening. In Florida, use Channel 9 to call *and* request a bridge opening.

Sound signals. If your boat has no radio or the tender doesn't answer, use your whistle or horn. Sound a prolonged (4- to 6-second) blast, followed immediately by a separate short (1-second) blast. The tender must reply with one of two signals:

Bridge will open: one 4- to 6-second blast and a 1-second blast
Bridge cannot open: five short blasts

SEA-CRET TIP

▶ Set your radio to 1 watt when calling a bridge tender. This prevents the transmission from interfering with others using the same VHF-FM radio channels.

Use the Secret of "Triple Timing" to Verify a Lighted ATON

You're underway on a wet, windy night, straining through the binoculars to sight an entrance buoy 4 miles away. Four-foot beam seas cause your 32-foot cruiser to pitch and roll. You and the crew are tired and just want to get into the harbor. There it is! You sight an intermittent blip, then another a few seconds later. Well, not quite the right interval, but it seems close enough—or is it?

In Chapter 1, you learned that lighted aids to navigation have periods of light and darkness. To time such an aid, use a watch or stopwatch to count from the first flash in the pattern to the first flash in the next repetition of the pattern. For instance, when sighting a buoy that flashed every 6 seconds, you would time from one flash to the next. Your watch should read 6 seconds. To time buoys with groups of flashes, you start the watch when you see the first flash of the group and stop it when you again see the first flash of the group. For example, if the listed pattern is Gp Fl (2) 20s, you will expect to measure an elapsed time of 20 seconds from the start of one pattern repetition to the start of the next. If the time you measure is 15 seconds, either you've measured wrong or this is not the light you thought it was.

But boats and buoys pitch and roll in heavy weather, making positive identification tough. Err on the side of safety. Slow down and get closer. Time light periods three times in a row to verify your landfall or to transit unfamiliar waters. Follow the steps below for a safe passage in these conditions.

1. Raise your height of eye so that you can see the light more consistently and at a greater distance when a sea is running.
2. Slow your approach; get closer so that you can see the aid's distinct light pattern.

3. Time the light period three times in a row. For example, if a navaid flashes every 4 seconds, verify three successive 4-second intervals. When sighting a midchannel light with its characteristic Morse (A) pattern, verify three consecutive sets of long-short flashes.

SEA-CRET TIP

▶ Check the Coast Guard Light List to find the sound-signal characteristic of any major light structure. Look in the far right column for the interval in seconds between successive blasts. Time the interval between blasts and compare it with the Light List time. Times should match within 0.1 second.

How to Use S.T.O.P. for Easy Orientation

On the water after sunset, our perceptions change. Height and distance become difficult to judge. It's a challenge to orient what we see on the chart to what we see on the water. Most of us are content to anchor or moor after dark and be done with it, but nighttime sailing offers peace and quiet, cooler summertime temperatures, and a special beauty all its own. Below are helpful tips for navigating after dark.

Supplies and Tools Needed for Navigating at Night

▶ parallel rulers or protractor (for measuring courses and bearings between ATONs)
▶ handheld spotlight (one million or greater candlepower, to pick up an ATON at night)
▶ handbearing compass (with night-light)
▶ small flashlight with red or blue lens (to prevent night blindness)
▶ highlighter and black felt-tip marker (for annotating your chart)
▶ Scotch Magic Tape or dull finish tape that accepts writing

PREPARATIONS FOR NAVIGATING AT NIGHT

With your highlighter, mark each light structure along your route on the chart. Tape the area of transit and tape over the aids to navigation (see Chapter 2 on marking charts). Draw a small circle around each light structure. Write the name, color, and light period alongside. This simplifies the full description by showing only the most important identification information. For example, the full charted description of R "22" fl R 4 sec 3M 16 ft could be simplified to "22" R4.

Home In on Leading Lights

In many channels you can steer from one light to another without fear of running into unlighted markers. First check the chart to make sure there is a clear path from light to light by laying a straightedge between the lights. Find the magnetic compass direction between the lights and label the trackline. Annotate the chart in any area where it's necessary to make a channel jog for safety. (See Chapter 4.) Lay a GPS waypoint to any channel jog point that is not next to a lighted beacon.

The Magic of S.T.O.P.

I got snookered one night when I confused a lighted buoy for a light structure. Both aids showed similar light characteristics and were within 100 yards of each other. As we proceeded south, we kept the flashing light ahead just off the starboard bow. Suddenly, our spotlight picked up the reflective tape of the light, 50 yards off the port bow!

We made a sharp left turn at the last moment to leave the light structure to starboard. We were high up on a flying bridge that night, looking down into the water, and the light structure got lost in the shore lights. From this incident was born the concept of S.T.O.P. It's easy to use and works almost anywhere.

S **is for slowing down to a crawl or stopping.** After arriving at a leading light or known marker, slow to bare steerageway, stop, or even anchor. This first step is essential for safety.

T **is for turning the boat or taking a bearing.** You should already have plotted your magnetic course to the next leading light. Turn the boat to that heading or take a bearing using a handbearing compass. With a handbearing compass, hold it to your eye and turn until the bearing matches the next course. You should see the light dead ahead. Time the light and use your spotlight to confirm color, name, and shape.

O **is for orientation of the big picture before moving on.** Before moving, turn off the spotlight and check the visual picture again. If necessary, repeat the steps under *T*.

P **is for proceeding only after being fully oriented.** Keep ahead of the boat. Verify the color, name, and shape of each unlighted beacon or buoy you pass. Do you turn left, right, or continue straight at the next light ahead? Does an emergency anchorage lie to the left or right of your current position? At all times, stay ahead of the boat. Stop if you are in doubt.

SEA-CRET TIP

▶ Avoid confusion by setting up simple signals between the navigator and the spotlight operator. On power vessels, you may need to send the spotlight operator forward. Use battery-operated headsets for quieter, hands-free communications between the spotter on the bow and the navigator.

Range Sector Strategy Secrets

It's 2030 on a summer evening. You've plotted a northbound course into the harbor. The chart shows a powerful range, visible from 5 miles at sea. It carries a quick flashing lower light and an isophase 6-second upper light. At 3 miles, you still haven't picked up the range. What's going on? (For a quick review on ranges, see Chapter 1, Ranges Lead You to Safety.) If you've checked the Local Notices to Mariners (LNTM) for reports of outages, the next step is to check the Light List. Take a look at this excerpt from the Light List for the Fort Sumter range.

Name & Location	Position	Characteristic	Height	Range	Structure	Remarks
FORT SUMTER RANGE FRONT LIGHT	32 45 04 N 79 52 15 W	Fl W (Day) Fl W 2.5s (Night)	26 38	5	On skeleton tower.	Visible 0.5°each side of range line. Lighted throughout 24 hours.
FORT SUMTER RANGE REAR LIGHT 3,665 yards, 298.4° from front light.	32 45 58 N 79 54 07 W	F W (Day) Iso W 6s (Night)	166 170		On skeleton tower.	Visible 0.5°each side of range line. Lighted throughout 24 hours.

The Light List will give you more detail than you can get from a chart on ranges for nighttime navigation.

In the Remarks column for the Fort Sumter range, note that the range is only visible within a narrow 1-degree arc (i.e., 1/2 degree on each side of the range line). Large, deep-draft vessels require such precise tolerances to keep from running aground. In a small boat, you can pick up a range like this by steering a course 90 degrees across the rangeline. Use a slow speed so that you can make a sharp turn to take you down the range line as soon as it becomes visible.

Red Sectors Give Instant Danger Bearings

Some lights have lenses divided into white and red sections, called *sectors*. The red sector covers a region of extraordinary danger to mariners; the white sector marks deep, safe water. Red sectors never flash, but show a steady, fixed red light. White sectors show one of the four common characteristics: *flashing*, *quick flashing*, *occulting* (a flash in which the duration of light exceeds the duration of darkness), or *isophase* (a flash in which the light and dark intervals are of equal duration).

Cartographers plot the red sector as an arc between two dotted lines (see chart illustration), radiating from the position dot of the light. The Remarks column in the Light List shows the bearing of each line (in degrees true) as observed from your vessel.

Name & Location	Position	Characteristic	Height	Range	Structure	Remarks
REBECCA SHOAL LIGHT	24 34 42 N 82 35 06 W	Fl W 6s (R sector)	66	W 9 R 6	Square skeleton tower on brown pile foundation.	Red from 254° to 302°

The Light List information for Rebecca Shoal Light. The Remarks column shows the true bearing to each red sector dotted line as observed from your boat.

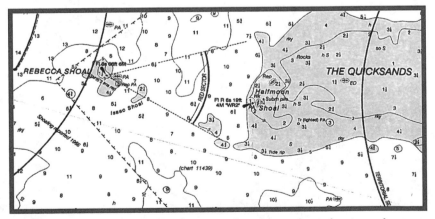

The chart showing Rebecca Shoal Light. Notice the red sector danger bearing and note that the shoals in the immediate vicinity of Rebecca Shoal are not marked by the red sector. It's up to the mariner to determine safe passing distance to keep his vessel clear of these dangers.

THREE STEPS TO AN INSTANT DANGER BEARING

You can use red sector arcs as danger bearings without having to plot them on your chart. Follow these three steps.

1. Look in the Light List under the Remarks column. Choose the correct bearing to use as a danger bearing.
2. Apply variation to the danger bearing.
3. Label the danger bearing with the prefix NLT (not less than) if the danger lies to starboard. Label the danger bearing NMT (not more than) if the danger lies to port.

You're bound northwesterly along the Florida Keys, en route to the Dry Tortugas. Without plotting, find a danger bearing using the Light List and Rebecca Shoal Light. The variation is 3 degrees west.

Look at the chart (see illustration on page 129) and note the two dashed arcs that radiate from the light. One bears to the northwest toward the light and one to the southwest toward the light. Choose the arc closest to your trackline—in this case, the arc that bears northwesterly. Turn to your Light List and look up Rebecca Shoal Light. Look in the Remarks column to find the exact bearing of the northwesterly arc (302 degree true). Apply variation to convert this to a magnetic bearing: 302 degrees true + 3 degrees west = 305 degrees magnetic. The danger bearing is NLT 305 degrees magnetic.

While on your trackline, take bearings with your handbearing compass to the light. As long as those bearings are greater than 305, you are in safe water. If, at any time, you sight a steady red light, or the bearings fall below 305, turn south to return to safety.

"Your Call, Skipper"

You're the skipper or most knowledgeable crewmember in each of the following situations. What actions would you take?

1. The tidal current tables indicate a strong flood running through the single-leaf bascule bridge 1 mile ahead. You'll pass through with the current astern. You've called the bridge tender, and he will raise the bridge for you. Name three things you would do before attempting passage.

2. You're entering an unfamiliar harbor with several channels branching from the main channel. You stop alongside a lighted buoy. What two methods could you use to find the next aid to navigation?

3. The Light List indicates the rear range going into Shelter Bay bears 187 degrees true from the front light. If the local variation is 14 degrees east, what is the magnetic course to steer directly onto the range? The range is visible 1 degree on each side of range line. What does this mean?

4. What unique light characteristic is shown in the red sector of a light marking a dangerous reef?

5. What do the prefixes NMT and NLT mean, and how do you label a danger bearing based on the side of your boat?

Answers

1. Check the horizontal clearance on the chart. A stern current makes steering difficult, so put your best helmsman on the wheel or tiller. Hang fenders on both sides. Watch for other vessels attempting passage from the upcurrent side. Test your engine(s) in reverse before you attempt passage.

2. Pivot your boat to the magnetic bearing or use a handbearing compass to locate the next aid to navigation.

3. The course is 173 degrees magnetic (187 degrees true −14 degrees east). The range is visible within a 1-degree band, in this case from 172 degrees magnetic to 174 degrees magnetic.

4. A fixed (steady) red light.

5. NMT stands for "not more than;" NLT stands for "not less than." Label port-side danger bearings NMT; label starboard-side danger bearings NLT.

AVOIDING COLLISION BY EYE OR RADAR

Most collisions result from the inability of one vessel to understand the intentions of another.

While crossing the Gulf Stream and heading to the Bahamas you sight a north-bound tanker traveling at 30 knots. The vessel appears to be headed straight for you! How many minutes do you have to maneuver? Which of the two action steps must you take to avoid collision?

In This Chapter, You'll Learn How To:
- ❀ Track any vessel, day or night, with visual drift bearings
- ❀ Avoid collisions using the magic of E.A.S.A. solutions
- ❀ Maneuver to safety if you are caught in a ship's blind spot
- ❀ Use three steps to decide when to cross a tug and tow
- ❀ Plot fast collision-avoidance solutions using your radar

The English Channel maintains a reputation as one of the busiest shipping lanes on earth. The Straits of Florida, which run between the Florida Keys and Cuba, are a close second. One of the Coast Guard captains I served under stated that every conning officer should experience at least a year in the Straits. He said it was as close to a baptism under fire as a pilot would ever experience.

He wasn't kidding. Piloting a vessel in the Straits is like riding a bicycle on an expressway. I ended up serving three years there and encountered every situation imaginable. Our 14-knot buoy tender encountered 20- to 30-knot tankers, cruise ships, tugs and tows, yachts, and commercial fishing fleets. Let's look at a few of the best techniques you can use anywhere to avoid collision.

Bearing Drift: A First Sign that Danger Exists

To judge the potential for a collision with another vessel, you need to know the bearing between your vessel and the other, and whether and how that bearing changes over time. Take a series of bearings, called *drift bearings,* to some fixed point on the other vessel such as its bow, stern, or—at nighttime—a light.

Make sure you take the bearing to the same part of the vessel (or same light) each time.

A series of drift bearings taken over a few minutes will show the vessel's *bearing drift* relative to your boat. If the vessel drifts to the right, it is said to have right bearing drift. If the vessel drifts left it is said to have left bearing drift. If the bearings show no change over time, the vessel has a steady bearing drift, which means you have a high risk of collision.

You must also observe the rate of drift. This *drift rate* is not a mathematical formula, but an observation. If the bearings change slowly, the vessel has a slow drift rate. If the bearings change rapidly, it has a fast drift rate. The faster the drift rate, the lower the risk of collision. Use drift bearings, bearing drift, and drift rate together to decide whether you must maneuver to avoid a collision.

One of three situations always exists between vessels:

Meeting: Two vessels are moving *toward* each other, end to end. This includes vessels bow to bow, bow to stern, or stern to stern.

Crossing: One vessel moves *against* the other. Vessels cross from left to right or from right to left.

Overtaking: A faster vessel is coming up from behind a slower vessel.

In a busy channel, harmless meetings between vessels can quickly change to dangerous crossing situations. For this reason, you must maintain a visual watch on any vessel until it no longer presents a risk of collision.

Download a Free Copy of the Navigation Rules

Add a copy of the Navigation Rules for International and U.S. Inland Waters to your onboard library. This book has but one purpose: to advise mariners on how to prevent collisions on any body of water on the planet. Download a free copy from the U.S. Coast Guard's Navigation Center at http://www.navcen.uscg.gov/mwv/navrules/download.htm.

Do this now, before reading further, and use the navigation rules to help you understand the concepts we discuss. Always keep a copy onboard your boat. (In fact, certain commercial vessels are required to keep a copy of the rules on board.) Before long, your copy of the rules will become one of the most highlighted, dog-eared nautical books onboard! And you'll find yourself referring to it time and again for advice on avoiding collision, vessel lighting, fog, and distress signals.

Note from the publisher: among the commercially published editions of the navigation rules is The One-Minute Guide to the Nautical Rules of the Road *(by Charlie Wing; 0-07-147923-6), which includes illustrations and interpretations along with the precise language of the rules, and which also highlights the few differences between the U.S. Inland Rules and the International Rules that apply in U.S. coastal waters and around the world. You can also find a condensed version of the rules in* Charlie Wing's Captain's Quick Guide: Rules of the Road and Running Light Patterns, *0-07-142369-9.*

Will that vessel off our starboard bow cross ahead or astern of us? How about the large power vessel coming toward us down the channel? Will we pass safely, port-side to port-side? Use the following techniques to determine if another vessel will cross ahead or astern of you or if the threat of a collision exists.

To determine bearing drift and drift rate:

Stanchion bearings. Use a stanchion or other fixed point to sight the other vessel. Watch the way the vessel drifts relative to the stanchion. Does it appear to drift to the left, to the right, or stay steady? If drifting, is its rate of drift fast or slow?

Compass bearings. Use your handbearing compass to shoot the bow of the vessel. Wait 30 seconds and shoot it again. Repeat the procedure one more time. Note whether the bearing drifts to the left or right.

In either of the above cases, if the bearing drifts toward our bow, the other vessel will cross ahead of us. If the bearing drifts toward our stern, it will pass astern of us. And if the bearing has little to no drift and remains constant, a risk of collision exists.

DOES A RAPID DRIFT RATE EVER INDICATE DANGER?

Rule 7 in the Navigation Rules for International and Inland Waters offers examples of what you use to determine if a risk of collision exists. For instance, it cautions that drift bearings could change rapidly in three cases and still result in a collision:

- Extremely large vessels
- Vessels close to you
- When you approach a vessel that is towing

To track large or close vessels with drift bearings, pick a prominent point on one end of the vessel. Shoot only this point each time you take a bearing. Do not hesitate to take defensive action if needed (see more on this below). We will discuss collision avoidance strategies for tugs with tows later in this chapter.

ACTION STEPS AND OPTIONS TO KEEP YOU SAFE

Mariners always have two action steps to avoid a collision:

Change course: Come right or come left

Change speed: Slow down (or stop) or speed up

Choose one or both action steps to control the situation. Take action earlier than you think necessary. That way, if things don't work out as planned, you have time to try something else.

If you change course, alter your course 60 to 90 degrees or more. If you increase or decrease speed, do so in a dramatic way. The goal is to make any action you take crystal clear to the other vessel. Most collisions result from confusion between vessels.

HOW TO CHANGE A DRIFT BEARING

A decreasing range along a steady bearing indicates that a risk of collision exists between vessels. You must get that bearing moving to the left or right. Remember that the action steps of changing course and/or changing speed are always available to you.

In a crossing situation, slow or stop your boat. In a meeting or overtaking situation, change course *away* from the other vessel. If needed, combine this with a speed change.

Use Sectoring to Track a Crossing or Overtaking Vessel

In many crossing situations, you will see the other vessel's red or green sidelight. Treat that light as if it were a traffic light. A red light warns you to stop or slow down. A green light indicates that you are the stand-on vessel; the rules prescribe that you should maintain your course and speed, and the onus to change course or speed is on the other vessel. But there are times when you will be unable to tell whether a vessel's sidelight is red or green. It may very well look white! At sea, red and green lenses decrease the range of a sidelight, or they might blend in with the white deck lights used on larger vessels.

Use a fast and easy concept called "sectoring," which works whether or not you can distinguish the color of another vessel's lights. Imagine dividing your boat into four equal parts, or sectors. Split it down the centerline, and then split it again across the middle (beam) of the boat. You now have four sectors: one from the bow to the starboard beam; one from the starboard beam to the stern; one from the stern to the port beam, and one from the port beam to the bow. Those sectors remain in place no matter how the boat turns (see illustration).

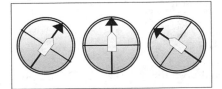

Using sectoring to track a crossing or overtaking vessel. As the boat turns, its sectors turn with it.

Sector colors: Our imaginary sectors will have colors similar to those used in a traffic light—red, yellow, and green. Your first sector is red; the next two sectors are yellow; and the final one is green (see illustration). Remember, no matter how you turn the boat, keep these sector colors in the same sequence.

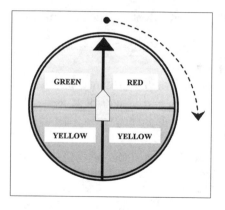

Start from the bow and designate the sectors red, yellow, yellow, and green.

Sighting Another Vessel in One of Your Sectors

Follow these three steps each time you sight a crossing or overtaking vessel:

1. Determine which sector contains that vessel.
2. Find the vessel's bearing drift.
3. Decide on the action steps to take to avoid collision.

Red sector. If another vessel is in your red sector, determine the bearing drift. You are the give-way vessel and must slow down, stop, or change course. Allow the other vessel to cross ahead; proceed after the other vessel enters your green sector.

Yellow sectors. If a vessel is in one of your yellow sectors, determine the bearing drift. Vessels behind you may be overtaking you at high speed. Assume they don't see you. If the bearing does not change as the range decreases, move out of the way. (See the section later in the chapter on how to use E.A.S.A.)

Green sector. If a vessel is in your green sector, determine the bearing drift. You are the stand-on vessel. You must maintain your course and speed unless the other vessel refuses to give way to you. If the bearing remains steady as its range decreases, slow or stop to let him pass ahead of you. He is in the wrong, but pressing the point might only cause you grief.

Caught in a Ship's Blind Spot!

You look straight up from your powerboat or sailboat to see the bow of a huge container ship. It looks as if the ship is headed right for you! But surely the crew is tracking you both visually and by radar. After all, the rules require a constant lookout by *all* means available.

Don't bet on it! Ships with long bows, aft bridges, and high freeboard often lose small contacts in a large blind spot forward of the bow called *freeboard shadow*. Freeboard, or the height of a vessel from its deck to the waterline, can exceed 100 feet on large ships. If the officer on watch is in a pilothouse near the stern, he's looking diagonally over the bow and may lose vessels in this freeboard shadow. Or the officer could be daydreaming—relying on the radar to sound an alarm if a target comes within range. In addition, radar signals travel in a straight line and can skip over a small craft below the line-of-sight plane.

Always assume a large ship does not see you. In this case, you must abandon the stand-on or give-way vessel rules and take action right away.

Change course 90 degrees. Immediately turn to bring the other vessel's bow abeam. If you see more of the vessel's starboard side, turn 90 degrees to keep its starboard side visible. If you see more of its port side, turn 90 degrees to keep its port side visible.

Increase to maximum speed. Power vessels should increase speed to the highest RPMs available. Sailing vessels under sail should start the engine and increase to maximum RPMs; if the engine fails to start or you have no engine, trim your sails for best speed.

Signal and illuminate. Sound the danger signal (continuous short blasts on the whistle or foghorn). In nighttime, turn on your cabin and deck lighting. Illuminate the flying bridge, hull, or sails.

All hands into life jackets. All hands on board should get life jackets on *now!* If you are wearing an inflatable, pull the CO_2 cartridge or use the manual tube to inflate the bladders.

Take constant drift bearings. Take constant drift bearings to the vessel's bow and stern. The bearing should change rapidly as each vessel moves away from the other.

SEA-CRET TIP

▶ It's tempting to jump on the radio, but this diverts your attention from the situation at hand. Establishing communications takes time. A 20-knot tanker half a mile away will run you over in less than 90 seconds. ($60 \div 20 = 3$ minutes to travel 1 mile, or 90 seconds to travel $1/2$ mile). Better move now!

How to Identify Motionless Contacts on Your Radar

Two types of contacts present hazards in our path: those with motion and those without. You've probably laid your track from buoy to buoy or light to light. So let's look at how to identify fixed or floating structures.

Imagine that it's nighttime, or that a fog and haze have set in. You turn to your radar and study the path ahead. You need to pick out that next buoy along your courseline. Up ahead, however, the radar shows a cluster of dots where your buoy should be. Which is the buoy, and which are other boats? To solve this puzzle, you first must understand relative motion.

Try some relative-motion practice in clear weather. Pick out a single buoy ahead and watch your radar as you move toward it. The buoy "appears" to move down the scope toward you. This movement is called relative motion, or relative speed. Now stop your boat and look at the buoy again on the radar scope. It has stopped all movement, so it not longer has any relative motion.

So how can you pick out motionless objects ahead, such as buoys, drifting boats, boats at anchor, fish stakes, and small islands? Remember these two secrets of a motionless contact.

Heading is the same, but opposite. On a radar, a stationary contact shows a reciprocal (opposite) heading, exactly parallel to yours. No matter how you turn, the stationary contact follows this rule.

Speed is the same as your speed. A stationary contact's relative speed is exactly equal to your boatspeed. Modern radars show range in nautical miles and tenths of a mile. In radar plotting you can use an easy concept called the "6-minute rule" to compute speed. Follow these steps:

- Measure the distance in nautical miles that a contact moves in 6 minutes.
- Multiply the result by a factor of ten.

For instance, if a contact appears to move 1.2 miles in 6 minutes, it has a relative speed of 12 knots (1.2×10). If a contact appears to move 3.2 miles in 6 minutes, it has a relative speed of 32 knots (3.2×10).

Your speed is 6 knots. A contact appears to be on a parallel heading to your course. At 2110, the range to the contact is 7.3 miles. You wait 6 minutes, and then take a second range. At 2116, the range to the contact closes to 6.7 miles. How can you tell if this is a motionless contact or not?

During that 6-minute span, the object appeared to move 0.6 mile (7.3 miles − 6.7 miles = 0.6). To find its relative speed, multiply 0.6×10 (or move the decimal one place to the right). The relative speed is 6 knots, the same as our own boat. This confirms that we are looking at a boat at anchor, adrift (drifting boats rarely have enough relative motion to matter in this calculation), or an aid to navigation.

Avoiding Collisions the E.A.S.A. Way

I honestly believe that a combination of *early action* and *substantial action*, or E.A.S.A., may be the cure-all for preventing collisions at sea anywhere on the globe. Below are some guidelines for making E.A.S.A. solutions part of your defense against collisions.

1. Determine the situation (meeting, crossing, or overtaking).
2. Determine the risk of collision (by drift bearings or vessel lighting).
3. Put an E.A.S.A. solution into play.

Meeting a Stationary Vessel

Imagine that you are approaching a vessel at anchor, dead ahead at a range of a quarter mile. Your boat speed is 3 knots. You must take action within 5 minutes to avoid collision ($60 \div 3 = 20$ minutes to travel 1 mile; $20 \div 4 = 5$ minutes to travel $1/4$ mile).

E.A.S.A. solution: Slow to bare steerageway and change course, aiming well astern of the vessel. Stop if necessary.

Meeting a Moving Vessel

Relative speed increases when two vessels are traveling toward one another from opposite directions. Determine bearing drift. A constant bearing indicates a high risk of collision. At nighttime, take action if you sight both red and green sidelights on a vessel. On larger vessels farther away, you may see two white masthead lights before you see the sidelights. If the masthead lights line up like a pair of range lights, this indicates that you are on a collision course.

E.A.S.A. solution: Change course 90 degrees to the right. Shoot drift bearings until you are clear.

Crossing Another Vessel

Determine bearing drift. Use sectoring (described earlier) to determine which vessel should stand on and which should give way. Another method to use during daytime is to picture the *nighttime* sidelight color of a crossing vessel. If the vessel crosses from left to right, you'd see

Small Vessel Basic Navigation Lights 101

Navigation Rule 23, Lights and Shapes, Power-driven Vessels Underway, and Navigation Rule 25, Lights and Shapes, Sailing Vessels Underway, describe the light patterns. Study the two illustrations with the captions: "Power-driven vessel underway—less than 50 meters" and "Sailing vessel underway. Same for Inland." Compare the similarities on both vessels. Notice that both vessels carry sidelights: red on the port side and green on the starboard side. Both vessels also carry a white sternlight. But only the vessel under power carries an additional white light, called a masthead light, above the sidelights and sternlight. If a sailing vessel turns on its engine, it becomes a power vessel and must switch on its white masthead light. Navigation lights show over a part of a circle called an *arc*. This prevents one light from blotting out another. To learn more about arcs on vessel lights, see Rule 21.

the green "go-light," and you are the stand-on vessel. If a vessel crosses from right to left, you'd see the red "stop light," and you are the give-way vessel.

E.A.S.A. solution: Slow or stop. This applies if you are the give-way vessel. It also applies if you are the stand-on vessel and the other vessel isn't giving way. In any case, shoot drift bearings until you are clear.

Being Overtaken by Another Vessel

It's alarming to glance astern and see a fast-moving powerboat or ship barreling toward you. In overtaking situations, relative speed is the *difference* between speeds. Determine bearing drift right away.

E.A.S.A. solution: As long as bearing drift has a high rate of change, maintain course and speed. If a collision appears imminent, change course 90 degrees. Shoot drift bearings until the danger passes.

How to Cross behind a Stern-Towing Tug

First you sight the tug, then you sight the tow; once you've sighted both sterns, then it's safe to go.

Lights describe a vessel's type, size, direction of travel, and nature of work or casualty. Towing vessels and their tows carry special light combinations, specified under Rule 24, Lights and Shapes. The drawings do not show the cluster of deck lights we often see on these workhorses. Use binoculars to pick out a towboat's navigation lights.

Lights tell the size and direction of travel of a power-driven vessel. Sidelights and stern light help define the heading of the vessel. Masthead lights tell us that the vessel is operating an engine. A power-driver vessel (PDV) less than 50 meters (164 feet) in length must show sidelights (green on starboard, red on port), a stern light, and a single (white) masthead light. A PDV over 50 meters adds a second masthead light aft of and higher than the forward light.

Tugs towing astern (hawser towing). Stern-towing tugs add lights above the masthead and stern lights to indicate that they are engaged in towing. Two white lights in a vertical line indicate a hawser (stern towline) with a length less than 200 meters (656 feet). Three white masthead lights in a vertical line show that the hawser exceeds 200 meters. Oceangoing tug hawsers may extend a quarter mile or more astern to ease tow loads. Most of the hawser lies beneath the surface, invisible to the eye or radar. Stern-towing tugs also carry a yellow light over the white stern light. Treat any yellow light on another vessel with caution. Use this mnemonic: "Yellow over white, my hawser is tight."

Barges or vessels being towed astern. Vessels being towed show a sidelight on each forward corner and a single stern light aft. They *never* show masthead lights, because they're not propelling themselves with an engine.

Pass a tug and tow only after you sight and identify all lights on each vessel. If necessary, stop, heave-to, or anchor. Use binoculars to scan the horizon astern for the vessel being towed. Follow these steps:

- **ON THE TUG** (towboat)

    Sight and count the white masthead lights.

    Make sure you count two or three masthead lights.

    Sight the yellow-over-white stern lights. Wait until you are positive you see the yellow light. These can be quite difficult to see from a distance (they look white).

- **ON THE TOW** (vessel being towed)

    Sight the sidelights. Remember that the sidelights might be at the forwardmost corners.

    Sight the stern light. Look low. Barge stern lights are difficult to sight in a seaway.

PDV

TOWING ASTERN < 200M

TOWING ASTERN > 200M

The lights on a power-driven vessel (PDV) help define the heading of the vessel. When a tug is towing astern, the light patterns define the distance of the towed vessel behind the tug.

Identify Vessels Towing Barges Alongside or Pushing Them Ahead

Tugs coming in from stern-towing along the coast or over the ocean often shorten their hawser once they are inside the jetties. For better control, they often lash the tow alongside. In extremely narrow channels such as the Intracoastal Waterway, tugs push barges ahead. This provides better control for turning and maneuvering through narrow bridges. Below are clues to the light patterns you will see on these types of vessels.

Tugs Towing Alongside or Pushing Ahead

Masthead lighting. Tugs towing barges alongside (on the hip) or pushing them ahead always show two white masthead lights in a vertical line. (This is the same masthead lighting as when a tug is towing a vessel less than 200 meters astern. See "Solve the Mystery of Two White Vertical Lights" below.)

Stern lighting. The stern configuration depends on the body of water. Tugs in inland water (see sidebar) replace the stern light with two vertical yellow lights. Tugs in international waters show a single white stern light.

Barges or Vessels Being Towed Alongside or Pushed Ahead

Towed alongside. Sidelights and stern light. A vessel not under its own power never carries a masthead light.

Pushed ahead. Drop the stern light to keep from blinding the tugboat captain. Add a yellow light between the bow sidelights. The yellow light flashes at least once every second. A vessel not under its own power never carries a masthead light.

Inland or International Waters?

Imaginary lines, called *lines of demarcation*, mark the boundary between inland and international waters. Look near the back of the Navigation Rules for the exact boundaries. On coastal charts the demarcation lines are printed as dashed magenta lines and labeled "COLREGS demarcation line" (COLREGS stands for Collision Regulations). Only the United States has its own set of inland rules, and thus, lines of demarcation. Parts of the U.S.—all of Alaska and parts of Hawaii and other Pacific possessions—follow international rules even on inland waters.

SOLVE THE MYSTERY OF TWO WHITE VERTICAL LIGHTS

Three white lights in a vertical line mean one thing: towing astern on a long hawser. But two white lights in a vertical line could mean pushing ahead, towing alongside, or towing astern on a short hawser. Use three easy steps to solve the riddle.

1. Slow to bare steerageway or stop. Grab your binoculars.
2. Study the tug's masthead. If you see two vertical white lights, look for a tow alongside or ahead. An additional pair of sidelights or sidelights and a yellow flashing light solve the mystery.
3. If you don't see the tow, assume it's astern. Scan the area behind the tug. Find that tow *before* you go!

Quick Guide for Sailboat-to-Sailboat Situations

Why are sailors subject to so many extra rules above and beyond those of power vessels? Many of these rules are carryovers from the days of square-riggers. These vessels needed lots of room to maneuver, and unlike many of today's sailboats, they had a difficult time sailing close-hauled. They also needed more room for tacking and *wearing* (turning the ship by passing the stern through the wind; these days called *jibing*).

We're stuck with these rules, so why not make it easy? A simple three-term memory aid will remind you which vessel must give way or keep clear in any meeting between two vessels under sail: *Port-Wind-O.* Here's what the three terms mean:

Port: In a meeting between two boats under sail on opposite tacks, the right-of-way is determined by what *tack* the boats are on. When a sailboat is on *starboard tack*, the wind is passing over the starboard side of the boat and the boom and mainsail are on the port side. When a boat is on *port tack*, the wind is passing over the port side of the boat and the boom is on the starboard side. Starboard-tack boats have right-of-way over port-tack boats. Said the other way, a port-tack vessel must stay clear of a starboard-tack vessel.

Wind. When two sailing vessels converge on the same tack, the *windward* vessel must stay clear. This is one of the rules left over from the days of square-riggers. Carrying full canvas, a ship could block the wind of a leeward vessel. The burden fell on the windward vessel to stay clear.

O. If you are *overtaking* another vessel, you must stay clear of it. This rule applies across the board, whether you're under sail or power. Even if you're under sail and overtaking a power-driven vessel, you must stay clear of it. If you are unable to tell if you are overtaking, assume you are and give way.

When in Doubt, Have a Way Out!

If you're unsure who has the right of way, maneuver as if you must stay clear. The rules are clear on this. Many times, I've simply fallen off to clear another sailing vessel whose bearing was steady while its range decreased. Make your move early and make it substantial!

Right-of-way for sailboats is based on the sailboats' tacks. A sailboat is on starboard tack when the wind is coming over the starboard side of the vessel. A sailboat is on port tack when the wind is coming over the port side of the vessel.

How to Become Sound Signal Savvy

When vessels are within sight of one another, they use sound signals to tell each other the action they are taking or intend to take. In low visibility, sound signals indicate a particular activity or status, such as dredging, sailing, anchored, or aground. All sound signals use distinct blast intervals, either alone or in combination. A short blast is about 1 second, and a prolonged blast lasts about 4 to 6 seconds.

In general, vessels use short blasts to indicate maneuvering or danger. In low visibility, vessels underway sound a prolonged blast alone or in combination with short blasts.

Below are the most common signals for maneuvering and a few low visibility signals. Refer to Rules 32 to 37 in the Rules of the Road for more extensive coverage of sound and light signals.

Memory Keys for Passing Sound Signals

These memory keys should help you remember what sound signal to use, whether you signal intent (Inland Waters) or take action (International Waters). First, think of how you want to keep the other vessel *relative to your own vessel.* In other words, do you want the other vessel off your port side or your starboard side?

port has one syllable = one short blast (to keep the other vessel off your port side)

star-board has two syllables = two short blasts (to keep the other vessel off your starboard side)

I'm-going-astern is three words = three short blasts (engines operating in reverse for astern propulsion)

d-o-u-b-t has five letters = five or more short blasts (uncertain situation or danger; see text)

SIGNALING INTENT ON INLAND WATERS

In inland waters, the signals you make to other vessels let them know that you *intend* to do something (except backing). This signal of intent must be answered by the other vessel, blast for blast. If you sound one short blast and the other boat agrees, they must give you one short blast in return (see key below). If the other vessel doesn't agree, they must sound the d-o-u-b-t signal of five or more short blasts. Then you may begin the sequence of "ask?-answer" to request to pass the vessel's other side. In any event, you don't execute the maneuver until you receive the same signal in return. Here are the signals that apply when two vessels meet or cross on inland waters:

One short blast: I intend to leave you on my port side
Two short blasts: I intend to leave you on my starboard side

Three short blasts: I'm operating with astern propulsion
Five short blasts: I d-o-u-b-t what you're doing is safe!

In inland waters, you may arrange passing signals on VHF-FM Channel 13 instead of sounding the whistle. Nothing changes as far as the rules' intent. You must ask for and receive permission before executing passage. If the other vessel does not answer the radio, go back to whistle signals. Remember to call the other vessel on Channel 16, establish communications, then shift to Channel 13.

SIGNALING ACTION ON INTERNATIONAL WATERS

In international waters you signal that you are *going* to do something. You don't need permission to maneuver in international waters. If for any reason, either vessel doubts that the maneuver is safe, it must sound five or more short blasts.

One short blast: I'm going to alter course to starboard (equivalent to saying
   I intend to leave you on my port side on inland waters)
Two short blasts: I'm going to alter course to port (equivalent to saying
   I intend to leave you on my starboard side on inland waters)
Three short blasts: I'm operating with astern propulsion
Five short blasts: I d-o-u-b-t what you're doing is safe!

WHAT IT MEANS

Maneuvering and Warning Signals in Sight   (• = one-second blast; — = four- to six-second blast)

INTERNATIONAL (ACTION BEING TAKEN) MEETING OR CROSSING AND ACTION IS REQUIRED (NO ANSWER REQUIRED):		INLAND (ACTION PROPOSED TO BE TAKEN) MEETING OR CROSSING WITHIN ½ MILE OF EACH OTHER AND ACTION IS REQUIRED (AGREEMENT BY SAME SIGNAL REQUIRED):	
I am altering course to starboard	•	I propose leaving you to port	•
I am altering course to port	• •	I propose leaving you to starboard	• •
I am operating astern propulsion	• • •	I am operating astern propulsion	• • •
OVERTAKING IN A NARROW CHANNEL OR FAIRWAY AND ACTION IS REQUIRED (AGREEMENT REQUIRED BEFORE ACTION):		OVERTAKING IN A NARROW CHANNEL OR FAIRWAY AND ACTION IS REQUIRED (AGREEMENT BY SAME SIGNAL REQUIRED BEFORE ACTION):	
I intend to overtake on your starboard	— — •	I propose overtaking on your starboard	•
I intend to overtake on your port	— — • •	I propose overtaking on your port	• •
I agree to be overtaken	— • — •	I agree to be overtaken	• or • •
Warning—I don't understand your intentions	• • • • •	Warning—I don't understand your intentions	• • • • •
Approaching a bend in a channel	—	Approaching a bend in a channel or leaving berth or dock	—

LOW-VISIBILITY SIGNALS

In low visibility, sound a prolonged blast (4 to 6 seconds) at intervals of 2 minutes. This lengthened signal makes sense, for you want to make sure another vessel knows where you are. Vessels never exchange maneuvering signals in these conditions because they are not in sight of one another. These are the three basic low visibility signals:

One prolonged blast: underway under power; making way through the water
Two prolonged blasts: drifting under power; not making way through the water
One prolonged blast and two short (1-second) blasts: sailing or in a special status (such as tugboats, commercial fishing vessels, vessels dredging, and others)

See Rule 35 for more coverage of low-visibility signals.

HOW TO ATTRACT ATTENTION TO AVOID DANGER

The rules allow you to use the whistle and light to get the attention of another vessel. You may need to do this to warn another vessel of danger or to avoid a collision. Be sure not to confuse the other boat by using a specific maneuvering or low-visibility signal.

How to Use the Three Factors of the Lookout

Every vessel shall at all times maintain a proper lookout by sight and hearing as well as by all available means . . .
—Navigation Rules for International and Inland Waters, Rule 5

Look over the quote from Rule 5 again. What do you notice about the priorities of the lookout? The three ingredients of a proper lookout are as follows:

1. sight (visual)
2. hearing (sound)
3. all available means (including radar if installed)

Each discussion of collision avoidance strategies in this chapter starts with visual assessment. You must track a vessel by sight until any threat of collision disappears.

When visibility drops, change your priorities to hearing. Send a crewmember forward, away from engine or wake noises. Keep noise to a minimum. On large vessels, use cordless headsets to communicate from the bow to the bridge.

Vessels equipped with radar must use it underway in all conditions, along with sight and hearing, to assess the possibilities of a collision. Admiralty courts do not excuse ignorance of operation. If there is a radar unit aboard and it works, you must use it for collision avoidance.

First, energize and optimize your radar (review the section in Chapter 3 on page 67). Change radar range scales up and down every few minutes. Lower the range to under 3 miles to pick up small targets close to you. (The maximum range at which your radar can pick up targets depends in part on radar antenna height above the water—see Appendix I, Radar Range Table.) Always combine radar observations with a 360-degree visual scan of the horizon. If you spot a contact, determine its bearing drift right away.

HOW TO DETERMINE VISIBILITY AND SAFE SPEED

Rule 6, Safe Speed, requires you to go slow enough that you can stop your vessel and avoid collision in the prevailing conditions of visibility, vessel traffic density, sea state, shore lights, and depth of water relative to draft. The most important of these factors is visibility, so you must estimate your range of visibility in order to determine a safe speed.

Radar can help with this. First you need to know how far your radar can "see." Base this on antenna height (see Appendix I). Then use your radar as follows to estimate range of visibility.

1. Scan the horizon with binoculars. Find a vessel or an object just barely visible in the fog or haze.
2. Take a bearing to the vessel or object.
3. Turn to the radar and set the cursor or *electronic bearing line* (EBL) onto that bearing. Move the *variable range marker* (VRM) out to the object and read the range. Subtract a half mile for safety, and call the result your range of visibility.

Having obtained this estimate, what do you do with it? One useful approach is to ensure that you can stop within half your range of visibility in yards (1 nautical mile equals approximately 2,000 yards). That requires a good estimate of your stopping distance as well as a good estimate of your range of visibility, however, which makes it a bit problematic in practice. I prefer to divide my estimated range of visibility by two, convert the result to a speed, and multiply that speed by 80%. Follow these examples:

> **Your visibility is 0.5 mile:** 1,000 yards ÷ 2 = 500 yards. To get your speed, move the decimal to the left two places, which gives 5 knots, and 5 knots × 80% = 4 knots.
>
> **Your visibility is 1.5 miles:** 3,000 yards ÷ 2 = 1,500 yards; 15 knots × 80% = 12 knots.
>
> **Your visibility is 0.25 mile or less:** bare steerage (just enough speed to steer the boat); every so often, stop the boat and listen.

THE DANGER OF USING "SCANTY INFORMATION"

Rule 7, Risk of Collision, warns the mariner not to be lazy. The rule explicitly states that you should make no assumptions based on "scanty information." If you sight a contact at 6 miles, don't blow it off. Start tracking the bugger as if it's an enemy U-boat! Here's why.

In the Straits of Florida the big boys are doing 25 knots, riding the Gulf Stream. Let's put one of these vessels into play with a 5-knot sailboat traveling eastbound for Key West.

A 25-knot freighter overtakes the 5-knot sailboat at 20 knots (25 knots – 5 knots = 20 knots).

Sighting the freighter at 6 miles, you have 18 minutes to maneuver (60 minutes ÷ 20 knots = 3 minutes per mile; 3 minutes × 6 miles = 18 minutes).

Since you only have 18 minutes (0.3 hour) to maneuver, you must act immediately to increase the passing range to 1.5 miles (5 knots × 0.3 hours = 1.5 miles).

A distance of 1.5 miles might sound large, but that is not the case. These ships eat up that distance in the blink of an eye. You must open your range to more than you think you need. If the ship changes course for some reason, you'll need even more time to maneuver to avoid collision.

SEA-CRET TIP

▶ Train your crew on basic radar plotting and drift bearings. If you're below deck and off watch, make sure they know when to wake you. On many large vessels, the watch must notify the skipper if a radar plot shows any contact that will pass within 2 miles.

Radar Scope Plotting

Plot directly onto the glass or plastic dome cover—called a *scope*—on your radar. This direct surface method, called *radar scope plotting* or *radar contact plotting*, gives fast, accurate results for collision avoidance. All radar plotting begins with a determination of another vessel's *closest point of approach*, or CPA. Once you acquire a target, begin a scope plot to answer theses four vital questions.

1. How close will the contact come to your vessel?
2. Is this a meeting, crossing, or overtaking situation?
3. How much time do you have to maneuver?
4. What is the best action to avoid collision?

<table>
</table>

Supplies and Tools Needed for Radar Scope Plotting

- grease pencil or overhead projector marker
- cotton rags
- tongue depressor or straightedge
- nautical slide rule
- handbearing compass
- binoculars

Your radar will need to be equipped with the following controls.

Fixed Range Rings. Turn these non-movable rings on. Use the fixed range rings to quickly estimate the range of the contact between marks.

VRM (variable range marker). This range device moves a dot, called a *bug*, out to the target. Use the VRM to plot the target. If your radar doesn't have VRM, use the fixed range rings for plotting.

EBL (electronic bearing line). This measures the relative bearing of the contact.

HEAD-UP MODE AND RELATIVE BEARINGS

Most radars show a *head-up* display, where land and targets appear relative to the bow of your boat. Some radars show a *north-up* display, where land and targets appear relative to true north. We'll discuss only the head-up mode here.

Relative bearings start at the bow with 0 degrees and run clockwise to the target. No matter how we turn, the bow is always at 0 degrees. If we have a target bearing 40 degrees on the radar scope, the target is 40 degrees off our bow, or 40 degrees relative. If we turn toward the target, its relative bearing decreases. If we turn away from the target, the relative bearing increases.

On your radar scope, you'll see a faint flash each time the antenna rotates. This *heading flash* stays aligned to 0 degrees relative on the bearing ring, even when you change course.

PRIORITY #1: VISUAL TARGET TRACKING

If visibility permits, acquire and track the target visually. First, convert the relative bearing to a magnetic bearing. Always add the relative bearing to your magnetic heading, and subtract 360 from any number greater than 360.

If your boat's magnetic heading is 110 degrees, and the radar target bearing is 56 degrees relative, what is the magnetic bearing to target?

110 degrees magnetic + 56 degrees relative = 166 degrees magnetic

Go on deck, hold the handbearing compass to your eye, and turn to 166 degrees magnetic. Acquire your target and check the bearing, then begin tracking the bearing drift.

If your boat's magnetic heading is 225 degrees and the radar target bearing is 190 degrees relative, what is the magnetic bearing to target?

225 degrees magnetic + 190 degrees relative = 415 degrees – 360 = 55 degrees magnetic

Go on deck, hold the handbearing compass to your eye, and find 55 degrees magnetic. Acquire the target, refine the bearing, and begin tracking the bearing drift.

RULE #1 OF HEAD-UP RADAR CONTACT PLOTTING

In a seaway, the contact will appear to move if your boat wanders off course. Before you mark the contact on the radar scope, have the helm steady up on course. When the helmsman is on course and calls "Mark!," use your marker or grease pencil to mark the target on the scope. Do this each time you place a mark on the target. The example below illustrates this procedure. Refer to the diagram as you read through the scenario. The boat at the center of the scope in the illustration simulates the radar's heading flash.

Your course is 020 degrees magnetic and your speed is 4 knots. Your radar is set to the 6-mile range. Each fixed range ring represents 1 nautical mile. Make your marks on the scope every 6 minutes. That way, you can use the 6-minute rule to calculate contact speed.

1. **Radar contact and the first mark.** At 1340, your radar picks up a target. Use either the variable range marker (VRM) or fixed range rings to find the target range. (Note that the VRM allows more precise measurements because you control the size of the range ring. The fixed range rings are set to the selected scale by the radar. The radar allows you to use either method individually or along with the other.) Ask the helm to steady up and sound out "Mark!" when the boat is on course. Place a mark onto the target with your marker. You find the range to be 4.8 nautical miles. Label this first mark 1340. Place the EBL onto your mark and read the contact's relative bearing: 22 degrees relative. Convert this to a magnetic bearing (020 degrees magnetic + 22 degrees relative = 042 degrees magnetic).

2. **Acquire visual contact and bearing drift.** Grab your binoculars and handbearing compass. Step outside and sight with the handbearing compass in the direction of 042 degrees magnetic. If you sight the contact, read and record the actual magnetic bearing. If not, drop the compass and scan with the binoculars to the left and right of the bearing. To see a small target 4.8 miles away, you need to raise your height of eye to 17 feet. If you still see nothing, try again in a few minutes. Remember, you need to mark the target again at 1346 (6 minutes after the 1340 mark). Return to the radar to get ready for the next mark.

3. **The second mark and the DRM Line.** At 30 seconds before the second mark, ask the helm to steady up on course. As soon as the helm says "Mark!," place your second mark on the target. Label this mark 1346. The range to the target is now 3.8 miles. Now you have everything you need to find range, bearing, and time to the closest point of approach, or CPA.

     Lay your straightedge along the two dots (1340 and 1346) and extend the line an inch or two past the center of the scope. This represents the contact's

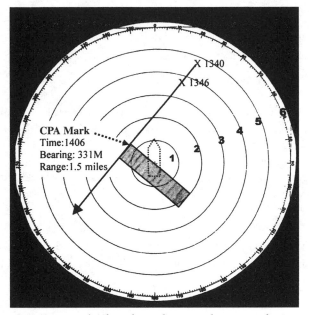

This radar screen is set to a scale of 6 miles and pictures the contact plotting scenario described in the text.

    direction of relative movement (DRM) line. As long as both vessels maintain course and speed, the vessel will plot down this DRM line.

4. **CPA mark along the DRM line.** To find the CPA, measure the closest point from the DRM to the center of your radar scope. To do this, place a straightedge (e.g., a batten or tongue depressor) perpendicular to the DRM line and back to the scope center. Mark this point along the DRM line. This establishes the closest point of approach, or the CPA mark (see illustration).

5. **Range and bearing at CPA.** Next, run the VRM out so that it just touches the DRM line. This shows a range at CPA of about 1.5 miles. Place the EBL onto the CPA mark and read the relative bearing: 311 degrees relative. The contact's magnetic bearing at CPA will be 331 degrees magnetic (020 degrees magnetic + 311 degrees relative = 331). Label the range and bearing next to the CPA mark.

6. **Relative speed of contact and time of CPA.** Find the relative speed of the contact. Take the range difference between the 1340 and 1346 marks: 4.8 miles − 3.8 miles = 1 mile. Move the decimal one place to the right. The relative speed of the contact is 10 knots.

Next, measure the distance from the 1346 mark to your CPA mark. Place your tongue depressor between the two marks and mark that on the depressor. Use the VRM or fixed range rings to estimate distance between the two marks on the depressor: 3.4 miles.

Find the time in minutes to the CPA:

3.4 miles at 10 knots = 20 minutes

1346 hours + 20 minutes = 1406

Label the time next to the CPA mark. Label the CPA mark 1406.

7. **Track the target until it is past the CPA.** Get a new relative bearing to the target with your EBL (make sure to coordinate with the helm). Convert this to a magnetic bearing and step back outside. Track the target by taking drift bearings every minute until the target reaches the CPA bearing: 331 degrees magnetic. Check the scope to make sure the target keeps tracking down the DRM line.

Situation Analysis

The contact will cross your bow from right to left. You are the give-way vessel. Unless he changes course and/or speed, he will clear your vessel by 1.5 miles.

Action to Avoid a Collision

To open the CPA farther, you must slow down, stop, or turn to the right by at least 60 degrees. Make the course change decisive so the other vessel has no doubt as to what you are doing.

Continue to track the vessel by radar and visual means. Use the handbearing compass between plots to determine the bearing drift. As long as the target keeps drifting to the left, risk of collision does not exist.

"Your Call, Skipper"

You're the skipper or most knowledgeable crewmember in each of the following situations. What actions would you take?

1.   You sight a large vessel off your port bow. With binoculars, you are able to see the vessel's green sidelight. You take drift bearings on the sidelight and notice a slow drift rate to the right of about 1 degree every 2 minutes. What action should you take?

2.   You are eastbound at 10 knots. You pick up the bow of a westbound tanker at 5 miles. Bearing drift is steady. Assuming the tanker is moving at 20 knots, how many minutes do you have to maneuver?

3.   A tug lies dead ahead in your path, showing three white lights in a vertical line. You stop the boat and scan astern for the tow. Even with good visibility, you see nothing astern. What do you tell your crew to watch for?

4.   Approaching San Francisco Bay in fog, you study the radar to find the sea buoy. You see eight contacts within a half mile of where the buoy should be. What two steps would you take to identify which contact is the buoy?

5.   When plotting a contact on the radar scope, what four questions must you answer to determine the risk of collision?

Answers

1.   You are the stand-on vessel, but you must take action because of the approaching vessel's slow bearing drift. Slow down to accelerate the drift rate. Allow the vessel to cross ahead of you. Continue to take drift bearings to make sure it drifts to the right. Proceed only after risk of collision no longer exists.

2.   You have 10 minutes. The relative speed is 30 knots (10 knots + 20 knots = 30 knots).

$$60 \text{ minutes} \div 30 \text{ knots} = 2 \text{ minutes per mile}$$
$$5 \text{ miles (range)} \times 2 \text{ minutes} = 10 \text{ minutes}$$

3.   Sidelights and stern light. Barges carry navlights low to the water because they lack superstructure. The range of these low lights is only 2 to 3 miles. Raise your height of eye and scan with the binoculars just above the horizon.

4.   Look for a contact that shows a heading parallel to your heading but in the opposite direction. The relative speed of a stationary contact must match your actual speed.

5.   The four questions you must answer are:

- How close will the contact come to your boat (CPA)?
- Is this a meeting, a crossing, or an overtaking situation?
- How much time do you have to maneuver?
- What action should you take to avoid collision?

DIESEL ENGINE MAINTENANCE AND POWERBOAT SEAMANSHIP

The secret to a trouble-free engine isn't knowing how to repair it, but knowing how to maintain it so you don't have to repair it.
—PETER COMPTON, TROUBLESHOOTING MARINE DIESELS

What five systems must you inspect before starting your engine? If your engine refuses to shut down, what two things do you look for? Are you prepared to cope with a runaway engine in restricted waters? What five steps must you take before entering an inlet anywhere in the world?

In This Chapter, You'll Learn How To:
- Inspect a diesel engine of any size quickly and thoroughly
- Attack a deadly engineroom fire with four powerful weapons
- Use the secrets of emergency wake breaking in a pinch
- Deal with the loss of one or both engines inside a breaking inlet
- Make a super-accurate fuel consumption graph for cruising

A Simple User's Guide to Inboard Diesel Engine Maintenance

This section examines the many things powerboaters and sailors can do to keep their engines in peak condition. Sailboat engines get abused much more than powerboat engines, simply because they are used less and run at lower throttle speeds. For example, my liveaboard Cape Dory 27 sloop was equipped with a tiny, 8-horsepower Yanmar 1GM diesel. At first I knew little about engines, but I did know enough to follow the owner's manual religiously when it came to preventive maintenance. So with my trusty manual, I stumbled around and found all the major components on the mini-diesel. I learned to change the oil, filters, impeller pump, and belts.

When it came time to check the fuel pump or injectors, I made an invaluable investment—I hired a mechanic to come out to the boat. The elderly gent had run a mobile business out of his van for years, and he always brought his pleasant wife. She kept him company, filled his coffee mug, and handed him the tools he needed.

While he worked, I asked questions about anything I wasn't quite sure of. He always had a smile and tons of patience. But his most memorable advice was, "Don't worry about anything if it's not in your owner's manual. But if it is, do it *before* the manual tells you to." That advice served me well. The little Yanmar ran flawlessly for the five years I owned *Winged Victory*.

Whether in an auxiliary-powered sailboat or a power vessel, you can achieve this same reliability by taking care of the five most important engine systems, the systems I call the Big Five: the cooling system, the lubrication system, the fuel system, the air system, and the charging system. Maintain these and your engine will run like a top. Ignore them and trouble is sure to follow. First and foremost, read and follow your owner's manual to the letter.

THE COOLING SYSTEM

My little diesel was straight raw-water cooled, which means that it lacked a heat exchanger. Instead, raw seawater circulated through the engine's internal passages, removing heat. These days most engines have a recirculating freshwater cooling system in which a mixture of fresh water and antifreeze circulates through the engine's internal passages. The heat removed from the engine by this coolant is then transferred to raw seawater through thin-walled tubes in a heat exchanger, and the heated seawater is then injected into the

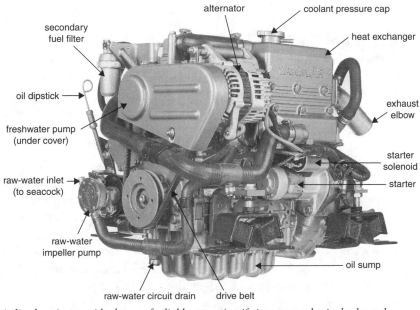

A diesel engine provides hours of reliable operation if given proper basic checks and preventive maintenance (see next page, too). (Yanmar Marine)

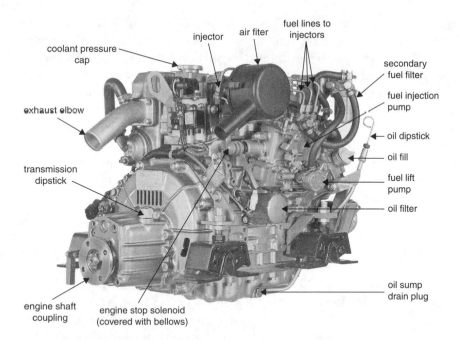

engine exhaust and sent overboard. Freshwater cooling makes your engine more efficient while sparing the engine's internal passages from the corrosive effects of salt water.

Cooling System Checklist

Check the raw-water seacock (before start-up and after shutting down). Do this before getting underway or starting the engine after anchoring. Move the handle to the closed position and back to the in-line position. If it's corroded, tap the handle lightly with a hammer or mallet. Shut off the seacock after shutting the engine down.

Check the hoses and clamps (before start-up). Shine a light along the hose and near the ends. Feel for hardening and look for cracks and kinks. Hardness and cracking indicate a hose near the end of its service life. Kinks restrict water flow and lead to overheating. All hoses and lines need two stainless steel clamps installed at each end. Clamps corrode over time. Left unattended, they'll become brittle and crack. Replace any questionable clamp right away.

Check the raw-water strainer (before start-up). To find the raw-water strainer, follow the line inboard from the raw-water seacock. The first filter(s) you come to will be the strainer. Shine a light through the strainer bowl. Clogged strainers cause most overheating problems. If it's dirty, remove the strainer filter (after making sure the raw-water seacock is closed!), clean it, and then reinsert it.

Check the freshwater cooling system (before start-up). Many engines have an externally mounted expansion tank that collects freshwater coolant as it circulates through the engine. Make sure the expansion tank coolant level stays within a half inch of the full mark (or at the level indicated by your manual). Next, check the engine coolant level through the oblong-shaped heat exchanger header tank on top of the engine. After making sure the header tank is cool to the touch, remove the radiator pressure cap on top of the tank and stick a finger in. Keep the coolant level within a half inch of the top. Also check the freshwater cooling hoses.

Check the radiator pressure cap (before start-up). Little things turn into big problems. Before putting the pressure cap back onto the header tank, turn it over and check the gasket seal. Worn seals lead to fluid leaks. Replace the entire pressure cap if you have a bad seal.

Check the drive belt (before start-up). The belts on the front of your engine drive the shaft, alternator, and freshwater pump. They stretch over time and may develop cracks on top and bottom. No belt should have more than a half inch of play when depressed with moderate fingertip pressure. Check your manual. Most belt adjustments are made by moving the alternator along its mounting bracket. Loosen the bolt and wedge a large screwdriver between the alternator and engine block. Lift up on the alternator. Adjust or replace the belt and retighten the bolt.

Check the stuffing box (before start-up, while underway, and after shutting down). The stuffing box forms a seal where the shaft exits the hull. With the shaft turning, a drop of water every 20 to 30 seconds (1 or 2 drops every minute) isn't cause for concern. This helps keep the shaft cool and lubricated. Excessive leaking indicates loose, worn, or missing packing material. First, try tightening the packing nuts on the shaft. You will need two oversized wrenches to accomplish this task. After tightening, restart the engine and check the leak drip rate again. If it's still excessive, you'll need to replace the packing inside the stuffing box. Do not use the engine until you address this problem. Always check the stuffing box before you leave the boat. Many boats sink at the dock or at anchor because this final, all-important inspection was neglected. (In Chapter 13, we'll look at strategies for dealing with flooding and other emergencies.)

Check the exhaust (after start-up). Bend over the transom or stern quarter to make sure there is a healthy flow of cooling water coming out of the exhaust. If the cooling water output is absent or restricted, your engine is not getting enough seawater, and you should shut it down. If the raw-water seacock, strainer, hoses, and belt are normal, the most likely problem is an obstruction (say, a plastic bag or seaweed) blocking the raw-water intake strainer on the outside of the hull. To check this, close the raw-water seacock, disconnect the hose, then momentarily open the seacock. If the flow is reduced or absent, there is an obstruction outside. If the flow is healthy, the problem must be upstream—perhaps in the raw-water pump (see below).

Cooling System Maintenance

Replace the raw-water impeller. The raw-water system pulls in seawater through a vane-type pump called an *impeller pump*. Over time the rubber vanes, or impellers, harden and crack. Keep a spare impeller onboard. Change the impeller once a year to prevent problems.

Change the drive belts. As mentioned above, these drive your shaft, alternator, and water pump. Change all belts once a year.

Adjust the stuffing box and replace the packing. Packing comes by the roll or in preformed rings. It's made of square-sided rope and used to fill the void between the shaft and shaft tube to seal out water. Replace the packing annually, or get the boatyard to do it for you.

THE LUBRICATION SYSTEM

Oil works as hard as or harder than any other fluid circulating through a diesel engine. It must lubricate parts, cool the engine, and trap dirt and grime. Without oil, vital parts would seize up and melt together, and the engine would cease operating. Contaminants would clog injectors and gum up cylinder walls, and the engine would surely overheat. Transmission fluid lubricates the hardworking parts of the gearbox for smooth, trouble-free shifting.

Lubrication System Checklist

Check the oil level and condition (before start-up). Time and again I see skippers start their engines without taking the few seconds to pull the oil dipstick. These skippers are missing two important clues as to what's going on inside their engines. First, you need to know if there's enough oil in the oil pan, or sump (the oil reservoir in the bottom part of the engine). The manufacturer puts those marks on the stick for a reason, so top it up if it's low. Second, you need to know the condition of the oil. If the dipstick readings are getting so dark that it's difficult to see the stick, this indicates that your oil is losing its ability to trap carbon, soot, and sulfur. Oil stops these villains to help the engine run cooler.

Check the oil pressure gauge and oil pressure warning light (after start-up). The gauge should read normally and the warning light should be out.

Check the transmission fluid level (before start-up). Look for the transmission gearbox on the back of the engine near the shaft coupling. Unscrew the dipstick on top of the gearbox. Make sure the fluid is clear; a milky color indicates water intrusion. Wipe the stick clean and reinsert it into the hole without screwing down the top. Pull it out and check the level. It should read to the top mark. Any reading other than full indicates transmission problems. Address this before using the engine.

Lubrication System Maintenance

Change the oil and filter twice a year. Follow these easy steps.

1. Start the engine and run it for a few minutes; then shut it down. This warms the oil and puts contaminants in suspension, and makes it easier to get all oil and contaminants out of the sump.
2. Remove the oil filter and the oil sump drain plug, and drain the old oil into a catchment container. (On some boats, especially auxiliary sailboats, the engine installation makes access to the drain plug difficult or impossible. In this case you may want or need to pump the old oil out through the dipstick tube, and marine retailers sell various manual and electric pumps for this purpose.)
3. Wipe the engine-block oil filter mounting surface clean. Smear a light coat of clean oil on the sealing gasket of the new oil filter.
4. Spin the oil filter onto the mounting. Hand-tighten it, then tighten it down by an additional half or three-quarter turn with an oil filter wrench.
5. Fill with new oil to the designated mark on the dipstick, run the engine for a couple of minutes, and check the oil pressure and level. Top off with more oil if necessary.

Transmission Gearbox Fluid

Change the transmission fluid once a year. Drain the old fluid in the same manner as described above. Replace with new fluid to the top mark on the dipstick. Take care not to overfill the gearbox.

THE FUEL SYSTEM

Diesel fuel helps lubricate an engine's internal parts too, but not as well as oil. Most engine problems result from dirty fuel. All fuel must be squeaky clean by the time it reaches your injectors. Water and dirt intrusions come from:

- Leaks around your deck fill cap
- Condensation on the walls of partially filled fuel tanks
- Poor fuel filtering at the dockside fuel pump (some foreign ports)
- Failure to change engine fuel filters when they are dirty or filled with contaminants (see below)

Fuel System Checklist

Fuel line and fuel shutoff valve inspection (before start-up). Start at the tank and check the fuel line connections. Fuel tanks have three or four flexible fuel lines on top.

SEA-CRET TIP

▶ The ideal fuel tank is designed with a beveled bottom that traps water and contaminants. A drain plug allows you to drain off the dirty fuel.

1. The largest is the fuel fill line. It leads to the deck fill.
2. The smallest is the fuel vent line. It leads aft or abeam.
3. The fuel supply line leads to the engine.
4. Some engines require a fourth line to return surplus fuel from the injectors to the fuel tank.

Check for leaks or crimped or cracked fuel lines. Inspect the doubled hose clamps. Follow the main fuel line to the fuel shutoff valve. This valve shuts off fuel supply to the engine in an emergency. Turn the valve to the off position (perpendicular to fuel line) and then back in line. If it is frozen from corrosion, spray some lubricant to get it working again.

First (primary) fuel filter (before start-up). Follow the fuel line to the first (primary) filter. Some primary filters have a clear separator bowl on the lower part of the filter. This traps water and contaminants and has a drain plug on the bottom. Shine a light through the bowl. If it's dirty, drain the water and contaminants. There's no easy way to check a solid, non-separator-type primary filter. You'll need to take a sample from the tank to analyze fuel quality. Do this once a year or anytime you suspect contaminated fuel.

Secondary fuel filter (before start-up). Continue to follow the fuel line to the secondary filter. It often resides on the engine block near the fuel injection pump. Check for fuel leaks, cracks in the fuel lines, or corroded hose clamps.

Fuel injection pump (before start-up). Follow the fuel line from the secondary filter to the fuel injection pump. Inspect the high-pressure fuel lines that lead from the pump to the injectors on top of the engine. Look for fuel seepage at the pump and at each injector. Use a flashlight to spot a sheen of leaking fuel anywhere around the engine body.

Engine drip pan (before start-up, while underway, and after shutting down). Any liquid or odor of diesel fuel indicates a possible fuel leak. Stick your fingers into the liquid and rub them together. Oily water indicates oil or fuel. Sniff your fingers. No odor indicates leaking lubricating oil or coolant fluid. Look around the engine body where the head of the engine joins the engine body. Black streak marks indicate a worn gasket. Keep an eye on this when underway. If it worsens, call a mechanic and ask him to replace the head gasket or check for more serious problems. Coolant leaks often result from loose caps or worn gaskets on the cap. This is no different than a leak from the cap on your car's radiator. You have to have a good seal or the fluid leaks from the top. Press down on the cap and tighten it. If it still leaks, the cap gasket may be worn, preventing a proper seal. Replace the cap before you use the engine.

Fuel System Maintenance

Replace primary fuel filter(s) (as needed). Locate the primary fuel filter. The top contains a basketlike filter. After many hours of use, the basket filter gets clogged and loses its trapping ability. Open the top cover, then pull out the filter element and gasket. Replace the element and gasket at the same time. When you change the fuel filter, air gets into the fuel lines. You must bleed all of the air from the system in order to start the engine. Each engine is different, so follow the process shown in your engine manual. Consider installing two primary separator filters right after the fuel tank. Dual filters allow you to keep the engine running while changing one filter at a time.

Replace the secondary fuel filter (as needed or at specified intervals). It's easy to forget the secondary filter, because it's often hidden on the side of the engine block. Follow your engine manual for the recommended filter change frequency. If the secondary filter is dirty, the primary filter is almost certainly dirty as well (though the converse is not necessarily true). And if the secondary filter is dirty and your fuel system includes an electric or manual lift pump between the primary and secondary filters, you should check the filter screen in the lift pump as well.

Replace the deck fill cap gasket (as needed). Keep your deck fill cap tightened and change out the gasket annually. Before fueling, make sure to surround the fill with absorbent pads, and wrap a rag or pad next to the nozzle body. Wipe off the deck fill cap threads before screwing the cap back down.

Hire an expert for 2 hours. If you've never worked with injectors or fuel systems, ask a mechanic to do the job. What if your engine runs like a top? Hire a mechanic for 2 hours once a year. Get him to look things over, make recommendations, and show you something new. The time and money are well spent.

THE AIR SYSTEM

Engines require great quantities of air to operate efficiently. The intake system needs filtration to keep dirt and dust out. The exhaust system must provide an unrestricted path to remove extreme heat and engine gases.

Air System Checklist

Check air filters and clamps (before start-up). Smaller engines often have the air filter housed inside a metal cover on the side of the block, and some small engines do not have an air filter. Some large power vessels carry external filters clamped to the air intake. Check the filter for excess dirt and grime. Clamped filters tend to loosen from engine vibration, so check the hose clamps often and tighten as needed.

Air System Maintenance

Clean or replace the air filter element. Annually, or more often if needed, remove the air filter and clean it as described in the instructions below:

Paper element filters. Tap the filter on its side to remove deposits. Continue to turn and tap the filter around its circumference. Replace as needed.
Foam element filters. Use a mild solution of detergent and water. Dry thoroughly before reinstalling.
Metal element filters. Wash the filter in solvent.

THE CHARGING SYSTEM
Charging System Checklist

Check covers and straps (before start-up, while underway). Each battery needs its own cover to protect the terminals from dropped tools, which could cause sparks and even an explosion. All batteries must have strong webbing tie-down straps that wrap around the batteries (over the covers) and are through-bolted to the battery shelf or box. Tie-downs must keep the batteries in place—even in a knockdown or broach. Replace defective or worn tie-down straps.

Check that the alternator is charging normally (after start-up). If you have an ammeter, it should show charging. If you don't have an ammeter, look at the charge warning light, also called the ignition light. This will extinguish as soon as the alternator comes on line. If it stays lighted, you have a problem. It may mean that the alternator belt has failed, and since this belt also drives the water pump, the engine will soon overheat.

Charging System Maintenance

In his book *Troubleshooting Marine Diesels*, Peter Compton recommends three steps for the maintenance of the lead-acid batteries found on most boats:

1. **Battery size and type.** Use batteries that are the correct size for the job at hand. If you have two batteries onboard, reserve one for no other duty than starting the engine. *Starting* batteries have to deliver a burst of power to start your engine. These batteries will show a rating of cold cranking amps. Compton recommends 2 to 3 cranking amps for each cubic inch of engine cylinder volume. Look in your engine manual for the cubic inch measurement.

The second battery, called a *domestic* or *house* battery, runs all lights and navigation electronics. For this you need a deep-cycle battery, which is capable of being discharged and recharged time and again (whereas automotive-type starting batteries will weaken if subjected to multiple deep discharges). House batteries must be capable of handling whatever electronics you have with plenty of juice to spare.

2. **Battery connections and ventilation.** Clean corrosion from terminals and make sure connections are tight. Keep batteries in a well-ventilated compartment outside the cabin. (Batteries can discharge hydrogen and oxygen with explosive potential, and should never be stored inside a cabin.)

SKIPPER TIP

▶ A battery selector switch allows power to be drawn from or recharged to one battery or the other, or both batteries at once. You must protect your starter battery from deep discharge. In other words, when you are underway, do not run electronics or lights with the starter battery. Use the house battery. And do not turn the battery selector switch from Battery #1 to Battery #2 through the OFF position while the engine is running. If you do this, you may very well fry your alternator diodes.

SKIPPER TIP

▶ Don't forget your underwater appendages. Salt, stray electrical currents, and incompatible metals pit, corrode, or crumble other metals if ignored long enough. Install one or more *sacrificial zincs* next to your propeller, shaft, and through-hulls to make sure corrosion attacks the zinc instead of these critical components. Once the zinc disintegrates, the corrosion starts up again. Change out zincs once a year. If you don't haul the boat, hire a diver. Spend a bit now to save a bunch later. Some engines use *pencil zincs* (long, thin zincs attached to a threaded screw) that screw into a hole in the engine body. As with any sacrificial zinc, you must change these every so often. Check the owner's manual or call your manufacturer to locate these on your engine.

What Tools Do You Need On Board?

For Daytrips or Weekend Cruising

Basic Everyday Toolkit: Carry an assortment of flat and Phillips-head screwdrivers, socket wrenches to fit all nuts and bolts, hammer, adjustable wrenches, and pliers.

Spare Parts Toolkit: Carry spare oil, transmission fluid, coolant, and a light lube oil (like WD-40). Carry these parts: oil filters, raw-water impeller, raw-water impeller gasket, primary fuel filter replacement element, secondary fuel filter replacement element, and an air filter replacement element. Add any other parts you feel necessary, such as an alternator.

Extended Cruising

Add to the lists above a full set of gaskets, as well as replacements for all fuel injectors and the freshwater pump. Again, this only touches on the essentials. The best source of advice for your particular engine is the manufacturer. Some companies, like Mack Boring, provide sailboat and powerboat owners hands-on seminars on inboard diesel engine repair and maintenance.

3. **Battery charge and the 50% rule.** Overcharging your batteries causes internal boiling and increases the discharge of hydrogen and oxygen gases. Undercharging weakens battery output. Keep each battery charged *above* 50% at all times. If your battery allows access to the cells, pry off the cell caps and check the electrolyte level. Fill with distilled water as needed.

Gel-cell and *AGM (absorbed glass mat)* batteries are often called "sealed" or "no-maintenance" batteries because they lack cell caps and provide no access to the cells. These batteries are unlike the traditional lead-acid batteries (also called flooded-cell or wet-cell batteries) discussed above in that the electrolyte is in gel or absorbed rather than liquid form. These batteries are less susceptible to leakage or gassing and require no regular maintenance, which makes them ideal for careless boatowners. They also recharge more quickly. However, their cost is higher, and they tend to be more sensitive to overcharging.

How to Manually Shut Down a Diesel Engine

We brought the big twin-engine Bertram alongside her berth and toggled the start switch to *off*, and nothing happened. The big Detroits kept humming at idle RPM. We tried again a few seconds later: same story—nada, nothing doing. Now what?

Fortunately, we were tied up when this incident occurred. Unlike their gasoline cousins, diesel engines run on any food deposits left in their cylinders. In this case, built-up carbon deposits provided all the oomph needed to feed those engines.

Once this happens, you need to cut off the fuel supply through the electrical solenoid or mechanical stop. Try these three easy steps:

1. **Safety first.** Remove jackets, rings, bracelets, watches, and necklaces from your person.
2. **Locate the solenoid or shutdown lever.** Open the engine access cover. Locate the fuel injection pump. Some engines have a spring-loaded rod that goes into a cylinder-shaped solenoid. This rod might have a bellowslike cover wrapped around it. (See photo on page 156.) Other engines have a spring-loaded lever attached to a cable.
3. **Shut down the engine.** Pull or push the rod or lever, whichever way offers the least resistance. Hold it in position until the engine shuts down. Repeat steps 2 and 3 with a second engine.

Make Your Emergency Engine Shutdown Easy to Find

Put this on your to-do list. Clean the shutdown lever or rod thoroughly. Scrape off any loose paint, rust, or corrosion. Paint it a Day-Glo yellow or red. Now it's easy to find, day or night, in an emergency.

How to Stop a Runaway Engine

Your engine RPMs increase suddenly. You pull back on the throttle and nothing happens. This indicates a runaway engine. Leaking oil gets sucked through the air intake into the cylinders. Engines will run as long as the oil supply lasts or until the engine seizes from lack of oil.

In the previous scenario, we were able to place the throttles into neutral position and the engines throttled down to idle speed. In a runaway diesel, you lose all control over throttle speed. The engine will not answer the controls, even if you bring them back to the neutral position. And, you will be unable to shut the engine down through the shutoff switch or fuel stop. No matter what you do, the engine will continue to run at high speed. This makes a runaway diesel a dangerous beast indeed!

Larger vessels, like Bertrams, have an emergency pull-stop lever at the console. This slaps a flap over the air intake, choking the engine and shutting it down quickly. Smaller vessels require manual methods. But this takes time, and in restricted waters you must prevent damage or injury to other persons, vessels, or property. First, get everyone into life jackets right away. Then use one of the methods described below:

CO_2 Shutdown Method

The engine needs oxygen for combustion, so you can stop it by substituting CO_2 for oxygen.

Fixed CO_2 firefighting system. Evacuate the engine compartment. Energize the CO_2 system with the auto switch or remote pull station.

Portable CO_2 fire extinguishers. Ventilate the compartment. Blast short bursts directly into the engine air intake.

Manual Shutdown Method

Equipment. Find a large cushion, a block of wood, or a life jacket.

Find the air intake. Locate the air supply. Look for a cylindrical- or discus-shaped filter mounted to large piping. Remove the filters.

Block the air intake. Air intakes create enormous vacuum pressure at the pipe opening. Keep your hands and fingers away from the opening. Lay the cushion, wood, or life jacket flat against the open air intake pipe. Use a solid object like a block of wood or hatch board if possible. If you have to use a soft object, take great care not to allow the object to get sucked into the intake.

Runaway Engines in Restricted Waters

If you have a runaway engine in restricted waters, remember these three steps.

1. **Sound the horn or whistle.** Assign one crewmember to continuously sound the danger signal on the horn or whistle. If your VHF has a loud hailer function, ask a crewmember to warn others in your path.

2. **Put the boat into a tight turning circle.** If you have room to maneuver, put the boat into a tight turn. Put the wheel hard over and leave it there. This gives you more time to use one of the emergency shutdown procedures described above.

3. **Consider an intentional grounding.** You might choose to ground the boat to prevent endangerment to others. Get the crew aft into the cockpit—in life jackets, squatting low, and grabbing any solid support. As you enter shallow water, make a narrow angle to the shoals. You want to ground the boat so that it slows down gradually before stopping. This prevents injuries associated with hard impact groundings.

Fighting Engineroom Fires by Remote Control

When fire strikes, you have about 30 seconds to get things under control. After that, it's too late. Some vessels have fixed CO_2 systems inside the engine compartment. (Note: halon is no longer authorized as an extinguishing agent in a *new* installation. Vessels with existing halon systems may use it, but must choose another system if they replace their existing system.) On your boat, do you have enough redundant systems in place as a backup? Train your crew on the operation of these four vital systems.

1. **Portable fire extinguishers.** Mount all fire extinguishers. Consider replacing dry chemical extinguishers with CO_2 extinguishers. Dry chemical puts out the fire, but the fine powder causes irreversible damage to any electrical equipment. CO_2 is clean and effective, but much more deadly because it displaces oxygen. You must use a CO_2 portable extinguisher in a well-ventilated compartment. Point out the location of each extinguisher to crewmembers. Check the gauge on each bottle and replace the extinguishing agent if the gauge reads low. To fight an engineroom fire, blast the extinguisher in short bursts into the outside engine intake vents, or try to find a crack or hole in the hatch through which to blast extinguishing agent.

2. **Fixed extinguisher remote pull switch.** If you have an installed, fixed extinguishing system, you must have a backup remote pull switch. Look in the cockpit or near the helm. Most remote pull switches have cover plates installed over the device to protect against unintentional operation. They are sometimes difficult to locate in the dark or in foul weather. Paint each cover plate a bright Day-Glo color. Make simple step-by-step instructions, laminate them, and post them next to each pull switch. Below is a sample instruction plate.

   E.S.P. for Engineroom Firefighting

   E-vacuate: Evacuate all persons from the compartment.
   S-eal off: Close doors, hatches, ports, and scuttles behind you.
   P-ull switch: If the fire is not out within 20 seconds, operate the remote switch.

3. **Remote electrical panel kill switch.** You must be able to shut down power to every electrical switch and panel in a fire. Live current feeds fires. Clearly mark the main breaker switch that shuts down everything aboard, including the generator. Point it out to your crew.

4. **Remote ventilation shutdown.** The deadliness of a convection fire cannot be overstated. Superheated gases shoot through ventilation and air-conditioning ducts, spreading fire from one space to another. Cruise ship fires spread from deck to deck by this method. Install a switch that shuts down the vessel's air ducts and ventilation system completely. Make sure to shut down exhaust and intake for the engine compartment. (If you keep the intake open, you feed oxygen to the fire; if you keep the exhaust open, you'll lose extinguishing agent from the compartment.)

How to Ventilate and Prepare for Fire Reflash

You must thoroughly ventilate any compartment after using any type of extinguishing agent. Immediately after a fire, the extinguishing product remains active for several minutes. Be aware that fire can reflash in a fraction of a second. Prevent this by taking the following precautions.

1. **Carry a portable extinguisher.** You need a backup extinguisher next to you (not in its brackets) anytime you access a space where combustion has occurred.

2. **Don heat-resistant gloves.** Put on heat-resistant gloves or hot-pot holders. The engineroom access hatch will most likely be extremely hot.

3. **Cool the access hatch.** Spray a water mist onto the engineroom access hatch. Wait to open the hatch until you no longer see steam rising from the hatch surface.

4. **Open the hatch and start a reflash watch.** After opening the hatch, set up a 15- to 20-minute reflash watch. Lay the extinguisher horizontally on deck and keep the pin in. This prevents bottle damage, rolling around, or accidental ignition. Wait at least 10 minutes before re-entering the compartment.

Stay Safe When Hooking Up Shore Power

When you hook up or disconnect from shore power, make the prevention of electrical shock your number one goal. Walk your crew through the procedures shown below, and follow these two safety rules before you begin:

Safety Rule #1. Never hold the live end of a shore-power plug.

Safety Rule #2. Shoreside receptacles are always LIVE! Some shoreside facilities have breaker switches to shut off the power; others have continuous live power. Assume they're all live and play it safe.

HOOKING UP TO SHORE POWER

1. **Go dead ship.** Shut down the engines and generator. Turn off switches first: lights, navigation equipment, and all accessories at the power panel. Check panels near the console on the flying bridge and in the cabin. Turn off breakers and rockers (main breakers) last.

2. **Plug into boat receptacle.** The receptacle on the boat has no power, so plug it in. Most plugs require a push and quarter turn to lock into place. The better plugs have a locking ring to prevent the plug from pulling out of the receptacle. On boats with multiple receptacles, consider color-coding the main shore-power plug and receptacle cover plate with Day-Glo paint.

3. **Plug into shoreside receptacle.** Ask the dockmaster to secure (turn off) the power momentarily. Whether you can secure power at the pier or not, go ahead and plug in. Check the plug and receptacle to make sure they mate. If not, ask the dockmaster for an adapter. Don't force things. If you get resistance, stop and find out why. Remember to give the plug a quarter turn and finish up with the locking ring.

4. **Energize power from pier to boat.** If not already energized, turn on the power at the pier. Return to the boat and turn on rockers. Then turn on the accessory and equipment switches.

DISCONNECTING SHORE POWER FOR GETTING UNDERWAY

1. **Go dead ship.** Turn off lights, nav equipment, and all accessories at the power panel. Check all power panels in the cabin and topside. Shut off the black or white rocker (breaker) switches last.
2. **Remove shoreside plug.** Ask the dockmaster to secure the power momentarily. If shoreside power cannot be secured, you can nevertheless pull out the plug from the shoreside receptacle.
3. **Remove boat plug; coil and stow.** Remove the plug on the boat. Screw the receptacle cover plate back over the receptacle. Coil and stow the shore-power cord in a dry area.
4. **Start engines and energize power.** Start the generator and engines. Turn on the main rocker switches first, then the accessory switches. Finally, turn on lights and navigation equipment.

Wake Control and Emergency Wake Breaking

There's nothing fun about fighting to stay inside a channel after being waked by a boneheaded skipper. This problem, however, is not going away anytime soon. Professional and recreational skippers have a responsibility to set the example.

First off, you are solely responsible for controlling your wake. You are responsible for any wake damage to vessels that are underway, at anchor, or moored. In the worst case, a person could end up falling overboard.

Most of us who operate power vessels have found ourselves faced with this dilemma: do I slow down or do I keep going? When I was a Coast Guard coxswain, no judgment was allowed; I was obligated to slow down near others, no matter what. We'd slow down to clear one group of vessels, then ramp up our speed for a while, slow down to clear another group, and then ramp it up again. Doing that only cost a few seconds and never impacted the outcome of our operations. Safety first—always.

WAKE CONTROL 101

Use your own boat's LOA (length overall) to determine when you should slow down to a minimum wake or to no wake at all. Follow these guidelines.

Slow down to minimum wake ($10 \times$ LOA). Displacement and semidisplacement power vessels tend to churn up the water astern. Slow to minimum wake when you are at a distance that is ten times your boat length (ten boat lengths) from another vessel. For example, if your boat is 20 feet long, slow down when you are within 200 feet of another boat. If you're 50 feet, slow when within 500 feet of another boat. Planing vessel skippers must use their discretion, since these vessels tend to throw larger wakes at displacement speeds than when up on plane. Make your decision based on proximity to other vessels and the depth of water (in shallow water, wake increases).

Slow down to no wake (2 × LOA). When you are two boat lengths from another vessel, slow to minimum throttle.

HOW TO DEAL WITH MEETING OR OVERTAKING SITUATIONS

Meeting or passing stationary vessels. Continue at a no-wake speed until you are two boat lengths past the other vessel(s).

Overtaking another vessel. Match the speed of the other vessel exactly. Sound the appropriate sound signal (see Chapter 7). In inland waters, you may use the VHF radio to arrange passing agreements. Remember, the other skipper is under *no* obligation to allow passage. They are, however, obligated to answer your signal.

Many operators are not familiar with the Navigation Rules. If you don't receive a response, ease up just off the other vessel's quarter. I've often done this and have been waved to go on ahead. But always start off by following the methods prescribed by the Navigation Rules.

After reaching an agreement to pass, increase your speed so it is slightly faster than the other vessel. Keep your wake to the absolute minimum to prevent the other boat from yawing (swinging from side to side of its course). Maintain a parallel course as you pass the other boat. Keep your passing speed consistent until you are two boat lengths past the other vessel's bow. Then increase to normal cruising or planing speed.

EMERGENCY WAKE BREAKING

If you are in between plane and displacement mode, you're probably throwing a huge wake. When you slow down from a plane, the vessel squats at the stern, dropping into a hole, and all that water has to go somewhere. Your wake train moves out laterally from the vessel, affecting anything in its path.

There's no guarantee that the wake-breaking method described below will work for your vessel. But in an emergency, it's better than doing nothing at all. Test it in an area clear of traffic before you use it in the real situation.

1. **Fast and smooth.** Bring the throttle or both throttles simultaneously back to neutral in a fast, smooth motion. This isn't a crash-and-burn stop. Keep it under control. You don't want to lose an engine here.
2. **Delay, then idle astern.** Allow 1 to 2 seconds in neutral, then put the engine into idle reverse propulsion and leave it there until all forward motion stops. Throttle back to neutral, and then proceed in displacement mode at a no-wake speed.

Decisions to Make Before Running an Inlet

Few things test the skipper's integrity like the final decision to enter an inlet.

No hard and fast rules exist for running inlets. Ultimately it comes down to the safety of your passengers, crew, and vessel. Do not enter any inlet in rough weather without local knowledge. Even then, you must consider the capability of your boat and crew.

Don't expect to find inlet buoys plotted on your chart or plotter. The Coast Guard tries to reposition inlet buoys as bar conditions change, but this requires good weather. It isn't unusual to find an inlet buoy out of position. Use this five-step evaluation process to guide your decision.

1. **Local knowledge.** Check the Local Notices to Mariners for the previous thirty days (see Chapter 1). When was the last recent buoy shift in the area? Have new shoals built up inside one of the buoys? If you're unsure, call your Coast Guard District Waterways and Management office. They're up to snuff and can tell you. Don't forget the local experts such as Sea Tow, TowBoatU.S., or tugboat operators. Be sure you let them know your draft and power capabilities.

2. **Visibility and buoy identification.** You must have enough visibility to identify all the characteristics of the inlet buoys, from entry to exit points. The Coast Guard often uses small, plastic unlighted and lighted buoys. This makes their job easier if they need to drag the buoy to a new position—but it makes your job more difficult. Check the color, shape, and name of each buoy. Use binoculars to find the next buoy in the sequence. Study the water for breaking seas. Ocean swells coming onto a beach or an inlet will form a breaking sea when they move over a bottom only one to two times their height. For instance, a 2-foot swell forms a breaking top in 2 to 4 feet of water. (For more on waves and swell, see Chapter 12.) Seas that break inside the buoy line of an inlet channel indicate that the sand has shifted. Stay clear and find an alternative route up or down the coast.

3. **Wind and sea.** Onshore winds and seas slam into an ebb current, creating steep breaking seas over the entrance bar. Study the tidal current and calculate the times of maximum ebb, maximum flood, and slack water. Wait for slack current or the beginning of a flood before you attempt the passage. (See Chapter 5 for how to obtain information about tides and currents; use this information for planning an inlet passage.) Know the height of the tide inside the inlet. Large displacement power vessels can touch bottom from going too fast in shallow water. Their stern sinks into the hole created behind them (called *squatting*). Slower, deep-keel vessels could touch bottom in the trough (deepest part of a wave train) between two waves.

Study the local winds and tidal currents—if they are in opposition, you can expect much rougher conditions inside an inlet.

Do not under any conditions base your decision on what you hear on a weather radio. Many forecasts are several hours old, and only you can see the conditions at this particular spot. Stop the boat and study the inlet with binoculars. Take your time and look for a wave pattern to develop. You will usually see a larger sea, followed by a series of smaller seas. If you get inside an inlet and must then turn around and head back out, this knowledge could prove crucial to prevent your boat from capsizing. If possible, avoid having to turn broadside to the seas inside an inlet. If you must turn around, your vessel needs to have enough power to make a 180-degree turn within a few seconds. Start the turn the moment the large sea in the sequence passes beneath your hull. Complete the turn and get your bow into the seas before the next large sea arrives.

If you have any doubt as to the safety of an inlet, play it safe and stay out!

4. **Boat and crew capabilities.** Underpowered boats have no business in any inlet with breaking waves across the channel. A boat must have the power to hold herself on the back of a wave and square herself before a breaking wave. In inlets, power and stability (see Appendices) take precedence over speed. Coast Guard surf boats depend on stability and brute power to negotiate the worst inlets in the nation.

   Your boat. You must maintain control of the vessel at all times. That means keeping the rudder and propeller in the water and the bow and stern squared to the seas. Use throttle bursts to dig the stern in and maintain perpendicular alignment to the wave crests. When exiting an inlet, avoid the crest of any breaking wave ahead of you by angling slightly left or right. When entering an inlet, slow down on the back of a breaking wave by throttling down so as not to overtake the crest. Tow warps (long loops of line) or a drogue to keep the stern square to a following sea. If the boat gets caught on the crest, your rudder and propeller break water and lose effectiveness, and you could *broach* (roll over onto your side and capsize). Or you might *pitchpole*, which is when the bow digs into a trough and the boat somersaults forward.

   Your crew. Some of your crew must be experienced working on the foredeck in an emergency. Do not leave the helm unattended, even for a moment. If you lose control inside a rough inlet, the boat could broach. Make preparations ahead of time to prevent this from happening.

5. **Ground tackle and fast deployment strategy.** Your vessel needs substantial ground tackle that sets immediately on short scope (see Chapter 11 for more on ground tackle and anchoring). Make the

following preparations before you approach an inlet. Attach 10 feet of chafing chain to the working anchor. Pull 75 feet of nylon rode out of the locker. Check for chafe and remove the kinks and *hockles* (twists). Coil it back down into the locker. Now you know it's ready to run free without jamming on the spill pipe.

Cockpit-rigged emergency anchor. Consider rigging the main, bow anchor to deploy from the cockpit. This keeps your crew off the pitching, rolling foredeck in an emergency. You don't want to experience a man overboard inside an inlet. To do this, set the chain stopper. Pull out 75 feet of anchor rode and lead the bight (loop of line) aft. Keep the line outside all rails, stanchions, shrouds, or other obstructions. Pull the line leading from the anchor taut, and cleat it off to a stern cleat. Coil the rest of the line near the stern cleat, ready to feed out. Go forward and release the chain stopper.

TWENTY SECONDS TO AVOID DISASTER

Here's the time factor: 10 seconds to get to the bow and pick up the anchor and 10 seconds for the anchor to set (if you're lucky). That gives you a total of 20 seconds before disaster strikes. And that's on a well-prepared vessel. Lose an engine or both engines in an inlet without the hook ready for an emergency set, and you'll probably pile up on a jetty or shoal. Let's look at an example and bring some previously learned nav-math into the mix.

The current inside the inlet is running at 4 knots, with shoals located just outside the 100-yard-wide channel. Our plan is to stay in the middle of the channel as we make our way in from seaward. But if we were to lose our engines, how far would we drift based on the tidal current speed?

In Chapter 3, you learned about the 3-minute rule. Use that method here. Add two zeroes to the right of a speed (in knots) to find the corresponding distance traveled (in yards) in 3 minutes. For instance, at 4 knots, distance traveled = 400 yards in 3 minutes. Now go to the example:

At 4 knots, we would drift 400 yards in 3 minutes. In 1 minute, we would drift 133 yards (400 ÷ 3).

In 20 seconds, we would drift 44 yards (133 ÷ 3). (See Drift Rate table, Appendix I.)

If we are midchannel when the casualty happens, we're 50 yards from disaster. Excluding the effects of vessel momentum or wind drift, we might make it if the anchor sets right away.

PREPARATIONS TO ENTER OR EXIT AN INLET

Now that you've gone through the evaluation checklist, make an entry/exit preparation checklist to get your crew and boat ready. This list has five critical tasks.

1. **Lash and stow.** Start inside the cabin. Stow or lash anything that might fly around when your boat is rolling and pitching in a seaway. Use bungee cord, small line, or marline. You can also stuff items into lockers, but make sure any such items stay in place. Shove towels, rags, clothing, or pillows inside to keep things from becoming movable ballast or unguided missiles. Lockers need positive latches to keep heavy gear from crashing through.

2. **Seal her up.** Make the vessel watertight. Start forward and work your way aft, checking these three positions:

   Up. Close and seal hatches. Remove the forward cabin ventilation cowl vents and screw on the cover plates. (Do not remove or seal engine intake and exhaust vents.)

   Sides. Close opening ports and windows. If portlights have cover plates, install them.

   Down and center. Check bilge access plates and covers to make sure they're properly seated and dogged (latched). Check the engineroom hatch. In sailing vessels, the companionway ladder often serves as the engine access hatch. Check the seating and dogs (twist latches). When you exit the cabin, close and latch the door or companionway hatch. On sailing vessels, install dropboards and close the main hatch. Secure the main hatch cover with an easily removed non-locking device. Check the exterior of the vessel for loose gear and open lockers. Imagine getting doused with a wave breaking on the bow or quarter. What needs a cover? Could something use an extra lashing?

3. **All hands into life jackets.** Everyone onboard should wear a life jacket (PFD)—properly tightened, clipped, and zipped. If you and your crew are wearing inflatable PFDs, fully inflate the bladders with the manual tube. If conditions warrant, rig port and starboard jacklines and don safety harnesses. Make sure that 75 to 100 feet of line is attached to a throwable PFD (ring, horseshoe). Bend the line to the aft rail or tie it off to a cleat.

4. **Keep crew low for safety and stability.** If you have a lower steering station, use it. Keep the crew off the flying bridge. You want the crew ready in the cockpit to handle any emergency. If you must steer from the flying bridge, have one crewmember stay with you to act as a messenger between you and the crew below.

5. **Rig warps or drogue.** Make the call now whether to rig warps or a drogue. The simplest warp consists of a large bight of line, rigged from one quarter cleat to the other. When towed astern, it provides some resistance and helps keep the stern square to the seas. Maintain a sharp lookout in the cockpit when you are towing warps in breaking seas. You don't want a line to wrap around your propeller shaft inside an inlet!

How to Make a Fuel Consumption Graph

Supplies and Tools Needed to Make a Fuel Consumption Graph

▸ accurate fuel flowmeter or fuel gauge
▸ clipboard and graph paper

In addition to making a speed/RPM table, as described in Chapter 3, you should also make a fuel consumption table. In power vessels, you must know the RPM boundary where your engine or engines become extremely thirsty. Think of this as a critical RPM setting. Stay below this limit and you'll get decent mileage. Run above that limit and your fuel needs increase heavily. Always measure fuel consumption in gallons per hour (GPH).

1. **Fuel tank gauges.** Before you start, you must have an accurate way to measure fuel consumption. See which of these methods apply to you.

   In-line fuel flowmeter. A fuel flowmeter installed directly onto the fuel line gives the most accurate readings.
   Transfer to day tank. If you have an odd-shaped fuel tank, transfer the fuel to a symmetrical day tank. The day tank should have square or round sides and a flat top and bottom. This avoids the problems with V-shaped bilge fuel tanks (see next method).
   Float gauge markings. Float gauges that measure fuel from a V-shaped bilge tank tend to give inaccurate readings. When you top off the tank, the float sits in the tank's widest area; consumption appears much slower. Once you are past the halfway point in the tank, however, consumption accelerates because you're near the bottom of the V.

   Sid Stapleton, author of *Stapleton's Powerboat Bible*, recommends running the tank down close to empty. Then add 20 gallons to the tank and stop. Mark the fuel gauge with a marker. Add another 20 gallons; stop and mark the gauge again. Keep marking in this manner until your tanks are topped off.
   Refine each mark by dividing it in half. Place smaller marks between the 20-gallon marks. That way, each gauge shows marks at 10-gallon intervals.
2. **Set up your consumption graph.** Set up the graph with fuel consumption in tenths on the left side and RPMs in hundredths on the bottom.
3. **Sea trial for fuel consumption.** It takes a lot of time to make an accurate fuel graph. If possible, make the graph in ideal conditions: flat seas and little wind or current. In less-than-ideal conditions, make each run headed into the elements, or make a run into the elements, then turn and make a reciprocal run with the elements, keeping the same RPM on both runs. You need to make two graphs for this method (see below).

Each run consists of 1 hour at a specific RPM. Record in your log: RPM, speed, GPH, wind, current, sea condition. Then bump the speed up or down to the next RPM, and again run for a full hour. When complete, plot your findings onto your graph. Note the weather conditions on the graph.

If you made reciprocal runs, you'll need to make two graphs. Label each graph with the conditions encountered (i.e., "Bow seas"; "Following seas"; etc.). When cruising, use the graph that most closely matches your current conditions.

Alterations and Fuel Provisioning

Remember that any alterations to your engine or boat—such as adding turbochargers, changing props, or provisioning for extended cruising—might affect the accuracy of your data.

Even without alterations, it's wise to overestimate fuel needs by 30% or more. This compensates for fighting wind, current, or seas, and for passenger and provision weight or running generators.

A FUEL CONSUMPTION GUIDE FOR SLOW BOATS

Sailboats and vessels with slow speeds needn't go through the process outlined above. The method outlined below gives a rough estimate at cruising RPM. Sailing vessels in particular need to run as often as possible at maximum throttle. Diesels hate babying, and serious problems crop up when a diesel is run continuously at idle speeds. For an accurate consumption calculation, get the engine up to maximum speed when you clear the no-wake zone. Your iron genny will reward you with longer life, better performance, and fewer problems.

1. **Top off the tank.** Fill your tank to 90% capacity. Mark the position of the fuel float gauge. Use a felt-tip pen and mark on or near the gauge.
2. **Log entries.** Make a log entry showing the date and time of filling. Describe the mark location on the fuel gauge in case it rubs off.
3. **Run at cruising RPM.** Run the boat at cruising RPM. Burn the fuel down to the quarter-tank mark on the float gauge.
4. **Find your consumption.** Return to the fuel dock. Record the date and time. Fill the tank back to the exact level shown by your mark on the fuel float gauge. Divide gallons taken on by the hours run under power between fills. Round the result up to the next higher tenth of a gallon.

You have finished the test and return to the fuel dock. It takes 15.4 gallons to fill your tank to the mark you made on the fuel gauge. Total time run was 33.8 hours. Divide the total gallons of fuel by the total hours run:

$$15.4 \text{ gallons} \div 33.8 \text{ hours} = 0.456 \text{ GPH}$$

Rounding to the next higher tenth gives you a result of 0.5 GPH at cruising RPM.

"Your Call, Skipper"

You're the skipper or most knowledgeable crewmember in each of the following situations. What actions would you take?

1. "Hey Skipper, the engine drip pan is full of water. It's clear but feels oily. What do we need to check?"

2. On an engine or a generator, how could you stop the engine if the pull stop failed?

3. You start the engine, proceed to the stern, and notice that only a trickle of cooling water flows from the exhaust. What four steps would you take next?

4. You're operating at full throttle on a 40-foot trawler, overtaking another vessel a half mile ahead. How can you use your boat length to effectively control your wake?

5. You've made the decision to enter Stono Inlet in South Carolina. You've studied the inlet and see no breaking waves across the bar. Now you'll get the crew ready for the run. What is the first thing you tell them?

Answers

1. Check the stuffing box first. The shallow stuffing box sump could have filled and overflowed into the drip pan. Clear but oily liquid indicates fuel or transmission leaks. Use your flashlight. Check hose connections for leaks.

2. Look for a cylinder-shaped solenoid. Pull or push the lever going into the solenoid and hold until the engine stops. Smaller engines have a stop lever on a cable that mounts to the fuel injection pump. Push or pull the lever and hold it in that position until the engine stops.

3. (1) Shut down the engine. (2) Check the seacock handle (the open position is in-line with hose). (3) If the seacock is open, shut it, open up the raw-water strainer, and check for a clogged filter. (4) Check for an obstruction of the raw-water intake strainer outside the hull. Shut the seacock, pull off the raw-water hose, and open the seacock for a moment. Weak (or no) flow indicates an exterior blockage, perhaps from weed or a plastic bag.

4. Start slowing when you are 400 feet astern (10 x LOA) of the other vessel. When you get within about 80 feet (2 x LOA) slow to idle, and then adjust throttle(s) to match the other vessel's speed. Call on the radio (in Inland Waters) or sound whistle signals to reach a passing agreement.

5. Everyone aboard will need to wear life jackets. Crew wearing inflatable vests should manually inflate the bladders to full volume.

9 SAILBOAT SEAMANSHIP

*I could watch the motions of a sail forever, they are so rich and full
of meaning. I watch the play of its pulse, as if it were my own blood
beating there.*
—Henry David Thoreau

Do you know the eight most critical components to check aboard any sailboat before casting off? How do we supercharge our sails to give us the best speed and power in any condition of wind and sea? How can we balance our boats in heavy weather so that they practically steer themselves? Are you prepared to handle the unexpected—such as sheets jamming on a winch, loss of steering, or an accidental jibe?

In This Chapter, You'll Learn How To:
- ❀ Inspect a sailing vessel of any size quickly and thoroughly
- ❀ Shape your sails for amazing power and speed
- ❀ Balance your boat in heavy weather in just three easy steps
- ❀ Confidently handle problems like jammed sheets or loss of steering

The Sailing Skipper's Eight-Component Inspection

Make a simple eight-component checklist for your boat. We're all anxious to get out there and start sailing, but it pays big dividends to check things first. Set up your checklist so you begin at the bow and work toward the stern.

1. **Ground tackle.** Our number one component—the anchor and its accompanying hardware—does double duty as a boat brake and insurance policy. It often gets overlooked, hidden on the bow roller or stowed in a locker. First, check the long arm, or *shank*, of the anchor for distortion. A bent shank means you have a useless hunk of metal that needs replacement. An anchor shank cannot be straightened without seriously compromising its strength. Check the screw-pin shackles at the top of the shank and the rope-to-chain connection. Seize shackle pins to the shackle's side with stainless seizing wire or nylon wire ties.

Next, pull out 5 or 6 fathoms of anchor line and inspect for chafe. Then coil it back down into the locker. If coiling three-strand line, twist your wrist

clockwise a quarter turn as you lay down each bight. This keeps the line free of twists, called *hockles*. Finally, dig down beneath the coils and make sure the bitter end of the rode is permanently tied to the eye at the bottom of the locker. (Anchoring is covered in Chapter 11.)

Check the seizings on your shackle pins.

2. **Furling drum, furling line, and sheets.** Like a roll-up window shade, furling gear needs to work smoothly, without jamming. Our number two component tends to bind up at the most inopportune times—and that often means a trip to the foredeck to fix the problem.

     Inspect the genoa sheets at the clew for proper bowlines and indications of wear. (Sheets should be connected to the clew with bowlines, not with shackles. If you have ever received a blow from a shackle in the clew of a flogging headsail, you already know why.) Check the integrity of the clevis and cotter pin on the furling mechanism. Look inside the drum to see if the coiled line comes off the drum evenly. Follow the furling line aft, checking for chafe or binding. Inspect the cockpit furling line cleat and get the coil ready to run free when you set the headsail.

3. **Lifeline integrity.** These flexible rails keep you and your crew aboard. The ends of the lifeline make or break the integrity of this component. Check the lifeline ends at bow and stern pulpits and gates along the sidedecks. Lifelines end in turnbuckles or pelican hooks. Check turnbuckle sleeves and swage fittings for bending, distortion, and missing cotter pins. Check pelican hooks to make sure the bail is firmly in place over the hook. Tape or lash the bail in place. Check along each lifeline for broken wire strands, called *meathooks*.

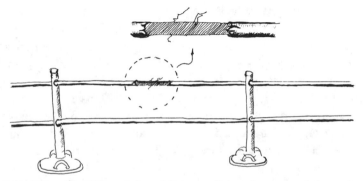

Check the integrity of the lifelines at the end fittings and along the expanses between stanchions.

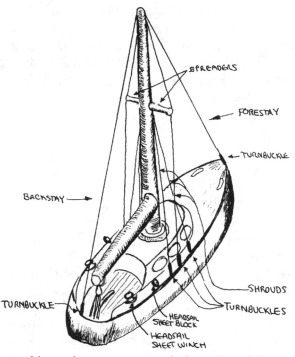

Check the integrity of the standing rigging on a regular basis. This includes checking the cotter pins in the turnbuckles and looking for signs of wear and bending on the stays and shrouds.

Cover meathooks with duct or rigging tape to protect hands and legs. Make a note to replace meathooked wires at the next opportunity.

4. **Stay and shroud integrity.** Nautical bobby pins, called *cotter pins*, keep your mast up. On deck, they are used in turnbuckles at the bases of shrouds and stays. Take your time when checking these. Also inspect the cotter pins in lifeline terminals, tackles, sheets, and shackles. Replace missing or broken cotter pins right away. Use a pin that fits into its hole snugly. Shorten the legs so that they stick out $1^1/_2$ times the diameter of the fitting. Bend the legs to form a "V" shape of about 25 degrees, but no more than that. This makes the cotter pin easy to remove for replacement or in an emergency.

5. **Deck hardware.** Deck hardware—such as winches, blocks, and the mainsheet traveler—represent your boat's throttles and gears. Like a finely tuned sports car, they need to operate smoothly to give you the ability to tune and trim your sails for acceleration and power. For instance, you can slide the headsail sheet block forward on its track to provide a fuller, more powerful headsail shape in a light to moderate breeze. In heavy weather, you can slide it aft to depower the headsail. (See "How to Shape Headsails for Power and Speed" later in this chapter.) Check screw pins or plungers

SEA-CRET TIP

▶ A medium-sized cruising sailboat may have twenty or more cotter pins just keeping stays and shrouds in place. Stay away from cotter rings, referred to as ring-dings. They tend to distort and vibrate out of their holes. Stick with the reliable cotter pin.

in each sheet block. Snatch blocks should open easily. Test each winch for smooth operation. Inspect halyards, mainsheets, topping lifts, and vangs.

Lines, too: Check for chafe where lines exit blocks, cam cleats, or clutches. Look for chafe at any eyesplice attached to a strap, becket, or shackle. Check the lines between the blocks (sometimes called *falls*) on boom vangs, mainsheets, and traveler cars. Falls may chafe where they contact the deck. Run the traveler car out to each end of the track. Check for smooth operation. If the car sticks, use a light waterproof lubricant on the track. Check the traveler car stops. Screw and plunger pin stops corrode if not exercised. Apply lubricant as needed.

INSPECTING HIDDEN EQUIPMENT

Our checklist continues with equipment often overlooked because it is hidden and not in plain view. Most of this gear lives in deck lockers, in aft lazarette spaces, or beneath the cockpit deck. Modify the list specifically for your own boat.

6. **Wheel quadrant system.** Our sixth component hides beneath the wheel. Pop open the round or square inspection port to inspect the steering gear. Move the wheel from stop to stop. Look for distortion or slack in the steering cables. Locate the emergency tiller access port. Place the emergency tiller in a location close to the helm.

SEA-CRET TIP

▶ Mark the access cover for the emergency tiller. Use a permanent felt-tip marker or reflective tape, which makes this easy to find by day or night.

7. **Battery compartments.** Batteries can release deadly hydrogen gas and must be secured in a ventilated compartment. Check each battery as a separate component. Each battery needs its own cover to prevent accidental arcing across the terminals from dropped metal items. Each battery also needs a tie-down strap to keep it from shifting or rolling around.

8. **Through-hull integrity.** Our last component gets forgotten as often as the wheel quadrant system. Check every handle on every seacock on every through-hull. You must be able to close any seacock with minimum effort. Move the handle from open (parallel to the hose) to closed (perpendicular to the hose) and back to open. If the handle is frozen, a gentle tap with a hammer or mallet often encourages smooth operation. Check scupper, sink, shower, head, and engine seacocks. Examine the hoses and stainless steel clamps at the top of each seacock. A tapered wooden plug should be lashed to each seacock with easily broken twine. If a seacock hose fails, you can drive the plug into the seacock bore. (For more on flooding, see "Handling Flooding Emergencies with M.A.T.E.," page 280, in Chapter 13.)

Clearing Up the Mystery of Apparent Wind

Sails operate in *apparent wind*, which is a combination of your boat's speed and the *true wind* (the wind you experience when your boat is not moving). To sail efficiently, sails must be trimmed to the apparent wind. Knowing this gives racing sailors an edge over their competition, and it enables cruising sailors to reach their destinations much faster. Let's break the mystery of apparent wind into four easy pieces.

Boatspeed changes. Picture yourself standing outdoors with the wind blowing against the left side of your face. Begin walking, and increase your pace until you reach jogging speed. Then slow down gradually until you're standing still.

What did you notice about the wind? When standing still, you felt the true wind against the left side of your face. As you increased your speed to a jog, the wind "appeared" to move toward the front of your face. Of course, the wind never really moved; rather, your own forward motion, or speed, caused this apparent wind. Remember these two facts about apparent wind.

If boatspeed *increases*, apparent wind moves *toward* the bow (or the front of your face).

If boatspeed *decreases*, apparent wind moves *away* from the bow (or away from the front of your face).

Boat course changes. If two vehicles traveling at 25 mph were to collide, the drivers would feel an impact of 50 mph. Similarly, when we are sailing *close-hauled* (as close to the wind as possible), our boat speed and the true wind speed are additive, and the apparent wind feels stronger than the true wind.

On the other hand, if both cars were traveling in the same direction and one hit the other, neither driver would feel much impact because the difference in their speeds would be negligible. Similarly, when we are running downwind (with the true wind behind the boat), our boatspeed partially counteracts the true wind speed, and the apparent wind is lighter than the true wind. Remember these two facts about course changes and apparent wind:

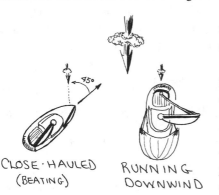

CLOSE·HAULED
(BEATING)

RUNNING
DOWNWIND

If you change course *toward* the true wind, apparent wind speed increases.

If you change course *away* from the true wind, apparent wind speed decreases.

When you are closed-hauled, the apparent wind is stronger than the true wind. When you are running, the apparent wind is not as strong as the true wind.

True wind speed changes. In sailing, we deal with three phases of true wind: the steady wind phase, the gust wind phase, and the lull wind phase. Gust and lull wind phases operate like the accelerator pedal in your car. If you need to pass another vehicle, you accelerate for a short while. If you need to slow down to allow a vehicle to pass you, you decelerate for a short while.

In Chapter 4 we learned about the basic concept of lifts and headers. Here we learn how lifts and headers can occur not just when wind direction changes, but when velocity changes as well.

A wind gust accelerates above the baseline steady wind for a short period of time. Sailors call a gust from the same direction as the baseline breeze a *velocity lift* because the apparent wind moves away from the bow. If you're sailing close-hauled, you can point your boat closer to your windward destination during a gust from the baseline wind direction. As your boat speeds up in response to the stronger wind, however, the apparent wind will move forward again—though perhaps not enough to force you all the way down to your previous baseline close-hauled course.

A lull decelerates below the steady wind for a short period of time. Sailors call a lull from the baseline wind direction a *velocity header* because the apparent wind moves toward the bow. When sailing close-hauled, you will have to respond by falling off the wind somewhat, which points you farther from the windward destination you are trying to reach.

The discussion of lifts and headers in Chapter 4 suggests that you should always tack on a header to keep moving toward your destination, but a velocity header and a header resulting from a change of true wind direction are different animals. A velocity header will cease to be a header once your boatspeed drops in response to the lull. As your boatspeed falls—and assuming the true wind direction remains steady—the apparent wind will move back aft to its previous position. Thus, tacking will gain you nothing *unless* sailing the other tack will get you into a stronger breeze. Look at the wind on the water ahead and to windward. Darker streaks denote areas of stronger breeze. Look at other sailboats too—do they seem to be heeling more and moving faster to windward or ahead? Weigh the evidence and decide whether the wind is more likely to fill back in if you hang with your current tack or switch tacks.

Remember these two facts about gusts and lulls:

If true wind speed *increases,* the apparent wind moves *away from* the bow
  (a velocity lift).
If true wind speed *decreases,* the apparent wind moves *toward* the bow
  (a velocity header).

True wind direction changes. The Chapter 4 discussion of true wind lifts and headers focuses on close-hauled sailing. But a change in the true wind direction has an equally significant though more subtle effect on offwind sailing. One thing that makes sailing downwind difficult is that a small change in true wind direction results in larger changes in apparent wind direction. Keep in mind that sailing vessels sail to the apparent wind. According to Steve Colgate, founder of the Offshore Sailing School, a 16-degree change in the true wind makes a 28-degree change in the apparent wind when you're sailing downwind. That's one reason boats sometimes roll from side to side when running before the wind. The person at the helm might be oversteering (moving the wheel or tiller too much) to try to keep the boat on a straight course. Oversteering in combination with a big apparent wind change could result in an accidental jibe, in which the boom swings across the boat with great force, possibly damaging the rig or causing serious injury. In gusty downwind sailing conditions, keep the wind over the stern quarter rather than directly over the transom, and rig a boom preventer (see "How to Prevent an Accidental Jibe" on page 198) or lower the mainsail and sail under headsail alone.

Remember this when sailing downwind:

When well off the wind, a small change in true wind direction causes a large change in apparent wind direction.

How to Determine Wind Forces

You're sailing in a light 5-knot southwesterly breeze with the wind on the quarter. The wind slowly increases to 15 knots throughout the day, but you hardly notice. With the boat level and the crew relaxed and content, what could be better? Near the end of the day, the wind shifts abruptly. You'll need to head up to make your destination. You change course with full sail set. Immediately the boat heels over, burying her rail. What happened?

When sailing downwind the apparent wind was relatively light. If the boat travels at 6 knots and the true wind is 15 knots, the apparent wind while you're sailing downwind will be 9 knots (the difference between the two speeds). As the boat turns upwind, the apparent wind increases (see "Clearing Up the Mystery of Apparent Wind" above) to just under 20 knots on a close-hauled course!

The force exerted on sails and rigging varies with the square of the apparent wind velocity. Thus the apparent wind force doesn't just triple between 5 and 15 knots, it increases by a factor of nine. Always look to windward for whitecaps before changing from a downwind course to a reach or close-hauled course. Reef or reduce sail before you turn toward the wind.

How to Shape the Mainsail, a Sailboat's Main Propulsion Unit

A balanced sailboat requires less than 4 degrees of wheel or tiller to keep her course.

The mainsail serves as a sailboat's primary propulsion engine. We have all the tools we need at our fingertips to move, shape, and trim that sail into a powerful machine, capable of taking us anywhere we choose to go. Our magic tools enable us to build a faster *speed shape* into the sail or a stronger *power shape* to meet any condition. But how do we determine the shape we need? How do we turbocharge our mainsail for daysailing, cruising, or racing in any weather?

CHOOSING MAINSAIL SHAPE FOR SPEED OR POWER

The *luff*, or leading edge, of a sail greets the wind first. A sailmaker can build the luff flat for speed or full for power, depending on where you sail. Flatter sails generally provide more speed and work well in smooth-water areas such as Long Island Sound or the Chesapeake Bay. Fuller sails provide more power to punch through a chop in areas such as San Francisco Bay, the English Channel, or the Caribbean.

But sail shape isn't totally in the hands of the sailmaker. Unlike an airplane wing, a sail is a flexible membrane, and you can make it fuller or flatter—within the limits imposed by the sailmaker—to respond to conditions on the water.

Draft control: The #1 secret to powerhouse sailing. Viewed from leeward, a sail is a convex curvature of cloth. Viewed from windward it is cupped in a shape that can be thought of as an invisible wedge. In the case of the mainsail, the base of the wedge is the main boom and the apex is the masthead.

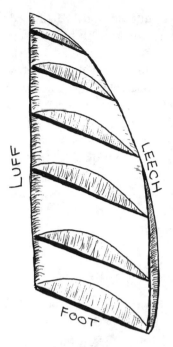

Adjust the draft in a mainsail according to wind and sea conditions.

Looking down at this wedge from above the mast, we can slice a cross section through at any height and draw a straight line from luff to *leech* (the after, trailing edge of a sail), parallel with the boom. Look along this line, which is called a *chord,* and find its point of maximum separation from the sail membrane. That point is the position of maximum depth, or draft, often called simply the *draft position.*

A mainsail's draft position should stay between 40% and 50% of the chord length aft of the luff. Use this table as a rough guide for setting draft in a mainsail:

40% (breezy to heavy winds)
45% (light to moderate winds)
50% (very light winds; "ghosting")

Think of the wind as a giant hand that presses on a mainsail. The pressure of the hand is greatest at the point of maximum draft, and in heavy air, if our draft is too far aft, the hand pushing on the sail tries to round the boat up into the wind. Weather helm—the tendency of the boat to round up into the wind—increases, and the boat heels more and becomes more difficult to steer.

In light air you want a fuller, more powerful sail (see below), and a deeper draft combined with a forward draft position would make it difficult for a light breeze to remain attached to the sail with laminar flow. The air would tend to detach and become turbulent, reducing the sail's effectiveness, so the best draft position is farther aft in light air.

Three Secret Systems to Give You Perfect Draft Control

Fortunately, most sailboats have three powerful control systems that enable us to move and shape draft to match any condition of wind or sea. Think of each sail edge—the luff, leech, and foot—as having a separate "control system" toolkit. You want a full, powerful shape in light air and a flat, depowered shape for heavy air.

1. **Mainsail luff control system.** Your sail's luff takes it on the chin. After all, this is where the wind first makes contact, so you'll need to control the luff more than any other sail edge.

Halyards. Set halyard tension until you just start to get a slight (but not deep) single vertical crease building along the luff. Stop tensioning at that point and cleat off your halyard. As wind increases, wrinkles—called *scallops* or *crow's feet*—may develop along the luff. Tension the halyard just enough to remove the wrinkles. This flattens the sail and also counteracts the tendency of a strengthening breeze to move the draft position aft.

Cunningham. A fabulous invention from the racing world, this simple device tensions the mainsail luff without using a halyard. It's a large ring installed about 8 to 10 inches above the mainsail tack. Run a line from the mast base up through the ring and back down to a cleat on the opposite side. Haul on the line to tension the luff. Larger boats should rig a small block and tackle. Adding luff tension with the halyard is often difficult or impossible when the mainsail is full of wind; it's a lot easier with a cunningham. Again, greater luff tension means a flatter sail with a more forward position of maximum draft, both of which are desirable in a strong breeze.

2. **Mainsail leech control system.** The leech is often the forgotten edge of sail trim, yet it plays a vital roll in proper draft control. Use the mainsheet, boom vang, and traveler to control the mainsail leech.

   Mainsheet. Just 60 feet above the water's surface, the apparent wind is up to 50% stronger than it is at sea level, and the true wind direction may therefore be 10 to 15 degrees farther aft than it is at deck level. We need to shape the upper half of each sail to this different apparent wind. To do this, we introduce twist into the top of the leech by easing the mainsheet. Before making this adjustment, sight up the mainsail leech. Is it cupped to windward along its entire length? If so, the sheet is too tight. Ease the mainsheet to put twist into the top half of the sail as follows:

   Light air. In light-air conditions of less than 6 knots, take care not to cup the leech. You need an "open" leech to keep that light and tenuous airflow moving across the mainsail and exiting without turbulence off the leech. Ease the mainsheet just until the uppermost batten opens slightly to leeward (i.e., until it is cocked slightly to leeward of the boom).

   Moderate wind. In a moderate breeze of 6 to 12 knots, adjust the mainsheet so that the uppermost mainsail batten lines up parallel with the boom.

   Heavy breeze. In heavier winds, use more twist. You want to spill some of that high-octane wind to reduce heeling and balance the boat for a light helm. Ease the mainsheet several inches. Then use the traveler

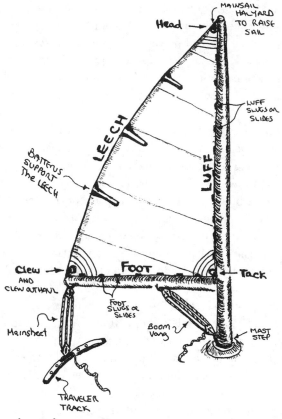

Mainsail parts and controls.

(when sailing on or off the wind) and the boom vang (when sailing off the wind) for further leech control.

Boom vang. When you're sailing off the wind and the boom is eased past the edge of the boat, the mainsheet becomes ineffective in limiting leech twist. Without some help, the end of the boom lifts up and the sail bellies like a pregnant whale. Enter the boom vang. Set vang tension just enough to keep the boom level and the leech under control. Leave a bit of slack in the vang to prevent boom distortion.

Traveler. Position the mainsheet traveler car on the traveler track to keep the boat balanced with good drive. In light to moderate winds, shape the leech first; then move the traveler car if you need to open up the leech as the wind freshens. Racing sailors often play the traveler more than the mainsheet when sailing close-hauled.

Light wind setting. Move the traveler slightly to windward. Adjust the mainsheet to keep the main twisted and the uppermost batten open just a bit (see above).

Moderate wind setting. In moderate winds of 6 to 12 knots, keep the traveler car centered.

Heavier wind setting. Ease the traveler car to leeward as wind speed increases. This maintains good drive yet keeps the boat on her feet.

3. **Mainsail foot control system—the outhaul.**
   The lower part of your mainsail contains the deepest draft. Increase or decrease the draft in the foot with the outhaul.

   Moderate and light wind trim. In light winds or when reaching or running, ease the outhaul to increase the draft and thus the power in the lower half of the sail

   Heavier wind trim. In heavier winds or when close-hauled, tighten the outhaul to decrease the draft and flatten the lower half of the sail.

The Luff-and-Sleep Trim Method

You need to tack through a narrow channel or reach across a waterway with the best speed and power. Is there a way to do this without setting numerous controls? You bet! Three quick steps will have your mainsail trimmed to a "good enough" status.

1. Keep your eyes on the luff of the mainsail.
2. When you are close-hauled, *pinch* (sail toward the wind) upwind a bit until the mainsail luff just begins to flutter. Fall off a hair to put the luff to sleep.
3. When you are reaching, steady up on course. Ease the headsail sheet until the luff just starts to flutter. Then, trim the sheet just enough to put the headsail luff to sleep. Next, trim the mainsail luff with the mainsheet in the same manner.

EVERY BOAT'S BEST BALANCE INDICATOR

▶ In all weather conditions, you should be able to hold your course with less than 4 degrees of rudder. If you can steer the boat by wheel or tiller with two or three fingertips, you've balanced her to perfection.

How to Shape Headsails for Power or Speed

Unlike a mainsail, a headsail has only one supported edge. But like the main, we need to make every effort to keep draft properly located.

Headsail luff control system. Control the draft of a headsail with halyard tension. Headsail draft should stay between 35% to 45% aft of the luff. Use the table below as a rough guide for setting headsail draft.

- 35% (breezy to heavy winds)
- 40% (light to moderate winds)
- 45% (very light winds; "ghosting")

Headsail leech and foot control. All headsail leech and foot trim needs to start from a "neutral" sheet-block position along the track. Use these three steps to find and mark the neutral position.

1. Mark the middle of the headsail luff with tape. On boats with roller furling, estimate by eye the center point of the luff. We'll refer to this point as your headsail's *mid-luff point.*

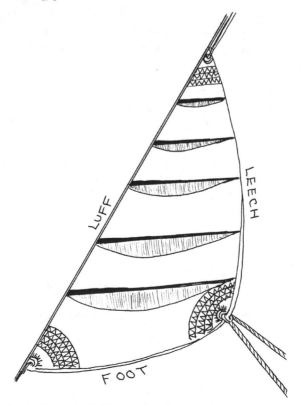

The draft of a headsail is controlled for speed and power.

2. Move the sheet block forward or aft on its track until the mid-luff point, the clew, the sheet, and the block describe a single straight line. You have found the neutral block position.
3. Mark this position on both genoa tracks. Repeat this procedure on trunk-mounted jib tracks (short strips of track mounted on the coachroof) for a smaller headsail if your boat has them.
4. Position both sheet lead blocks at the neutral position. Trim the headsail leech as shown above according to wind conditions. Always try to match the headsail and mainsail leech curves after trimming. Take care not to overtrim the headsail, which will cause the main to *backwind*, or bubble along its luff.

Medium-air trim; lead blocks in neutral position. In 6 to 10 knots of wind, keep the blocks at the neutral position. This evenly distributes foot and leech tension.

Light-air position; lead blocks forward of neutral position (power up). In light air, move the blocks forward. This places less tension on the foot and more on the leech, resulting in a fuller sail and more forward drive to punch through a chop.

Heavy-air position; lead blocks aft of neutral position (depower). As winds increase, start moving the blocks aft. This tensions the foot more than the leech, resulting in a flatter sail with more leech twist aloft.

SEA-CRET TIP

▶ Make sheet lead block changes one track hole at a time. Move one stop and check your speed. Repeat until you are satisfied.

▶ Always move *both* lead blocks together. Set the working sheet lead block; then match the lazy sheet lead block. If the working sheet block is under too much tension to be moved, adjust the lazy sheet lead block, then tack and adjust the former working block, which is now lazy. If you have a furling headsail, you might need to reposition the blocks after you partially furl the sail to a reefed position.

Take Note of Your Boat after Trimming Your Sails

After you trim any sail, make sure to check these three things:

Did the boat accelerate or decelerate? Watch the relative motion of objects (piers, boats) against the shoreline. In very light winds, observe your boatspeed relative to your wake trail bubbles. Look astern and note if the bubbles appear to leave the boat faster than before. Or watch flotsam in the water, such as leaves or seaweed. Keep the sails full and drawing by moving the crew to leeward and a bit forward.

What are those luffs telling you? Do you see a smooth or fluttering luff on each sail? A fluttering luff suggests an undertrimmed sail. A sail with a smooth luff might be in perfect trim, but it might also be overtrimmed, or stalled. Overtrimmed sails cause the boat to move sideways more than ahead. Use the luff-and-sleep trim method described earlier to trim to perfection.

How does the helm feel? The helm should remain light (fingertip pressure) and the boat easy to control. A well-balanced boat will almost steer herself, even when the going gets tough.

Three Easy Steps for Heavy Weather Control

To sail well is to have complete control over the sailboat at all times.
—STEVE COLGATE, *MANUAL OF BASIC SAILING THEORY*

As the wind freshens, go through a three-phase system to balance your boat to perfection. Follow the guidelines discussed earlier in the chapter to set the draft position, draft depth, and leech twist. If the boat still labors, reduce sail (outlined below) right away.

After any change, check the feel of the helm and the behavior of the boat. Did the helm lighten up, or is the helmsman fighting white-knuckled with both hands to keep the course? Did the boat become more level, or is she still digging the leeward rail in the water when a gust hits? Let your boat tell you when things are right.

1. **Draft position and depth.** Position the draft of your mainsail and headsail as described earlier in this chapter. Set mainsail draft at 40% and headsail draft at 35%. Flatten your sails when a freshening breeze heels the boat excessively or builds up excessive weather helm.
2. **Leech twist.** Twist both sails to keep the upper half flat. Ease the mainsail and headsail sheets. Move the mainsheet traveler car to leeward; position both headsail sheet blocks aft of the neutral position.
3. **Reduce sail area.** Reef earlier than you think necessary. It's easier to shake out a reef than to tie one in when the wind is howling, the deck is pitching, and spray is blasting the crew. Follow the steps below to reef your main and headsail.

Reducing Mainsail Area (Jiffy Reefing)

Jiffy reefing speeds the time it takes to reduce the area of a mainsail. This system uses only two lines to reduce the sail's size. With practice, you can jiffy reef a mainsail by yourself in under three minutes.

Note: some modern boats have mainsails that roll up onto a vertical furling unit inside the mast. This method will not work with the horizontal battens that stiffen a mainsail's leech and give it its characteristic convex profile, or roach. Without battens a mainsail can have no roach, and without roach it becomes a smaller sail, so in-mast furling requires a modest sacrifice in performance. (Ways around this have been developed, including vertical battens and deflatable battens, but these are not yet mainstream solutions.) Its great advantage is that it is easy and convenient when it works right, and many a shorthanded crew swears by in-mast furling. However, it adds a lot of complexity to reefing, so you will need to work out an alternative way of sailing, or sail under headsail alone, if the mechanism fails.

To jiffy reef:

1. Set the topping lift to maintain a horizontal boom when the main is lowered. Slack the mainsheet and boom vang.
2. With the mainsail luffing, ease the main halyard until you can haul the reefed tack cringle down to the tack position, where it is secured either by the reefing line or by passing the cringle over the windward ram's horn (a curved hook attached to the boom).
3. Retension the halyard. The tack and head cringles need to take all the loads in a reefed sail.
4. Pull on the clew reef line to haul the boom up to the clew reef cringle. Set the clew with good outhaul and downhaul tension. Ease the topping lift so it is no longer taking a strain. Trim the reefed sail.

SEA-CRET TIP

▶ Don't concern yourself with furling the excess material in a reefed mainsail foot right away. Get the boat balanced and level first.

▶ Before furling the bunt of the reefed main, sheet the boom in hard to the centerline. This gives the crew a solid handhold.

▶ Keep the reef tie points *very* loose. This keeps the sail from tearing at the tie point or along a nearby seam.

Reducing Headsail Area

Either partially furl your roller-furled headsail to a reefed position, or change to a smaller headsail to reduce your headsail area. If the latter, hank on a lapper (mule), working jib, or spitfire (storm jib): A lapper is a small, short-luff, high-clewed genoa with a 110% to 130% overlap. It provides excellent power in a chop combined with good visibility under the foot.

In either event, reposition the sheet lead blocks: Especially with high-clewed headsails, you may need to move headsail blocks forward to keep the leech from flogging.

ADDITIONAL SAIL REDUCTION OPTIONS

Sail under mainsail alone (beating or reaching). If you choose to sail under mainsail alone, you must still have the ability to point, tack, and maneuver. No boat will point as high under mainsail alone. But you won't have to worry about headsail trim or venturing onto a wet, pitching foredeck to change a sail or remove a knot from a jammed furling unit. Sail under mainsail alone in calmer weather to make sure you have good control on all points of sail.

Sail under headsail or staysail alone (reaching or running). You will need lots of sea room to sail under a solitary headsail, with no possibility that you may need to sail to windward to stay off of a dangerous lee shore. Sailing under headsail alone when reaching often balances the helm to fingertip pressure. You no longer must concern yourself with taking another reef in the mainsail. If you choose to sail under genoa, you will want to raise the genoa tack 12 to 18 inches off the deck with a wire-rope pendant. This will give you good visibility under the foot, and a boarding sea won't stress the sail seams. Ask your sailmaker to make up one or two wire-rope pendants with eyes and stainless shackles in each end.

KEEP FURLING GENOAS FURLED IN HEAVY AIR

▶ Roller furling ranks as one of sailing's greatest innovations. It's also very complex, needs periodic maintenance, and jams unexpectedly. Furling sails set and perform well when completely unfurled. When they're partially rolled to reefed positions, however, windward performance suffers. For extended cruising, consider a removable forestay just inboard of the furling drum. If you need to work to weather in a blow, furl your genoa, set the forestay, and hank on a working jib or storm sail.

How to Remove a Jammed Sheet from a Winch

An improper lead from a jib or genoa sheet lead block to the sheet winch can cause a line to jam, or *override*, on the winch drum. Once these turns jam up, you'll find it virtually impossible to remove the turns by hand, except in the lightest air. Overrides can occur when a sheet block is positioned above the winch, causing the line to lead at a downward angle to the winch drum. Change the lead angle by passing the line through another block that is even with or lower than the winch. Keeping fairlead angles greater than 90 degrees prevents most override problems.

When an override does occur, follow these steps to clear those frozen turns.

Luff-up or limited-time method. First, pinch up into the wind, luff the headsail, and attempt to unwrap the override. Reposition the sheet block to provide a good angle to the leeward winch as described earlier.

Block and sheet winch method. Use this method if the luff-up method fails to work. (See illustration next page.)

1. Position a snatch block on the leeward rail aft of the jammed winch.
2. Using a length of line of equal diameter to the sheet, bend a rolling hitch (see Chapter 11) onto the jammed sheet between the headsail lead block and the override.
3. Lead this new line through the leeward snatch block and across the cockpit to the windward sheet winch (boats with a second winch on the same side should lead the line to that winch).
4. The crew working the windward winch should position themselves outside the bight of the line. Grind on the windward winch to remove the load from the jammed sheet. Remove the override. Reposition the sheet lead block to give a proper lead angle to the leeward winch before taking turns on the winch.

SEA-CRET TIP

▶ Take care that crew do not place themselves in the bight of a line under load. Rig the line, block, and winch to remove an override with this in mind. Always stay to the outside of a loaded bight of line—never inside.

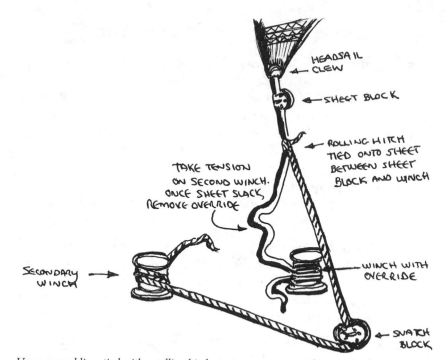

Use a second line, tied with a rolling hitch, to remove an override on a winch.

How to Sail Home if the Steering Fails

My little O'Day Javelin, at 13½ feet, skimmed across the blue-green waters of Biscayne Bay. Picture perfect it was, with puffy cumulus cotton balls pitched here and there across the blue sky over the Atlantic. After a couple of hours of sailing, I was getting a bit bored and decided it was time to teach myself something new.

I leaned over the transom and released the rudder pintles that were seated in the transom gudgeons, and hauled the rudder aboard. Now I was rudderless. For a terrifying moment I felt helpless. I'd just neutered my boat and was holding its main underwater appendage in my bloody hands! I'd recently read about practicing sailing without a rudder, but could it be done? Sure enough, I was able to beat, tack, and reach by alternately tensioning or easing the jib and main.

This is a valuable skill to practice, and while my little Javelin had a tiller, many sailboat wheels operate the rudder through a complex system of quadrant gears and cabling. If a wire snaps, a skipper needs an alternate steering method. Of course, you do have that oddball emergency tiller crammed in one of those sail lockers, don't you? But have you tried it out? You may need to remove the wheel from the steering pedestal to get enough room to move the emergency tiller from side to side. Test this at the dock and underway.

With a bit of practice, you can steer, turn, tack, and jibe a boat with just her sails. In a small boat, make steering under sail more effective by shifting crew weight forward or aft. This raises one end of the boat higher than the other. The wind will blow against the higher end, moving the low end in the opposite direction. Follow these easy-to-learn steps:

1. **How to sail in a straight line.** Practice straight-line steering first. Sail onto a close-hauled or close-reaching course. Lock the wheel or lash the tiller amidships. Line up the forestay or bow pulpit on two distant objects. Try to stay lined up on your natural range.

   Heading up. Trim the mainsheet and ease the jib or genoa sheet. Move the crew forward to lower the bow and raise the stern.

   Falling off. Trim the jib or genoa and ease the mainsheet. Move the crew aft to lower the stern and raise the bow.

2. **How to fall off the wind**

   Sail trim. Ease the main and keep the headsail sheeted in. If needed, backwind the headsail to push the bow to leeward. If the boat refuses to fall off, reef the main or change to a larger headsail.

   Crew position. Move the crew aft.

3. **How to head up toward the wind**

   Sail trim. Sheet in the main and ease the headsail.

   Crew position. Move the crew forward.

4. **How to tack**

   Sail trim. Sheet in the main and ease the headsail. When almost into the wind, pull on the windward headsail sheet to backwind the jib and help turn the bow through the wind.

   Crew position. Move the crew forward. After tacking, move the crew aft.

5. **How to jibe**

   Sail trim. Turn the boat off the wind as described above (see step 2). With good momentum, you should be able to pass the stern through the wind. Just before the jibe, sheet the main flat amidships and let the headsail fly free. Quickly ease the main immediately after the jibe to prevent your boat from rounding up to windward.

   Crew position. Move the crew aft.

How to Prevent an Accidental Jibe

With the weather going foul and the glass (barometer) plummeting, the owner roused the crew to shorten canvas and make the deck weather-ready. We were flying along in the Gulf Stream, broad reaching at 7 knots. This was the second day of our delivery from Norfolk to Miami aboard a brand-new Ted Brewer–designed Oceanic 43. Being the youngest of the crew, I went forward to assist the owner with reefing the main. The elder statesman of the crew—a gent in his 70s—manned the helm. The boat yawed like a drunken sailor as the swells lifted its quarter, shoving it to and fro. As soon as we finished the main, I made my way back to the cockpit. Perhaps trimming the sails would help ease the motion.

Whack! The boom whistled across the deck, missing my head by an inch or two. We quickly hauled in the mainsheet to center the boom. After lashing a line (called a *preventer*) to the boom's end, we led the line forward to a snatch block and then aft to the cockpit. The boom was eased, the preventer line was tensioned, and the boat came alive again.

That uncontrolled jibe came close to knocking me off the boat. Lucky I ducked. Our mistake was not rigging our boat for deep reaching or running from the get-go. If you intend to sail well off the wind for any period of time, you need to think about safety and rig a preventer from the main boom to a belay point or turning block forward to help prevent an accidental jibe.

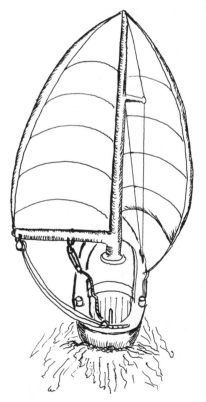

Preventer Rigging Methods

Mainsheet bails at the end of the boom make strong attachment points for preventers. Vessels with mid-boom mainsheets should rig the preventer to the end of the boom. Use a bail or attach a shackle to one of the holes near the end cap.

Smaller vessels might use the boom vang or lead a separate block and tackle to a strong deck-mounted padeye near amidships. Use nylon line for extra stretch and shock absorption. A fiddle block with a cam cleat on the lower part of the tackle allows easy adjustment from the cockpit.

Larger vessels need something beefier. Lead a line—at least twice as long as the boat—from the end of the boom, forward to a snatch block near the bow,

You can use a boom vang as a preventer on smaller sailboats.

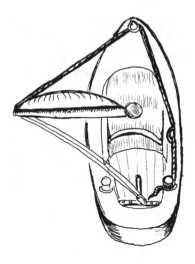

A bird's-eye view of an end-of-boom preventer on a large sailboat.

and then back to a cleat or winch in the cockpit. Pass the preventer outboard of all lifelines and shrouds.

Boom Overload Protection

As important as the preventer may be, too much tension could cause a distorted or snapped boom. Keep an inch or two of slack in the preventer line or block and tackle to prevent most problems. In heavy air, fashion a small 9- to 12-inch strop as a weak link. Use cotton small stuff, rotted line, or doubled bungee cord.

With block-and-tackle preventers, attach the strop between the deck padeye and the tackle. With end-of-boom preventers, lash the strop to the boom and then attach the preventer to the strop.

How to Short Tack in a Narrow Channel

Know your boat and crew intimately—their capabilities, strengths, and idiosyncrasies.

Most modern sailboats are capable of tacking in narrow channels less than 100 yards wide. But you must know your boat and crew intimately—their capabilities, strengths, and idiosyncrasies. When short tacking, you have to sail upwind through a narrow expanse of water. The crew has to work together quickly and smoothly, for as soon as one tack is completed, it's likely you'll have to get ready to execute the next one! Let's look at the successful techniques I've used time and again with experienced and inexperienced crews.

SIMPLE COMMANDS AND THE IMPORTANCE OF BACKWINDING

Before taking on a narrow channel with a new crew, practice short tacking in an area that challenges the crew to work as a team. Rotate each person through the sheet-trim position and the helm. Decide on a group of tacking commands that everyone finds easy to remember. Explain the importance of the three-part structure of any tacking command: prepare, answer, execute. The helmsman needs to tell the crew he is *preparing* to tack; the crew needs to *answer* that they are in position and ready; and the helmsman needs to then *execute* the tack.

The following old-fashioned commands follow the prepare-answer execute pattern: the helmsman's "Ready about?" prompt; the crew's answer of "Ready"; and the skipper's command, "Hard alee!" But I've found it best not to insist on these old-style commands; I've seen novices get so tongue-tied they forget to tack altogether! Let the crew work it out among themselves. As long as they have the prepare-answer-execute structure in place, things will work well. I've seen simpler exchanges work out just fine, such as: "Ready?" "Ready!" "Here we go!"

Show the headsail sheet trimmers how to allow just a bit of backwinding before releasing the jib and trimming it to the new leeward side. Doing this helps swing the bow through the wind quickly. Explain to the helmsman how, before tacking, to first look directly abeam to find a reference point to line up on once she has tacked; then turn the boat onto the new tack. Point out the importance of keeping the jib luff full and without flutter on the new tack. With only seconds until the next tack, you'll want to get up to speed quickly.

MOVE TO THE CONDUCTOR'S PLATFORM

As skipper, it is best to call the shots from a spot near the bow, away from the cockpit activity. First, take care to select your boat driver. Make your choice based on three things: good reflexes, the ability to follow directions without hesitation, and good concentration. Now you've found your ideal short-tack boat driver.

When you feel that the crew has things down pat, move to the bow. This gives good visibility as a lookout, keeps you out of a crowded cockpit, and puts you in the best position to handle emergencies. The skipper stays at or near the bow and performs four functions on each tack:

1. **Looks out for shoals and boats.** (Position: bow, holding onto forestay or pulpit.) At the bow, you have the best spot on the boat to see how much distance is left on each tack. The helm and crew have the disadvantage of being way back in the cockpit.
2. **Directs the helm by arm signals.** (Position: bow, holding onto forestay or pulpit.) Extend one arm straight out and help direct the helm to keep the jib luff full and drawing without flutter. You must do this to build up enough speed to get the bow through the wind on the next tack.

3. **Calls all tack commands.** (Position: bow; then mast as stated below.) In short tacking, the skipper should call the tacks. Call the *prepare-answer* part at least 10 seconds before the *execution* part. This gives a new crew time to get set. After you call for the execution of the tack, immediately move to the leeward, aft side of the mast. Keep your feet behind both headsail sheets.

4. **Manually backwinds the headsail (as needed).** (Position: mast [if necessary]; otherwise, return to bow.) If necessary, grab the sheets and back the jib to help force the bow through the wind. Your position next to the mast provides the ideal location to help the trimmer in this maneuver. As soon as the bow passes through the wind, take up position at the bow once again. Then repeat all steps.

DECISIONS TO MAKE BEFORE YOU BEGIN

If short tacking in areas with lots of boat traffic, you must not get in the way of other vessels. It does not matter that you are under sail. Rule 9 of the Navigation Rules states, "A vessel of less than 20 meters in length or a sailing vessel shall not impede the passage of a vessel that can safely navigate only within a narrow channel or fairway."

Do not attempt to short tack in areas that do not allow room to maneuver. You must have room to turn in a complete 360-degree circle under complete control. If in doubt, start your engine and place it in neutral, but remember that this changes your status to powerboat under the Navigation Rules (see Chapter 7). If you have no engine, anchor and wait for a wind shift to take you down the channel in safety. Know what the tidal current is doing (Chapter 5). Short tack during a slack or fair (on the stern) current if possible.

STUCK IN IRONS, SHEET JAMS, AND GROUNDING

Discuss with the crew what to do if things go wrong. Concentrate on three possible scenarios: getting stuck in irons, a sheet jam (override) on the winch, and a grounding. Make a few simulations to test the crew's grasp of each scenario.

Stuck in irons. If you get *stuck in irons* (the boat is stopped into the wind with sails luffing) and your boat stalls halfway through a tack, backwind the headsail. On a tiller-steered boat in a light breeze, you might feather the rudder to help get the bow around. Another option is to fall off right away and head downwind. When clear, head up, build up momentum, and start the tack sequence again.

Sheet jams. If you get a sheet jam on the winch, the helmsman should luff up slightly to take the load off the sheet. Hopefully the sheet trimmer can then remove the override. When it's clear, the helmsman falls back to the close-hauled course.

Grounding. If you ground, attempt to turn away from the shoal. If unsuccessful, slack the main and headsail sheets, drop the sails (the skipper is already at the mast), and assess whether to put out your anchor. Decide whether to use the sails or your engine to get off the shoal. Shift weight forward and to the low side of the boat in order to heel the boat and decrease its draft.

When you're comfortable, let the crew practice what they've learned in the real world. There are few sailing skills as satisfying as the ability to short tack through a narrow, winding channel under complete control.

"Your Call, Skipper"

You're the skipper or most knowledgeable crewmember in each of the following situations. What actions would you take?

1. "Skipper, the anchor shank seems to have a bit of a bend over to the left side. Looks okay to me; just thought I'd mention it."

2. "Skipper, I just checked those seacocks last night before we anchored. Do we really need to check them again before sailing today?"

3. You're sailing under full main and genoa in a moderate breeze. The boat seems a bit sluggish, and you just don't believe she's reaching her best speed. Name three things you might try to ramp up boat speed and power.

4. You're tacking up a narrow channel, and you alone are working both headsail sheets. As the boat comes about, the leeward sheet jams into an override. You have about 45 seconds to the next tack. What do you do now?

5. With winds increasing, you're starting to heel more. The helmsman is white-knuckled, and weather helm is increasing. You don't want to reef just yet. What steps could you take to balance the boat and get it back on its feet?

Answers

1. Turn the anchor into a lawn ornament or a large paper weight. In any case, don't cast off without replacing your anchor!

2. "Check 'em again, sailor!" Make sure they're operational and leak-free—each time, every time; before and after getting underway.

3. Check the luff of the mainsail. If it's backwinding, ease the headsail. Use the luff-and-sleep trim method. Match the mainsail and headsail leech twist. After each adjustment, check your speed by observing relative motion against the shoreline or your wake bubbles.

4. Pinch up to luff the headsail. Manually clear the override and rewrap the turns. Fall back to the close-hauled course. After the next tack, change the sheet lead angle.

5. Pinch up in the gusts to depower both sails. Move the mainsheet traveler to leeward. Move the jib block aft one or two stops. Check the helm. Reefing is the next step!

10 DOCKING SEAMANSHIP

Master boat handlers use little or no rudder during restricted maneuvers. Ninety percent of the time, they hold wheel or tiller to one side or set it amidships.

How well do you know your boat's close-quarters capabilities? Do you have a backup plan ready if your engine quits unexpectedly when entering a marina? How many emergency moorings did you spot on your way in or out?

In This Chapter, You'll Learn How To:
- ❀ Back a single-screw boat into a slip with complete control
- ❀ Hold any size boat alongside a pier with one line
- ❀ Sail into a slip under mainsail or headsail
- ❀ Moor between two boats with only inches to spare
- ❀ Dock a twin-screw vessel after losing one engine

Single-Screw Boat-Handling Secrets

Manufacturers name propellers (also called props or screws) right-handed or left-handed to indicate the direction of rotation in forward gear. Imagine standing astern of your boat. Shift into forward gear and watch the direction the propeller rotates. If each blade turns to the right at the top of its swing (i.e., clockwise), it's right-handed; if it rotates to the left, it's left-handed. When you shift into reverse gear, the propeller's direction of rotation reverses. A right-handed propeller rotates counterclockwise in reverse gear.

THE SECRETS OF PROP WALK, RUDDER, AND PIVOT POINT

Master boat handlers use as little rudder as possible in restricted maneuvers. Ninety percent of the time, the rudder is left either amidships or hard over to one side. This frees the driver to concentrate on stern control and pivot-point alignment. The wheel or tiller comes into play only if and as needed.

One way to minimize rudder use is to make prop walk work for rather than against you. *Prop walk* is the tendency of a propeller to "walk" the stern in the direction of its spin. Think of it this way: The blades of a right-handed prop travel to the right at the top of their rotation (in forward gear) and to the left at the bottom of their rotation. The water they encounter at the bottom of their rotation is slightly denser and less aerated than the water nearer the surface, so the prop blades get a better "grip" over the bottom half of their swing. The result is to direct the prop wash slightly to port rather than directly astern, and the tendency of that net thrust to port is to push the stern to starboard.

It doesn't matter if your boat is moving forward or backing up. If the propeller rotates to the right, the stern moves to the right. If the propeller rotates to the left (as a right-handed prop will do when the engine is operated in reverse gear), the stern moves to the left.

Before maneuvering any single-screw vessel, determine its prop rotation direction in reverse gear. Place the rudder amidships and shift into reverse gear. If the stern "walks" to the left, you have a right-handed prop. If the stern walks to the right, you have a left-handed prop. Right-handed props are more common than left-handed.

Next, understand what happens to the rudder under the water when you turn the wheel or tiller. When you turn your wheel to the right, the trailing edge of the rudder blade also turns right, and this turns the bow to the right when the boat is moving forward. The opposite happens when you turn the wheel to the left. Tillers connect directly to the rudderpost, so when you push a tiller to the left, the trailing

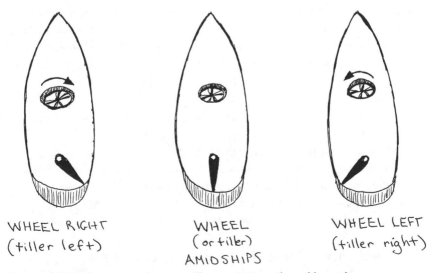

WHEEL RIGHT
(tiller left)

WHEEL
(or tiller)
AMIDSHIPS

WHEEL LEFT
(tiller right)

Turning the wheel on a powerboat or sailboat repositions the rudder as shown.

edge of the rudder pivots to the right. If you want to initiate a right turn while your boat is moving forward, turn a wheel right (just as in a car), but push a tiller left.

All vessels have an imaginary point, called a *pivot point*, about which they turn. Knowing the location of your boat's pivot point (it's usually about one-third of the way aft from the bow) will help you dock in a slip, avoid a collision, or turn in a tight channel. Try this exercise:

1. Throw a life ring or life jacket (also called a personal flotation device, or PFD) into the water. Bring the object abreast of a point about one-third of the way back from your bow.
2. Put the wheel hard over toward the object and hold it in place.
3. Shift into idle forward gear and try to make a circle around the object without hitting it. You want to keep it lined up with your pivot point throughout the circle. Make slight adjustments as necessary to find the magic spot. Then go to the next exercise.

FIVE STEPS TO BACK AND FILL ANY SINGLE-SCREW BOAT

Single-screw vessels often need to pivot 180 degrees or more by *backing and filling*. This technique uses the helm, gearshift, and throttle in combination to turn your boat in a tight space. Practice backing and filling in an open area until you are comfortable with the procedure.

1. Turn your wheel all the way toward the direction you want to turn and hold it there. If you are using a tiller, hold it hard over on the side opposite the intended turn. Do not move the wheel or tiller throughout the maneuver.
2. Sight a natural range abeam (e.g., a nearby mooring buoy or navaid lined up with a more distant pier, house, or steeple). Try to keep the range lined up with your pivot point during the maneuver. Use this range to gauge how long you can keep the boat in forward or reverse gear without moving forward or backward.
3. Shift to forward gear for about ½ to 1 second. In a breeze, give the engine a burst of throttle. You want the boat to start to turn in the desired direction without gaining headway. Check your range alignment.
4. Shift into neutral, then immediately shift into reverse gear. Leave the engine in reverse just long enough to stop any forward momentum. Give a burst of throttle if needed, and check your range alignment.
5. Repeat steps 3 and 4 continuously until you turn the boat through 360 degrees. How did you do with your range alignment?

THE SECRET OF A TIGHT TURNING CIRCLE

Use the five steps above to perform a full 360-degree turn. Make a full turn to the right, then to the left. What did you notice about the diameter of your boat's turning circles? You should have noticed that your boat can make a tighter pivot in the direction of its propeller hand. To understand why, let's break it down.

Assume your boat has a right-handed prop and you want to pivot to the right. In forward gear, prop walk tries to move the stern to the right (opposite the direction you want to turn), but in forward gear your prop wash is directed onto the rudder blade, which is hard over to the right. Since the force of the prop wash on the blade is much stronger than prop walk, your turn to the right begins or proceeds as planned. When you shift into reverse, the prop wash is directed forward, not aft, and no longer impinges on the rudder blade. Since your boat has little or no forward or backward motion, there is therefore no flow of water over the rudder, and the rudder is effectively taken out of the equation. That leaves prop walk in control, and prop walk in reverse gear pushes the stern to port and the bow to starboard—exactly what you want to have happen. Prop walk works *with* you to help pivot the boat.

This doesn't mean you can't pivot left with a right-handed prop—only that it's more difficult and will require a turning circle of larger diameter. By the same token, a single-screw boat with a left-handed prop will make tighter pivots to port than to starboard. Use this information when deciding in which direction to execute a tight maneuver in a narrow canal, channel, or basin. All other things being equal, the skipper on a boat with a right-handed propeller would chose to pivot to the right.

MARINA ENTRY AND EXIT STRATEGIES

When you enter or leave a marina, you often have little room to maneuver. The space is tight to begin with, and you need to contend with boats moving in and out of the channel, slips, and docks. Use the following checks to prepare for most any situation you might encounter.

Check wind and current. Use flags, waves, or wind indicators on boat masts to get an idea of wind conditions inside the marina. If sailing in, this is critical for decision making (see "Working into a Slip under Main or Headsail" below). If under power, this enables you to judge which slip or dock approach you need to use. If your engine fails, you will know which way your boat will drift. Study the bases of pilings for clues to current flow. Current tails (streams that flow off a piling) reveal current strength and direction. If in doubt as to whether current or wind is the stronger element, stop the boat for a moment to identify the stronger of the two.

Locate pivot areas. Look for pivot areas for backing and filling. Remember that on a boat with a right-handed propeller (which is the norm), the stern walks to the left in reverse gear, and the boat therefore turns better to the right. Thus, you should scope out a pivot area on the left side of a constricted basin or channel. Boats with left-handed props should look for pivot areas on the right side. This takes advantage of your boat's prop walk and helps you pivot tighter and faster.

Look for emergency moorings and slips. Rig spring and stern lines on both sides of the boat. Hang fenders along each side. Attach a length of line to a spare fender and direct one crewmember to carry it about the boat (rove), fending as needed. Look to the right, left, and ahead for open docks, slips, or single pilings. If you lose propulsion, you'll need a place to park. Concentrate on the downwind side of the channel. Most vessels maintain some steerage with a wind blowing between the beam and stern.

Rig anchor(s) for instant use. If your engine fails, you'll want an anchor ready to lower and set within seconds. Always have the bow anchor ready. You might rig a dredging anchor astern. Dredging involves dragging a small anchor astern, letting it bump along the bottom without getting a bite. Use it to slow the boat when the wind or current is from astern. To stop the boat, pay out a few feet of anchor line and snub it to a cleat. Take care not to foul your dredging anchor in your prop or rudder.

THE REPEATABLE SLIP BACKING MANEUVER

I know of few mariners who look forward to backing their vessels into a slip. Add a capful of wind and pour in some current, and things get dicey in a hurry. Not long ago I was out with a group of people who were interested in boning up on their single-screw boat-handling skills. The wind was blowing into the slips, so I looked forward to a challenging afternoon of boat handling. We climbed aboard a stout little single-screw power vessel, putted out into the canal, and proceeded down the channel. Upon our return, they were anxious to practice backing the vessel into its berth without any help from me. They did well but weren't quite able to get the boat lined up for entry.

They would stop the vessel within a boat length or two of the slip entrance. Then they tried to use the wheel to back the boat between the pilings and into its berth. The wind toyed with us, pinning the boat against a piling or twisting it sideways in the canal. Sailors in particular know the frustration of trying to back their boats in this way. An auxiliary sailboat backing under power through a crosswind often behaves like a sailor topped off with one too many rum punches.

The secret to success starts with knowing what happens under the water. When you shift into forward gear, the propeller shoots water directly onto one side of the rudder blade. This is the prop wash we spoke of earlier, and your boat responds instantly to the wheel or tiller: propeller + rudder = maximum control. The moment you shift into reverse gear, however, you lose the power-house combo of propeller plus rudder. Instead your propeller throws all of that precious water toward the bow, where no rudder exists. How do you maintain maximum control in close quarters? Use the combination of propeller thrust, rudder, pivot point, and prop walk.

Ready a roving fender. Assign a crewmember to work a roving fender where the boat meets the piling during the maneuver.

Align your pivot point to the piling. Approach the slip parallel to a line drawn between the outer pair of pilings. (Assuming you have a right-handed prop, this will be much easier if the slip is on your port side.) Stop the boat with the outer piling on the far side of the slip about 1 or 2 feet away, directly abreast of your pivot point. Turn your rudder away from the slip and hold it there.

Pivot the boat around the piling. Shift into forward gear just long enough to start the bow turning, but not long enough to disrupt the alignment of the piling to the pivot point. Stand facing the stern. Have the bow crew keep an eye on things up forward. Shift into neutral; then immediately shift into reverse gear at idle speed. Give a burst of reverse throttle if needed to maintain the turn or counteract the wind. Shift back into neutral when forward momentum stops. Repeat the cycle as necessary, slowly working the stern inside the slip. Pass or grab the spring line (see "Docking and Undocking with One Spring Line" below) and cleat it with slack. Snub it if necessary.

Work the boat into the slip. Work the stern back an inch or two during each forward-reverse pivot cycle. Leave the engine in reverse gear a bit longer during each successive pivot. Keep the boat moving back a few inches deeper into the slip each time. When the boat is almost square, use the wheel or tiller to bring it alongside the finger pier.

After demonstrating this technique to the crew that day, I handed the helm back over to them. Time after time, each one made a picture-perfect entry into the narrow slip. That crew left with smiles on their faces that day. And that's the way boat handling should be—fun, simple, and repeatable!

SEA-CRET TIP

▶ When you're pivoting a boat, the time spent in each gear is quite short—about 1 second. It might help to count seconds using a simple repeated phrase such as "one thousand and one": 1001 (forward)—1001 (neutral)—1001 (reverse)—1001 (neutral)—1001 (forward)—1001 (neutral)—1001 (reverse)—1001 (neutral), etc.

Twin-Screw Boat-Handling Secrets

Twin-engine boats (or "twin screws") have the advantage of a second engine to offset the effects of prop walk. Another advantage is that if you lose one engine, you can still limp home on the other. Here are a few points to remember before you take the helm of a twin-screw vessel.

Propeller rotation = no prop walk. Most twin-screw boats carry a right-handed screw on the starboard side and a left-handed screw on the port side. If you could stand astern and place both engines into forward gear, you would see both props rotate outboard. With the wheel amidships and both engines in forward gear, the boat will go in a straight line (assuming no wind or current). Put both engines into reverse gear, and the screws rotate inboard. If you place the wheel amidships, the boat will back in a straight line (again, assuming no wind or current). This is because twin-screw boats have no net prop walk.

Center your wheel. Inside tight maneuvering areas, learn to handle your twin-screw boat without any rudder. In the boat-handling scenarios in this chapter, keep your wheel amidships, unless otherwise specified.

Inboard engine vs. outboard engine. On a twin-screw boat, the inboard engine is that engine on the *inside*, or closest to the pier, piling, or seawall. The outboard engine is the one on the *outside*, or farthest away from the pier or piling. This relationship holds no matter which side you dock or undock on.

Your boat is docked port-side to the pier. You are ready to leave and want to pivot to clear the stern. How do you do this? Go forward on the outboard engine and reverse on the inboard engine. Both propellers will work in concert to walk the stern to starboard, away from the pier. You can then back clear of your berth.

Next, let's try a scenario without reference to a specific side. You approach a pier at a slight angle. You get your bow up to the pier and need to get your stern in. How would you do this? Go ahead on the inboard engine and reverse on the outboard engine. Regardless of whether your approach is starboard side or port side to, prop walk will pull the stern to the pier.

MASTERING YOUR BOAT'S HANDLING CHARACTERISTICS

Find a wide-open area to practice these maneuvers.

Straight-line maneuvering. Use only forward or neutral gear. Keep the wheel amidships. Pick a fixed object to aim for (such as a pier or buoy). Place both engines in forward gear and get her moving ahead. If she wanders, put one engine in neutral for a second or two. To push the bow to the right, use just the port engine; to push the bow to the left, use just the starboard engine.

Repeat the maneuver in reverse gear. This time, use only reverse and neutral gear. Leave the wheel amidships. Turn sideways so that you can see astern. Pick a fixed object to aim for (pier, buoy). Start off by placing both engines in reverse and get her moving astern. If she wanders, put one engine in neutral for a second or two. To push the stern to the right, use just the port engine; to push the stern to the left, use just the starboard engine

Port and starboard pivot (wheel amidships). Stop the boat. Pick a range or an object off the beam. Place the wheel amidships. Pivot to starboard by placing the port engine in forward and the starboard engine in reverse. Check your range alignment. Stop the boat. Pivot to port by placing the starboard engine in forward and the port engine in reverse. Check your range alignment.

Port and starboard pivot (full rudder). Repeat the maneuver, but this time use full rudder. Turn the wheel completely to starboard and leave it there during the starboard pivot. Turn it completely to port and leave it there during the port pivot. Maintain alignment with the range.

Use full wheel for a fast, tight pivot in high wind or in an emergency. Otherwise, keep the wheel amidships for close-quarters maneuvering or transits in and out of a marina.

Engine delay and forward surge. Does your boat's prop turn immediately after putting it in gear, or does it hesitate? One Bertram I skippered had a full 1-second delay on its big Detroits. Then again, it also carried 27-inch props. When the boat went into gear, it let you know it! Plan your maneuvers in tight quarters a bit early if your boat has a clutch delay like this.

The more powerful thrust of forward propulsion causes the boat to surge, or jump ahead, when pivoting. To offset this, engage the reverse engine a fraction of a second *before* you engage the forward engine. Or, back off a hair on the forward engine's throttle during the pivot. Either method works to keep you aligned in tight maneuvers.

Docking and Undocking with One Spring Line

In the early 1990s, refugees fled the terrible conditions in Haiti, making their way out to sea in tiny, leaky rafts. Because of U.S. policy, the president ordered the Coast Guard to find, rescue, and repatriate the refugees back to Haiti. A message from the State Department warned of violence in the capital city of Port-au-Prince. Our orders were to get in, transfer the refugees to Red Cross vans waiting on the pier, and then get underway immediately for sea. We devised a plan for a fast, temporary mooring that would allow quick departure.

We took a single spring line to a bollard on the pier, leading it back to the ship so that we could control it onboard. This kept our line handlers out of harm's way. Using our rudder and engine to hold the ship alongside, we quickly lowered the gangway and escorted the refugees ashore. Then we hauled the gangway aboard, slipped the spring line, and backed away from the pier. This method worked time and again throughout that dangerous patrol.

For a quick stop alongside a pier in any weather, nothing beats an *after-bow spring line*—i.e., a line led aft from a cleat forward of amidships to a cleat on the dock or pier. You can dock and undock quickly with this line alone. Select a cleat a third of the way back from the bow, near your boat's pivot point. Prepare the spring line before your approach by cleating the inboard end and passing the line under any rail or lifeline and then back aboard over the rail or lifeline. Assign a crewmember to work a roving fender.

DOCKING

1. Aim for a point on the pier one-third of a boat length aft of where you want to end up.
2. Pass a loop of the spring line around a cleat or piling on the pier, well aft of your onboard spring line cleat. Pull the line back aboard and take a round turn onto the spring line cleat. Stand forward of the cleat to keep out of the bight of the line.
3. All wheel-steering boats should turn the wheel hard away from the pier. Tiller-steered boats should hold the tiller hard toward the pier.
4. Single-screw boats should shift the engine into forward gear at idle speed. Twin-screw boats should go ahead on the inboard engine.
5. Slacken or tension the spring line to warp the boat flush against the pier. Then, cleat off the spring line. Keep the engine idling in gear and the wheel or tiller hard over.

UNDOCKING

1. Rig an after-bow spring line as described above. If room allows, work the boat slowly up to a corner of the pier. This makes springing more effective and protects bowsprits and protruding ground tackle.
2. Use a roving fender to cushion the boat-to-pier contact point. The line handler should stand forward of the deck cleat to keep clear of the bight. Remove the cleat belay, but leave a full round turn around the cleat; hold the bitter end with moderate tension.
3. Wheel-steered boats should turn the wheel toward the pier. Tiller-steered boats should hold the tiller hard away from the pier.
4. A single-screw boat should engage the engine in forward gear at idle speed. A twin-screw boat should power ahead on the outboard engine at idle speed. Face the stern.

5. With the rudder toward the pier, the stern should swing away from the pier. When the stern clears, place the engine into neutral long enough to cast off the spring line and bring it aboard. Then back away and clear the pier.

SEA-CRET TIP

▶ For short stops, keep the engine in gear to hold the boat against a single spring line alongside a pier. When undocking, wait until Step 5 to take the engine out of gear. Both docking and undocking against a spring line require a combination of engaged engine and turned rudder.

Working into a Slip under Main or Headsail

In case your auxiliary engine bites the dust, you should know how to sail your boat back to her slip. Successful mooring under sail requires careful preparation before you enter the marina.

1. **Estimate wind for the approach.** Figure out what point of sail you will be on as you enter the marina. Reaching or running works well in most situations. Going in close-hauled might be out of the question if the entry is through a narrow canal. Wind shadows and headers could cause loss of control. If the wind is blowing straight out of the entrance, you might want to anchor or beg a tow. Current adds to the challenge. In most cases, you should wait for a mild or slack current before you enter.

    When you make the turn into the slip, the wind will affect you in one of four ways. If the wind is from ahead, the wind will help brake the boat. Wind off the port or starboard side will set the boat downwind. If it's astern, you'll need to use some method to stop the boat.
2. **Preset two "braking" spring lines.** Cleat two lines at the bow to use as port and starboard spring lines. Lead the springs through the bow chocks and outside all lifelines, stanchions, and shrouds on the port and starboard sides, respectively. Pull the lines aft to about two-thirds the length of your boat. The springs need to stop the boat well short of the seawall at the head of your slip. Make a large 2-foot-diameter bowline (see Chapter 11) in the end of each line to drape over the outer slip pilings.
3. **Preset ground tackle.** Set up your bow anchor so that any crewmember can deploy it in under 10 seconds. Check the anchor line to make sure it runs without jamming inside the locker or spill pipe.

Have a small, light kedge-type anchor ready to toss over the stern. A small Bruce, Danforth, or grapnel will work well to slow or stop the boat. Make sure the anchor line leads from the cleat, outboard, and back over the stern pulpit to the anchor.

4. **Ready your fenders and boathook.** Many boats enter marinas with fenders neatly hung, yet there is no crewmember ready with a portable roving fender. Bend a line onto a spare fender and direct one crewmember to move about the boat (rove), fending as needed. Have the boathook ready and on deck. Stress to the crew that they are not to use their hands or feet for fending off.

5. **Mainsail, headsail, or bare poles?** A single- or double-reefed mainsail should provide more than enough momentum for steerage during your approach. Depower the main by lowering it just enough so the boat remains under complete control. If you have lazyjacks, keep the battens clear of the rigging when you lower the main. If you are reaching or running, lower the main completely once you have good steerageway. Many boats sail quite well under bare poles. After lowering the main, raise the topping lift and sheet the boom

When entering a slip under sail, rig two spring lines on the bow and slip them over pilings as soon as possible upon entering the slip. Precautionary measures to take include rigging a stern anchor and making sure your bow anchor and tackle are ready to deploy. Have crew ready with roving fenders and a boathook.

hard amidships. Drape the sail over the boom to keep a clear line of sight forward from the helm.

Using a headsail alone is an option for boats with roller furling or boats that handle poorly under mainsail alone. Just remember that this clutters the foredeck with sheets and flapping canvas. Your crew must be on the bow during the entry and docking phase. If you feel you might need to head up in an emergency, stick with the mainsail.

6. **Turn into the slip, and feather the rudder if necessary.** Instruct the crew to pass the spring lines over the outer slip pilings to port and starboard as soon as possible. If your approach is a bit fast, move the rudder rapidly in a continuous motion from hard left to hard right. This maneuver, called *feathering*, helps slow the boat.

   You can also feather to move the bow quickly in one direction. For example, to make a fast starboard pivot, spin the wheel swiftly from amidships to the right. Hold it for a second, until the bow starts to turn. Then move it smoothly back to amidships and throw it hard over to starboard again. Continue this rhythm as long as necessary. Helmsmen on a tiller-steered boat in this case would move the tiller from amidships hard to port, then back to amidships, repeating as needed. You'll be amazed at how fast the boat will turn in the desired direction.

How to Parallel Park between Two Boats

There is delight to be had from handling a boat well—and being seen to handle her well.
—DES SLEIGHTHOLME, *BETTER BOAT HANDLING*

The dockmaster directs you to park between two vessels with only inches to spare, both ahead and astern. Gusting wind and strong current add to the fun. Now what, skipper?

SECRETS OF SUCCESS IN UNFAMILIAR MARINAS

You turn the corner into the marina and notice swirling water at the piling bases streaming toward you. But a strong wind blows from astern. Which element should you choose to face? Should you moor port- or starboard-side to the fuel pier?

Keep the following in mind in all docking sequences.

Before entering the marina basin. Rig lines on all four corners of the boat. Hang two or more fenders on each side and assign a crewmember to work a roving fender. You'll notice that each of the following scenarios begins with the first line to get ashore. But you also need to set up your deck for the unexpected.

Upon entering. Stop all momentum and drift for a few seconds. Observe whether wind or current dominates. If possible, always make an approach into the stronger of the two elements.

Side control. Think of any vessel, power or sail, as having three "sides"—bow, stern, and sides. As long as we face into the wind or current with bow or stern, we control the vessel. We give up some of that control the moment we expose *part* of one side to either element. We give up complete control once we expose one whole side to these forces. With this in mind, let's look at how to deal with four specific docking situations.

SEA-CRET TIP

▶ Watch overhanging gear, such as anchors in roller chocks, bow pulpits, and bowsprits. These can bump or snag on pilings or pier cleats. It's difficult to judge how far your bow is from the pier. Have the bow crew use hand signals or fingers for the number of feet to the pier.

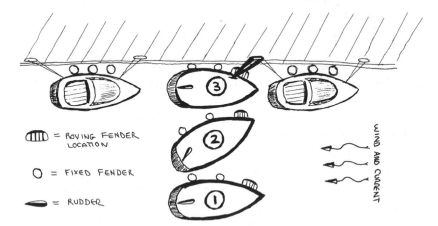

When docking with the wind and current coming from ahead, align your boat parallel with the dock (1). Angle the bow slightly toward the pier momentarily to allow the wind and current to push it toward the pier. Then, turn your rudder away from the pier and use your engine to crab the boat across wind and current into the berth (2). Control your boat's position to prevent her from setting down onto the boat astern (3).

DOCKING WITH WIND AND CURRENT FROM AHEAD (PARALLEL WITH THE PIER)

1. Have a crewmember ready with the bow line, since this will be the first line ashore. Approach parallel with the pier. Line the boat up abreast of your berth and about one to two boat lengths away, using forward gear to hold the boat in this position. Next, angle the bow slightly toward the berth so that wind and current begin to move the bow toward the pier.

2. Turn your rudder away from the dock, and use a short burst of propulsion if necessary to keep your bow-toward-pier angle modest. You don't want your bow to be blown or pushed directly toward the pier. Keep this angle constant and modest so that the boat crabs across wind and current into the berth. Watch your position relative to the boat astern. Use short bursts of ahead propulsion to help you maintain your angle and position against the wind and current.

3. Get the bow line ashore to a dock cleat or piling forward of the bow. Use idle reverse gear, along with wind and current, to bring the stern into the pier.

DOCKING WITH WIND AND CURRENT FROM ASTERN (PARALLEL WITH THE PIER)

1. Have a crewmember ready with the stern line, since this will be the first line ashore. Approach parallel with the pier and position your boat abreast of your

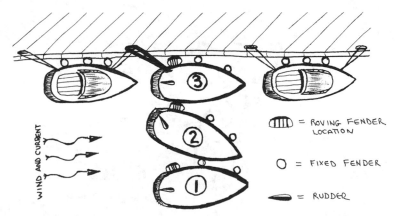

When docking with the wind and current coming from astern, align your boat parallel with the dock (1), turn the rudder toward the pier (2), and hold your station abreast of your berth with reverse gear while the wind and current push your stern toward the dock. Pass a stern line ashore (3) as soon as possible.

berth and about one to two boat lengths away. Use reverse gear to hold the boat in this position.

2. Ease the rudder toward the pier, allowing the stern to be set bodily in toward your berth by the wind, current, or both. Control the speed of your set by increasing or decreasing the rudder angle. Use your engine(s) to keep your boat abreast of its berth and clear of the boats docked ahead and behind.

3. Get the stern line ashore to an aft cleat or piling. Then use idle forward gear to bring the bow in.

DOCKING WHEN THE WIND AND CURRENT ARE SETTING YOUR BOAT ONTO THE PIER

1. Have a crewmember ready with the after bow spring line, since this will be the first line ashore. Approach the pier at a steep angle and aim for a spot just aft of the boat that is immediately forward of your berth. Use reverse idle gear to slow your momentum.

2. When the bow reaches the pier, turn the rudder away from the pier, and let the wind or current begin to push your stern in. As soon as possible, loop the after bow spring line around a cleat or piling near the after end of your berth and cleat it aboard. Twin-screw boats can assist this by pivoting for a moment with the inboard engine in forward and the outboard engine in reverse.

3. Hold the boat alongside with the spring line technique described earlier. Put out other lines to secure your position.

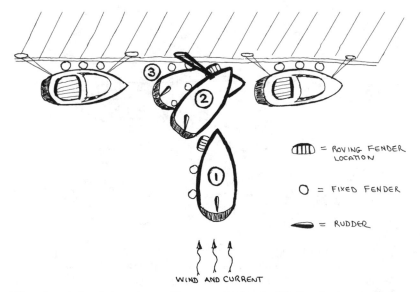

When the wind and current are setting you onto the pier (1), the after bow spring line goes ashore first (2). Allow the wind to push your stern in (3).

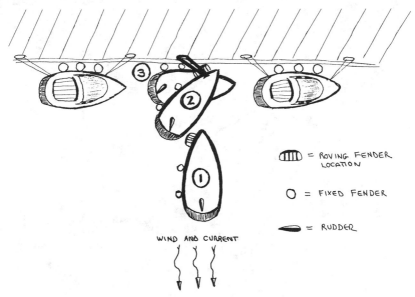

= ROVING FENDER LOCATION

= FIXED FENDER

= RUDDER

WIND AND CURRENT

When the wind and current are setting away from the pier (1), the after bow spring line goes ashore first (2).

DOCKING WHEN THE WIND AND CURRENT ARE PUSHING YOU AWAY FROM THE PIER

1. Have a crewmember ready with the after bow spring line, since that will be the first line ashore. Approach at a steep angle, aiming about for the middle of your berth. Use forward idle gear to maintain progress and steerage with minimal momentum.
2. When the bow reaches the pier, loop the after bow spring line around a cleat or piling near the after end of your berth and bring it aboard. Turn the rudder away from the pier. Work the spring line and use idle forward gear against the spring line to walk the stern into your berth between the two boats. Twin-screw boats can pivot with the inboard engine in forward and the outboard engine in reverse.
3. Hold the boat alongside with the spring line technique described earlier. Put out other lines to secure your position.

UNDOCKING WHEN PARALLEL PARKED

When ready to leave, choose one of two methods, depending on wind and current direction.

- With wind or current off the dock or from ahead, rig a forward quarter spring line—i.e., a line led forward from the boat's inboard quarter to a cleat or piling on the pier.
- With wind or current on the dock or from astern, rig an after bow spring line.

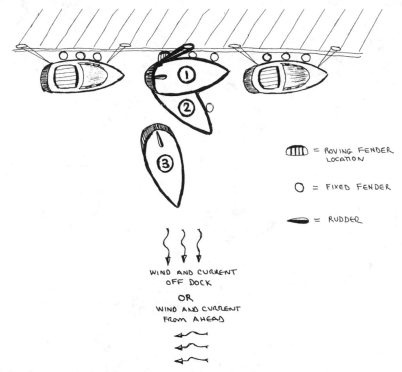

When leaving a dock with wind or current from ahead or off the dock, rig a forward quarter spring line.

UNDOCKING WITH WIND OR CURRENT OFF THE DOCK OR FROM AHEAD

1. Use a roving fender to cushion the boat near the stern. Rig a forward quarter spring line to keep the boat from setting down onto the boat astern. Take the slack out of the spring line and hold it with a full round turn. Bring all other lines aboard.
2. Keep the rudder amidships. The elements will push the bow away from the dock.
3. When the bow is out far enough, cast off and retrieve the spring line. Then, shift into idle forward gear and make sure you are clear of all dangers.

UNDOCKING WITH WIND OR CURRENT ONTO THE DOCK OR FROM ASTERN

1. Use a roving fender to cushion the bow. Rig an after bow spring line to keep the boat from moving ahead toward the boat in front of yours. Take the slack out of the spring line and hold it with a full round turn. Bring all other lines aboard.
2. Turn the rudder toward the pier.
3. Shift the engine into forward idle gear. Twin-screw boats should pivot with the outboard engine idling forward and the inboard engine in reverse.

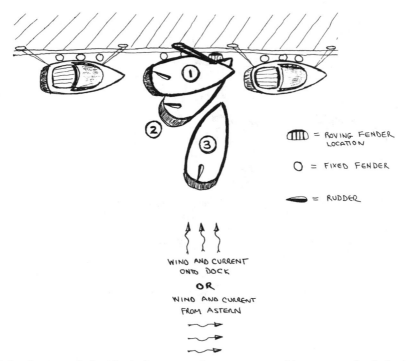

When leaving a dock with wind or current from astern or pushing you onto the dock, rig an after bow spring line.

4. Face the stern. When the stern is out far enough, shift into neutral, cast off the spring, and bring it aboard. Then, shift to reverse idle gear and back clear of the berth.

How to Warp a Boat around a Pier or Piling

Sometimes the only available berth is at the end of a pier, and it may be shorter than the boat. When we tie up, our bow or stern will stick out from the end of the pier. If you have a choice, extend the bow past the pier to protect the bowsprit and anchor.

In a case like this you may have to land on the end of the pier and then warp your boat around the corner and into its berth. Use a forward-leading spring line from a cleat at or just aft of amidships to work the boat around the corner. The same approach can help you work your boat around a piling and into its slip.

1. Attach a forward-leading spring line to a cleat at or just aft of amidships. If you lead the line from too far aft, you might lose control of your bow.
2. Hang several fenders near the point where your boat will pivot around the pier corner or piling, and have a roving fender at the ready. Rest alongside the pier corner or the piling at the corner of your slip.

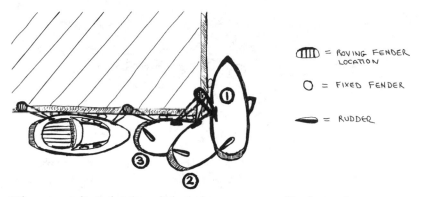

When space is limited at the end of a dock, you can use a piling for turning.

3. Loop your spring around the corner piling, then run it back to the beam cleat and take a full round turn.
4. On a single-screw boat, turn the rudder slightly toward the pier and shift into reverse idle gear. On a twin-screw boat, reverse the outboard engine.
5. Adjust your spring-line tension as necessary. Attach a stern and bow line as soon as the stern reaches the pier.

How to Dock a Twin-Screw Boat with One Working Engine

If a single-screw power vessel loses an engine, you must repair it or arrange for a tow. A twin-screw boat still has another engine, but its propeller and rudder are offset from the centerline. This creates a boat-handling challenge. You have the options of anchoring, being towed, or limping home with a single offset engine.

BEFORE ENTERING THE MARINA
Perform the following steps before entering the marina.

1. **Contact the dockmaster.** Call the marina on the VHF, explain the situation, and request line-handling assistance at your slip.
2. **Lines and anchors.** Set up bow and stern lines on both sides of the boat. Rig a bow spring line to either side. Make each spring line about two-thirds the length of the boat, and tie large-diameter bowlines in their ends.
   Make up two short-scope anchors at the bow and stern. These need to be small anchors, easy to deploy and retrieve. If you lose control on the way in, you'll appreciate having an anchor to toss astern to stop your momentum.
3. **Side and bow fenders.** Hang fenders on both sides. Tie lines to the eyes on each end of your largest fender, and lash it horizontally across the bow.

This protects you in the event of a collision. Assign one crew to work a roving fender. Have a fully extended boathook ready on deck.

4. **Signaling equipment.** You must have a means of warning others in your path. Use your radio, whistle, or loud-hailer to communicate.

ENTERING THE MARINA

1. While you are in clear water, start moving the boat at bare steerageway toward the channel. It takes a considerable amount of time to get a vessel with an offset screw steering straight. Depending on the rudder size, it may be 50 yards or more before your boat straightens and answers the helm.
2. Favor the same side of the channel as that of the operating engine. If the good engine is your port engine, favor the left side of the channel. If the good engine is the starboard engine, favor the right side. This gives you room to turn or pivot.
3. Keep the engine in gear as long as possible. If you need to take it out of gear, do so in an in-and-out motion: ahead-neutral, ahead-neutral, ahead-neutral. Do not under any circumstances allow the boat to lose steerage. The smaller your rudders, the more critical this becomes. Maintain control.
4. Use your peripheral vision to spot emergency moorings—piers, pilings, empty slips, or seawalls—on the way in. Keep your options open.

SLIP DOCKING

Put aside any notion of trying to back into the slip. With one working engine, bow-first is the only feasible approach.

If Your Good Engine Is on the Side Toward the Slip

1. Start your turn into the slip earlier than you think you should. Use full rudder and use short bursts of throttle in reverse gear to pivot the bow into the slip. Pass *both* bow spring lines around their respective outer pilings as soon as the bow enters the slip. (A bow spring line leads aft from a cleat on the bow to a piling or dock cleat.)
2. Put the engine into reverse to slow the boat, but shift back to neutral before the spring lines take a strain. Let the spring lines stop and center the vessel. Fend off as necessary, and get your other lines ashore.

If Your Good Engine Is on the Side Away from the Slip

1. Delay turning into the slip. Once you turn the wheel, the bow will make a fast turn toward the slip. Time this to square the boat and enter between the outer pilings.
2. Pass *both* bow spring lines around their respective outer pilings as soon as the bow enters the slip.
3. Back down, slowing the boat. Shift into neutral *before* the spring lines take a strain. Let the spring lines do their job to stop and center the vessel. Fend off as necessary, and get your other lines ashore.

"Your Call, Skipper"

You're the skipper or most knowledgeable crewmember in each of the following situations. What actions would you take?

1.   You enter a marina off the Intracoastal Waterway to take on fuel. It's a blustery day and you've been bucking a stiff ebb current for the past 2 hours. You rig lines and fenders. What's the first thing you should do once inside the marina?

2.   In a single-screw boat with a right-handed prop, what is the preferred direction to pivot, and why? What is the preferred side to make an approach to a pier, and why?

3.   The dockmaster directs you to tie up your 35-foot single-screw boat between two yachts. The wind is blowing at a steep angle off the dock. It's just you and your mate. How would you handle this situation?

4.   Two hours later, you prepare to leave. The wind has shifted almost 180 degrees and is now gusting onto the dock. Again, it's just you and your mate. What would you do to clear the yachts and pier safely in these conditions?

5.   After a great sailing day, you're ready to lower the mainsail, but the engine won't start. Using binoculars, you check the wind direction inside the marina. You'll have a light wind off the port beam, so sailing in should work. How would you direct the crew to make up lines for entering your slip?

Answers

1.   Stop the boat and drift for a few seconds to find out if the wind or current dominates. Make your approach with the bow facing the stronger of the two.

2.   The preferred direction is to the right. The boat will back to port during the pivot, and this helps get it around more quickly. For docking, favor port-side to. Prop walk will bring the stern in as soon as you shift into reverse gear.

3.   Have an after bow spring line ready to drape over a piling near the after end of your berth. Bunch fenders at the bow, but keep one fender ready on deck. Approach into the wind with just enough momentum for control. As the bow reaches the pier, loop the spring line around the aft piling and back to the boat. Turn the rudder away from the dock and idle ahead against the spring line to walk your stern into the dock. Once berthed, keep the rudder over and the engine engaged until other lines are set.

4.   Turn the rudder toward the pier. Retrieve all lines except the after bow spring. Remove the spring line's belay, but leave a full round turn around the cleat. Put the engine into idle forward gear and let the stern clear the pier by at least 60 degrees. Shift into neutral, cast off the spring, and bring it aboard. Back away and clear the pier.

5.   Rig a "braking" spring line from each bow cleat. Make each spring line two-thirds of the length of the boat, one leading aft on the starboard side and one leading aft to port. Form bowlines with a large eye in the end of each line. Drape these eyes over the outer pilings of the slip as soon as possible.

ANCHORING AND MARLINSPIKE SEAMANSHIP

Anchor in an emergency, when doubtful of your position, or when weary.
Nothing seems to give quite as much comfort in times of stress or uncertainty.

Have you checked all five factors to make sure you've chosen the safest anchorage in gusty weather? What two things increase the holding power of a single anchor in a crowded anchorage? How would you tie a clove hitch to a piling to make it stronger than the mighty bowline?

In This Chapter, You'll Learn How To:
- Put together a powerful all-weather ground tackle system
- Approach a crowded anchorage under power or sail
- Prevent an anchor from dragging by one of four methods
- Unground a boat with two throwable kedge anchors
- Tie five of the most useful knots, bends, and hitches

How to Choose the Right Anchors for Your Boat

The market bombards us with the newest, high-tech, perfectly designed anchors. The fact is any anchor will drag under certain conditions. And unless you physically dive on the anchor and bury it beneath the seabed, you should assume it will drag. Wind and current shifts, heaving ground swell, boat wakes, and a fouled or inconsistent bottom unite against you. The anchor must reset itself in the shortest distance in a matter of seconds. It can only do this with the help of other components.

The best way to understand anchoring is to see how all the components work together. First, choose the right anchors for your cruising ground. Match the anchor to the boat, seabed, and the amount of shelter of a given anchorage. Carry at least two anchors and keep them ready for immediate deployment.

WHAT SIZE ANCHOR DO YOU NEED?
Most tables in marine-store catalogs or literature from anchor manufacturers recommend anchor size based on boat length and displacement. But you should take into consideration freeboard (height of the hull above the water) and

Anchor Nomenclature 101

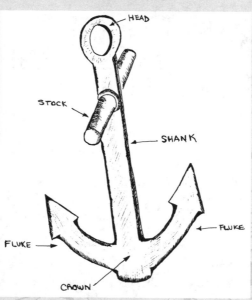

Shank. The longest arm of the anchor provides weight to help the flukes dig into the bottom.

Head. The top of the shank. The head has a hole or ring for *bending on* (attaching) chain.

Flukes. This "sharp end" of the anchor digs deep into the seabed. Depending on design, the flukes may be U-shaped, fork or claw shaped, or plow shaped. Ideally, no part of the flukes should be visible once the anchor sets.

Crown. In flat anchors, like the Danforth (see description), the shank joins the flukes at the crown.

In other anchors, like the Bruce (see description), the crown lies where the shank turns down toward the flukes. In some anchors, you will see a small hole drilled near the crown for a trip line (used to retrieve the anchor if it gets stuck, or *fouled*, on the bottom).

Stock. Some anchors carry stocks— long bars perpendicular to the shank— to help the flukes dig in. These bars stabilize the anchor to keep it from *capsizing* (turning onto its back). Other anchor designs are quite stable and don't require stocks. Stockless anchors include the Bruce, CQR, and Delta (see descriptions).

underwater configuration. Vessels with high freeboard tend to "sail" around their anchors. So do vessels with flat bottoms or light keel ballast. Choose an anchor one size heavier than that recommended in a manufacturer or boating retailer's table.

HOW WILL YOU USE YOUR ANCHORS?

All anchors fit into one of three general categories. These define how you use the anchor.

Working Anchor. The main bow anchor, called a working anchor or *bower,* is the boat's workhorse. Use this anchor for long stops or overnight anchoring. Some boats carry a second, lighter working anchor, nicknamed a *lunch hook.* Use a lunch hook for brief, temporary stops, but never for overnight stays.

Kedging Anchor. Kedge anchors are used to pull you off a shoal if you go aground. The word *kedge* is a general term, not an anchor design. Some mariners prefer to choose a large kedge, such as the Luke or Admiralty Pattern anchor that looks like the anchor in a sailor's tattoo. They load the kedge into a dinghy, row it out, and deploy it in deep water. On small boats, you might choose to go with a light throwable kedge (see "How to Use Casting Kedges for Ungrounding" below). Make sure your kedge has these capabilities:

Easy to handle and deploy in foul weather.
Digs and holds in the seabeds of your cruising area.
Quick to retrieve after ungrounding.

Storm Anchor. Use your largest anchor to hold the boat in exposed, unprotected areas (more on this later), or in storm conditions. Choose the largest anchor that you are comfortable handling alone in heavy weather. The Paul E. Luke Company states that most mariners can handle anchors up to 80 pounds without a windlass. We will discuss special storm anchoring techniques later in this chapter.

TYPES OF ANCHORS

Lightweight Anchors

Danforth. Lightweight anchors model themselves after the famous Danforth anchor. The incredible Danforth helped win World War II by getting our troops in and out of Normandy on D-Day. Each landing craft, filled with men and supplies, dropped a huge Danforth just outside the surf line. Then, the coxswain would back the boat into the beach, close enough to put our soldiers ashore. When they were done, they winched themselves back through the surf, weighed anchor, and were off again.

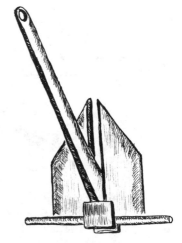

Danforth and Fortress anchors are lightweight and easy to stow.

Lightweight anchors are great in softer bottoms, such as soft sand, mud, and clay. Their design is not made for hard bottoms, such as grass, kelp, rock, or coral. They tend to *sail* (float or skip) across such bottoms instead of digging in and holding. Softer bottoms allow the forklike flukes to bury with ease.

Fortress. Newer, lighter-alloy anchors include the aluminum Fortress anchor, which allows you to adjust the fluke-to-shank angle. With ordinary tools, you can increase the angle for more powerful holding power. For instance, in soft mud, adjust the flukes up to 45 degrees from the shank for deeper penetration.

Plow and Claw Anchors

> For the primary anchor . . . we recommend the CQR plow. Our second choice . . . is the Bruce.
> —TECHNICAL COMMITTEE OF THE CRUISING CLUB OF AMERICA, FROM *DESIRABLE & UNDESIRABLE CHARACTERISTICS OF OFFSHORE YACHTS*

Use a plow-or claw-type anchor in hard bottoms or heavy weather conditions. These anchors have no *stock* (stabilizing bar) near the flukes. Because of this, you will often hear them referred to as "stockless" anchors. When they drag, they will roll back onto their flukes and reset into the seabed. The CQR (plow) and Bruce (claw) are the most common anchors used by cruising vessels worldwide. Both have good reputations as working anchors.

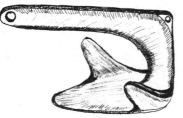

Bruce anchor.

Bruce. The Bruce's one-piece construction gives it great strength. The fluke looks like a large fork with three blunt prongs and resets itself quickly if it breaks out of the bottom. Use the Bruce anchor in firmer mud or sand bottoms where the Danforth might have difficulty digging in.

CQR (plow) anchor.

CQR. Unlike the Bruce, the CQR has a hinge between the shank and crown. It has a single, pointed, plow-shaped fluke. Long a favorite of long-distance cruisers, the CQR handles harder bottoms like hard-packed sand or mud with ease.

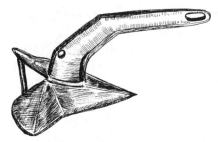

Delta anchor.

Delta. Unlike the CQR, the Delta has no hinge joining the shank to the crown. The front part of the fluke is sharper than the CQR, and the back is much wider. This gives the Delta an edge (pun intended!) when digging into poor bottoms like kelp or grass. The lighter Delta makes it a contender to the CQR and Bruce. One manufacturer claims that a 22-pound Delta holds as well as a 45-pound CQR! It beat out other anchors in testing done in coastal Georgia, which is notorious for its poor holding ground and swift currents.

Kedge Anchors

This traditionally shaped anchor—called a yachtsman, fisherman, or Admiralty Pattern anchor—can also be used as a storm anchor. If rocks, coral, or kelp make up the seabed of your cruising ground, this Hercules of anchors deserves a berth aboard your boat.

Luke anchor.

Luke. The Paul E. Luke Company in Maine makes an excellent kedge-type fisherman anchor for small cruising vessels. Their drop-forged steel masterpiece breaks down into four pieces (shank, flukes, stock, and shackle). It stows below or on deck in a locker and assembles in minutes on deck.

Choose the Proper Anchor Rode for Safety

The umbilical cord between anchor and cleat (or windlass) makes up your *anchor rode*. The integrity of shackles, chain, and rope determine the overall strength of the system. You don't want weak links anywhere in this area. Anchor rode is made up of all rope, all chain, or some combination of these two.

Rope. Use all-rope rode only for dinghy anchoring. All-rope rode is unsuitable for larger vessels because it lacks weight and chafe protection near the anchor. The weight of chain helps maintain the necessary horizontal load on an anchor.

Chain. Charter companies typically outfit their yachts with all-chain anchor rodes. Coral and rock seabeds dominate in cruising grounds in the Caribbean. Large, heavy-displacement yachts over 40 feet long with wide, buoyant bows make up many of these charter fleets, and these vessels easily carry 300 to 600 extra pounds of steel chain in their forward anchor lockers. They are Sherman tanks with Ramada Inn accommodations; it's a good thing those steady trade winds dominate in the region!

So what does all this mean for the rest of us? We can learn a few things about chain from these charter companies. Chain rodes serve as a chafe guard against bottoms that could easily saw through rope rodes (think coral, sharp rock outcroppings). Also, the weight of chain helps maintain horizontal loads on the anchor. These companies realize many of their clients know little about putting out the proper scope (see "Scope Solutions and Careful Calculations" later in this chapter). But even on short scope, an all-chain rode usually gives enough curvature, called *catenary*, to help keep the anchor set.

Many anchorages in the Caribbean give only partial protection from the elements. Large ground swells are not uncommon. That makes the yacht surge up and down, imposing enormous shock loads on its ground tackle. The sheer weight of chain absorbs a lot of these loads.

Combination rope and chain. A combination rode makes the best sense for most small craft by providing the best of all worlds: strength, chafe protection, relatively low weight, excellent shock absorption, and easy stowage.

In a system that combines chain and rope, the anchor rode needs a bottom-chafing chain length equal to the boat's waterline length. More is better, but that's the minimum for anchoring overnight. For storm anchors, stow an extra length two to four times as long. Spend the bucks and get *BBB chain*. It's more expensive than proof-coil or high-test chain, but it has many advantages. The tight link diameter discourages fouling if the chain piles up on the bottom. It also feeds smoothly in and out of anchor wells and marries well to windlasses. Cheaper chain breaks without warning. BBB chain, on the other hand, gives you fair warning of breakage by first deforming. Replace the chain right away if you notice any elongation in the links.

The other required elements for a combined anchor rode are detailed below.

ANCHOR CHAIN SIZE RECOMMENDATIONS	
Boat Length	**Chain Diameter**
25–30 feet	1/4″
30–35 feet	5/16″
35–40 feet	3/8″
40–45 feet	7/16″
45–50 feet	1/2″

Shackle Choices

Use only galvanized steel shackles. Stay away from stainless steel shackles—their pins have a nasty habit of backing out when subjected to shock loads. Stainless deteriorates in salt water when immersed for extended periods. Shackles should be a size larger than the chain you use. For example, if you are using ¹/₄-inch chain, purchase ⁵/₁₆-inch shackles.

ROPE SELECTION, CORDAGE CARE, AND CHAFING GEAR

When choosing anchor rope for your anchor rode, use nylon because of its ability to stretch up to 25% under load and recover without damage. Choose either three-strand or double-braid cordage.

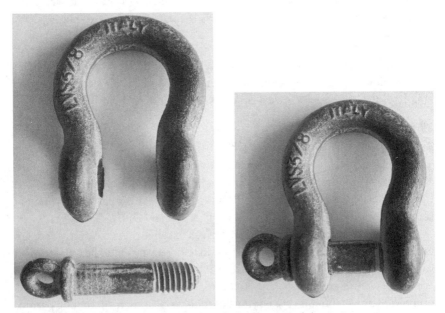

A ⁵/₈-inch galvanized steel shackle shown with the pin out and the pin in.

Rope Size

As a general rule of thumb, $1/8$ inch of diameter for every 9 feet of boat length gives a good starting point for rope size selection. For vessels with high freeboard or extremely heavy displacement, add an additional $1/16$ inch of diameter. These vessels tend to sail or hobbyhorse at anchor and need larger line to handle shock loads. For instance, a 36-foot medium- to heavy-displacement cruising sailboat with high freeboard would need $9/16$-inch nylon rode ($1/8$ inch times four, plus $1/16$ inch). Before buying large-diameter nylon line, make sure it's compatible with your bow cleats and windlass.

Coiling Down and Faking

Many sailors prefer three-strand line because it's quick and easy to splice. But it requires some attention prior to anchoring because three-strand nylon tends to kink and might jam when running out of the anchor locker. Prevent this by *coiling down*.

Pull the amount of line you need from the locker and lay it on deck. Then carefully coil it *clockwise* back down into the locker. As you coil, twist your wrist a quarter turn clockwise at the beginning of each bight. This helps flatten the coil and keeps the kinks out. You might prefer to coil or *fake* the line on deck just before anchoring. To fake the line, lay down long, narrow bights next to one another. It uses more room than coiling, but the line runs free of kinks every time.

Double braid usually runs out much more easily without binding, hockling, or jamming. Coil down double braid *without* the quarter turn of the wrist. The coils look similar to a figure eight, which is the natural lay of this cordage.

Cordage Care

Wash and dry your anchor line with fresh water (rainwater works). This helps prevent fiber deterioration and hardening from salt and dirt abrasion. Before you coil the line back into the locker, dry it by faking it over the rail or lifelines.

Thimble Choices

To protect the line from chafe, insert a thimble at the end of the rope rode. Thimble material choices include steel, nylon composite, and bronze alloy. Try to find thimbles with *keeper* arms, which hold the rope securely inside the channels. Make your eyesplice tight against the thimble apex to prevent the line from jumping off the thimble.

Steel. Galvanized or stainless steel gives excellent service and stands up under heavy loads. Galvanized thimbles tend to deteriorate after heavy use in salt water or damp stowage in a locker. Once they start corroding, rusting, or pitting, eye-splice chafe soon follows. Cut off the splice, resplice the eye, and replace the thimble. Stainless thimbles are not the best choice if submerged for long periods in salt water. They tend to rust and deteriorate through galvanic corrosion. Always wash galvanized or stainless thimbles and anchor rode with fresh water at the first opportunity. Dry thoroughly before coiling back down into the anchor locker.

Nylon composite. It's best not to use plastic thimbles with heavy ground tackle, because they flex a lot under load. Limit them to light-duty jobs such as anchoring the dinghy.

Bronze alloy. Top-of-the-line bronze thimbles with keepers offer the best combination of strength, resistance to saltwater deterioration, and chafe protection. They are the Mercedes-Benz of rope thimbles—superior to all other types!

Chafing Gear

In heavy wind and sea, your anchor rode saws like the devil in the chocks, and many a boat has been lost from inadequate chafing gear. Wrap chafing gear around the rope part of the rode where it passes through chocks or over the rail. Use old hose, canvas, or—in a pinch—duct tape. Nylon line elongates under load, so you want chafing gear that moves with the line. Inspect your chafing gear frequently, and add more if necessary.

Most foredecks have two bow cleats. Lead the bitter end of the rode across the deck to the far cleat for a better fairlead. Change the chafe point in the chocks every now and then. Simply take in a little slack or ease off a bit of rode, then reposition the chafing gear to the new contact point.

Horizontal Loading: The Secret to Drag Prevention

Whether ground tackle holds or drags depends on the relationship between the anchor shank and the rode. To see this in action, try this experiment. Find an area of sand or soft dirt. Attach a 20-foot piece of line to the shank of a small anchor. Set the anchor on the ground, bend over so you are in line with the shank, and pull in the line. Watch the flukes of the anchor. Even if the anchor rolls onto its side, as long as you keep a horizontal load on the anchor, the flukes try to dig into the ground.

Now let the line out again. This time, stand up and place some tension on the line; walk toward the anchor and gather line as you go. This simulates a vertical load. Note the angle between the line and the shank. As the line gets shorter, it pulls vertically on the end of the shank. The flukes rise, break out of the seabed, and drag. This demonstrates why you must do everything possible to keep only horizontal loads on your anchor. Vertical loads not only result in dragging but place enormous strain on deck gear such as cleats and windlasses.

SCOPE SOLUTIONS AND CAREFUL CALCULATIONS

We can easily ensure that we have this horizontal alignment by putting out enough *scope,* which is the ratio of rode to a combination of three factors: water depth, tidal range, and bow freeboard. The average scope for a combination chain/rope rode should be 7:1, or 7 feet of rode for each foot of the above-mentioned factors. Make the scope 10:1 in exposed anchorages or storms.

You are going to anchor in an area where the water is 15 feet deep at low tide, the tidal range is 8 feet, and your boat has 3 feet of freeboard. For a 7:1 scope, you'd use 182 feet of rode, as shown in the equations below:

$$15 + 8 + 3 = 26 \text{ feet}$$
$$26 \text{ feet} \times 7 = 182 \text{ feet}$$

Notice what happens if you forget to factor in the tidal range and freeboard.

$$15 \text{ feet} \times 7 = 105 \text{ feet}$$
$$105 \div 26 = 4:1 \text{ scope}$$

The Five-Factor Guide to a Secure Anchorage

The following five factors add up to a secure anchorage.

1. **Seabed.** Your anchor must be able to penetrate the seabed and hold. In Chapter 1, we discussed how to interpret seabeds on a chart. Study the chart to choose the best anchor based on the type of bottom. The best holding ground consists of hard mud or clay. When in doubt about the seabed quality, use a larger plow or claw anchor.
2. **Wind, sea, and groundswell protection.** The ideal anchorage provides wind and sea protection from at least three sides. In areas with steady winds, choose a cove protected from the dominant wind direction. In areas with shifting winds, make sure you will be protected after the wind changes direction. In the Caribbean, many anchorages are exposed to a constant groundswell. You must use more scope to keep the anchor from breaking out. Make sure you leave an escape path open in case of a wind shift. For instance, with wind out of the northeast, you might choose a two-sided headland to the north. But if the forecast calls for a wind shift to the south, you must understand that the headland could become a dangerous lee shore.
3. **Tides and currents.** You need to know the tidal range to compute adequate scope. Rising tides could break out an anchor with inadequate scope. Lower-than-normal tides could increase scope to the point where the boat swings onto a shoal or into another boat. In areas with shifting currents, set two anchors. Always be aware of changes in direction and strength of wind, current, waves, and swell when at anchor. (See Chapter 12, "Weather and Water Wisdom.")
4. **Swinging room.** Take the time to circle the anchorage and see if boats are using one or two anchors. In areas like the Bahamas where currents shift 180 degrees, many boats anchor with two anchors. This cuts down their amount of swing to about one boat length. In this case, you too would want

to follow suit so that your boat swings with the tide in a small radius. Make sure when your boat swings to a single anchor that it clears other boats and shoals. If you put out 250 feet of anchor rode, then you should expect to swing in a circle with a 250-foot radius or 500-foot diameter. Stay clear or upwind of any boat that you suspect has put out inadequate scope.

5. **Drag indications and bearings.** After you have set your anchor (if you are doing this under power, see "Secrets to Anchoring under Power"), and after the rode takes strain, check your anchor line for dragging. Extend your arm out over the rode and place the back of your hand on the rode. Any vibration indicates dragging. Pay some line out, cleat it off, and repeat the drag test. Next, take a *drag bearing* off the beam. Look for a natural range—it doesn't have to be charted. The end of a pier in line with a large tree can work. As long as they stay in line, you aren't dragging. In areas without ranges, take a bearing to a single object off the beam. Record the bearing in your log and check it often. At night, use lighted objects abeam. Anytime the wind or current causes the boat to swing, select a new range or object abeam. As a backup, set the GPS or radar alarm to alert you if you start to drag. Use electronics as a backup only, unless you are in low visibility or a remote location without visual landmarks. If you start to drag, *veer* (let out) scope right away.

Trip Lines

Before you lower the anchor, you might want attach a trip line to the crown. This marks your anchor position and helps you retrieve a stubborn anchor. Make the trip line longer than the expected height of water at high tide. Attach one end to the anchor crown. Attach a float to the other end (a plastic jug, Styrofoam buoy ball, or similar). Stream the trip line first, *before* you lower your anchor.

How to Increase an Anchor's Holding Power

In crowded anchorages, you might need to use shorter scope. Or perhaps a blow is coming and you need to make sure your anchor stays buried. Try one of these techniques to increase your anchor's holding power.

Send Down a Sentinel

1. Gather heavy chain, shackles, or lead weights. Place them into a canvas or nylon bag.
2. Attach your largest snatch block to the rope rode so that the sheave will ride down the rode. Attach a strong, light line, as long as your scope, to the block.

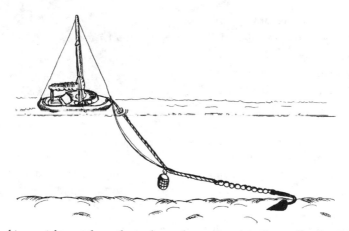

A sentinel is a weight sent down the anchor rode on a line that places a bend in the rode. This pushes the rode toward the seabed to keep the anchor dug in.

3. Open the block's snap shackle and attach the weighted bag's handles.
4. Lower the sentinel. When the line becomes slack, you've reached the rope-to-chain joint. Pull the line up a few feet and cleat it off.

Rig a Shock-Absorbing Buoy System

1. Purchase a large mooring buoy with a solid core rod and bails at both ends.
2. Make up a line with a length equal to one half of the intended scope of the rope part of your ground tackle. For example, if the rope part of your tackle will be 40 feet, make up a separate 20-foot length with a proper eye splice and thimble in one end.
3. Cleat the bitter end of this line and shackle the eye at its other end to the top end of the mooring ball.

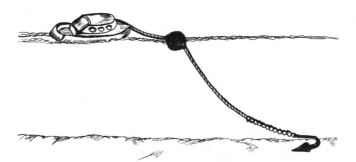

Rigging a large mooring buoy into your anchoring system helps minimize strain on your deck.

4. Make up an eye splice and thimble in the top end of the anchor line that's connected with the chain. Shackle this thimbled eye splice to the submerged bail on the buoy.
5. Lower the anchor and set it deep into the seabed. This system keeps the load on the rode and off the deck gear.

How to Rig a Two-Anchor Mooring System

Set down two anchors in reversing currents, tight anchorages, or narrow channels.

   Bahamian moor. In a narrow waterway with limited swinging room, or in areas with currents that reverse 180 degrees, the Bahamian moor provides superior security. Follow these steps:

1. Lower and set the first anchor from the bow, paying out rode as the boat drifts aft. When you pass your *calculated rode point*—the amount of rode you expect to use—mark that point on your rode with tape, marker, or a rag, but keep on paying out rode.
2. Pay out rode until you have dropped back twice as far as your calculated rode. Cleat off the rode.
3. Drop a second anchor from the stern. Now pull the vessel toward the bow anchor, slacking the stern rode as you move the boat forward. When you're back to your calculated rode point on the bow anchor, stop and cleat off the bow rode. Move the stern rode to the bow. Install chafing gear on both rodes.

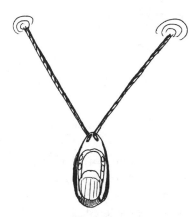

Modified Bahamian moor. This arrangement keeps swinging room to a minimum and takes up less room than the full-blown version. This variation of the Bahamian moor sets two anchors from the bow, 45 to 60 degrees apart.

Modified Bahamian moor.

1. Drop the first anchor and fall back to your calculated rode point. Cleat off the anchor rode and back down under power or back the mainsail under sail to set the anchor deep into the seabed.

2. Keep the rode under moderate strain while you power or sail across the wind. When the anchor rode bears a few degrees abaft the beam, stop and lower your second anchor.
3. Fall back on the second anchor until its rode length equals that of the first rode. Cleat it off. Then back down under power or back the mainsail to set the second anchor deep into the bottom. Install chafing gear on both anchor rodes.

Secrets to Anchoring under Power

Make preparations as described previously: calculate scope and prepare anchor rode, estimate swinging room, and select the best anchor for the type of seabed. Approach your anchorage spot from downwind, round up into the wind, and stop all forward motion. Lower the anchor until the rode slackens. The wind will push the vessel aft, or you can use the engine in idle reverse gear. Slack the rode as the boat falls back until you reach your calculated scope, and cleat the line off.

Now back the engine at idle speed. When you feel the anchor digging in, slowly *increase* RPMs to place a heavy load on the ground tackle. Watch ranges carefully abeam and astern to check for dragging. Slowly ease off on RPMs. Have a crewmember check the anchor rode for vibration (as described earlier in this chapter) with the back of his hand.

If you are dragging, decrease RPMs to idle, pay out more scope, and then slowly increase RPMs. Keep checking the rode and drag bearing until you are set. When the anchor is dug in, slowly *decrease* RPMs back to neutral and secure the rode on the cleat.

Anchoring under Mainsail or Headsail

When anchoring under sail, always make your approach under a single sail—either your mainsail or a small headsail. Read on for simple steps you can follow to anchor under sail. First, regardless of which sail you choose, keep the following three things in mind:

Control your speed. Close reaching allows the best combination of speed control and simplicity. Sheet in to increase speed; luff to slow down.
Plan your approach tack. Plan your approach tack to the anchorage so your sails are on the opposite side from your anchoring gear. For example, if you intend to lower the anchor from the port bow, make your approach on port tack. That way, your luffing sails are out of the way of the foredeck crew.
Plan an escape route under sail. Choose an approach to your anchorage spot that allows for a safe way out if things don't go as planned. Keep the halyard bent onto the lowered sail so it's ready for hoisting.

MAINSAIL-ONLY APPROACHES

1. Drop or furl your headsail. Flake and lash the sail to one side to keep the deck clear.
2. Approach on a close reach. Within two to three boat lengths of the desired anchoring spot, ease the mainsheet completely and drift to a stop. On a close reach, you can luff completely to stop the boat. When you lower the anchor, it might angle to one side of the bow. Allow the boat to fall back, and ease the anchor line to the intended scope. Cleat off the anchor line.
3. Back the mainsail against the wind by pushing it toward the shrouds. Push on one side for a few seconds, then swing the boom and push it out to the other side. Repeat this method until the anchor digs in. Check for dragging as you backwind the mainsail, and check again when you are done. Lower the mainsail when the anchor sets.

HEADSAIL-ONLY APPROACHES

1. Make your approach downwind with a small headsail, staysail, or bare poles. Keep your speed as slow as possible.
2. It's easier on a downwind approach to deploy the anchor from the cockpit. Rig the anchor on the side opposite the headsail. In the illustration, the anchor is rigged to port with a headsail on the starboard side. This clears the deck for the crew. Move the anchor back to the cockpit, making sure to keep all rode outside the stanchions and shrouds. Pull back enough anchor line for a cockpit deployment, which means at least three times the water depth. Coil or fake any excess anchor rode in the cockpit. Cleat off the anchor line at the bow.
3. Start your approach upwind of your chosen spot. Just before reaching your spot, release the headsail sheet to let the jib fly free. Turn the boat slightly *toward* the side you'll be lowering the anchor on. This helps keep the ground tackle clear of the hull.

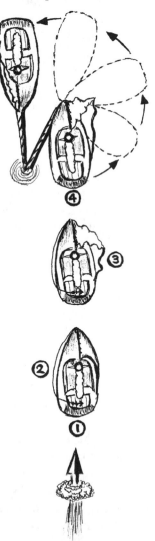

Approaching a downwind anchorage under headsail alone (see text).

4. Lower the anchor and feed the rode out rapidly as the boat sails past the anchorage position. When the rode takes a strain the boat will spin 180 degrees and turn into the wind. Go to the bow and veer the remaining scope. Check for dragging before you lower the headsail.

How to Use Casting Kedges for Ungrounding

TGIF! Friday had finally arrived. Soon we'd be off, just my little beauty and I, sailing out into the serenity and splendor of the Chesapeake. Casting off, I pointed toward one of my favorite secret hideaways, a perfect anchorage tucked just off the Poquoson River. The anchor set deeply into the hard muddy bottom early that evening. As I sipped a cup of joe in the cockpit, the sun seemed to wink "Good night"—just before slipping beneath the horizon.

Sunrise greeted us with a brisk southwester, promising a fine sailing day. After a lazy breakfast, I hoisted the main, weighed anchor, and reached out of the perfect cove. Just outside the entrance, I lashed the tiller and went forward to raise the working jib. The little sail went up without a hitch, and I made my way back to the cockpit. And that's when I heard the thunder.

The whole foot of the jib was shaking violently, pouring over the leeward rail. I had forgotten to set the tack into the stemhead shackle. Glancing at the chart, I guessed that I could continue another few hundred yards before I needed to tack to clear the shoal ahead. I charged up to the mast, slacked off a couple of feet of jib halyard, and started moving toward the forestay. A moment later my boat slammed into the mud, stopping with a jolt that almost knocked me off my feet.

Down came the jib and main to keep the boat from driving any farther onto the mud. Out came two 2.5-pound Bruce anchors from the aft lazarette. I quickly tied the bitter end of the line from one of these tiny anchors to a stern cleat, coiled the line, and climbed on top of the lazarette hatch cover. I heaved the anchor out toward deep water and pulled until the flukes dug in. Then I led the line to a sheet winch, took a couple of wraps, and started cranking. The boat started creeping foot by foot toward the anchor. As the boat closed in on the little Bruce, I stopped cranking and readied the second mini-hook.

I cast the second anchor, pulled until it took a hefty bite on the bottom, and then led it to the other sheet winch. I then pulled up the first anchor and hoisted it aboard. Then I heaved around on the second anchor. I repeated this sequence several more times, finally sliding off the muddy shelf into deeper water. Free at last! Upon inspecting the bilges, I found that the boat was dry as a bone, so no harm done. The little casting kedges had come through like champs to save the day!

Kedge anchors have a great history of helping free grounded ships from rocky shoals. The traditional kedge looks like one of those sailor tattoos, with U-shaped flukes and a long shank. Smaller vessels often need something light and throwable.

Most groundings aren't serious, just aggravating. But all of us ground now and then. Read on for advice on choosing a casting kedge anchor and rode, followed by simple steps on how to use a casting kedge for ungrounding your boat.

Casting kedge anchor selection. You'll need to purchase two throwable kedges. The 2.5-pound Bruce anchor is ideal. It has no moving parts and sets quickly. You might also try a strong folding or fixed grapnel anchor.

Casting kedge line selection. Use two 100-foot lengths of $5/16$- or $3/8$-inch nylon line. Bend a shackle onto the ring at the end of each shank. Tie a bowline to the shackle and coil the line.

1. **Coil and cast.** Pass the bitter end of your line over and back under the stern rail and secure it to a quarter cleat. Coil the remainder of the line (coil toward the end with the anchor). Brace yourself at the stern rail. Break the coil in half, with the nondominant hand holding that part of the coil closest to the cleat. Taking care not to snag the backstay, throw the anchor as far as possible toward deeper water. If the first throw falls short of where you intended, haul in the anchor, re-coil the rode, and try again. When the anchor touches bottom, tug on the line a few times until you feel the flukes dig in.
2. **Take the bitter end to a winch.** Remove the bitter end from the quarter cleat and move it to a sheet winch. Take at least three wraps on the drum, then cleat the line (standard winch) or pass it over the stripper arm and into the self-tailer jaws (self-tailing winch).
3. **Shift crew weight to the bow.** Move your crew to the bow and onto the same side as your line and winch. This heels the boat, lifts the stern, and decreases draft.
4. **Start grinding slowly.** Grind until you have a lot of strain on the line. When the rode is taut, stop grinding. If you see no apparent movement, have the crew shift their weight from side to side while staying in the forward half of the boat. When the boat begins to move astern, continue grinding slowly, maintaining a constant strain on the kedge. Stop grinding when you're within a few yards of the anchor, because further grinding would risk breaking out the anchor.
5. **Cast out the second kedge.** Use the same process and cast out the other kedge as far past the first as possible. Take the second kedge line to the remaining sheet winch and make it taut. Retrieve the first kedge and repeat the procedure until you are free.

How to Make a Snubber Bridle for an All-Chain Rode

To relieve shock loads on an all-chain anchor rode, rig a nylon line snubber bridle. This takes the strain off the rode and keeps things quieter in the cabin. All-chain rodes without snubbers tend to rub and bang on the hull, and this can cause a racket down below.

Making your snubber bridle. Splice a 1-foot-diameter eye in one end of each line. Splice a thimbled eye into the other end of each line. Attach your thimbled eyes to the oversized galvanized shackle. Stow your bridle.

Using your snubber bridle.

1. Set the anchor in the usual manner.

> ### Tools Needed to Make a Snubber Bridle
>
> ▸ 2 12-foot lengths of 3-strand ¹/₂-inch nylon line
> ▸ 2 stainless steel thimbles
> ▸ 1 galvanized shackle (same size as used on your anchor rode)
> ▸ 1 oversized galvanized shackle

2. Pass the large eye of each bridle end under your bow cleat legs and around the horns.
3. Use the second, regular-sized shackle to bend the apex of the bridle (i.e., the oversized shackle attached to the two thimbled eyes) onto the chain rode near the windlass.
4. Ease the chain rode out by hand or with the windlass until the bridle takes all strain.
5. Wrap chafing gear around the bridle lines where they rub the edge of the deck or inside the chocks.

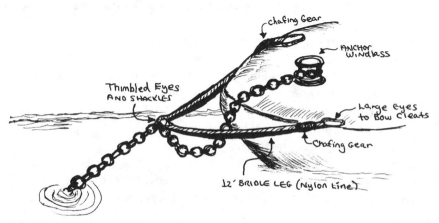

A snubber bridle for an all-chain rode.

The Five Kings of Marlinspike Seamanship

The seaman's abilities are put to the test with the grace and speed with which he turns the knot, bend, or hitch.

Few subjects seem more hotly debated by sailors than the subject of which knots you need to know. Most of us might settle with the advice of a learned world cruiser or racer we know, but it often seems their counsel applies to their unique vessel. Better candidates might be those knots used across the board, which are practical for both power and sail and useful enough that they're seen on most every type of commercial and recreational vessel. Here's how to tie the five kings of marlinspike.

CLEAT HITCH

Considered the king of knots for lines that are always under load, cleat hitches serve as belaying points for heavily loaded sheets, halyards, docking lines, and anchor rodes. We often have to partially undress the hitch under tension to spring a boat into a dock or veer anchor rode.

1. **Touch the "far side" first.** Always start this hitch by pulling the line to the cleat horn *farthest* from the load. Then, loop the line around the cleat base, under and around the opposite horn. If under tension, make sure you stand on the far side, facing the load.

Line Lingo

Bitter end—either end of a piece of line (all line has two bitter ends)

Standing part—the idle, inactive part of a line

Bight—a loop in a line; coils are multiple loops or bights

Knot—a general term for knots, bends, and hitches

Bend—bends tie a line onto another line, mast, boom, becket, block, or rail

Hitch—passing a bight of line over something; a line is hitched to a post, rail, boom, spar, or hook, usually over or under the same line

Splice—nautical weaving; unlay the strands from a bitter end and pass them under and over the strands of a line

Whipping—passing twine around either or both bitter ends to keep them from unraveling

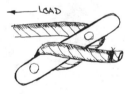 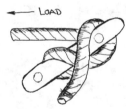 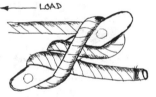

Tying a cleat hitch.

Cleat Hitch without the Final Half Hitch

There are instances where you would not want to make a final "locking turn" on the cleat hitch. For example, lines used on sailboat sheet winches usually shouldn't include the final half hitch. Dock lines that surge (strain) with a large range of tide or in storms should not be half hitched. In either case, you risk having the half hitch freeze onto the horn. But you must use caution if making up a cleat hitch without one. Use extra figure eights around the horns and then snug up the bitter end by passing a full turn around the cleat base. The cleat must be large enough to accept extra turns and allow a full round turn at its base. Let each situation guide your decision.

2. **Make a figure eight.** Wrap one full figure eight from horn to horn. It's not necessary to make more than one.
3. **Lock the half hitch to the lay.** Finish with a half hitch. The bitter end should lie parallel alongside the first hitch. Remove all slack.

BOWLINE

It was another perfect November day for frostbiting—until that 25-knot gust struck out of nowhere! With no time to release the mainsheet, I flipped the boat in shallow water, about 200 yards from shore. The tiny 14-footer rolled 180 degrees before planting its mast firmly into the muddy bottom of Charleston Harbor. The boat resisted every attempt to right her. As tempting as that lee shore looked, I decided to stick with the boat and wait it out. It turned out to be a good decision.

I pulled myself up onto the boat's whale-belly bottom, wrapped one arm around the centerboard, and waved like a fool with the other. Since I was well outside the channel proper, no one saw me. And it was getting colder by the minute. Matter of fact, I was quickly losing feeling in my submerged legs. I prayed that help would arrive soon.

Finally I saw them, riding that glorious white thoroughbred with a flaming-red racing stripe. Aye, with a bone in her teeth she was steaming dead for me! They came alongside and asked me how I was. "Hi guys, thanks for stopping by!" was about all I could mutter between blue lips and chattering teeth.

SEA-CRET TIP

▶ Sometimes you need to make up two lines to one cleat. First, decide which line will be the last to cast off. Make an eye in that line; pass it between the cleat legs and over the horns. Then, make a cleat hitch with the second line.

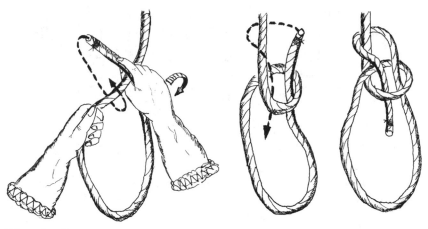

Tying a bowline.

They tossed me a hawser and I dove beneath the hull. Of course, there could only be one knot to tie around the boat's mud-sucking spar: the bowline. They hauled me aboard and stowed me down in the warmth of the cabin to thaw. Gazing through the porthole, I saw the coxswain take a strain, and my lovely righted herself. Free at last! The knot I used, the bowline, is the one I consider the king of knotland.

1. **Bitter end on top.** Start the bowline as shown. Face the standing part. Hold the standing part with your nondominant hand. With your other hand, loop the bitter end and place it on top of the standing part. Hold it in place with your palm facing down and your thumb underneath, as shown in the first illustration.
2. **Twist away.** Keep the line held in your nondominant hand a bit slack (notice in the first illustration, the nondominant hand allows slack in the standing part). With your other hand, twist your wrist away from you and at the same time, pass the bitter end under the bight to form a small loop (first and second illustration).
3. **Loop around and through.** Pass the bitter end around the standing part and back down into the small loop. Keep the bitter end 4 to 6 inches long to prevent the knot from untying when shocked.

ROLLING HITCH

Next to the bowline, the rolling hitch easily makes the list of most reliable knots. I consider it the king of get-out-of-trouble knots. Tie this knot to a post, another line, or a rail, and you needn't worry about slippage. Use it to take out a nasty override from a jammed sheet winch. If you need to go aloft, use this hitch to secure your safety line. Lash your fenders to a lifeline with a rolling hitch and they won't slide.

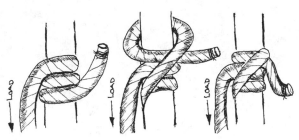

Tying a rolling hitch.

Many variations exist, but I like the following version for security and simplicity. Remember the steps as R-O-L-L:

> **R = roll**
> Roll those first two turns toward the load you want to lift.
> **O = overlap**
> Overlap the two turns with a hitch away from the load.
> **L = lash**
> Lash the hitch with one or two half hitches; remove all slack.
> **L = lower**
> Lower strain onto the hitch slowly to avoid slippage.

CLOVE HITCH

Tie it with one hand, hang a fender, toss two horizontal bights around a piling or bollard: the clove hitch is the king of temporary knots, and tying one is a must-have skill. This hitch needs a constant load or it will start to untie.

1. **Round turn and a hitch.** Take a full round turn around a rail, lifeline, or spar, and then pass a hitch over the turn.
2. **Lock the hitch.** Pass the bitter end under the hitch to finish off. Cinch tight by hauling on both ends.

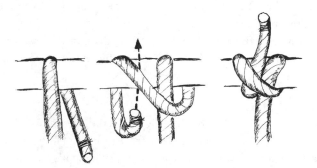

Tying a clove hitch. Left: the start of a turn; center: the turn is completed and the hitch is finished (the line coming under the hitch); right: pulling the hitch tight from the bitter end.

3. **Add some security.** For more security, pass two or three half hitches around the standing part. Take out the slack and slide them up flush beneath your clove. This turns your clove hitch into a powerhouse hitch, capable of holding your vessel securely in any berth.

DOUBLE BECKET BEND

The king of "joinery" is the double becket bend, also called the double sheet bend. You can use two bowlines or the double becket bend to join two lines together. Bowlines, however, take up more room and require more line than the double becket. Use the double becket when joining two lines of different sizes or two lines of the same size in cases where two bowlines are impractical.

1. **Larger line is the teardrop.** Make a teardrop shape with the larger of the two lines. Hold the teardrop with your nondominant hand, with the pointed side of the teardrop facing up.
2. **Bend on the smaller line.** Pass the smaller line through the back side of the teardrop and pull toward you. Form a loop with the smaller line, leaving 6 to 9 inches of bitter end. Pass the bitter end around the back of the teardrop and through the loop. Pass it a second time around the back of the teardrop and through the loop (see illustration).
3. **Make it tight and compact.** Pull on the standing parts and bitter ends of both lines. Get all the slack out to make the bend compact.

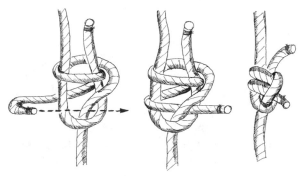

A double becket bend.

"Your Call, Skipper"

You're the skipper or most knowledgeable crewmember in each of the following situations. What actions would you take?

1. You send a crewmember forward to get the anchor rode ready for running. He pulls the rode from the locker and begins coiling down on deck. He's having trouble getting the line to coil without knotting. What might be the problem?

2. You arrive in a crowded anchorage near sunset. You'll need to anchor in a soft bottom on a short scope of 4:1. What two things could you do to help prevent dragging?

3.   Right after setting the anchor, what two things must you check to make sure it is holding? If you are dragging, what is the number one thing you must do right away?

4. How do you approach your anchorage under mainsail alone? After the anchor is down, you drift astern, put out maximum scope, and cleat off the line. How would you use the mainsail to set the anchor?

5. You are tying up to a dock and need another line about 20 feet long. You have two pieces of line left onboard (same diameter), one 15 feet long and another 10 feet long. What two methods could you use to join the two lines together?

Answers

1.   Show him how to twist the wrist a quarter turn clockwise each time before laying down a bight.

2.   Send a sentinel halfway down the rode (use chain, shackles, or any heavy ballast). In deeper water, rig a mooring buoy with a solid rod core between the boat and anchor.

3. First, take a strain on the anchor rode and check for vibration with the back of your hand. Vibration means you're dragging; veer (let out) scope. Next, take drag bearings abeam. Use a natural range or take a bearing to a single object with a handbearing compass. A change in bearing indicates dragging, so veer scope right away.

4. Approach on a close reach. Dig the anchor in by backwinding the main. Push the boom out toward the shrouds for a few seconds. Then backwind it to the other side. Repeat this method until the anchor sets. Check rode vibration and drag bearings before lowering the main.

5. Tie two bowlines together or tie a double becket bend.

WEATHER AND WATER WISDOM

What will the weather bring? Is the yacht and her crew fully prepared?
—ERROLL BRUCE, *THIS IS ROUGH WEATHER CRUISING*

A falling barometer and southerly winds warn of a low-pressure system headed your way. What do you need to do to get out of its path? How far from a cliff face must you stay to avoid deadly "ricochet" winds? What four things must you do to prepare for an approaching squall line under power or sail?

In This Chapter, You'll Learn How To:
- ❁ Use a barometer and wind direction to avoid storms at sea
- ❁ Maneuver during the fury of a line squall
- ❁ Modify a sea state forecast for greater accuracy
- ❁ Use terrain effects to safely forecast cruising weather
- ❁ Predict rough weather on the lee side of an island anchorage

A Mariner's Most Essential Weather Predictor

The barometer is to weather forecasting what a knife is to the sailor. This simple instrument measures the weight of a column of air at the sea surface. Modern barometers convert this weight to millibars or inches. Normal sea level pressure is 1013 millibars or 29.92 inches. If you observe changes above or below these average pressures, you can predict wind, waves, and precipitation.

WIND CREATION
Wind occurs when the air masses over two locations contain different barometric pressures. Small changes in pressure between two locations usually result in light to moderate breezes. Large pressure changes can brew reefing breezes and a steep chop in protected waters, or heavy seas offshore.

BAROMETRIC READINGS—TRACKING THE TREND
Base your forecasts on the trends you detect in a series of hourly barometric readings. Note whether the barometric pressure remains steady, rises, or falls.

Also note the speed of the trend—rapid, slow, or steady. An hourly rise or fall of 1 millibar (0.03 inch) is considered a slow rate of change. This usually indicates good weather; in some cases, it signals the approach of a weak frontal system. On the other hand, an hourly change of 2 millibars (0.06 inch) foretells strong wind and possible precipitation. To make accurate forecasts, you need to log at least 3 hours of observations. A series of readings gives a clear indication of what the future holds (see table).

BAROMETRIC TRENDS		
Time	Reading	Trend
1700	1010 mb	—
1800	1010 mb	steady
1900	1009 mb	falling slowly
2000	1007 mb	falling rapidly

Many mariners prefer to log inches instead of millibars. Indeed, many barometers read in inches. Yet most weather maps show pressures in millibars. Just remember that 1 millibar equals 0.03 inch.

Diurnal Pressure Variations in the Tropics and U.S. Waters

During the day, temperatures rise and the atmosphere becomes less dense. During the evening, temperatures fall and the atmosphere becomes more dense. This causes a subtle shift in barometric pressure, called the diurnal (daily) variation. The amount of variation depends on the time of day and your location relative to the equator. At 0400 and 1600, readings are slightly lower than normal. At 1000 and 2200, readings are slightly higher than normal. From the equator to a latitude of 23 1/2 degrees north or south (between the Tropics of Capricorn and Cancer), the diurnal variation averages about 3 millibars (or 0.09 inch). The farther north or south you travel from the equator, the less the diurnal variation. Over most of the U.S., the diurnal variation averages 1 to 2 millibars. In Northern Europe you might find only 1 millibar of diurnal variation. Always take diurnal variation into consideration when tracking the trend of your barometer. Here's an example:

You are cruising in the Caribbean. Because you are near the equator, use 3 millibars (mb) of diurnal variation. You take barometric readings between 1600 and 2200. What is the actual rise or fall in the barometric readings shown below? What is the trend?

1600: 1015 mb
2200: 1012 mb

The actual fall was 6 mb. Think of the 1600 reading as a datum line. Because of the diurnal change, you would start your calculation 3 mb *above* this datum line. Call this your starting point. At 2200, the reading has fallen 3 mb below the datum line. Call this your endpoint. The total fall from the starting point to the endpoint is 6mb. The barometric trend is thus a slow fall at 1 millibar per hour (6 mb in 6 hours).

ISOBARS: AREAS OF EQUAL PRESSURE

Meteorologists draw concentric circles, called *isobars*, on weather maps (and synoptic charts, which is a term used for the wider area weather maps often used by mariners). These circles show areas of equal atmospheric pressure. Look along the isobar circle for the pressure in millibars. You'll most often find isobars plotted at 2- or 4-millibar intervals. Adjacent isobars increase toward the center of a high-pressure area and decrease toward the center of a low. Highs normally bring gentle to moderate breezes and cooler, dryer air. Lows generally bring squally, unsettled weather.

Gradient and Surface Winds

At an altitude of 1,500 feet above the earth's surface, winds blow along (parallel with) isobars. These high-altitude winds are called *gradient winds,* since their behavior depends entirely on the pressure gradient. At ground level, however, friction from terrain and water slows the wind to about two-thirds of its pressure-gradient speed, and the earth's rotation deflects these reduced surface winds so that they cross the isobars at an angle of 15 to 20 degrees.

In the Northern Hemisphere, the surface winds rotate clockwise around a center of high pressure (counterclockwise in the Southern Hemisphere) but are deflected 15 to 20 degrees *away* from the high-pressure center. Conversely, Northern Hemisphere winds spin counterclockwise around a center of low pressure (clockwise in the Southern Hemisphere) but are deflected *toward* the low-pressure center. You can think of the winds around a low as spiraling inward, and the winds around a high as spiraling outward from the center.

SEA-CRET TIP

▶ The distance between adjacent concentric isobars tells you the relative wind strength you can expect. Widely spaced isobars indicate weak gradients, bringing light to moderate winds. Isobars close together indicate steep gradients and higher winds.

Using a Weather Pattern Log

For both sailboats and powerboats, weather remains one of the primary factors in decision making. Do we leave or stay? Do we change routes to avoid a frontal system? How soon before precipitation begins and waves increase?

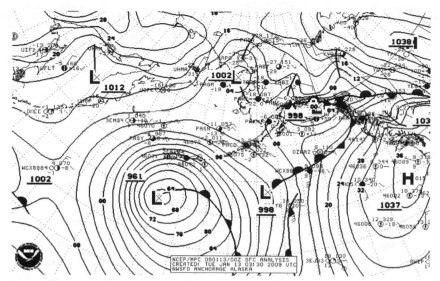

A synoptic chart of the northern Pacific Ocean: the tightly spaced isobars to the west of the 961 mb low-pressure system indicate winds that will be stronger than those that precede the passage of the front.

Do we have enough time to make port or should we move farther offshore to gain sea room?

You can make a simple weather pattern log to organize the information you need to make decisions (see illustration). Use your horizontal rows for your hourly observations, setting up blocks for 3-hour intervals. Set up vertical columns for Temperature, Barometer, Pressure Change, Wind (direction and speed), Cloud Type, Cloud Cover (%), Waves, and Visibility. You can add a large comments space at the end of each 3-hour interval. Below are some guidelines for filling out your log.

WEATHER PATTERN LOG SUBJECT FIELDS

Temperature. Note whether temperature is rising, steady, or falling.

Barometer. Observe the barometric pressure trend over the 3-hour period. Record the direction and speed of movement as follows: steady, rising slowly or rapidly, or falling slowly or rapidly. Note a pressure rise or fall of more than 1 millibar (0.03 inch) during the 3-hour period. Remember that in an area of significant diurnal variations, as discussed earlier, the readings at 0400 and 1600 hours will be slightly lower than baseline, and those at 1000 and 2200 hours will be slightly above baseline.

Winds. Estimate the direction and average speed over the previous 3 hours and record those details as follows: backing (shifting counterclockwise); veering (shifting clockwise); steady; increasing; decreasing.

Date: / Time	Temperature	Barometer	Pressure Change	Wind	Cloud Type	Coverage %	Waves	Visibility
1200	75°	30.06	—	NW/8	Ci; As	50%	2-3/N	6
1300	77°	30.06	0	NW/8	Ci; As	55%	2-4/N	6
1400	77°	30.05	-.01	NW/10	As; Ac	65%	3-5 N	6
TREND	75°-77°	30.06 TO 30.05	STEADY, THEN FALLING SLOWLY	STEADY NW 8-10	Ci/As/Ac	50-65%	2-5 N	6 miles
1500	77°	30.05	0	NW/10	Ac; Cu	75%	3-5/N	6
1600	76°	30.03	-.02	NNW/10	Ac; Cu	75%	3-5/N	6
1700	76°	30.03	0	NNW/12	Ac; Cu	75%	3-5/N	6
TREND	77°-76°	30.05 TO 30.03	FALLING SLOWLY, THEN STEADY	VEERING NW-NNW 10-12	Ac/Cu	75%	3-5 N	6 miles
1800	74°	30.03	0	NNW/12	Ac; Cu	75%	2-3/N	6
1900	74°	30.02	-.01	N/15	Cu	75%	2-3/N	6
2000	73°	30.01	-.01	N/15	Cu	—	2-3/N	6
TREND	74°-73°	30.03 TO 30.01	FALLING SLOWLY	VEERING NNW-N 12-15	Ac LOWERING TO Cu	75%-SUNSET	2-3 N	6 miles
2100	75°	30.02	+.01	N/12	—	—	1-2N	6
2200	68°	30.04	+.02	N/12	—	—	1-2N	6
2300	68°	30.04	0	N/10	—	—	1-2N	6
TREND	71°-68°	30.02 TO 30.04	RISING SLOWLY THEN STEADY	STEADY N 10-12	UNABLE TO OBSERVE	UNABLE TO OBSERVE	1-2 N	6 miles

A sample weather pattern log. In this example, diurnal variation is negligible.

The cardinal directions on this compass card will help in your recording of wind direction and determining whether the wind is backing or veering.

Cloud Identification

HIGH-ALTITUDE CLOUDS

The highest clouds appear to be solid white and are composed entirely of ice crystals or flakes.

Cirrus (Ci). These clouds, the highest of the earth's visible clouds, resemble short strokes from a delicate artist's brush.

Cirrocumulus (Cc). Mimicking the scales on a fish with their white, mottled appearance, these clouds are often referred to as a mackerel sky. Catch a glimpse of these near sunset for a stunning display of light and color.

Cirrostratus (Cs). Milky white and wispy like cirrus, these clouds show much longer brushstrokes. Sailors call these mare's tails, because of the resemblance. Check the sky throughout the day and look for thickening: an indication of stormy weather ahead. Sheets of cirrostratus often blur the image of the sun or moon, resulting in a halo around the body.

MIDDLE-ALTITUDE CLOUDS

Lumpiness marks the first sign of the middle cloud layers. The reflection of land casts a gray shadow onto their bases.

Altocumulus (Ac). These form long, narrow bands or rolls—like conveyor belts—lumped together. The center of each band may appear slightly darker than its ends.

Altostratus (As). These look like a cloud sheet covering the sky with little shape or form. When the sun or moon shines behind these clouds, it looks like a light behind a glass shower door. This often warns that precipitation lies ahead.

LOW-ALTITUDE CLOUDS

These form long rolls, giant towers, or shapeless forms.

Cumulus (Cu). Sailors tend to call these cotton balls fair-weather clouds—and as long as they remain independent, they usually are. If they band together and lower, they may rapidly change to a more formidable thunderhead.

Stratocumulus (Sc). These "roll" clouds often form at sunset and foretell of a fine evening with quiet weather. Spectacular sunsets accompany their presence. Soon after the sun sets, they disappear, leaving clear, star-filled skies in their wake.

Stratus (St). This shapeless wonder hugs the earth like a cloak, with a consistent gray color covering its underbelly. Rarely is the sun or moon visible, unless the cloud breaks apart. Stratus may hover less than 1,000 feet above earth's surface, making it the lowest cloud.

Nimbostratus (Ns). These are a gray sheet cloud accompanied by steady rain, and often herald the arrival of a warm front.

Cumulonimbus (Cb). Get ready to rumble. Though the bases of these clouds are at low altitude, their tops may reach 40,000 feet or higher. Towering thunderheads and anvil tops sheered off by super-high-velocity winds mark this wonder of nature. They finally erupt in light, sound, and hard rain.

Cloud identification. Do your best to identify the cloud types you are seeing. Note in the 3-hour trend whether clouds lower and thicken, or have vertical development. Also, log the percentage of sky covered by the different types of clouds. (The international symbol for each cloud type is given in the accompanying sidebar.)

Wind waves and swell. Winds that blow over the water for a period of time create waves, called *wind waves*. After many hours or days, the wind stops blowing at that location. The waves continue moving in the same direction, but they are now called *swell* or *swell waves*. Swell might travel thousands of miles before breaking onto a beach, coral reef, or cliff.

Take a bearing in the general direction of wind-driven sea waves. Height is much more difficult to estimate. Enter sea wave height in feet or meters into your weather log. Swell do not break on their tops, but roll in a generally steady direction beneath any sea waves.

Visibility. Estimate your visibility in nautical miles (see the table Horizon Distance Based on Height of Eye in Appendix I).

BASIC FIVE-FACTOR FORECASTING FROM A WEATHER PATTERN LOG

Use your weather log observations to give you an idea of the weather to come. Concentrate on these five factors:

Barometer: Steady, falling, or rising? What is the rate of change (fast or slow)?
Temperature: Steady, falling, or rising?
Wind Direction: Divide a compass into four parts (called quadrants); N to E; E to S; S to W; W to N. Place the wind into one of those quadrants.
Wind Shift: Is the wind steady, backing, or veering?
Clouds: The pattern of clouds can show the advance of a warm or cold front, indicate fair weather, or warn of an impending thunderstorm.

- Winds from an eastern quadrant (N to E or E to S) with a falling barometer foretell stormy weather.
- Winds from a western quadrant (S to W or W to N) with a rising barometer foretell clearing weather.
- When the barometer and temperature are both falling, expect stormy weather; when both are rising, expect clearing or fair weather.
- Sluggish barometer readings—inconsistent, slow rising, or slow falling—often indicate wet weather just ahead.
- A rapid fall in the barometer indicates a storm on the way accompanied by high winds. The faster the rate of fall, the more intensity you can expect from the storm.

- Puffy cumulus clouds that dot the sky signal fair weather. If the cumuli mass together and develop into a rising vertical column of nimbostratus clouds, expect a thunderstorm.
- The approach of a warm front is heralded by high clouds: cirrus first, followed by cirrostratus, altostratus, and finally nimbostratus. Your first sign will be cirrus that lower and thicken into cirrostratus (mare's tales).
- Cold fronts give much less warning of their approach. When cumulus clouds band together to develop into towering cumulonimbus, stand by for heavy weather!

Weather Information Resources for Mariners

For inland waters, you might use Internet marine weather sites (listed below), or marine weather forecasts (see below). For distance cruising, start with a general overview from Coast Pilots (see Chapter 1), Cruising Guides, or Reeds Almanac. Next, use resources from the Internet, along with offshore radio broadcasts (see below). In either case, include your own observations to revise forecast predictions.

U.S. Coastal Marine Weather Forecasts
NOAA Weather Service broadcasts 24 hours each day on VHF-FM radio. Most modern FM radios have a WX1 and WX2 button. Push one or the other and select the clearest channel. Radios not so equipped should try one of the following frequencies: 162.400, 162.425, 162.450, 162.475, 162.500, 162.525 or 162.550 FM. Coverage includes the coastline of the United States, Great Lakes, Hawaii, and the populated coast of Alaska offshore to 25 nautical miles.

U.S. and Caribbean Offshore Forecasts
For a graphical point-and-click forecast extending several hundred miles offshore, click on: **http://www.weather.gov/om/marine/zone/wrdoffmz.htm**

In addition, mariners can download weather briefing packages (these include forecasts extending out 96 hours, and include surface analysis charts, wind and wave charts, as well as upper-air charts) from the National Weather Service website in the radiofax section (for example, you can get one for Boston, MA, at **http://weather.noaa.gov/fax/marine.shtml**).

High Seas Offshore Forecasts
Access the NOAA marine weather site at **http://www.nws.noaa.gov/om/marine/home.htm.** Scroll to the lower half of the page for links that show upper side band (USB) frequencies for high seas offshore marine weather forecasts. (This is the home page of the NOAA site—here you will find many resources.)

European Coastal and High Seas Forecasts

Coastal broadcasts are given by the Coastguard MRCC/MRSC stations via NAVTEX (a nautical information station on upper side band radio). Forecasts on marine VHF and medium frequency band radios provide coverage 200 to 300 miles offshore. BBC Radio 4 supplements these broadcasts with an inshore weather forecast and (offshore) shipping weather forecast.

Marine Weather Websites for Cruise Planning

http://www.buoyweather.com/
http://www.passageweather.com/
http://www.oceanweather.com/

How to Predict Wind Shifts in Low-Pressure Systems

In North America, most high-pressure systems move west to east and then progress out over the Atlantic Ocean. Lows typically move west to east over the continent but then bend northeasterly along the eastern seaboard toward the colder waters of the North Atlantic. Fast-moving lows travel up to 500 miles per day. East Coast sailors should keep a sharp watch on any low draped over the Mississippi Delta region. Expect these systems to catch up to you within 48 hours, bringing reefing breezes and rough seas.

DETERMINING A LOW-PRESSURE SYSTEM'S LOCATION

Dutch meteorologist Christoph Buys-Ballot devised a clever method for finding the direction to the center of any low-pressure system. If on land, at a dock, or anchored you can find this without using a compass.

1. Stand with your back to the wind.
2. Point your left arm straight from your side (in the Southern Hemisphere, use your *right* arm).
3. Move your arm back 10 to 20 degrees. Now you're aiming at the low-pressure center.

If you are underway and making way, you'll need to use a compass:

1. Power vessels should turn to bring the wind astern.
2. Sailing vessels should fall off to a run.

Glance at your steering compass and subtract 110 degrees (in the Southern Hemisphere, add 110 degrees).

> You are in the Northern Hemisphere and need to track the location of a nearby low-pressure system. Fall off dead downwind and read your steering compass: 127 degrees magnetic.

127 degrees magnetic – 110 degrees = 017 degrees magnetic

Apply variation to convert this answer to true degrees, then plot a line in that direction from your position. It shows you are south and slightly behind the low's center.

WIND AND BAROMETER SIGNALS

Winds may back, veer, or stay steady—depending on where you are in location to a center of low pressure. Barometers fall slowly or rapidly to indicate where you are relative to the low's center. Below is an outline of the signals you are likely to see if the low is bearing south, north, or west of your position.

Low-Pressure Center Bears South (Northern Hemisphere)
Wind signals

> Winds are backing—i.e., shifting counterclockwise.
> If the winds are southeast, the system is approaching.
> If the winds are easterly, the center is due south of you.
> If the winds are northeasterly, the center has passed you.

Barometer signals

> The barometer will be lower than normal and dropping slowly.
> If your track parallels an isobar, the barometer will be steady, with a slight drop.
> When the barometer starts to rise, the low center has passed by.

Action to take (Northern Hemisphere): Head farther north or hold position. The counterclockwise winds will help drive you away from the storm path.

Low-Pressure Center Bears North (Northern Hemisphere)
Wind signals

> Winds are veering—i.e., shifting clockwise.
> If the winds are southwest, the system is approaching.
> If the winds are westerly, the center is due north of you.
> If the winds are northwesterly, the center has passed by.

Barometer signals

> The barometer will be lower than normal and dropping slowly.
> If your track parallels an isobar, the barometer will be steady, with a slight drop.
> When the barometer starts to rise, the low center has passed by.

Action to take (Northern Hemisphere): Make best speed and head south to take yourself out of the storm path. Keep heading south until the winds shift to the northwest and the barometer begins to rise.

Low Pressure Center Bears West (Northern Hemisphere)
Wind signals

> The wind will be steady; no wind shift will occur until the center passes.
> If the winds are southerly, the system is approaching.
> If the wind shifts 180 degrees, the center is passing over you.
> If the winds are northerly, the center has passed by.

Barometer signals

> The barometer will be lower than normal and dropping rapidly.
> When the barometer bottoms, the center lies over you.
> When the barometer rises rapidly, the center has passed by.

Action to take (Northern Hemisphere): Make best speed and head north to take yourself out of the storm path. Keep heading north until the winds shift to the northwest and the barometer begins to rise.

Meeting a Line Squall

You've watched those jagged-edged clouds building to the west for the past hour. A flattish roll cloud signals that this line squall is moments away. Don't be fooled when no rain comes from these clouds. First, you'll feel the temperature drop. Then, the winds will veer 60 to 90 degrees to the right, accompanied by torrential rain, lightning, and thunder. One of Mother Nature's most spectacular sound and light shows has begun.

WHAT TO EXPECT AND HOW TO PREPARE
Make preparations when you first sight a squall line to the west of your position. Below is a list of weather elements you should prepare for, followed by specific steps to take, depending on whether you are in coastal or inland waters. You can expect the following:

> wind direction shifts clockwise 60 to 90 degrees
> wind speed is 35+ knots
> visibility is less than 100 yards
> lightning and thunder is intermittent
> the squall will last less than 45 minutes

Follow one of the two preparation and action steps below. If in inland, restricted waters use the first method. Vessels in open waters or offshore should use the second method.

Line Squall Response for Inland or Restricted Waters

1. Don foul-weather gear and life jackets. Close hatches, doors, and ports. Stow or lash equipment and gear.
2. You might make harbor, but you must be moored *before* the squall arrives. I've been caught inside a marina during a squall, trying to maneuver. We were fortunate to sustain only minor damage to our boat. If you have any doubt as to whether you have enough time to make port, anchor as described in the next step.
3. Anchoring offers an excellent restricted-waters alternative. Check for room to swing and plan for the possibility of dragging downwind. Set two anchors, 60 to 70 degrees apart. Power vessels and sailing vessels with engines should keep the engine ticking over in case you need to relieve strain on the anchor rode.
4. Have a whistle or horn ready to warn others of your location. The Navigation Rules require sound signals in or near areas of reduced visibility.

Line Squall Response for Coastal or Unrestricted Waters

1. Don foul-weather gear and life jackets.
2. Close hatches, doors, and ports. Remove cowls and stow them below. Lash dinghies or shorten painters. Check and stow loose gear below. Secure the galley stove or cooktop.
3. Prepare for the expected abrupt wind shift. Power vessels should reduce speed and keep the wind off the port bow. Sailing vessels should reef their sails. If you are running or broad reaching, get onto port tack; prevent an accidental jibe by rigging a preventer (see Chapter 9 for more on preventing accidental jibes).
4. Have a whistle or horn ready to warn others of your location. The Navigation Rules require sound signals in or near areas of reduced visibility.

Lightning Timing and Protective Strategies

Beware of any cumulonimbus clouds to the west of your position. Track the movement of these dangerous clouds and time the difference between the thunderous volleys and the white-hot flashes of supercharged energy. The most dangerous lightning lies in the back half of the cloud base.

HOW FAR ARE YOU FROM THE NEXT LIGHTNING BOLT?

To determine your distance to the lightning, time the period from a clap of thunder to the flash of lightning. Use one of two methods to determine range in nautical miles:

Divide the number of seconds by 5, or

Multiply the number of seconds by 0.2.

You have timed the interval from boom to flash, and the time period is 26 seconds

$$26 \div 5 = 5.2 \text{ nautical miles.}$$

You get the same result from using the second method

$$26 \times 0.2 = 5.2 \text{ nautical miles.}$$

IS LIGHTNING HEADED YOUR WAY?

Storm clouds to the west or northwest of your position indicate that a storm is headed your way. Take a series of bearings on successive bolts of lightning. Constant bearings indicate the storm will pass overhead. If the storm lies to the south or southeast, it should pass clear of you.

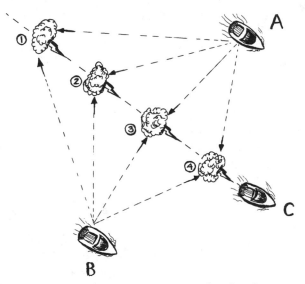

When a lightning storm approaches, monitor its progress by taking bearings on the lightning strikes. Vessels A, B, and C are several miles apart. They all sight a lightning strike on the horizon at position 1. Using a handbearing compass and radar (if equipped), each vessel tracks the lightning's direction, or bearing drift (for more on bearing drift, see Chapter 7), relative to their position. If unable to take a bearing at the moment of a strike, they shoot the cloud surrounding the strike position. When lightning strikes at position 2, vessel A notes that the bearing has changed to the left. Vessel B observes a bearing change to the right. But vessel C shows a steady bearing. This indicates that the lightning is on a collision course with vessel C. But vessels A and B should not relax yet. They must continue to take bearings until the lightning and associated clouds are well past their positions (position 4). Vessel C must take evasive action now, changing course 90 degrees to the north or south and increasing speed while continuing to take bearings visually and by radar (if equipped) to ensure the bearing drift moves to the right or left.

Protection Systems and Grounding Tips

The best lightning protection comes from forming a cone over the boat with the apex at the boat's highest point. Ground the mast to the bonding point. In sailboats, this should be the keel; in a powerboat, it might be the keel or a separate grounding block in the bilge. Always check with the manufacturer to find out if your boat is grounded for lightning protection. Otherwise, consider running a proper grounding wire for safety. In *Stapleton's Powerboat Bible*, Sid Stapleton recommends using #8 copper wire and cautions to run the wire in as straight a line as possible, avoiding sharp bends. For safety, keep the bonding wire behind fiberglass liners or bulkheads. Sailing vessels without proper grounding installations might try attaching chain, copper wire, or battery cables to the shrouds and the backstay. Feed it over the side and into the water to provide a ground path if lightning strikes.

How to Predict Wave Heights for Cruising

You're preparing for that long-awaited cruise, just a short hop up the coast. The weather forecast calls for seas running 3 to 5 feet. What does that height range really mean, and how should you prepare for it?

THE ANATOMY OF A WAVE

Waves are created entirely by wind. Every wave has four parts: back, crest, front (face), and trough. Know this and you can estimate the height of a wave, measured from the bottom of the trough to the crest.

The Wave Period

If you plan on a trip outside the jetties, check the *wave period* first. The wave period is the time it takes two crests to move past a fixed point. The shorter the wave period, the less comfortable the sea is for small craft. Use a 12-second period as a gauge for comfort. Comfort levels decrease the closer the period gets to 0 and increase closer to 12 seconds. For example, a 4-foot sea with a 3-second period means tough going for most small craft, but a 4-foot sea with

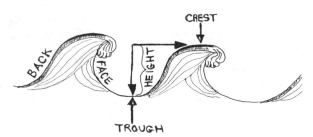

The parts of a wave.

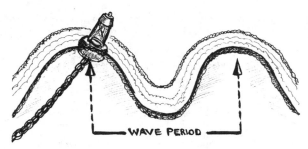

Wave period.

a 10-second period gives a much smoother ride on both power and sailing vessels.

If you are caught out in high, short-period waves, slow the boat and change direction to prevent pounding. Sailing and power vessels can tack across waves for better control.

Significant Wave Height (SW) and Wavecasting

Waves increase to a fully developed state—called *significant wave height*, or *SW*—after about 24 hours of wind. Significant wave height represents the average height of the highest one-third of all waves in the area, and it will vary according to the average wind strength over the previous 24 hours.

1. **Find SW.** Use the highest height of waves given during a marine forecast or from a weather text message. If the forecast says "Seas 4 to 6 feet," use 6 feet as SW. If it says "Seas 4 to 6 feet, building to 8 feet," use 8 feet as SW.
2. **Correct SW to give the full wave spectrum.** Use the accompanying wave spectrum formulas and apply corrections to SW. This gives you the range of wave heights you can expect to encounter.

WAVE SPECTRUM FORMULAS
Significant Wave Heights (average of one-third of the higher seas): SW
Average Wave Heights (average of two-thirds of the smaller seas): SW × 0.6
Three Higher Wave Heights (these seas will run higher than SW):
10% of seas encountered: SW × 1.3
1% of seas encountered: SW × 1.7
Highest occasional wave: SW × 2.0

The forecast calls for 3- to 4-foot seas, building to 6 feet during the afternoon and into the night. What conditions should you expect to encounter? Below is the spectrum of expected seas based on a SW of 6 feet:

Average wave height = 3.6 feet as follows: SW= 6; 6 × 0.6 = 3.6 feet
10% of highest waves = 7.8 feet as follows: SW= 6; 6 × 1.3 = 7.8 feet
1% of highest waves: 10.2 feet as follows: SW= 6; 6 × 1.7 = 10. 2 feet
Extreme possibility: 12.0 feet as follows: SW= 6; 6 × 2 = 12 feet

---

SEA-CRET TIP

▶ Estimate significant wave height (SW) by squaring the wind speed over the past 24 hours and then multiplying by 2%. For example, a 15-knot wind blowing for 24 hours develops a SW of about 4^1/$_2$ feet. A 30-knot wind develops an 18-foot significant wave height after 24 hours.

Swell Secrets

Swell—A long crestless wave or series of crestless waves in the open sea.
—MERRIAM-WEBSTER'S DICTIONARY

Swell (also called *swell waves*) form after the wind in a specific area ceases to blow. For instance, if the wind blows from the north for 48 hours, wind waves form during that period. These waves build in height and move with great speed to leeward. When the wind dies, the water continues to move through momentum as a swell. The swell may travel hundreds or even thousands of miles before it makes contact with some obstruction: a shoal, an island, coastal beach, or a cliff. If the land causes the swell to break, it loses much of its energy. But if the land offers only modest resistance, the swell continues past with much of its energy intact.

SWELL AND BREAKER FORMATION
Swell waves form as the environment surrounding the wind waves changes. Three factors give birth to swell waves:

Dying wind
Wind waves that are moving into a calmer area
Wind waves that are moving into a region with different wind and wind-
    wave directions

Swell moves slightly faster than the wind-driven waves that created them. Deepwater swell have well-rounded tops and gentle motion. Their height decreases by about half every 24 hours, and their periods increase considerably. Swell slow, and cluster together, and begin to steepen as they approach land. If the sea bottom rises to within one to two times of their height, the crest of the swell breaks; this creates extremely hazardous conditions in inlets for small craft. For example, a small 3-foot swell passing through an inlet begins to break when it passes over a sandbar 3 to 6 feet below the surface.

Some harbors are open to the sea, with little protection from natural or man-made breakwaters. A ground swell may roll into such areas, straining mooring lines or ground tackle.

AVOID CROSS-SWELL MADNESS

A cross swell results from high wind waves blowing across the top of an undeveloped swell. This creates havoc for power and sailing craft alike.

Plan any Gulf Stream transit with great care in the fall, winter, or early spring. Every few weeks, cold fronts march across North America, bound for the Atlantic coast. As the front approaches, southerly winds begin to blow, and within 24 hours the waves are fully developed. Just as that sea starts to develop into swell, the cold front passes. Winds shift northwest, velocity increases, and a steep northwesterly sea builds on top of the undeveloped southerly swell. Throw in some northerly Gulf Stream current flowing against that northwesterly gale and you have complete chaos. Many seasoned mariners have lost their lives under these circumstances.

If a cold front is headed your way, wait to make the Gulf Stream crossing. Delay departure 12 or more hours after the front passes before casting off.

BEWARE OF ROCK AND ROLL AREAS CAUSED BY SWELL

You're island-hopping in the Lesser Antilles and expect to make your next stop late this afternoon. Last night, an uncomfortable groundswell turned your idyllic anchorage into a stay at the Hard Roll Café. You were on the protected lee side, so why did this happen? How can you use the topography of an island to warn you of this in the future?

As swell approach a flat or continuous coastline, rising bottom contours slow their forward motion. Swell approaching a beach obliquely have different speeds on their offshore and near-shore sections. The offshore section, traveling in deeper water, experiences less friction with the seabed and is therefore faster than the near-shore section. As the swell approaches the beach, therefore, its crestline becomes less oblique and more nearly parallel with the shore. In general, swell will crest and break parallel to the coast.

Refraction of a Swell

Roundish islands that are surrounded by gently rising bottom contours, however, present another problem. As swell roll into the beach, they meet little resistance from the bottom. Instead they bend, or refract, on each side of the island and then continue wrapping around the back side. When the

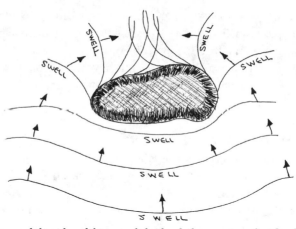

Waves wrap around the sides of this roundish island, then meet on the island's back side to form a cross swell.

divided crests meet each other on the island's lee side, a cross swell develops. Many a mariner has spent an uncomfortable night at anchor, rolling and hobbyhorsing in a cross swell. If you are sailing in a trade wind region, study the chart and look for irregularly shaped islands with indentations or coves on their lee sides, or find islands with steeper bottom contours on one side than the other. Such islands offer prospects of secure lee-side anchorages.

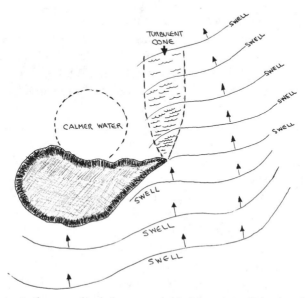

Avoid anchoring in the cone of turbulent water behind the points of islands or breakwaters. The center of the lee side of this island will have much calmer water because no cross swell exists, unlike the island in the previous illustration.

Diffraction of a Swell

Stay well clear of the area just behind the pointed ends of islands or breakwaters. Wave energy carries beyond the point into a shadow zone. This results in an abrupt change in wave height, called *diffraction*. A cone of turbulent water forms just behind each point. Swell height and strength quickly diminish beyond this area. Move to the center of the lee side before you lower your anchor.

How to Use Terrain Effect in Cruise Planning

A landmass changes the prevailing wind direction and strength; it also decreases or increases wave heights. Use these elements in cruise and voyage forecast planning. Annotate your charts (see Chapter 2) to indicate landmass areas that might cause any of these effects.

Sea breeze effect. Steady, prevailing winds blowing parallel along the coastline warn of rough conditions by afternoon. After the sea breeze fills in, the wind shifts to a direction between the two winds. Wind speed may increase by 50%. For example, a steady, 20-knot northerly wind blows along a western coastline. In the afternoon, a westerly sea breeze blows toward shore. By late afternoon, the prevailing wind and sea breeze combine into a 30-knot northwesterly gale.

Cliff effect. On your chart, cliffs appear as *hachures*, which resemble teeth-like serrations on a saw blade (see Chapter 1). Use caution anytime your charted position brings you close to these symbols. Cliff effects can change wind speed and direction in three ways:

1. Winds blowing onshore at narrow angles often change direction and increase in speed near a cliff base.
2. If a wind rolls down the face of the cliff wall, it sends high, gusty winds far offshore.
3. High winds that blow *onto* a cliff wall create a ricochet effect, and can send gale force winds offshore to a distance equal to ten times the cliff height. For example, if you are passing a 600-foot cliff in a breeze, stay at least 1 mile offshore (10 × 600 feet = 6,000 feet or 1 nautical mile).

Island effect. Study the cloud layers over islands with high terrain, such as mountains or cliffs (and remember that mountainous regions appear on the chart as non-concentric circles; sometimes the elevation is written somewhere along the circles, but not always). Low clouds near the peaks, covering all sides of the island, signify rough conditions on the lee side. Clear skies to leeward indicate calm waters (a wind shadow).

Mountain effect. Fall winds form in Pacific and northern Mediterranean regions with coastal mountain ranges. These winds rise over the snowcapped peaks and rush down the other side to the sea. They have local names—a *williwaw* in Alaska, a *Santa Ana* in Southern California, or a *mistral* in the Mediterranean. At the surface, fall winds reach gale to hurricane force. Vessels 30 miles at sea in an Alaskan williwaw have reported winds up to 90 knots!

Breaker effect. Narrow, docile bays turn chaotic when the wind opposes the current. High winds blowing into a bay against the current cause breakers to form across the mouth. Small craft must not attempt to cross the breakers until the current slackens and conditions moderate.

Cape effect. When a prevailing wind blows parallel to the coast and runs into a cape, winds and seas increase. Cliff-lined capes may have huge seas and winds twice as high as the prevailing wind. Small craft must stay several miles offshore for safety.

Strait effect. Winds increase in velocity when squeezed between two land-masses. Some examples include two islands, the mainland and an island, or a narrow, high-sided canal.

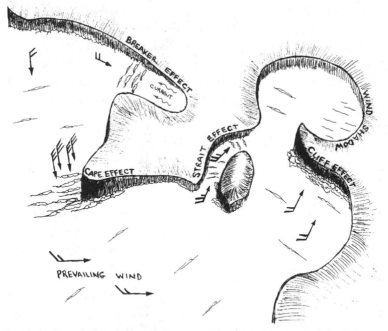

Land disrupts wind strength and direction. On this idealized coastal sketch (and on actual weather charts), wind arrows are used to show direction and wind speed. The shaft and arrowhead show direction. Each tail feather, called a barb, represents 10 knots. One-half of a tail feather is 5 knots. Note the increase from 15 knots of prevailing wind to 30 knots at the cape (gale force). Speed also increases inside the strait between the island and mainland. Study your chart and track the weather to help determine the safest path to follow.

"Your Call, Skipper"

You're the skipper or most knowledgeable crewmember in each of the following situations. What actions would you take?

1. You were sailing southbound for the islands but decided to anchor to wait out a storm to the south. What two signs would indicate the storm center has passed and it's safe to proceed?

2. The latest weather forecast calls for 2- to 3-foot seas this afternoon, building to 5 feet by evening. What average wave height would you expect this evening? What is the highest possible sea after nightfall?

3. A 20-knot breeze is predicted to blow onto the 1,200-foot cliffs close to your trackline. How far away should you stay to avoid a possible dangerous "ricochet" zone?

4. You are approaching a mountainous island in a gusty 15-knot breeze. Winds will increase later this afternoon. A low cloud layer has settled over the island on all sides. What effect could this have in the anchorage on the lee side?

5. You're sailing in the Caribbean and need to find a good anchorage for this evening. You pull out the largest scale chart and study the area. What features would warn you to expect a heavy groundswell caused by refraction?

Answers

1. The winds will back to the northeast (in the Northern Hemisphere) after the eye passes. The barometer will begin to rise slowly.

2. The smallest seas should average 3 feet (60% × 5 feet). Occasionally, you may experience a 10-foot sea (200% × 5 feet).

3. Two miles: 1,200 feet × 10 = 12,000 feet; 12,000 feet ÷ 6,000 feet (per mile) = 2 miles

4. Expect a rough anchorage. A low cloud layer on all sides funnels high winds around the island. Use storm ground tackle or tie up pierside.

5. A roundish island with gently sloping bottom contours all around its circumference is a candidate for heavy groundswell caused by refraction. Try to find long, narrow islands or islands with protected coves or lagoons or their lee sides.

PREVENTING AND HANDLING EMERGENCIES

I am looking to see whether anything is out of order. There will be no time to look for what is missing or out of place when a storm comes up at sea.
—Phoenician seaman, 334 BC

Does your crew understand how to safeguard against the possibility of a fire aboard your boat? How can you prevent the deadly "domino effect" in a flooding emergency? Are you certain that your crew knows the top survival techniques if they fall overboard?

In This Chapter, You'll Learn How To:
* Pressure test a propane stove system to prevent a fire
* Approach a person in the water under power or sail
* Use the magic of N.O.W. to prevent overboard emergencies
* Turn your engine into a high-capacity dewatering pump
* Survive in cold water with five lifesaving techniques

Fuel-Fire Prevention Techniques

Marine firefighters estimate that you have less than 30 seconds to get a fire on any boat under control. Many items on your boat burn extremely hot, including fiberglass. It takes no time for liquids like diesel, gasoline, propane, or kerosene to reach flash point and give off combustible vapor. At that point, one spark causes combustion.

On vessels, most serious fires start during fueling or cooking. Fuel fires almost always are the result of improper pre-fueling and post-fueling procedures. Galley fires combine improper preheating, storage, vapor ventilation, and failure to monitor cooking activities.

A basic checklist goes a long way in preventing common emergencies. Make it simple and keep it in a three-ring binder. Laminate the lists, or put them into document protectors, and separate the lists with tabbed inserts.

Below are the tools and steps required for safely fueling your boat.

1. Run blowers for 5 minutes to rid bilges of vapors. Close hatches, opening ports, vents (including dorades), and doors. On sailboats, insert dropboards into the companionway opening and close sliding hatch.

2. Keep a fire extinguisher ready for immediate use. Remove one of the portable extinguishers from its bracket. Lay it on deck, on its side, to keep it from rolling around.

3. Place diapers or absorbent pads over downhill scuppers and drains. This prevents fuel from spilling from the deck and into the cockpit and overboard.

4. Assign one crewmember to watch the fuel gauge. V-shaped fuel tanks cause gauge readings to be somewhat erratic. The gauge rises quickly when you start fueling, and then slows to a crawl near the tank top.

5. Place a rag around the nozzle or fuel fill hole. Insert the nozzle and maintain contact with the fill to prevent buildup of static electricity. When you are three-quarters full, assign a crewmember to monitor the fuel vent. Have him or her hold an absorbent pad or diaper under the vent in case of overflow. Top off each tank to 90% to allow for expansion.

6. Replace the nozzle and wipe up any spills. Check the cap gasket for cracks and proper seating. A cracked or worn gasket leads to water intrusion into the fuel tank. Replace and tighten down the fill cap. Check all around the boat's waterline for fuel spills. Cleanup any spill immediately with absorb pads. Do not—*under any circumstances*—use a dispersant. (This is a U.S. federal law.)

7. Open all vents, hatches, opening ports, and doors. Run the blowers for 5 minutes. Tour the vessel and sniff for vapor fumes. If you smell fuel, locate the source *before* you start the engine. After starting the engine, check the waterline again for spills—paying particular attention to the area beneath each fuel vent. Check the engine compartment for fuel leaks.

Galley Stove Safety Secrets

Stove fires are the second-most common cause of boat fires and explosion. Most galley fires result from failure to maintain a cooking watch. If you cook, whether in port or underway, always be next to the stove, ready to snuff out flare-ups (a flame shooting up from the cooktop), burning food, or grease fires.

OPERATING AN ALCOHOL STOVE

You must preheat an alcohol burner before lighting it to prevent a flare-up. Most two-burner alcohol stoves have three devices used in the priming process: a pressure/fill cap, a pump, and burners.

1. Open the fill cap slowly to allow the pressure to release. Stoves with a separate tank have a pressure relief valve. Use a penlight or tongue depressor to check the fuel level. Keep the tank filled to within a half inch of the top. Replace the fill cap. Close all valves and burner controls.
2. Operate the pump until you feel heavy resistance. Stoves equipped with pressure gauges should be pumped to between 15 to 20 psi.
3. Crack open the desired burner valve for an instant, then close it. You want to release just enough alcohol to cover the bottom surface of the burner cup. If your stove has a separate fuel tank, open the valve 90 degrees counterclockwise before opening the burner valve.
4. Light the burner cup and let the alcohol burn off completely. Then immediately crack open the burner valve. If you hear a steady, unbroken "s-s-s-s-s," you've done things right. Light the burner immediately. If you hear a broken, gurgling hiss, allow the burner to cool; then go through the preheat steps again.

SEA-CRET TIP

▶ Alcohol fires may be extinguished with water, so keep a bucket nearby. Baking soda works too.

▶ Use *fiddles* to secure pots and pans in place. Keep food levels below the three-quarters-full mark in pots and pans. Add tight-fitting or strapped lids to pan or pot tops.

PROPANE STOVES AND OVEN SAFETY

Check your propane locker. It should be completely airtight and top-loading. Make a strong, secure installation of tank, regulator, pressure gauge, and solenoid. Install a vent tube to carry propane gas overboard in case of a leak. Periodically check the integrity of all fittings. First, pressurize the system but keep all appliances off. Brush a soapy water solution onto every fitting, from the tank valve to the galley. Bubbles indicate leaks, and you must repair these as soon as possible.

Start-up and Cooking

1. Check that the main tank valve and stove burners are off.
2. Ventilate the galley area for 5 to 6 minutes. Open all hatches, vents, opening ports, and doors. Run blowers.

3. Crack the main tank valve about a quarter turn.
4. Turn on the solenoid switch at the galley station to allow fuel flow from the main tank. Light the stove or use the electronic ignition. Keep the flame visible even at low levels. You don't want a burner turned on with only gas vapor pouring into the cabin.

Shutdown and Securing

1. Shut off the oven. Keep one burner going with a medium flame. Shut off all other burners.
2. Secure the solenoid switch and wait until the flame dies out at the burner.
3. Turn off stove burner valve. Double-check that all other burners and oven are off.
4. Turn off main tank valve.

SEA-CRET TIP

▶ While cooking underway, wear chest-high bib foul-weather trousers. Shove a square cushion down the front of the bib to protect your chest; then take the slack out of the top of the overalls. You don't want boiling liquid or grease pouring down the top or splashing up against the thin front section.

Overboard Recovery and Reality Checks

Remind your crew of the techniques that give them the best chance of remaining aboard: crouch when moving fore and aft, crawl when conditions warrant, grab and hold, then move . . .

It's nearing midnight on a blustery evening and you're at the end of your watch. You set the autopilot and go below to wake the crewmember taking the next watch. When he gets to the cockpit, you agree to reef the mainsail to better balance the boat.

He moves forward to the mast to adjust the luff reef cringle, and you start getting the clew cringle ready. Within seconds, a gust from nowhere heels the boat to starboard, burying the rail in white water. You hear a shriek and twist around, only to see your friend somersault backward over the starboard lifelines.

The loose-footed mainsail, partially reefed, blows wildly out of control to leeward, blocking your vision of the lost crewmember. Now you're alone on deck, with one other crewmember still aboard, below and sound asleep. Read on for tips on how to handle crew overboard situations.

TIME: ENEMY #1 IN AN OVERBOARD EMERGENCY

Always assume the following three conditions for any person who falls into the water—even if you suspect otherwise:

Injured. The victim might have sustained an injury when he fell over the side. Contact with lifelines, stanchions, toerails, or the hull result in lacerations, broken bones, or a concussion. This leads to, or adds to, the seriousness of the next two factors.

Unconscious. Unless you hear the victim's shouts, you won't know his state of consciousness. Without a life jacket, an unconscious victim will drown. Automatic, inflatable life jackets must fully inflate to roll a person from a face-down to a face-up position.

Hypothermic. Hypothermia, the cooling of the body below its normal temperature of 98.6°F (37°C), causes loss of motor skills. Even in Key West, Florida, water temperatures during late fall and winter average around 70°F (21°C) to 75°F (24°C). Within 5 minutes, a victim may lose the ability to grasp any flotation device thrown to him or her (see "Signs of Hypothermia and Cold-Water Shock" later in this chapter).

CREW OVERBOARD APPROACH METHODS

No approach method works every time for every vessel. Choose your approach based on crew number and ability, wind and wave conditions, and vessel handling characteristics.

Power Vessel Approach

1. Turn the wheel toward the victim (to kick the stern away).
2. Throw flotation (life jacket, life ring, cushion, fender); assign crew to maintain continuous visual contact with the man overboard.
3. Slow the boat to a crawl (bare steerageway) when you are halfway through the turn and spot the person abeam; use just enough power for control.
4. Stop near the victim. Tie a large bowline in one end of a line and heave that to the person. Pull him or her alongside and tie off the line. If the person is

In a powerboat, approach an overboard crewmember by turning the wheel toward him.

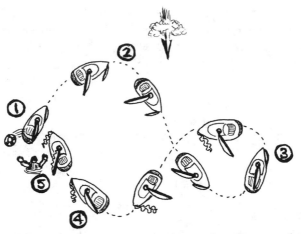

On a sailboat, one way to approach the overboard crew is by sailing onto a broad reach, tacking, broad reaching, and making the final approach on a close reach. Luff the mainsail to slow the boat to a stop.

unconscious, you must make an approach to bring him or her right next to the boat. Stopped in a seaway, a boat lies beam to the seas, and this causes it to roll from side to side. To prevent injury, place fenders or cushions on the recovery side of the hull before you bring the person alongside. Loop a line around the person and under his/her arms. Cleat off the line until you work out a way to get the person onto the boat (see the section on recovery methods).

Sailing Vessel Approaches

REACH-TACK-REACH METHOD

1. Throw flotation (life jacket, life ring, cushion, fender); assign crew to maintain continuous visual contact.
2. Fall off to a broad reach.
3. Wait until you sail about five boat lengths from the person; then perform a quick tack. Fall off to a broad reach and luff the headsail completely. You need to be downwind of the person before turning up toward them.
4. Head up onto a close reach as soon as possible. When within one or two boat lengths, luff both sails to stop the boat and bring the person alongside.

QUICK-STOP METHOD

1. Throw flotation; maintain continuous visual contact.
2. Tack immediately and fall off to a run. Do not release the headsail sheet. Sheet the mainsail to the centerline to flatten and depower the main.
3. Jibe; release the headsail sheet.

The Leeward-Windward Approach Debate

So, which is the safer side to approach a person in the water? Some may argue that you must make all approaches to leeward of the person. This approach has its merits under sail, in that the sails will luff to leeward and clear the recovery area. Under sail or power, there is less chance for injury because the hull will drift downwind.

But what if you drift away from the person before you are able to get a line to him or her? In cold water or with an unconscious victim, even a short delay could cause grave danger (see "Signs of Hypothermia and Cold-Water Shock" below). On the other hand, an approach to windward of the person creates a lee (calm area) for them because the boat hull blocks the wind. If you are off by a few feet on a windward approach, the boat could still drift down to the person. And, you could attach a line to a flotation aid and float it downwind to the person. In either case, base your decision on wind and sea conditions, boat-handling characteristics, and the number and capability of your crew.

4. Head into the wind alongside the man overboard, or continue circling the victim with a trailing line (see the Lifesling Method below).

HEAVE-TO

Not all vessels perform the quick-stop method effectively. For inexperienced or shorthanded crews, try heaving-to (see below). Then perform these four steps:

1. Throw flotation.
2. Get a bearing on the victim *before* you lose contact.
3. If more crew are below, get their attention by shouting or using a whistle or horn.
4. If you are alone, use the Lifesling recovery method discussed below.

LIFESLING METHOD: POWER OR SAILING VESSEL

The Lifesling—a horseshoe-shaped, throwable device with a polypropylene trail line attached—offers an easy way for inexperienced crews to bring a person alongside for recovery. If you do not have a Lifesling aboard, you can still use this method for recovery.

1. Powerboats should turn the wheel toward the person, slow to idle speed, and continue to turn. Make a circle around the person in the water. Sailboats should use the quick-stop maneuver described above, but continue to sail around the person in a circle.
2. Throw the buoyancy device on the trail line (or a flotation device attached to a line) inside the circle, toward the person. Continue around the circle until the person in the water grabs the device.
3. Stop the boat immediately. Powerboats should place both engines into neutral. Sailboats should luff up and drop sails. After the person dons the

Lifesling device, pull the person alongside. Tie off your end of the line to a cleat.

4. Drop lifelines in the recovery area. Sailing vessels may be able to recover the person by attaching the main halyard to the top of the Lifesling and winching the person aboard. In any kind of seaway, however, the person may swing out and slam back into the hull. Decide on the best recovery method to prevent injury.

How to Heave-to in a Sailboat

Heaving-to stops the forward momentum of a sailboat. Use this to recover persons in the water, in heavy weather, or to go below to take a break or make a meal.

1. Sail onto a close-hauled course.
2. Tack the boat but do not touch any sheets. Allow the jib to backwind.
3. Adjust the helm so that the boat tries to head up into the wind, but the backed jib pushes the bow away from the wind.

The boat will lie beam-to the seas and make a zigzag drift to leeward at about 1 or 2 knots. This also creates a slick to windward to calm the seas.

RECOVERY WITH A LARGE DOSE OF REALITY

Most crews practice overboard recovery in controlled conditions, such as:

- Daylight
- Smooth water and light to moderate winds
- With a lightweight "victim," such as a fender
- With crew on deck and anticipating the exercise
- Recovery using a boathook

Imagine lying on your belly and holding onto the boat with one hand. Now, reach down and pull 150 to 200 pounds up 2 to 3 feet of freeboard and onto the boat. Throw in a gale-force wind and heavy seas. This might be the reality of what you face in a live overboard recovery.

How about swim grids or ladders? On powerboats, swim platforms can become sledgehammers as the boat rises and falls in heavy seas. Sailing vessels with reverse transoms could present the same problem. All vessels should exercise caution when recovering from the stern with a swim ladder. In all but the calmest seas, move the swim ladder to a location between the beam and stern quarter to prevent crushing-type injury.

CROUCH AND GRASP BEFORE YOU MOVE

The difficulties and hazards of recovery demonstrate the need to practice preventive measures in all types of weather. These tips will help keep you and your crew on board:

1. Keep one hand for the boat and one for yourself.
2. Grasp a solid, through-bolted object at all times.

3. When moving, crouch to lower your center of gravity and keep your knee creases below the upper lifeline levels (most upper lifelines on production boats, however, are too low).

4. During night watches or when the weather worsens, don a safety harness, clip it to jacklines whenever you're outside the cockpit and to padeyes whenever you're in the cockpit (see next section), and crouch even lower to the deck. In extreme conditions, crawl to and from the foredeck.

Use N.O.W. and Keep Crewmembers Alive and Well

N.O.W. conditions are *Nighttime*, *Offshore*, or *Weather* with high wind, sea, or precipitation. Heighten your crew's awareness during these conditions and use the following ten-step guide to keep them safe:

1. **Don life jackets (PFDs).** All crew on deck after sunset or during blustery weather should wear a personal flotation device. Equip PFDs with waterproof lights and whistles on lanyards. Cover the outside of the jackets with long, wide strips of reflective tape. If you fall overboard, a spotlight will pick up this tape long before the crew sees your face and body.

2. **Rig jacklines.** Jacklines are long lengths of line, webbing, or wire rope run from bow to stern. The crew in a safety harness (see next) clips to the jackline to move about the boat without fear of falling overboard. Run your jackline from the largest bow cleats to stout fittings aft. These might be quarter cleats, genoa track slides, or deck padeyes with backing plates. Do not use the weak eyes found on the inboard side of stanchion bases.

3. **Don safety harnesses (with dual tethers).** Safety harnesses must be worn by any crewmember working on deck at night or in heavy weather. Don the harness before coming on deck from below. When moving forward and aft, always clip onto the windward jackline. Harnesses need two tethers so the crew remains attached even when going around the mast or other obstructions. Clip the lead tether before you unclip the trailing tether.

4. **Engine test and familiarization.** All hands need to know how to start the engine and use the throttle, shifter, and fuel stop. Let each person use the shifter—moving from forward to neutral, to reverse, and back to neutral.

5. **Rig swim ladders.** Unfold collapsible swim ladders. Set up strong lashings to hold the ladder on both sides of the boat in the recovery area.

6. **Throwable device.** Tie 100 feet of polypropylene line to a throwable device—such as a life ring—and secure the bitter end to the rail. Attach and test a waterproof light and whistle to the gear.

7. **Extra life jackets.** Place several life jackets in port and starboard cockpit lockers and near the steering station. Place extras near the helm. The life jacket is the most important throwable device aboard. If the victim

enters the water without a life jacket, he or she might quickly succumb to hypothermia. Show all crewmembers the special technique for donning a life jacket in the water (described later in this chapter).

8. **Tow a grab line.** Stream at least 150 feet of bright orange or yellow polypropylene line astern. (Sometime earlier in the season, make up a large 3- to 4-foot eye splice in the bitter end of this line. Stow the line near the wheel or tiller.)

9. **Half inflate the inflatable.** If you are carrying an inflatable, partially inflate it and tie at least 100 feet of line to the towing eye. This makes it much easier for a person in the water to crawl inside the inflatable, as opposed to getting onboard with full air chambers. Tow it astern on a short scope but have the line ready to pay out. Consider towing a rigid dinghy astern; if not, make the dinghy ready for immediate deployment.

10. **Mount a handheld GPS near the helm.** Install a bracket for a handheld GPS near the helm. Keep spare batteries in a waterproof container nearby. Brief the crew on how to activate the MOB (man-overboard) function on the GPS receiver to record your precise position at the time of the accident.

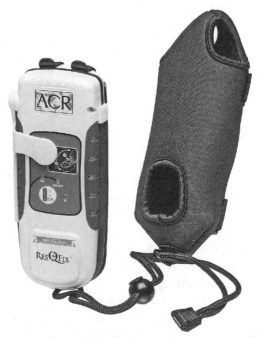

Personal locator EPIRBs (called personal locator beacons or PLBs), with GPS interface, are another way to track the position of crew overboard. PLBs are small enough to clip to a life jacket, batteries last up to 5 years, and the distress signal activates for up to 40 hours. PLBs require manual activation by the person in the water. The GPS antenna on the PLB must be held clear of the water for the best signal. (ACR Electronics, Inc.)

Handle Flooding Emergencies with M.A.T.E.

It's been a fine boating day, and you're nestled in the perfect anchorage, just you and your beauty. With a mug o' rum and a fine imported stogie, it just doesn't get better than this. You stare lazily up at the canopy of twinkling prisms above your head. Every so often a shooting star streaks across the gilded background. Ah, this is the life! Thirty minutes later, you pick yourself up and meander down the companionway. You never make it past the last step . . .

You tumble onto your hands and knees in 6 inches of ice cold, brackish water. It's pouring in—but from where? You push the switch on the cabin lights and nothing happens. Where's the damn flashlight? You desperately pull out drawer after drawer. Contents spill into the salty liquid, which is already creeping steadily above your ankles. Finally you find a small flashlight, tear away the engine cover, and shine the light at the raw-water seacock. It's closed and the hose looks intact. Sweeping the lantern from right to left, you locate the source of the problem.

The sink overboard discharge hose has blown off its seacock. Water gushes in through a 1-inch hole, 1 foot below the waterline. Every hour, you're taking on 1,200 gallons of seawater. In just 60 minutes your boat's displacement will increase by 10,200 pounds!

Grabbing the seacock handle, you push it forward to shut it off, but nothing happens. Desperately flailing at the frozen fitting, your skin and fingernails tear away, bloodying the brackish water below. Where did you stow the hammer? Turning back to the cabin, the lantern begins flickering, blinking once, twice . . . then it dies. You push the button on and off. Nothing. Now you have no lantern, no batteries, and no hammer.

Insurance companies claim that 50% of vessel sinkings occur to moored or anchored vessels. Undersized bilge pumps rarely keep up with water flooding in from stuffing boxes, blown seacock hoses, or broken gate valves. Most emergencies result from little things overlooked or ignored. In our scenario above, the deadly domino effect turned an easy-to-solve problem into a serious emergency.

The typical production boat has six to eight holes drilled below her waterline, with average diameters of $1/2$ inch, 1 inch, or 2 inches. These *through-hulls* accommodate the engine raw-water intake, sink and shower drains, cockpit scupper drains, and instrument impellers. The graph shows hourly water-flow rates through a 1-inch-diameter hole at various depths below the waterline.

Each gallon of seawater flowing into your hull adds about 8.5 pounds to your displacement. For a real eye-opener, multiply this by the flow rate per hour. With enough water or liquid sloshing fore and aft or left to right, you can capsize. Big ships have this problem unless they keep their liquid cargo tanks filled. You need to have an attack plan in place before a flooding emergency strikes. Start with a map of all hull penetrations above and below your waterline.

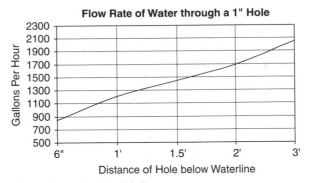

The flow rate of water through a 1-inch hole.

M *is for mapping from a bird's-eye view*

Make a simple drawing of every through-hull in your boat, showing locations of seacocks, ball valves, and exhaust vents. Include rudderposts, stuffing boxes (shaft exits), transducers (depth sounders and speed measuring instrumentation). If the fitting penetrates the hull, add it to your sketch. Start forward and work your way aft, removing every inspection cover or port. Look inside lockers and beneath berths and settee seats. Follow the water and head hose lines from entry to exit points. Neaten up your rough sketch, mount it in the cabin, and show it to your crew.

A *is for attack preparation*

Make every piece of flood-fighting equipment accessible and keep it in good working order. Brief your crew on the locations of the equipment described here and hold mini-demos on how to use it.

Seacock valve handles. Test every fitting with a seacock at least once a month. Test the most common fittings—such as the head, sink, and engine raw-water intake—more frequently. Don't forget hidden ones such as the cockpit scupper drain seacocks or the generator raw-water intake seacock. Move the handle the full 90 degrees from open to closed position several times. A light tap with a hammer usually frees up frozen handles. Disassemble and repack every seacock during your annual haulout. Apply a waterproof silicone grease to lubricate internal parts.

Mechanical (electric) bilge pumps. Install the largest-capacity mechanical pump possible. With two electric pumps in the same bilge, mount the larger of the two on a shelf over the smaller one. Test all float switches before and after getting underway.

Cockpit-mounted manual (diaphragm) bilge pump. Sailing vessels and small open powerboats should install a large-capacity manual, diaphragm-type bilge pump in the cockpit. Choose one with a 15- to 30-gallon-per-minute capacity. (The Gusher 10, made by Whale, for example, has a capacity of 17 GPM.) Before installing this fixed pump, test the handle clearance to make sure it doesn't interfere with the helm or sheets. Keep two or three handles aboard, mounted on deck and below. Before you cast off, point out their locations to your crew.

Portable pumps. Invest in at least two portable pumps with 6 to 15 gallon-per-minute capacities. The rigid pump body should be 2 to 3 feet long, and the flexible hose should be 4 to 6 feet long. Screen the intake to keep the pump from clogging. Use nylon mesh screening, and attach it to the end with stainless hose clamps.

Two buckets. Keep two buckets aboard with strong bails (handles) to which lines are attached. When other dewatering devices fail, these buckets can save your boat. Have the damage-control crew bail from below. As soon as they fill one bucket, pass it up to the on-deck crew. The below-deck crew keeps bailing with the second bucket. When full, they exchange it for the one just emptied by the on-deck crew.

Softwood plugs. Lash a wooden plug with light line to the body of each seacock. Be sure the line will break with a good tug. Softer woods swell up when wet, forming a better seal around the hole.

Cotton rags. For holes with jagged edges, you'll need filler to block the space around the perimeter of the wooden plug. Stow a bag of cotton rags in a fishnet bag in the forward and main cabin areas.

Pounding tool. Mount a hammer or mallet in the forward and main cabin. Install it in brackets outside a toolbox. Paint the handle a bright or Day-Glo color. Better still, cut thin strips of reflective tape and stick it onto the handle.

Lights and batteries. Have waterproof flashlights on board. Keep one lantern available with battery replacements in waterproof bags. Headband-type lights free up your hands and pinpoint the damage location. Purchase the Cyalume-type "break-'n-shake" lights from camping stores. They're bright and waterproof, and they illuminate a small area for several hours.

T *is for testing preparations and training the crew*

Get your crew together and show them your map of the boat's through-hulls. Explain actions to take and demonstrate how to use the equipment. Do they easily understand your drawing and action plan? If not, revise the plan to make it clear enough for all hands to follow.

E *is for execute and evaluate*

In an emergency, put your plan into action. Afterward, determine the cause of the problem and think of ways to improve things. Do you need to shorten preventive maintenance intervals? How did your equipment work out?

How to Use Your Engine as a Dewatering Pump

With a few simple preparations, your engine can serve as a large-capacity dewatering pump. Some authorities recommend using the raw-water hose without a separate flexible hose. But most raw-water exhaust hoses are short and won't reach flooded areas like forward bilges. You can make a more effective system for vessels with deep bilges or forward bilge compartments by attaching a longer, flexible hose to the raw-water hose as described next. If you choose to use only the raw-water hose, disregard the steps involving the flexible hose.

Tools Needed for Using Your Diesel as a Dewatering Pump

- 8- to 10-inch length of PVC (to fit raw-water hose and flexible hose)
- 6 hose clamps
- flexible hose (4 to 8 feet, or distance to the forward bilge)
- fine-mesh netting or flexible screening

1. Shut down the engine.
2. Close the raw-water seacock.
3. Pull off the raw-water hose from the top tailpiece of the seacock. (If you are using only the raw-water hose, screen the end and go to step 5.)
4. Insert the PVC tube 2 inches into the raw-water hose, and secure it with two stainless steel hose clamps. Insert the other end of the PVC tube 2 inches into the flexible hose and clamp it in place with two stainless clamps. Use stainless clamps to hold the screen material over the intake end of the flexible hose. (To save time in an emergency, make up the flexible hose ahead of time, and install the screen and compression tube.)
5. Stick the screened intake end deep into the bilge. Start the engine. The flexible hose will pull the floodwater into the engine and exhaust it at the stern. Check astern to make sure you have exhaust water flowing at a good rate.
6. Assign one crewmember to keep an eye on the exhaust water flow at all times. If you lose suction or exhaust water fails to flow, shut the engine down right away. To prevent this, keep the intake end of your pump beneath the water and watch for clogs from debris.

Other Strategies for Staying Afloat when Damaged

How else can you reduce or eliminate floodwater? If you ever sustain a below-the-waterline hole in your hull, make these final two points part of your damage-control strategy.

Jack up (shift) the damaged side. Flow rates taper off the closer the hole gets to your boat's waterline. If you raise a 1-inch hole from 1 foot below the waterline to 6 inches below the waterline, the hourly flow rate drops by 300 gallons. Shift your crew and ballast to the undamaged side. If you have damage in the bow or stern, shift weight to the opposite end of the boat. Power vessels might pump fuel, fresh water, or gray water into tanks on the undamaged side. Sailing vessels should sail on the same tack as the damaged side. For example, if the damage is on the port side, get onto port tack to raise the hole.

Shore up the damaged side. Some of the finest damage-control advice comes from the Navy and Coast Guard. After plugging a crack or hole, they suggest bracing the damaged area with lumber and wedges to prevent water pressure from blowing out the patch. To shore a patched hole, use a *strongback* and a brace. First, cover the hole with the strongback, made from cushions, hatch boards, or life jackets. Brace the strongback with a paddle, an oar, a spinnaker pole, or a boathook. Push one end of the brace into the strongback and wedge the other end onto an overhead or a bulkhead. Keep an eye on the shoring to make sure it holds.

Signs of Hypothermia and Cold-Water Shock

> *The risk of immersion hypothermia in North America is nearly universal during most of the year.*
> —DR. ALAN STEINMAN, MARITIME MEDICINE AND SEA-SURVIVAL EXPERT

You may be surprised to learn the truth about annual seawater temperatures. The average annual seawater temperature throughout the United States is only 65°F (18°C). That's not just during wintertime—but all year long. (See the accompanying graph.) And what happens when we sail across the Gulf Stream to the Bahamas? The beautiful water surrounding those jewels in the stream averages only 85°F (29°C) in midsummer! So why the fuss over such warm water?

Whether you are on land or on the deck of a vessel, your body works with the environment to maintain your core temperature by transferring heat back and forth. Evaporation cools you, and the atmosphere transfers warmth back to you through radiation. This stabilizes your core temperature to 98.6°F (37°C). On a hot day, trimming sheets, grinding winches, or pulling up a heavy anchor means you'll sweat more to stay cool. In cool weather or after sunset, your body shivers if necessary to warm itself to its core temperature.

Think of your body as having three layers: first the skin, then an insulating layer or shell, and finally the core of vital organs. Blood is our "warming fluid" and moves slowly between core and shell and back again. If we're too cool, blood flow increases and moves toward the layer that needs warming.

IMMERSION HYPOTHERMIA: WATER TEMPERATURES 95°F (35°C) TO 78°F (26°C)

Hypothermia is the loss of body heat resulting in a cooling of the body core below 98.6°F (37°C). It's important to note that a person can become hypothermic in air or

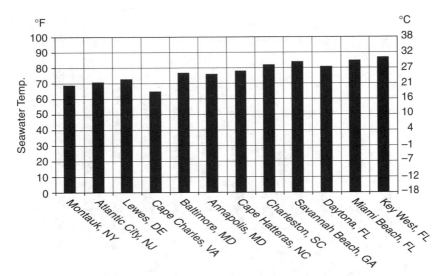

These statistics from the National Oceanographic Data Center show average summer seawater temperatures along the central and southern Atlantic coasts.

water. Wet conditions such as rain, sleet, snow, or waves that splash aboard accelerate hypothermia in air. But what happens when you fall into the water unprotected? In water, your body loses heat twenty-five times faster than in air. You'll eventually become hypothermic in water temperatures under about 95°F (35°C)!

You must take every precaution to prevent overboard emergencies. Be on the lookout for the visual warning signs of hypothermia in the accompanying chart. Later in this chapter, we will discuss survival tactics and treatment of individuals in various hypothermic stages.

COLD-WATER IMMERSION: WATER TEMPERATURE 77°F (25°C) AND BELOW

Boating in cold water calls for special precautions. The accompanying statistics from the National Oceanographic Data Center show average winter seawater

Severity	Body Core	Visual Signs
Mild	98.6F (37C)–96F (36C)	Shivering; difficulty moving or completing simple tasks
	95F (35C)–1F (33C)	Shivering uncontrollably; slurred speech; amnesia
Medium	90F (32C)–86F (30C)	Shivering stops completely; unable to move; muscles not responsive
	85F (29C)–81F (27C)	Irrational behavior; respiratory system slows dramatically
Severe	80F (27C)–78F (26C)	No reflexes; unable to communicate; heart arrythmia
	78F (26C) or less	Death

The visual warning signs of hypothermia.

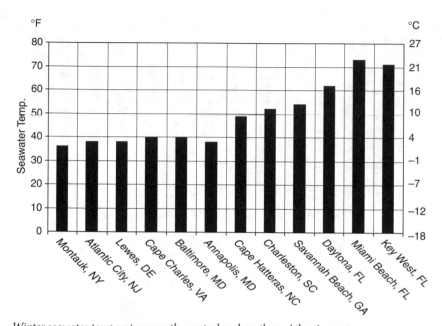

Winter seawater temperatures on the central and southern Atlantic coasts.

temperatures along the central and southern Atlantic coasts. In the British Isles, water temperatures in early fall range from 14°C (57°F) to 18°C (64°F). Winter water temperatures can plunge below 10°C (50°F). Mariners in wintertime must wear anti-exposure clothing and have survival equipment ready to use in an instant.

How Heat Loss Accelerates in Cold Water
Three things happen within seconds of falling into water with temperatures of 77°F (25°C) or less:

1. The body sends huge quantities of blood from the core to the shell area in an attempt to warm up the skin layer.
2. The shell area shrinks to shorten the distance the blood has to travel to get to the skin. It tries to help—but the end result is just the opposite! The core becomes *more* exposed because of less shell insulation.
3. The warm blood near the skin transfers heat to the surrounding water. The blood cools near the skin and flows back to the core, cooling it in turn. This cycle continues back and forth between core and shell. The longer you stay immersed, the cooler your core becomes.

Cold-Water Shock and Loss of Motor Skills
At 2:20 am, Monday, April 15th, 1912, the *Titanic* slid beneath the waves of the Atlantic, leaving her passengers and crew fighting for their lives in 31°F (−1°C)

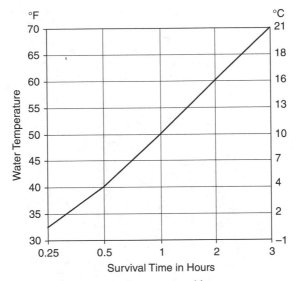

Minimum survival times for unprotected persons in cold water.

water. Most never had a chance and survived only a few minutes (see graph). Drowning—not hypothermia—is the real threat in cold water. An unprotected person (wearing regular street or boating clothes) goes through severe trauma during the first few minutes of immersion:

- Gasping or hyperventilation could lead to drowning.
- Disorientation and panic could cause cardiac problems.
- Fingers stiffen. You will soon be unable to grasp flotsam, flotation, or a trail line.

Wearing a life jacket can make all the difference in your ability to survive in cold water anywhere in the world.

Skipper's Immersion Survival and Treatments Guide

The skipper has a responsibility to keep passengers and crew safe in all conditions. Unlike many illnesses, hypothermia tends to sneak up on a person with little warning. This section gives you valuable tips on survival skills and the best treatments after recovering a person from the water.

1. **Protect body heat-loss zones.** Heat loss will be greatest from six major body zones: head, neck, sides of chest, armpits, groin, and behind the knees. The head loses 90% of all body heat. Carry a watch cap or ski cap in your pocket. If you fall overboard, you need to keep your head out of the water—and protected. A jacket or PFD collar protects the back of the neck. In a pinch,

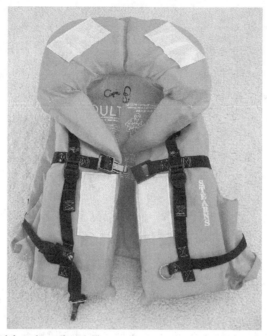

The bulky Type I life jacket offers the best protection of your heat-loss zones. It is the only true "life jacket" and turns an unconscious person from a face-down to a face-up position.

use a towel or scarf. A jacket or PFD protects the chest sides. To protect the remaining zones: armpits, groin, and behind the knees (see below: Use the H.E.L.P. survival position), you must be wearing a life jacket. A Type I PFD/life jacket is the most effective PFD available (see photo).

2. **Reduce body-core immersion.** Attempt to get as much of your body out of the water as possible. Pull yourself up onto large pieces of flotation or flotsam. The more body zones that you free from immersion, the slower your body will cool.

3. **Reduce movement.** The University of Victoria in British Columbia conducted extensive tests on cold-water survival times. The results showed that a person in motion lost heat 82% faster than when still. If someone falls overboard, you must get a PFD to them right away. Remember, they might soon lose the ability to grasp an object or don a life jacket.

4. **Train your crew on in-the-water PFD donning.** Show your crew how to don a PFD if they fall overboard. This requires a totally different approach than donning one on dry land. Use a Type I or II PFD during practice. For more realism, get onto your knees in front of a table. This places the table top near chin height and simulates the water surface for a person in the water.

Gathering your extremities into a ball, as shown here in the H.E.L.P, helps conserve body heat.

- Lay the jacket on the table and turn it face up. Grab the collar and pull it toward you. Unfasten all straps and snaps. Open the jacket and flatten it so that you can only see the inside.
- Stick your arms deep into the armholes.
- Raise both arms together in a smooth, rapid motion above and slightly behind your head.
- Close the jacket with zipper, buckle, and straps. Tighten fasteners to mold the jacket to your body. This helps prevent heat loss.

5. **Use the H.E.L.P. survival position.** The *Heat Escape Lessening Position,* or H.E.L.P., slows body cooling and protects those vital heat-loss zones. It simulates the fetal position. You must wear a PFD to use this survival method:
   - Don a PFD to protect the neck and chest zones. Put on your watch or ski cap to protect the head zone.
   - Keep both arms close to your sides, but clasp your hands together at the chest. This helps protects the armpit zone.
   - Cross your legs at the ankles and bend your knees up toward the chest. This protects the groin and knee zones.

HYPOTHERMIA TREATMENTS

Insulate the survivor from further heat loss and allow him to recover slowly, aided only by his own body warmth.
—DOUGAL ROBERTSON, *SEA SURVIVAL*

The big rule here is, easy does it! Treat hypothermia victims with extreme care. Don't be tempted to rub arms and legs to stimulate warmth because this sends cold blood back to the vital organs at the core. Review the chart of the visual signs of hypothermia on page 285 before you decide on the best treatment.

Mild Hypothermia

1. Remove wet clothing. If the clothing is tight, don't try to *peel* it. This could stimulate the cold surface blood at the skin layer and send it back to the core. Cut off the clothing using scissors, knife, or a razor.

2. Wrap the person in a wool blanket, sleeping bag, or space blanket.
3. Give a warm nonalcoholic or non-caffeinated beverage. You might add a bit of sweetener.

Medium Hypothermia

1. Remove wet clothing as described above.
2. Use body-to-body warming. Crawl into a sleeping bag or under a blanket and hug the victim from behind.
3. Treat the victim for shock (elevate feet 12" above head/cover with warm blanket), even if it is not apparent. Keep the head slightly lower than the feet.
4. Do not use hot-water bottles or heating pads to speed warming. The skin of a hypothermic person is as fragile as glass. Artificial heating methods may cause second- or third-degree burns.

Severe Hypothermia

1. If there's no time to remove clothing, leave it on. It still provides some insulation. Get the person down into the cabin, covered and out of the elements.
2. Treat the victim for shock (lower the head and raise the feet).
3. Monitor pulse and respiration. If the person is breathing on his or her own, gently exhale your breath down their throat as they inhale.
4. If the person is not breathing, begin CPR right away.

We've covered a lot of material in this book, and I hope that much of it is thought provoking. Every skipper, even in the best of times, must keep thinking about "what ifs." What if the wind changes? What if a boat or ship changes direction? What if the chart doesn't match the visual picture? The more prepared you are, the more pure enjoyment you receive aboard any vessel, power or sail. And isn't that what it's all about?

Many seamanship recommendations seem black and white, but often nature gives us another challenge—wind or current we didn't count on—forcing you to rethink the recommendations to fit your particular situation.

It's OK to be unsure. No one is sure all the time. That's just one more reason to drop the anchor, heave-to, or lie adrift. If something doesn't look or feel right, stop the boat. Take a breather to work things out. You will often find that solutions come more easily when you need not concern yourself with the forward motion of your boat.

To all of my readers, I extend my warmest thanks for coming along on this journey. I sincerely wish each of you the best. May you always stay safe and sound on the waters of the world.

"Your Call, Skipper"

You're the skipper or most knowledgeable crewmember in each of the following situations. What actions would you take?

1. What four ways could you use absorbent pads, rags, or cotton diapers before, during, and after fueling?

2. You are finished using the propane stove and ready to secure (shut everything down). Before shutting off the main tank valve, how can you ensure that no gas flows from the stovetop?

3. You are sailing along the New England coast. You've invited a friend along, but he's new to sailing. Which overboard emergency recovery method would be best for him to use if you fell overboard?

4. How can you use shoring to brace a patch on a hole or crack in the hull?

5. What is the *first* sign of mild hypothermia in your crew? How do you treat it? What is the *first* sign of medium hypothermia? How do you treat it?

Answers

1. Use these items to cover scuppers and drains downhill of the fill. Use them to line the fuel fill hole or wrap the fuel nozzle. Place them under fuel vents to catch overflow. And use them to clean up fuel spills in the water.

2. Turn off the oven. Turn off all burners *except* one. Leave a low flame burning. Then, shut off the solenoid switch at the stove. Watch the flame burn out, and then shut off the burner. Double-check that all burners and the stove are off. Shut off the main tank valve.

3. Show your friend how to heave-to. Also, show him how to start, shift, throttle, idle, and stop the engine.

4. Make a strongback with a cushion, life jacket, hatchboard, book, or full sailbag. Place the strongback over the damaged area. Brace it in place with an oar, a paddle, a spinnaker pole, or a boathook. Jam one end into the strongback and the other into a bulkhead or the overhead.

5. The first sign for *mild hypothermia* is shivering. Have them warm up for a few minutes down below. Have them drink warm water or juice (no alcohol or caffeine). After recovery, get them into coats or foul-weather gear and have them wear caps. In *medium hypothermia*, the shivering stops. Get a victim of medium hypothermia below right away. Wrap him or her in a blanket or sleeping bag and treat for shock. You might use the body-to-body warming method.

 APPENDIX I

USEFUL TABLES

Horizon Distance Based on Height of Eye of the Observer

(See Chapter 4, How to Determine When You Will Make Landfall)

Enter the table under the HE (Height of Eye) column with your height above sea level, or the height of a charted object above sea level that has been corrected for tide. Read the distance in nautical miles under the Horizon column.

You can also use the table to estimate the distance you will first see an object of known height, called *geographic range*. This does not take into account any element that reduces visibility such as haze, fog, or precipitation.

For example, when standing on your flying bridge, your height of eye is 16 feet. You are searching for a lighthouse with a charted height of 125 feet. At what distance might you expect to sight the light on a clear night?

HE of 16 feet = 4.7 miles

HE of 125 feet = 13.1 miles

To find geographic range, add the two values: 4.7 + 13.1 = 17.8 miles

For safety, compare the geographic range to the nominal range shown on the chart next to the light. Use the lower of the two ranges to estimate sighting. Or use the special technique, described in the reference above.

For heights greater than the table shows, multiply the square root of the object height by 1.17.

VISUAL (HE) TABLE

HE	Horizon	HE	Horizon	HE	Horizon	HE	Horizon
1	1.2	26	6.0	55	8.7	180	15.7
2	1.7	27	6.1	60	9.1	185	15.9
3	2.0	28	6.2	65	9.4	190	16.1
4	2.3	29	6.3	70	9.8	195	16.3
5	2.6	30	6.4	75	10.1	200	16.5
6	2.9	31	6.5	80	10.5	205	16.8
7	3.1	32	6.6	85	10.8	210	17.0
8	3.3	33	6.7	90	11.1	215	17.2
9	3.5	34	6.8	95	11.4	220	17.4
10	3.7	35	6.9	100	11.7	225	17.6
11	3.9	36	7.0	105	12.0	230	17.7
12	4.1	37	7.1	110	12.3	235	17.9
13	4.2	38	7.2	115	12.5	240	18.1
14	4.4	39	7.3	120	12.8	245	18.3
15	4.5	40	7.4	125	13.1	250	18.5
16	4.7	41	7.5	130	13.3	255	18.7
17	4.8	42	7.6	135	13.6	260	18.9
18	5.0	43	7.7	140	13.8	265	19.0
19	5.1	44	7.8	145	14.1	270	19.2
20	5.2	45	7.8	150	14.3	275	19.4
21	5.4	46	7.9	155	14.6	280	19.6
22	5.5	47	8.0	160	14.8	285	19.8
23	5.6	48	8.1	165	15.0	290	19.9
24	5.7	49	8.2	170	15.3	295	20.1
25	5.9	50	8.3	175	15.5	300	20.3

Maximum Target Radar Range Based on Height of Radar Antenna [H(ra)]

(See Chapter 7, Avoiding Collisions the E.A.S.A. Way and Radar Scope Plotting)

Before deciding on radar height installation, check the manual or talk with the manufacturer or installing electrician. Make a final decision based on these factors:

Vertical and horizontal offset. A gain in target range by increasing height also means a loss in acquiring close-quarters targets. Radar vertical beam width is quite narrow. For example, install an antenna 30 feet off the water and expect to lose targets inside a 50-yard radius.

Sailing vessel heel. Without an antenna leveling device, expect loss of target acquisition on the side of tack. On starboard tack, the beam will shoot over starboard-side targets and vice versa. This problem increases with radar height.

Power vessel squat. Squatting in the stern causes the antenna to aim skyward, missing targets close to the boat. Use trim tabs to keep the bow down or slow the boat to acquire targets in reduced visibility.

How much height do you need?

Mount your radar antenna high enough to acquire targets at a range that allows time to maneuver. The following recommendations are conservative, in that they only take into account your own radar's horizon distance. In most circumstances, you will pick up large vessels at somewhat greater distances. This depends on many factors, such as hull reflectivity, radar signal output, sea height, and atmosphere.

Small power vessels: 11 feet (minimum height above water) = 4-mile radar horizon.

Small sailing vessels: 24 feet (minimum height above water) = 6-mile radar horizon.

If sailing near shipping lanes, fall off to a deep reach every so often to level the radar antenna. Check for targets on the radar; if you are clear, return to your course. Otherwise, perform collision avoidance maneuvers described in the chapter sections noted above.

MAXIMUM RADAR TARGET RANGE BASED ON HEIGHT OF RADAR ANTENNA H(ra)

H(ra)	Range	H(ra)	Range	H(ra)	Range	H(ra)	Range	H(ra)	Range
1	1.2	16	4.9	31	6.8	46	8.3	61	9.5
2	1.7	17	5.0	32	6.9	47	8.4	62	9.6
3	2.1	18	5.2	33	7.0	48	8.5	63	9.7
4	2.4	19	5.3	34	7.1	49	8.5	64	9.8
5	2.7	20	5.5	35	7.2	50	8.6	65	9.8
6	3.0	21	5.6	36	7.3	51	8.7	66	9.9
7	3.2	22	5.7	37	7.4	52	8.8	67	10.0
8	3.5	23	5.9	38	7.5	53	8.9	68	10.1
9	3.7	24	6.0	39	7.6	54	9.0	69	10.1
10	3.9	25	6.1	40	7.7	55	9.0	70	10.2
11	4.0	26	6.2	41	7.8	56	9.1	71	10.3
12	4.2	27	6.3	42	7.9	57	9.2	72	10.4
13	4.4	28	6.5	43	8.0	58	9.3	73	10.4
14	4.6	29	6.6	44	8.1	59	9.4	74	10.5
15	4.7	30	6.7	45	8.2	60	9.5	75	10.6

Speed over a Measured Mile

(See Chapter 3, How to Make a Speed Graph in Three Easy Steps)

1. Find a measured mile range or a straight distance of 1 nautical mile between two prominent objects.
2. Start the watch and maintain RPM under power or heading under sail. After arriving at the object, enter the table across the top with minutes and on either side with excess seconds. The intersection gives the speed for one leg. Under sail, this gives average speed over ground, on that point of sail in those conditions.
3. If under power, repeat the method back to the first object. Enter the table again and find speed. The average of the two speeds gives the vessel's speed through the water at the selected RPM.

SPEED OVER A MEASURED MILE (1–11 MINUTES)

Sec.	1 Min.	2 Min.	3 Min.	4 Min.	5 Min.	6 Min.	7 Min.	8 Min.	9 Min.	10 Min.	11 Min.	Sec.
0	60.0	30.0	20.0	15.0	12.0	10.0	8.6	7.5	6.7	6.0	5.5	0
1	59.0	29.8	19.9	14.9	12.0	10.0	8.6	7.5	6.7	6.0	5.4	1
2	58.1	29.5	19.8	14.9	11.9	9.9	8.5	7.5	6.6	6.0	5.4	2
3	57.1	29.3	19.7	14.8	11.9	9.9	8.5	7.5	6.6	6.0	5.4	3
4	56.3	29.0	19.6	14.8	11.8	9.9	8.5	7.4	6.6	6.0	5.4	4
5	55.4	28.8	19.5	14.7	11.8	9.9	8.5	7.4	6.6	6.0	5.4	5
6	54.5	28.6	19.4	14.6	11.8	9.8	8.5	7.4	6.6	5.9	5.4	6
7	53.7	28.3	19.3	14.6	11.7	9.8	8.4	7.4	6.6	5.9	5.4	7
8	52.9	28.1	19.1	14.5	11.7	9.8	8.4	7.4	6.6	5.9	5.4	8
9	52.2	27.9	19.0	14.5	11.7	9.8	8.4	7.4	6.6	5.9	5.4	9
10	51.4	27.7	18.9	14.4	11.6	9.7	8.4	7.3	6.5	5.9	5.4	10
11	50.7	27.5	18.8	14.3	11.6	9.7	8.4	7.3	6.5	5.9	5.4	11
12	50.0	27.3	18.8	14.3	11.5	9.7	8.3	7.3	6.5	5.9	5.4	12
13	49.3	27.1	18.7	14.2	11.5	9.7	8.3	7.3	6.5	5.9	5.3	13
14	48.6	26.9	18.6	14.2	11.5	9.6	8.3	7.3	6.5	5.9	5.3	14
15	48.0	26.7	18.5	14.1	11.4	9.6	8.3	7.3	6.5	5.9	5.3	15
16	47.4	26.5	18.4	14.1	11.4	9.6	8.3	7.3	6.5	5.8	5.3	16
17	46.8	26.3	18.3	14.0	11.4	9.5	8.2	7.2	6.5	5.8	5.3	17
18	46.2	26.1	18.2	14.0	11.3	9.5	8.2	7.2	6.5	5.8	5.3	18
19	45.6	25.9	18.1	13.9	11.3	9.5	8.2	7.2	6.4	5.8	5.3	19

(Continued)

SPEED OVER A MEASURED MILE (1–11 MINUTES) (CONTINUED)

Sec.	1 Min.	2 Min.	3 Min.	4 Min.	5 Min.	6 Min.	7 Min.	8 Min.	9 Min.	10 Min.	11 Min.	Sec.
20	45.0	25.7	18.0	13.8	11.3	9.5	8.2	7.2	6.4	5.8	5.3	20
21	44.4	25.5	17.9	13.8	11.2	9.4	8.2	7.2	6.4	5.8	5.3	21
22	43.9	25.4	17.8	13.7	11.2	9.4	8.1	7.2	6.4	5.8	5.3	22
23	43.4	25.2	17.7	13.7	11.1	9.4	8.1	7.2	6.4	5.8	5.3	23
24	42.9	25.0	17.6	13.6	11.1	9.4	8.1	7.1	6.4	5.8	5.3	24
25	42.4	24.8	17.6	13.6	11.1	9.4	8.1	7.1	6.4	5.8	5.3	25
26	41.9	24.7	17.5	13.5	11.0	9.3	8.1	7.1	6.4	5.8	5.2	26
27	41.4	24.5	17.4	13.5	11.0	9.3	8.1	7.1	6.3	5.7	5.2	27
28	40.9	24.3	17.3	13.4	11.0	9.3	8.0	7.1	6.3	5.7	5.2	28
29	40.4	24.2	17.2	13.4	10.9	9.3	8.0	7.1	6.3	5.7	5.2	29
30	40.0	24.0	17.1	13.3	10.9	9.2	8.0	7.1	6.3	5.7	5.2	30
31	39.6	23.8	17.1	13.3	10.9	9.2	8.0	7.0	6.3	5.7	5.2	31
32	39.1	23.7	17.0	13.2	10.8	9.2	8.0	7.0	6.3	5.7	5.2	32
33	38.7	23.5	16.9	13.2	10.8	9.2	7.9	7.0	6.3	5.7	5.2	33
34	38.3	23.4	16.8	13.1	10.8	9.1	7.9	7.0	6.3	5.7	5.2	34
35	37.9	23.2	16.7	13.1	10.7	9.1	7.9	7.0	6.3	5.7	5.2	35
36	37.5	23.1	16.7	13.0	10.7	9.1	7.9	7.0	6.3	5.7	5.2	36
37	37.1	22.9	16.6	13.0	10.7	9.1	7.9	7.0	6.2	5.7	5.2	37

38	5.2	5.6	6.2	6.9	7.9	9.0	10.7	12.9	16.5	22.8	36.7	38
39	5.2	5.6	6.2	6.9	7.8	9.0	10.6	12.9	16.4	22.6	36.4	39
40	5.1	5.6	6.2	6.9	7.8	9.0	10.6	12.9	16.4	22.5	36.0	40
41	5.1	5.6	6.2	6.9	7.8	9.0	10.6	12.8	16.3	22.4	35.6	41
42	5.1	5.6	6.2	6.9	7.8	9.0	10.5	12.8	16.2	22.2	35.3	42
43	5.1	5.6	6.2	6.9	7.8	8.9	10.5	12.7	16.1	22.1	35.0	43
44	5.1	5.6	6.2	6.9	7.8	8.9	10.5	12.7	16.1	22.0	34.6	44
45	5.1	5.6	6.2	6.9	7.7	8.9	10.4	12.6	16.0	21.8	34.3	45
46	5.1	5.6	6.1	6.8	7.7	8.9	10.4	12.6	15.9	21.7	34.0	46
47	5.1	5.6	6.1	6.8	7.7	8.8	10.4	12.5	15.9	21.6	33.6	47
48	5.1	5.6	6.1	6.8	7.7	8.8	10.3	12.5	15.8	21.4	33.3	48
49	5.1	5.5	6.1	6.8	7.7	8.8	10.3	12.5	15.7	21.3	33.0	49
50	5.1	5.5	6.1	6.8	7.7	8.8	10.3	12.4	15.7	21.2	32.7	50
51	5.1	5.5	6.1	6.8	7.6	8.8	10.3	12.4	15.6	21.1	32.4	51
52	5.1	5.5	6.1	6.8	7.6	8.7	10.2	12.3	15.5	20.9	32.1	52
53	5.0	5.5	6.1	6.8	7.6	8.7	10.2	12.3	15.5	20.8	31.9	53
54	5.0	5.5	6.1	6.7	7.6	8.7	10.2	12.2	15.4	20.7	31.6	54
55	5.0	5.5	6.1	6.7	7.6	8.7	10.1	12.2	15.3	20.6	31.3	55
56	5.0	5.5	6.0	6.7	7.6	8.7	10.1	12.2	15.3	20.5	31.0	56
57	5.0	5.5	6.0	6.7	7.5	8.6	10.1	12.1	15.2	20.3	30.8	57
58	5.0	5.5	6.0	6.7	7.5	8.6	10.1	12.1	15.1	20.2	30.5	58
59	5.0	5.5	6.0	6.7	7.5	8.6	10.0	12.0	15.1	20.1	30.3	59

SPEED OVER A MEASURED MILE (12–22 MINUTES)

Sec.	12 Min.	13 Min.	14 Min.	15 Min.	16 Min.	17 Min.	18 Min.	19 Min.	20 Min.	21 Min.	22 Min.	Sec.
0	5.0	4.6	4.3	4.0	3.8	3.5	3.3	3.2	3.0	2.9	2.7	0
1	5.0	4.6	4.3	4.0	3.7	3.5	3.3	3.2	3.0	2.9	2.7	1
2	5.0	4.6	4.3	4.0	3.7	3.5	3.3	3.2	3.0	2.9	2.7	2
3	5.0	4.6	4.3	4.0	3.7	3.5	3.3	3.1	3.0	2.9	2.7	3
4	5.0	4.6	4.3	4.0	3.7	3.5	3.3	3.1	3.0	2.8	2.7	4
5	5.0	4.6	4.3	4.0	3.7	3.5	3.3	3.1	3.0	2.8	2.7	5
6	5.0	4.6	4.3	4.0	3.7	3.5	3.3	3.1	3.0	2.8	2.7	6
7	5.0	4.6	4.3	4.0	3.7	3.5	3.3	3.1	3.0	2.8	2.7	7
8	4.9	4.6	4.2	4.0	3.7	3.5	3.3	3.1	3.0	2.8	2.7	8
9	4.9	4.6	4.2	4.0	3.7	3.5	3.3	3.1	3.0	2.8	2.7	9
10	4.9	4.6	4.2	4.0	3.7	3.5	3.3	3.1	3.0	2.8	2.7	10
11	4.9	4.6	4.2	4.0	3.7	3.5	3.3	3.1	3.0	2.8	2.7	11
12	4.9	4.5	4.2	3.9	3.7	3.5	3.3	3.1	3.0	2.8	2.7	12
13	4.9	4.5	4.2	3.9	3.7	3.5	3.3	3.1	3.0	2.8	2.7	13
14	4.9	4.5	4.2	3.9	3.7	3.5	3.3	3.1	3.0	2.8	2.7	14
15	4.9	4.5	4.2	3.9	3.7	3.5	3.3	3.1	3.0	2.8	2.7	15
16	4.9	4.5	4.2	3.9	3.7	3.5	3.3	3.1	3.0	2.8	2.7	16
17	4.9	4.5	4.2	3.9	3.7	3.5	3.3	3.1	3.0	2.8	2.7	17
18	4.9	4.5	4.2	3.9	3.7	3.5	3.3	3.1	3.0	2.8	2.7	18
19	4.9	4.5	4.2	3.9	3.7	3.5	3.3	3.1	3.0	2.8	2.7	19

20	4.9	4.5	4.2	3.9	3.7	3.5	3.3	3.1	3.0	2.8	2.7	20
21	4.9	4.5	4.2	3.9	3.7	3.5	3.3	3.1	2.9	2.8	2.7	21
22	4.9	4.5	4.2	3.9	3.7	3.5	3.3	3.1	2.9	2.8	2.7	22
23	4.8	4.5	4.2	3.9	3.7	3.5	3.3	3.1	2.9	2.8	2.7	23
24	4.8	4.5	4.2	3.9	3.7	3.4	3.3	3.1	2.9	2.8	2.7	24
25	4.8	4.5	4.2	3.9	3.7	3.4	3.3	3.1	2.9	2.8	2.7	25
26	4.8	4.5	4.2	3.9	3.7	3.4	3.3	3.1	2.9	2.8	2.7	26
27	4.8	4.5	4.2	3.9	3.6	3.4	3.3	3.1	2.9	2.8	2.7	27
28	4.8	4.5	4.1	3.9	3.6	3.4	3.2	3.1	2.9	2.8	2.7	28
29	4.8	4.4	4.1	3.9	3.6	3.4	3.2	3.1	2.9	2.8	2.7	29
30	4.8	4.4	4.1	3.9	3.6	3.4	3.2	3.1	2.9	2.8	2.7	30
31	4.8	4.4	4.1	3.9	3.6	3.4	3.2	3.1	2.9	2.8	2.7	31
32	4.8	4.4	4.1	3.9	3.6	3.4	3.2	3.1	2.9	2.8	2.7	32
33	4.8	4.4	4.1	3.9	3.6	3.4	3.2	3.1	2.9	2.8	2.7	33
34	4.8	4.4	4.1	3.9	3.6	3.4	3.2	3.1	2.9	2.8	2.7	34
35	4.8	4.4	4.1	3.9	3.6	3.4	3.2	3.1	2.9	2.8	2.7	35
36	4.8	4.4	4.1	3.8	3.6	3.4	3.2	3.1	2.9	2.8	2.7	36
37	4.8	4.4	4.1	3.8	3.6	3.4	3.2	3.1	2.9	2.8	2.7	37
38	4.7	4.4	4.1	3.8	3.6	3.4	3.2	3.1	2.9	2.8	2.7	38
39	4.7	4.4	4.1	3.8	3.6	3.4	3.2	3.1	2.9	2.8	2.6	39
40	4.7	4.4	4.1	3.8	3.6	3.4	3.2	3.1	2.9	2.8	2.6	40
41	4.7	4.4	4.1	3.8	3.6	3.4	3.2	3.0	2.9	2.8	2.6	41

(Continued)

SPEED OVER A MEASURED MILE (12–22 MINUTES) (CONTINUED)

Sec.	12 Min.	13 Min.	14 Min.	15 Min.	16 Min.	17 Min.	18 Min.	19 Min.	20 Min.	21 Min.	22 Min.	Sec.
42	4.7	4.4	4.1	3.8	3.6	3.4	3.2	3.0	2.9	2.8	2.6	42
43	4.7	4.4	4.1	3.8	3.6	3.4	3.2	3.0	2.9	2.8	2.6	43
44	4.7	4.4	4.1	3.8	3.6	3.4	3.2	3.0	2.9	2.8	2.6	44
45	4.7	4.4	4.1	3.8	3.6	3.4	3.2	3.0	2.9	2.8	2.6	45
46	4.7	4.4	4.1	3.8	3.6	3.4	3.2	3.0	2.9	2.8	2.6	46
47	4.7	4.4	4.1	3.8	3.6	3.4	3.2	3.0	2.9	2.8	2.6	47
48	4.7	4.3	4.1	3.8	3.6	3.4	3.2	3.0	2.9	2.8	2.6	48
49	4.7	4.3	4.0	3.8	3.6	3.4	3.2	3.0	2.9	2.8	2.6	49
50	4.7	4.3	4.0	3.8	3.6	3.4	3.2	3.0	2.9	2.7	2.6	50
51	4.7	4.3	4.0	3.8	3.6	3.4	3.2	3.0	2.9	2.7	2.6	51
52	4.7	4.3	4.0	3.8	3.6	3.4	3.2	3.0	2.9	2.7	2.6	52
53	4.7	4.3	4.0	3.8	3.6	3.4	3.2	3.0	2.9	2.7	2.6	53
54	4.7	4.3	4.0	3.8	3.6	3.4	3.2	3.0	2.9	2.7	2.6	54
55	4.6	4.3	4.0	3.8	3.5	3.3	3.2	3.0	2.9	2.7	2.6	55
56	4.6	4.3	4.0	3.8	3.5	3.3	3.2	3.0	2.9	2.7	2.6	56
57	4.6	4.3	4.0	3.8	3.5	3.3	3.2	3.0	2.9	2.7	2.6	57
58	4.6	4.3	4.0	3.8	3.5	3.3	3.2	3.0	2.9	2.7	2.6	58
59	4.6	4.3	4.0	3.8	3.5	3.3	3.2	3.0	2.9	2.7	2.6	59

Duration of Slack Water

(See Chapter 5, Slack Intervals: Nature's Gift to Mariners)

Correct tidal current time and velocity to your substation (see reference above).

Write down max current speed on each side of your intended transit time. Write down the time of slack water that falls between the two max current times.

Enter this table in the first column with the higher of the two max current speeds (round to the closest half knot). Then, slide over to the second column. Write down the minutes of slack water.

Subtract and add the minutes of slack water to the time of slack water you found from the tables. The third column shows the total amount of time you have to make your transit.

Example

You need to find the best time to enter an unfamiliar but well-marked inlet in the afternoon. The current tables show the following data:

1100 max flood 2.3 knots

1415 slack

1710 max ebb 3.8 knots

Enter the first column below with the maximum speed: 3.8 knots (round to the nearest half knot): 4.0 knots.

Enter the second column on the same line: 15 minutes. Add and subtract this to the time of slack water.

1415 − 15 = 1400

1415 + 15 = 1430

Make your transit between 1400 and 1430.

DURATION OF SLACK WATER

Maximum Current (knots)	Add and Subtract to Time Slack Begins (minutes)	Total Transit Time in Slack Water (minutes)
1.0	60	120
1.5	40	80
2.0	30	60
2.5	24	48
3.0	20	40
3.5	17	34
4.0	15	30
4.5	13	26
5.0	12	24
5.5	11	22
6.0	10	20
6.5	9	18
7.0	9	18
7.5	8	16
8.0	8	16
8.5	7	14
9.0	7	14
9.5	6	12
10.0	6	12

Drift Rate

(See Chapter 8, Decisions to Make Before Running an Inlet)

Use drift rate for close-quarters maneuvering. You could also use the table to estimate drift caused by current in critical situations (see reference above).

Example

You are entering a narrow marina channel at 2 knots of boatspeed. You are having problems with the transmission, and reverse gear is unreliable. How far would you expect to drift 10 seconds after placing the engine(s) into neutral gear?

Enter the Seconds column and find 10 seconds.

Move over to Speed 2 knots column.

Drift distance: 11.1 yards, or about 33 feet.

DRIFT RATE IN YARDS

Seconds	SPEED 1 knot Drift Distance (in yards)	SPEED 2 knots Drift Distance (in yards)	SPEED 3 knots Drift Distance (in yards)	SPEED 4 knots Drift Distance (in yards)	SPEED 5 knots Drift Distance (in yards)	SPEED 6 knots Drift Distance (in yards)	SPEED 7 knots Drift Distance (in yards)	SPEED 8 knots Drift Distance (in yards)	SPEED 9 knots Drift Distance (in yards)	SPEED 10 knots Drift Distance (in yards)	Seconds
1	0.6	1.1	1.7	2.2	2.8	3.3	3.9	4.4	5.0	5.6	1
2	1.1	2.2	3.3	4.4	5.6	6.7	7.8	8.9	10.0	11.1	2
3	1.7	3.3	5.0	6.7	8.3	10.0	11.7	13.3	15.0	16.7	3
4	2.2	4.4	6.7	8.9	11.1	13.3	15.6	17.8	20.0	22.2	4
5	2.8	5.6	8.3	11.1	13.9	16.7	19.4	22.2	25.0	27.8	5
6	3.3	6.7	10.0	13.3	16.7	20.0	23.3	26.7	30.0	33.3	6
7	3.9	7.8	11.7	15.6	19.4	23.3	27.2	31.1	35.0	38.9	7
8	4.4	8.9	13.3	17.8	22.2	26.7	31.1	35.6	40.0	44.4	8
9	5.0	10.0	15.0	20.0	25.0	30.0	35.0	40.0	45.0	50.0	9
10	5.6	11.1	16.7	22.2	27.8	33.3	38.9	44.4	50.0	55.6	10
11	6.1	12.2	18.3	24.4	30.6	36.7	42.8	48.9	55.0	61.1	11
12	6.7	13.3	20.0	26.7	33.3	40.0	46.7	53.3	60.0	66.7	12
13	7.2	14.4	21.7	28.9	36.1	43.3	50.6	57.8	65.0	72.2	13
14	7.8	15.6	23.3	31.1	38.9	46.7	54.4	62.2	70.0	77.8	14

15	8.3	16.7	25.0	33.3	41.7	50.0	58.3	66.7	75.0	83.3	15
16	8.9	17.8	26.7	35.6	44.4	53.3	62.2	71.1	80.0	88.9	16
17	9.4	18.9	28.3	37.8	47.2	56.7	66.1	75.6	85.0	94.4	17
18	10.0	20.0	30.0	40.0	50.0	60.0	70.0	80.0	90.0	100.0	18
19	10.6	21.1	31.7	42.2	52.8	63.3	73.9	84.4	95.0	105.6	19
20	11.1	22.2	33.3	44.4	55.6	66.7	77.8	88.9	100.0	111.1	20
21	11.7	23.3	35.0	46.7	58.3	70.0	81.7	93.3	105.0	116.7	21
22	12.2	24.4	36.7	48.9	61.1	73.3	85.6	97.8	110.0	122.2	22
23	12.8	25.6	38.3	51.1	63.9	76.7	89.4	102.2	115.0	127.8	23
24	13.3	26.7	40.0	53.3	66.7	80.0	93.3	106.7	120.0	133.3	24
25	13.9	27.8	41.7	55.6	69.4	83.3	97.2	111.1	125.0	138.9	25
26	14.4	28.9	43.3	57.8	72.2	86.7	101.1	115.6	130.0	144.4	26
27	15.0	30.0	45.0	60.0	75.0	90.0	105.0	120.0	135.0	150.0	27
28	15.6	31.1	46.7	62.2	77.8	93.3	108.9	124.4	140.0	155.6	28
29	16.1	32.2	48.3	64.4	80.6	96.7	112.8	128.9	145.0	161.1	29
30	16.7	33.3	50.0	66.7	83.3	100.0	116.7	133.3	150.0	166.7	30

APPENDIX II

ADDITIONAL CONCEPTS AND FORMULAS

The Three Primary Motions of a Yacht

Boats rotate on three primary axes: one runs fore and aft, a second runs athwartships, and a third runs vertically. Any motion may act independently or combine with another.

ROLLING

Step aboard any moored vessel and you induce roll motion. The *roll axis* lies along the centerline of the boat, extending from bow to stern. A good indicator of vessel stability is the roll period test.

1. Stand with another person on the side of a vessel. Push hard up and down on the gunwale to get the boat rolling.
2. Step back and time one complete roll period from right to left to right. Conduct a second test and make sure it agrees with your first test. Compare your results with those shown below.

John Vigor, author of *The Practical Mariner's Book of Knowledge*, gives handy formulas for average roll periods:

Power vessels. Divide the vessel's beam by 3.3. For example, if your power vessel beam is 12 feet, 12/3.3 = 3.6 seconds. Compare this to your roll period test. Then read the section following the sailboat formulas.

Sailing vessels. Sailing vessel roll period depends on vessel design and the ballast/displacement (B/D) ratio. To determine the B/D ratio, divide the weight of the ballast by the weight of the vessel. For example, if the ballast is 2,500 pounds and the vessel weighs 10,000 pounds: 2,500/10,000 = 25% (B/D ratio).

Heavy displacement sailboats
B/D ratio 25% or less
Average roll period = (beam/3.3) × .95

B/D ratio 25% to 35%
Average roll period = (beam/3.3) × .90
Medium displacement sailboats
B/D ratio 35% or more
Average roll period = (beam/3.3) × .85
Cruiser/racer sailboats
B/D ratio 35% or more
Average roll period = (beam/3.3) × .80
Racing sailboats
Deep draft and low deck profiles
Average roll period = (beam/3.3) × .75

Longer-than-average roll periods indicate an inherently unstable vessel. These vessels are called *tender* or *crank*, and for good reason: they're top heavy. Even moderately tender power vessels heel over to one side when making turns in flat water. Any seaway imposes the threat of capsize.

Shorter-than-average roll periods indicate excessive stiffness. These vessels give an uncomfortable ride with short, snappy rolls. They are designed to carry extremely heavy ballast and light topsides. Only a few vessels in the world need this extreme stiffness. One of these, the Coast Guard motor lifeboat, carries most of its weight in the keel and is designed to recover from a 360-degree rollover.

PITCHING

A vessel pitches, or rises and falls up and down, on its athwartships axis. This uncomfortable motion often results from loading one end more than the other. Hull design also plays a role. Boats with long overhangs tend to pitch more, and might *hobbyhorse* (rise up and down in place when slowed by a sea). Pitching causes crew fatigue and induces seasickness. The smallest tasks take tremendous effort to perform. Move weights from the bow and stern and place them near the keel. Slow down and change course slightly to improve pitching motion.

YAWING

A boat rotates horizontally around a vertical axis in a motion called *yawing*. Sailing vessels experience yawing while running downwind in gusty weather. Power vessels running before seas and swell may yaw from side to side. Add weight astern to help cure yawing. In large seas when running before the wind, consider towing warps; in extreme conditions, stream a drogue.

Weight Distribution and Performance

Throughout the loading process, make a continuous check on your boat's list and trim. *List* is the tendency for a boat to lean permanently to one side. Even a small list of 1 to 2 degrees can affect underway performance. A boat is *trimmed* when it shows no inclination at the bow or stern. Boats out of trim pitch and hobbyhorse in a seaway.

Check list and trim before loading. Before you start to load, check your list and trim. Do you notice any differences in the waterline bootstripe on port and starboard sides? Stand in front of the bow or stern and see if the boat leans to one side. If you see a list, determine the source. Do you need to shift chain, canned goods, or tools to level the boat on its waterline? Check the bilges, seacocks, and stuffing box for leaks. Then, check off-centerline fresh- and gray-water tanks. Is one full and the other dry?

Fill water and fuel tanks and recheck. Once the boat is trimmed, fill freshwater and fuel tanks. When you are done, recheck list and trim.

Load provisions. Load low, beginning near the keel and work fore and aft and athwartships. Load half of all provisions and then step off the boat and check the list and trim again. Redistribute provisions if necessary. Finish loading and conduct a final check.

AMOUNT OF CREW WEIGHT AND PROVISIONS TO IMMERSE THE WATERLINE

How much weight does it take to lower your waterline by 1 inch? Use this chart to get a rough estimate of your crew and provisions weight. Then work through the formula below.

PROVISIONING AND CREW WEIGHT ESTIMATES FOR SAFE LOADING

Consumables

Canned and bottled goods = 1 pound per item

Fresh produce = best estimate

Crew and personal gear

Crew/passengers = 175 pounds per person

Personal gear (each person) = 100 pounds

Ground tackle

Anchor chain (up to 5/16 inch) = 1 pound per foot

Nylon line (common sizes):

  5/16 inch = 3 pounds per 100 feet

  3/8 inch = 4 pounds per 100 feet

  7/16 inch = 5 pounds per 100 feet

  1/2 inch = 7 pounds per 100 feet

Sails, sailing hardware, tools = best estimate

Tankage

Fresh water = 8 pounds per gallon

Waste water = 9 pounds per gallon

Diesel fuel = 7 pounds per gallon

Gasoline = 6 pounds per gallon

Use the following steps to determine how much weight it takes to lower your ~~w~~aterline by 1 inch.

1. Determine waterline length (LWL).
2. Calculate waterline beam (BWL). Multiply .90 × boat beam.
3. Multiply (LWL) × (BWL) × .75 = waterplane area (WPA).
4. (WPA) × 5.3 = weight to immerse the waterline 1 inch.

Your boat has a 25-foot waterline (LWL) and a 10-foot beam:
.90 × 10 feet = 9-foot waterline beam (BWL)
25 feet × 9 feet × .75 = 168.8 waterplane area (WPA)
168.8 (WPA) × 5.3 = 895 pounds to immerse the waterline 1 inch

LASH AND STOW

Make sure your provisions stay in place. Use bungee chord, twine, Velcro, foam wedges, sponges, towels, and fiddles. Shifting weights create danger to your boat and crew. In extreme conditions they could lead to a capsize.

Coast Guard Coordination Centers

Coast Guard Coordination Centers (RCC) monitor, plan, and execute searches over large regions. Think of an RCC as the mothership, with all of the CG stations, CG ships, CG aircraft, other military aircraft, and state and federal agencies within that area (see third column next page), at their disposal. Manned 24 hours a day, RCC controllers stay in constant contact with all units under their control.

Most VHF and USB radio calls from vessels in distress are received by the smaller units. These units monitor distress frequency channels 16 (VHF) and 2182 (USB) 24 hours a day. If the small units need extra resources, they call the RCC. Within minutes, the RCC can send planes, deploy CG cutters, divert merchant ships, and ask Air Force, Navy, Marine, or Army units to assist in the rescue. The RCC plans all major offshore searches and assigns rescue units to sea and air search sectors and maintains contact with family members.

Overseas, Her Majesty's Coast Guard (HMCG) covers inland, coastal, and offshore waters of England, Ireland, Scotland, and Wales. This region is broken down into nine Search and Recue (SAR) areas. Each area contains two Maritime Rescue Coordination Centers (MRCC). They monitor a broad band of distress communications, including VHF channels 16, 70 (DSC), 62A (land SAR), USB frequency 2182, and telephone number 999.

In all other areas, use channel 16 (VHF) or 2182 (USB) to place a distress call. Through international agreement, those two frequencies are monitored by rescue units worldwide.

COAST GUARD RESCUE COORDINATION CENTERS (RCC)

USCG RCC	Location	Area of Search and Rescue Coordination Responsibility	Phone
ATLANTIC AREA COORDINATOR	Portsmouth, Virginia	Overall responsibility for areas covered by RCC Boston, RCC Norfolk, RCC Miami, RCC San Juan, RCC New Orleans, and RCC Cleveland plus a portion of the North Atlantic Ocean out to 40 degrees west longitude.	(757)398-6231
RCC Boston	Boston, Massachusetts	New England down to and including a portion of Northern New Jersey plus U.S. waters of Lake Champlain.	(617)223-8555
RCC Norfolk	Portsmouth, Virginia	Mid-Atlantic states including the majority of New Jersey down to the North Carolina / South Carolina border.	(757)398-6231
RCC Miami	Miami, Florida	Southeast states from the South Carolina / North Carolina border around to the eastern end of the Florida panhandle plus a large portion of the Caribbean Sea.	(305)415-6800
RCC San Juan	San Juan, Puerto Rico	Southeast portion of the Caribbean Sea.	(787)289-2042
RCC New Orleans	New Orleans, Louisiana	Southern states including the Florida panhandle to the U.S. / Mexico border in Texas plus the inland rivers including the Mississippi, Missouri, Ohio, and tributaries.	(504)589-6225
RCC Cleveland	Cleveland, Ohio	U.S. waters of the Great Lakes, their connecting rivers, and tributaries.	(216)902-6117
PACIFIC AREA COORDINATOR	Alameda, California	Overall responsibility for areas covered by RCC Alameda, RCC Seattle, RCC Honolulu, and RCC Juneau.	(510)437-3700
RCC Alameda	Alameda, California	California and Eastern Pacific Ocean waters assigned by international convention off the Coast of Mexico.	(510)437-3700
RCC Seattle	Seattle, Washington	Oregon and Washington.	(206)220-7001

RCC Honolulu	Honolulu, Hawaii	Hawaii, U.S. Pacific Islands, and waters of Central Pacific Ocean assigned by international convention (extending from as far as 6 degrees south to 40 degrees north latitude and as far as 110 west to 130 east longitude).	(808)535-3333
Sector Guam (under RCC Honolulu)	Guam	Guam and other U.S. territories and possessions in the far western Pacific Ocean.	(671)339-6100
RCC Juneau	Juneau, Alaska	Alaska, U.S. waters in North Pacific Ocean, Bering Sea, and Arctic Ocean.	(907)463-2000

Mayday Calls: Step by Step

In any emergency situation, make a decision to call a Mayday (distress) call based on this question: "If you do not make this call, will the situation most likely result in a loss of life or the loss of your vessel?" If you can answer yes to that question, then make the call.

Use Channel 16 VHF or Channel 2182 USB.

You must give your position immediately so that rescuers can get moving toward your position. This is often forgotten in the heat of the moment. Assume that you'll lose power, so transmit this vital information early in the distress message. Follow the format in the script below.

1. Mayday-Mayday-Mayday (three times)
2. This is *Freedom-Freedom-Freedom* (vessel name, three times)
3. Mayday, motor vessel *Freedom* (severity/name, one time)
4. My position is 32°14.5'N, 67°12.5'W (if lat/long is unknown, give range and bearing from land, a landmark, a buoy, or a dead reckoning position)
5. We are sinking (state the nature of the emergency)
6. Request immediate assistance
     Release the transmit button and listen for a response (20 to 30 seconds). If nothing is heard, repeat steps 1 to 6. *After* rescuers respond to your call:
7. Give amplifying information: number of crew, nature of injuries, action taken, and survival equipment aboard.

Digital Selective Calling (DSC) Procedures

All new VHF-FM radios come equipped with the latest Digital Selective Calling (DSC) technology. It shortens the amount of time needed to hail another vessel and allows continuous distress broadcasting in an emergency. Think of DSC as a calling and distress frequency. It's not for chatter or routine communications. Use it to establish initial communications or in life-threatening emergencies.

To use DSC, both you and the receiving party must have a nine-digit identification number, called a MMSI (Maritime Mobile Service Identity). It's similar to a telephone number. If you know another boat's MMSI, you simply dial it into your DSC-equipped radio and it transmits a signal to it. It receives a tone and message, showing your MMSI, similar to a cellular phone caller-ID display.

Here's a sample of the basic steps for establishing routine, nonemergency communications with another DSC-equipped vessel. Your radio might have slightly different procedures, so always check the manual:

HOW TO MAKE A ROUTINE CALL USING DSC

1. **Select from the DSC menu:** Click on the DSC Menu and select *Individual Call* to call one boat or *Group Call* to call several DSC-equipped vessels. Let's say we want to talk to a single boat. We select Individual Call. Press Enter to go to the next menu.

2. **Select from the MMSI menu:** This shows all boats we've programmed into our radio, listed by MMSI number. Select one MMSI number. Press Enter to go to the next menu.
3. **Choose a working channel:** Choose one of the working channels from the menu listing. This clears the airways for other DSC users. Press Enter to make the call.
4. **Call receipt and reply by other boat:** The other boat receives a tone, notifying it of an incoming DSC call. It replies by pressing Enter (or its radio's reply button). Once it acknowledges receipt, DSC automatically shifts to your selected working frequency on *both* radios.

HOW TO MAKE A DISTRESS CALL WITH DSC

DSC sends a preformatted distress message to DSC-equipped stations, vessels, and Rescue Coordination Centers. The message broadcasts automatically and continuously, requiring no user action. If you're incapacitated, this feature alone could very well save your life and those of your crewmembers.

1. **Make a lifesaving link:** Prepare beforehand. Link your DSC-equipped radio to a GPS and the distress message continuously sends an updated distress position and position time. In most emergencies, you want to have time for handling the problem at hand. Make this link now, ahead of time, to save you valuable time in a crisis.
2. **Lift red Distress cover and press button:** Locate the red cover labeled *Distress* on the radio panel. This prevents accidental Mayday transmission. Lift the cover. Press and hold the button until the display stops flashing (about 5 to 6 seconds). This sends a preformatted distress message showing your MMSI. If you haven't linked your DSC to your GPS, go to step 3.
3. **For DSC radios not linked to a GPS:** For units not linked to GPS, rescue units need your position in order to start moving toward you. Manually enter your latitude and longitude (see your equipment manual on procedure). Push the Enter key to transmit your location to DSC-equipped vessels and stations.

BIBLIOGRAPHY

Bruce, Erroll. *This Is Rough Weather Cruising*. Boston, Massachusetts: Sail Books, Inc., 1980.

Burch, David. *Radar for Mariners*. Camden, Maine: International Marine, 2005.

Calder, Nigel. *Marine Diesel Engines*. Camden, Maine: International Marine, 1992.

Chapman, Charles F., and Elbert S Maloney, ed. *Chapman's Navigation, Seamanship and Small Boat Handling*. New York: Hearst Marine Books, 2007.

Colgate, Steve. *Manual of Basic Sailing Theory*. New York, NY: Van Nostrand Reinhold Company, 1973.

Compton, Peter. *Troubleshooting Marine Diesels*. Camden, Maine: International Marine, 1998.

Cunliffe, Tom. *The Complete Yachtmaster*. London, England: Adlard Coles Nautical, 2006.

Defense Mapping Agency. *The American Practical Navigator (Bowditch)*. Bethesda, Maryland: Defense Mapping Agency Hydrographic/Topographic Center, 1995.

Everitt, Dick, and Rodger Witt. *This Is Boat Handling at Close Quarters*. Basel, Switzerland: United Nautical Publishers, 1984.

Grant, James Lowell. *Jibsails: Their Design and Construction*. Churubusco, Indiana: Sailrite Enterprises, Inc., fifth edition, 2003.

Hancock, Brian. *Maximum Sail Power*. Norwich, VT: Nomad Press, 2003.

Henderson, Richard. *Sea Sense*. Camden, Maine: International Marine, 1972.

Hendrickson, Robert. *The Ocean Almanac*. New York, NY: Doubleday, 1984.

Kemp, Peter, ed. *The Oxford Companion to Ships and the Sea*. London, England: Oxford University Press, 1976.

Ross, Wallace. *Sail Power*. Toronto, Canada: Random House of Canada, Ltd. 1975.

Rousmaniere, John. *The Annapolis Book of Seamanship*. New York: Simon and Schuster, 1999.

Sleightholme, Des. *Better Boat Handling*. Great Britain: Stanford Maritime, Ltd., 1983.

Sloane, Eric. *Eric Sloane's Weather Book*. New York: Hawthorn Books, Inc., 1952.

Smith, Hervey Garrett. *The Marlinspike Sailor*. Clinton Corners, NY: John de Graff, Inc., 1971.

Stapleton, Sid. *Stapleton's Powerboat Bible*. Camden, Maine: International Marine, 2002.

Sweet, Robert J. *GPS for Mariners*. Camden, Maine: International Marine, 2003.

Technical Committee of the Cruising Club of America, *Desirable and Undesirable Characteristics of Offshore Yachts*. Markham, Ontario: Penguin Books Canada Ltd., 1987.

Toss, Brion. *The Complete Rigger's Apprentice*. Camden, Maine: International Marine, 1998.

Vigor, John. *The Practical Mariner's Book of Knowledge*. Camden, Maine: International Marine, 1994.

Watts, Alan. *Wind and Sailing Boats*. Great Britain: David and Charles Publishers, 1965.

INDEX

Numbers in **bold** indicate illustrations